D1617124

COOPERATION AMONG DEMOCRACIES

PRINCETON STUDIES IN INTERNATIONAL HISTORY AND POLITICS

Series Editors
Jack L. Snyder and Richard H. Ullman

RECENT TITLES

Strong Nation, Weak State: The Rise of America to World Power by Fareed Zakaria

Changing Course: Ideas, Politics, and the Soviet Withdrawal from Afghanistan by Sarah E. Mendelson

Disarming Strangers: Nuclear Diplomacy with North Korea by Leon V. Sigal

Imagining War: French and British Military Doctrine between the Wars by Elizabeth Kier

Roosevelt and the Munich Crisis: A Study of Political Decision-Making by Barbara Rearden Farnham

Useful Adversaries: Grand Strategy, Domestic Mobilization, and Sino-American Conflict, 1947-1958 by Thomas J. Christensen

Satellites and Commisars: Strategy and Conflict in the Politics of the Soviet-Bloc Trade by Randall W. Stone

Does Conquest Pay? The Exploitation of Occupied Industrial Societies by Peter Liberman

Cultural Realism: Strategic Culture and Grand Strategy in Chinese History by Alastair Iain Johnston

Cooperation among Democracies: The European Influence on U.S. Foreign Policy by Thomas Risse-Kappen

The Korean War: An International History by William W. Stueck

The Sovereign State and Its Competitors by Hendrik Spruyt

America's Mission: The United States and the Worldwide Struggle for Democracy in the Twentieth Century by Tony Smith

Who Adjusts? Domestic Sources of Foreign Economic Policy during the Interwar Years by Beth A. Simmons

We All Lost the Cold War by Richard Ned Lebow and Janice Gross Stein

Mercenaries, Pirates, and Sovereigns: State-Building and Extraterritorial Violence in Early Modern Europe by Janice E. Thomson

The Limits of Safety: Organizations, Accidents, and Nuclear Weapons by Scott D. Sagan

COOPERATION AMONG DEMOCRACIES

THE EUROPEAN INFLUENCE ON U.S. FOREIGN POLICY

Thomas Risse-Kappen

PRINCETON UNIVERSITY PRESS

PRINCETON, NEW JERSEY

PUBLISHED BY PRINCETON UNIVERSITY PRESS, 41 WILLIAM STREET,
PRINCETON, NEW JERSEY 08540
IN THE UNITED KINGDOM: PRINCETON UNIVERSITY PRESS,
CHICHESTER, WEST SUSSEX

LIBRARY OF CONGRESS CATALOGING-IN-PUBLICATION DATA
RISSE-KAPPEN, THOMAS.
COOPERATION AMONG DEMOCRACIES : THE EUROPEAN INFLUENCE ON U.S.
FOREIGN POLICY / THOMAS RISSE-KAPPEN.
P. CM. — (PRINCETON STUDIES IN INTERNATIONAL HISTORY AND POLITICS)
INCLUDES BIBLIOGRAPHICAL REFERENCES (P.) AND INDEX.
ISBN 0-691-03644-6
ISBN 0-691-01711-5 (PBK.)
1. UNITED STATES—FOREIGN RELATIONS—1989– 2. EUROPEAN COOPERATION.
3. SECURITY, INTERNATIONAL. I. TITLE. II. SERIES.
JX1417.R57 1995
327.73'009'045—DC20 94-41976

THIS BOOK HAS BEEN COMPOSED IN CALEDONIA

PRINCETON UNIVERSITY PRESS BOOKS ARE PRINTED ON ACID-FREE PAPER AND
MEET THE GUIDELINES FOR PERMANENCE AND DURABILITY OF THE
COMMITTEE ON PRODUCTION GUIDELINES FOR BOOK LONGEVITY
OF THE COUNCIL ON LIBRARY RESOURCES

SECOND PRINTING, AND FIRST PAPERBACK PRINTING, 1997

PRINTED IN THE UNITED STATES OF AMERICA

3 5 7 9 10 8 6 4 2

CONTENTS

PREFACE

EACH BOOK has its intellectual and personal history. This one has two origins. First, when I began to study the European influence on American foreign policy, I concentrated on NATO's nuclear decisions, particularly the Intermediate-Range Nuclear Forces issue (INF).[1] To my surprise, I found disproportionate European, particularly German, impact on the transatlantic decision-making process. I decided to study the subject further and to focus on "tougher cases," that is, wars, crises, and strategic arms control where supreme American interests were at stake. This book is the result.

Second, there is a political reason for this book. As a research associate at the Peace Research Institute Frankfurt, Germany, during the 1980s, I frequently encountered people who shared an almost intuitive anti-Americanism together with the conviction that "poor Germany" was utterly helpless when confronting the "superpowers." I try to demonstrate in this book that the Europeans have formed a community of liberal democracies firmly entangling the United States and influencing American foreign policy. They should continue to do so in the post–Cold War environment.

Since this book results from a project started in the late 1980s, there are many people and institutions to whom I am enormously grateful. Robert Jervis, Claudia Kappen, Elizabeth Kier, Andrew Moravcsik, Bruce Russett, and an anonymous reviewer read the entire manuscript and provided invaluable comments, criticisms, and suggestions. I am deeply indebted to them as well as to Malcolm DeBevoise on whose support I relied at Princeton University Press. I also thank David Nelson Blair, who copyedited the manuscript, and Sterling Bland, the production editor. In addition, Thomas Christensen, Ernst-Otto Czempiel, Dieter Dettke, Matthew Evangelista, John Garofano, Raymond Garthoff, Isabelle Grunberg, Helga Haftendorn, Robert Herman, Michael Howard, Peter Katzenstein, Catherine Kelleher, Robert Keohane, Audie Klotz, Jeffrey Knopf, Stephen Krasner, Gert Krell, Mark Laffey, Richard Ned Lebow, David Meyer, Harald Müller, Don Munton, M. J. Peterson, Judith Reppy, Steve Ropp, Nina Tannenwald, Janice Thomson, Alexander Wendt, and Michael Zürn read various chapters and/or commented on the project on different occasions. My thanks go to all of them. I also presented papers and tossed out ideas at a variety of places. Audiences at the Brookings Institution, Cornell University's Peace Studies Program, the Peace Research Institute Frankfurt, Yale

[1] See Thomas Risse-Kappen, *The Zero Option* (Boulder, Colo.: Westview, 1988).

University's International Security Program, as well as the annual meetings of the American Political Science Association, the International Studies Association, and the Pan-European Conference on International Relations were particularly important for the evolution of my ideas. Since this book is to a large extent based on archival research, I am very grateful to the staffs of various libraries, particularly at the Manuscript Division of the Library of Congress, Washington, D.C., the National Archives, Washington, D.C., the National Security Archive, Washington, D.C., and the Public Records Office, London. I also thank Dorothee Heisenberg, Richard Hauser, Susanne Kupfer, Birgit Locher, Nandini Sathé, Heike Scherff, Claudia Schmedt, Hans-Peter Schmitz, Richard Tanksley, and Daniel Thomas for valuable research assistance and/or for helping me with preparing the index.

Funding for various parts and time periods of the project was provided by a Social Science Research Council Advanced Research in Foreign Policy Fellowship and by research grants from Cornell University's Peace Studies Program and Yale University's International Security Program (in both cases provided by the John D. and Catherine T. MacArthur Foundation). Additional support came from the Peace Research Institute Frankfurt, the Brookings Institution, and the Department of Political Science at the University of Wyoming. I am deeply indebted to these institutions.

I had originally planned to submit the manuscript as my *Habilitationsschrift* to a German university. In the meantime, however, I received the offer and decided to join the faculty at the University of Konstanz as professor of international politics.

Konstanz, December 1994
Thomas Risse-Kappen

ABBREVIATIONS

ACDA	U.S. Arms Control and Disarmament Agency
AEC	Atomic Energy Commission
ATBT	Atmospheric Test Ban Treaty
CIA	Central Intelligence Agency
CINCFE	Commander in Chief, Far East
CINCUNC	Commander in Chief, United Nations Command
CMC	Cuban Missile crisis
CND	Campaign for Nuclear Disarmament
CSCE	Conference on Security and Cooperation in Europe
DEFCON	Defense Condition (nuclear alert status)
DDEL	Dwight D. Eisenhower Library, Abilene, Kansas
ENDC	18 Nation Disarmament Committee, Geneva
ExComm	Executive Committee, National Security Council (Kennedy administration)
FAS	Federation of American Scientists
FRUS	Foreign Relations of the United States
GDP	Gross domestic product
GDR	German Democratic Republic (East Germany)
ICBM	Intercontinental ballistic missile
IHT	International Herald Tribune
IMF	International Monetary Fund
INF	Intermediate-range nuclear forces
IRBM	Intermediate-range ballistic missile
JCAE	Joint Committee on Atomic Energy (U.S. Congress)
JCS	Joint Chiefs of Staff
LTBT	Limited Test Ban Treaty
MC	Military Committee (NATO)
MLF	Multilateral force
MRBM	Medium-range ballistic missile
NA	National Archives, Washington, D.C.
NATO	North Atlantic Treaty Organization
NORAD	North American Air Defense System
NSA	National Security Archive, Washington, D.C.
NSA:CMC	National Security Archive, Washington, D.C., Cuban Missile Crisis Microfiche Collection
NSA:NNP	National Security Archive, Washington, D.C., Nonproliferation Collection
NSC	National Security Council
OAS	Organization of American States

OECD	Organization of Economic Cooperation and Development
POW	Prisoner of War
PRO	Public Records Office, London
PRO:CAB	Public Records Office, London, Cabinet Files
PRO:FO	Public Records Office, London, Diplomatic Correspondence Files
PRO:PREM	Public Records Office, London, Prime Minister Files
PSAC	Presidential Scientific Advisory Committee
SACEUR	Supreme Allied Commander Europe
SALT	Strategic Arms Limitation Talks
SANE	Committee for a Sane Nuclear Policy
SCUA	Suez Canal Users' Association
SEATO	South East Asian Treaty Organization
SIPRI	Stockholm International Peace Research Institute
SPD	Social Democratic Party, Germany
TTBT	Threshold Test Ban Treaty
U.K.	United Kingdom
UN	United Nations
U.S.	United States of America
USSR	Union of Socialist Soviet Republics
WAH	W. Averell Harriman Papers, Manuscript Division, Library of Congress, Washington, D.C.

COOPERATION AMONG DEMOCRACIES

ONE

INTRODUCTION AND OVERVIEW

CAN SMALL STATES INFLUENCE the preferences and policies of great powers in alliances among unequals, and under what conditions? Are alliances among democracies special? How do democratic states influence each other in cooperative institutions? How do institutionalized norms affect the interaction patterns in alliances? How do domestic politics and interstate relations interact when liberal democracies deal with each other?

In particular, do the West Europeans have any significant impact on American foreign policy, and under what conditions? How does membership in the North Atlantic Treaty Organization (NATO) affect the discourses defining American interests and preferences in the world? Does it make a difference that NATO constitutes an alliance among democracies? How do alliance norms affect the transatlantic relationship? What about the interaction between alliance relations and domestic politics in NATO?

This book attempts to establish two major claims in addressing these questions. First, the West European and Canadian allies exerted greater influence on American foreign policy during the cold war than most analysts on both sides of the Atlantic usually assume. They did so even during the 1950s and 1960s, when the United States enjoyed undisputed economic and military supremacy in the alliance. The Europeans affected security decisions concerning vital U.S. interests in cases such as the 1950–1953 Korean War, the 1958–1963 test ban negotiations, and the 1962 Cuban Missile crisis. These cases were not directly related to European security and confirm findings with regard to NATO decisions involving military strategy and weapons deployments. The European allies influenced American foreign policy routinely and not just in some isolated incidents.

Second, I argue that traditional alliance theories emphasizing strategic interactions and power-based bargaining provide insufficient explanations for the European influence on American foreign policy. Even sophisticated realist approaches based on hegemonic stability and bargaining theories do not appear to offer satisfactory accounts of the "big influence of small allies" in NATO.[1] While they rightly focus on the process of intra-

[1] This is the title of an essay by Robert Keohane in *Foreign Policy* 2 (1971): 161–82.

alliance interactions rather than inferring outcomes directly from underlying power structures, they treat states as unitary actors with exogenously given interests and preferences.

I claim that the interaction processes in the transatlantic relationship can be better understood on the basis of *liberal* theories of international relations. These approaches link domestic political structures systematically to the foreign policy of states. They argue that liberal democracies are likely to form "pacific federations" (Immanuel Kant) or "pluralistic security communities" (Karl W. Deutsch).[2] The liberal approach has to be complemented by *institutionalist* arguments emphasizing the role of norms and communicative action.[3]

I argue that the transatlantic alliance constitutes a community of liberal democracies, which has deeply affected the collective identity of its members including the United States. This sense of community helped the Europeans to influence American policies through three mechanisms. First, norms committing the allies to timely consultation guided the transatlantic interactions as well as the decision-making processes in Washington. When such "alliance norms" were violated, U.S. superior power usually won interallied confrontations, as I demonstrate with regard to the 1956 Suez crisis. Second, while using material power resources in bargaining situations was considered inappropriate among democratic allies, domestic pressures were frequently used to increase one's leverage in transatlantic interactions.[4] Third, neither the Europeans nor the United States can be treated as unitary actors. Rather, transnational and transgovernmental coalitions among societal and bureaucratic

[2] See Immanuel Kant, "Perpetual Peace: A Philosophical Sketch," in *Kant: Political Writings*, 2d. ed., ed. Hans Reiss (Cambridge: Cambridge University Press, 1991), 93–130; Karl W. Deutsch et al., *Political Community and the North Atlantic Area* (Princeton, N.J.: Princeton University Press, 1957). For overviews on liberal approaches to international relations, see, for example, Ernst-Otto Czempiel, *Friedensstrategien* (Paderborn: Schöningh, 1986); Andrew Moravcsik, *Liberalism and International Relations Theory*, 2d ed., Working Paper Series (Cambridge, Mass.: Center for International Affairs, Harvard University, 1993); Bruce Russett, *Grasping the Democratic Peace* (Princeton, N.J.: Princeton University Press, 1993). For details, see chapter 2.

[3] See, for example, Robert O. Keohane, *International Institutions and State Power* (Boulder, Colo.: Westview, 1989); Friedrich Kratochwil, *Rules, Norms, and Decisions* (Cambridge: Cambridge University Press, 1989); Harald Müller, "Internationale Beziehungen als kommunikatives Handeln: Zur Kritik der utilitaristischen Handlungstheorie," *Zeitschrift für Internationale Beziehungen* 1, no. 1 (1994): 15-44. My use of the terms *liberal* and *institutionalist* in this book differs from the way these terms are often utilized in the international relations literature. In particular, I reserve the notion of "liberal" for approaches systematically linking domestic and international politics. For details, see chapter 2.

[4] For a theoretical argument on such processes, see Robert Putnam, "Diplomacy and Domestic Politics: The Logic of Two-level Games," *International Organization* 42, no. 3 (Summer 1988): 427–60.

actors frequently tipped the domestic "balance of power" in Washington in favor of allied demands.[5]

This book concentrates on the impact of the alliance community and its normative framework on U.S. foreign policy during the cold war as the dependent variable. As a result, less emphasis is placed on the origins of this community among Western Democracies. I present a deductive argument in chapter 2 that links liberal domestic structures to the emergence of "pluralistic security communities." But I do not try to explain the historical origins of the Western Alliance and NATO, because I am primarily concerned with the *impact* of the community on the foreign policy of the member states, particularly the United States. There is only so much that can be done in one book.

This study contributes to various theoretical and empirical debates in the field of international relations. First, there is the ongoing dispute in international relations theory between various realist, liberal, and institutionalist approaches.[6] This study tries to systematically evaluate the empirical validity claims of two versions of realism against liberal and institutionalist arguments. *Structural realism* in the Waltzian sense[7] provides the "null hypothesis" of this book, according to which small states are not expected to exert much impact on great power decisions in alliances under bipolarity. Using insights from *traditional realism*, hegemonic stability theory, and realist bargaining theory, however, one can posit a "big influence of small allies" under certain specified conditions. This latter version of realism privileges bargaining processes rather than exclusively focusing on outcomes. It can, therefore, be evaluated against liberal and institutionalist propositions emphasizing a community of liberal democracies, collective identities, alliance norms, "two-level games," and transnational politics.

While Joseph Grieco focused on European-American trade relations to test neoliberal institutionalism,[8] I examine the transatlantic *security* rela-

[5] On transnational and transgovernmental relations, see Robert O. Keohane and Joseph S. Nye, Jr., eds., *Transnational Relations and World Politics* (Cambridge, Mass.: Harvard University Press, 1972); Keohane and Nye, "Transgovernmental Relations and International Organizations," *World Politics* 27 (1974): 39–62; Thomas Risse-Kappen, ed., *Bringing Transnational Relations Back In* (Cambridge: Cambridge University Press, 1995).

[6] See, for example, David A. Baldwin, ed., *Neorealism and Neoliberalism* (New York: Columbia University Press, 1993); Robert O. Keohane, ed., *Neorealism and Its Critics* (New York: Columbia University Press, 1986); Richard N. Lebow and Thomas Risse-Kappen, eds., *International Relations Theory and the End of the Cold War* (New York: Columbia University Press, 1995).

[7] See Kenneth N. Waltz, *Theory of International Politics* (Reading, Mass.: Addison-Wesley, 1979).

[8] See Joseph Grieco, *Cooperation among Nations* (Ithaca, N.Y.: Cornell University Press, 1990).

tionship to probe approaches based on material power structures and claiming to be particularly relevant in the security area. While Robert Cox maintained that the postwar *pax americana* established U.S. hegemony combining material capabilities and cultural values in an "empire of consent,"[9] I want to know whether this consensus stemmed from hegemonic rule or from cooperation among democracies. While Joseph Nye argued that European influence on American foreign policy resulted from U.S. concerns about the Soviet Union during the cold war,[10] I examine whether Nye's emphasis on "soft power" resources such as values, norms, and knowledge might provide a better explanation for the allied impact than the perception of external threats. While John Ikenberry and Charles Kupchan claimed that America used "socializing power" to establish its hegemony,[11] I take the opposite perspective and investigate how Europeans "socialized" the United States.

The second debate to which this book contributes refers to ontological and epistemological concerns in the study of world politics. It has become fashionable to distinguish between "rationalist" and "reflectivist" approaches to international institutions.[12] The so-called rationalist school takes state interests as either fixed or exogenously given. International institutions and norms are expected to merely influence the cost-benefit calculations of actors and to constrain their behavior. "Social constructivists" argue instead that key structures of international relations are social and intersubjective rather than material.[13] The social and communicative practices of actors helps them to identify their interests and to create norms and international institutions. At the same time, norms of appropriate behavior affect the practices by enabling interaction and communi-

[9] See Robert Cox, *Production, Power, and World Order* (New York: Columbia University Press, 1987), chaps. 6, 7. See also Geir Lundestad, *The American "Empire"* (Oslo: Norwegian University Press, 1990).

[10] Joseph S. Nye, Jr., *Bound to Lead* (New York: Basic Books, 1990), 90–91.

[11] G. John Ikenberry and Charles A. Kupchan, "Socialization and Hegemonic Power," *International Organization* 44, no. 2 (Summer 1990): 283–315.

[12] On this distinction, see Keohane, *International Institutions and State Power*, 158–79. I do not find the term *reflectivism* particularly helpful, though. It lumps together approaches that need to be distinguished according to their ontological and epistemological claims—from social constructivist to critical as well as poststructural theories. In the following, I concentrate on "social constructivism" emphasizing norm-governed communicative practices in international relations. See, for example, Kratochwil, *Norms, Rules, and Decisions*; Müller, "Internationale Beziehungen als kommunikatives Handeln;" Alexander Wendt, "The Agent-Structure Problem in International Relations Theory," *International Organization* 41, no. 3 (Summer 1987): 335–70; Wendt, "Anarchy Is What States Make of It," *International Organization* 46, no. 2 (Spring 1992): 391–425. My thinking on the subject has been strongly influenced by a collaborative project directed by Peter Katzenstein. See Katzenstein, ed., *Norms and International Security* (forthcoming).

[13] See Alexander Wendt, "Collective Identity Formation and the International State," *American Political Science Review* 88, no. 2 (June 1994): 384–96.

cation based on collective understandings. International institutions and the social structure of world politics in general then contribute to defining actors' identities and interests.

The theoretical difference between the two approaches leads to a different emphasis in the study of international norms and institutions. "Rationalists" tend to focus on behavior and policy outcomes, while "social constructivists" concentrate on communicative action and the discourses of actors. However, it seems to me that the differences between the two approaches have been overstated.[14] To the extent that "rationalists" and "social constructivists" make different substantive claims, these propositions can be evaluated empirically. In this book, for example, I compare "rationalist" assumptions about the "big influence of small allies" with claims about cooperation among democracies developed from an interpretation of liberal theory that incorporates insights from "social constructivism." Moreover, the difference between the two approaches ought not to be that "rationalists" emphasize deeds and behavior, while "social constructivists" focus on words and norms. Rather, the latter should be as interested as the former in explaining state behavior in international relations. "Social constructivists" argue, however, that state actions cannot be adequately understood without taking the communications and self-understandings of actors seriously. This book then tries to explain the European influence on American foreign policy as the behavioral consequences of communicative practices.

The third area to which this study contributes concerns the empirical analysis of the transatlantic relationship. While the literature on NATO is enormous, surprisingly little has been written on the mechanisms and processes of intra-alliance cooperation. The overwhelming majority of studies on the transatlantic relationship focuses on European security issues and the U.S. contribution.[15] Nobody disputes that American foreign policy decisively shaped European security after 1945. But there is very little available on the impact of NATO and the European allies on American foreign policy. In addition, many of these studies are more than twenty years old.[16] This book contributes to closing an important empiri-

[14] See Keohane, *International Institutions and State Power*, 158–79; Friedrich Kratochwil and John Ruggie, "International Organization: A State of the Art on an Art of the State," *International Organization* 40, no. 4 (Autumn 1986): 753–75.

[15] For overviews see, for example, David Calleo, *Beyond American Hegemony* (New York: Basic Books, 1987); Alfred Grosser, *The Western Alliance* (New York: Continuum, 1980); Lawrence S. Kaplan, *NATO and the United States* (Boston: Twague, 1988); Elizabeth Sherwood, *Allies in Crisis* (New Haven, Conn.: Yale University Press, 1989); Douglas Stuart and William Tow, *The Limits of Alliance* (Baltimore: Johns Hopkins University Press, 1990).

[16] See, for example, William R. Fox and Annette B. Fox, *NATO and the Range of American Choice* (New York: Columbia University Press, 1967); Richard Neustadt, *Alliance Politics* (New York: Columbia University Press, 1970). There are two more recent studies, though, that reach conclusions similar to those of this book. See Fred Chernoff, *After Bi-*

cal gap in the literature on the transatlantic relationship. While most studies emphasize the American impact on European politics, this analysis looks the other way round and examines how West European governments and NATO membership in general have affected U.S. foreign policy.

Finally, there is the policy debate about the future of the transatlantic relationship. As the cold war is over, many expect the break-up of the Western alliance into competing trading blocs such as the United States, the European Community, and Japan. They argue that the Soviet threat was the glue that held NATO together. The bipolar structure of the international system and nuclear weapons kept the "long peace" (John Lewis Gaddis). As the system moves toward multipolarity, many fear that it will be increasingly difficult to contain ethnic and nationalist rivalries. In sum, those who believe in the anarchic and inherently conflictual nature of international relations, expect a rather nasty and brutish post–cold war world.[17]

In contrast, liberal theorists argue that peace and cooperation among the OECD nations are likely to be sustained, since they are not based on the power structure of the international system, but on the democratic domestic orders of these states. To the extent that the Central Eastern European countries and the successor states of the Soviet Union move toward democracy and market economies, they will be increasingly integrated in the peace order of liberal democracies. The liberal countervision for the post–cold war world expects a community of democratic nations with highly institutionalized and interdependent relationships from San Francisco to Berlin, Vladivostok, and Tokyo.[18]

It is futile to decide between these visions at a time when international relations in the post–cold war world are still in flux. But one can look at liberal democracies in the past and evaluate which theoretical approach offers a more plausible explanation for their interaction patterns. The evidence from the 1950s and 1960s presented in this book suggests cautious optimism that the "democratic peace" will hold in a changed interna-

---

polarity (Ann Arbor: University of Michigan Press, 1994); and Helga Haftendorn, *Kernwaffen und die Glaubwürdigkeit der Allianz* (Baden-Baden: Nomos, 1994).

[17] For this argument see John Mearsheimer, "Back to the Future: Instability in Europe after the Cold War," *International Security* 15, no. 1 (1990): 5–56. On the "long peace" see John Lewis Gaddis, *The Long Peace* (New York: Oxford University Press, 1987).

[18] See, for example, Emanuel Adler, "Europe's New Security Order: A Pluralistic Security Community," in *The Future of European Security*, ed. Beverly Crawford, (Berkeley: University of California Center for German and European Studies, 1992), 287–326; Dieter Senghaas, *Friedensprojekt Europa* (Frankfurt/M.: Suhrkamp, 1992); Steven Van Evera, "Primed for Peace: Europe after the Cold War," *International Security* 15, no. 3 (Winter 1990–1991): 7–57.

tional environment—to the extent to which generalizations from a specific historical context are at all possible. The picture emerging from the transatlantic relationship in the past closely resembles Kant's "pacific federation" and Deutsch's "pluralistic security community." But various interallied confrontations of the 1950s, in particular the Suez crisis, also suggest that maintaining such a community requires conscious efforts.

The next chapter provides the study's theoretical framework and elaborates three sets of propositions about interaction patterns in alliances among unequals derived from realist and liberal approaches to international relations. Waltzian structural realism argues that, under bipolarity, the international distribution of power by and large determines the distribution of influence in alliances among unequals. Smaller states should only have limited influence on the alliance leader. Traditional realism as well as hegemonic stability theory, however, assume that great powers need allies to compete in a global hegemonic rivalry such as the cold war. Small states are then expected to influence great powers under circumstances specified by realist bargaining theory.

Liberal theories also posit a disproportionate influence of small allies, but for different reasons. Alliances among democracies become democratic alliances shaping the collective identity of the actors. Institutionalism adds the role of consultation norms in allied interactions and expects transnational as well as transgovernmental coalitions among societal and bureaucratic actors to flourish when democracies deal with each other in a highly institutionalized setting such as NATO.

Chapters 3 to 6 contain four in-depth case studies. At the end of each case study, I summarize the findings in light of the propositions developed in chapter 2 and also investigate alternative explanations such as power-based accounts, domestic politics, and leadership beliefs.

Chapter 3 examines the 1950–1953 Korean War. The West European and Canadian allies prevented various courses of U.S. action that would have escalated the war into China, including the use of nuclear weapons. The allies also crucially influenced the American position during the armistice negotiations. The case study disconfirms the argument about the limited influence of small allies. Liberal propositions about cooperation among democracies provide a slightly better understanding for the allied interactions during the Korean War than realist bargaining theory. But this case alone does not provide sufficient evidence to decide between the two sets of propositions.

Chapter 4 examines the most important allied confrontation of the 1950s, the 1956 Suez crisis. The United States won the dispute by using its superior economic power and coerced the British and the French into giving up their military attempts to regain control of the Suez Canal.

While the outcome confirms the structural realist view, I claim that the *process* leading to the confrontation can only be understood in the context of liberal and institutionalist arguments. The interallied confrontation resulted from the gradual breakdown and mutual violation of alliance norms culminating in the temporary collapse of the sense of community among the actors. When the normative arrangements shaping the transatlantic alliance are no longer honored, however, U.S. superior power is likely to prevail.

In contrast to the Suez crisis, the 1958–1963 test ban negotiations represent another case of significant European impact on American foreign policy (chapter 5). The British decisively influenced American negotiating behavior toward arms control. Most compromise proposals originated in London and were eventually adopted by the United States. In particular, transnational and transgovernmental coalitions between British and U.S. actors significantly affected the domestic power balance in Washington. The case study confirms liberal and institutionalist propositions, while alternative explanations are implausible. The chapter also compares the British influence supporting a test ban agreement with the impact of the French and West German opposition against an accord. While the Germans were bought off by the United States to secure their signature to the test ban treaty, the French impact was rather limited.

The case of the 1962 Cuban Missile crisis also supports the general argument of this book (chapter 6). Formal interallied consultations were limited during the crisis with the exception of British input. But the sense of allied community and the normative underpinnings of the transatlantic relationship played a significant role in the internal debates among U.S. decision-makers. Questions of European security including the fate of Berlin were among the most important foreign policy items on the American agenda outside the direct confrontation with the Soviet Union and Cuba. Alliance considerations influenced crucial U.S. decisions during the crisis including the secret "missile swap" to remove the Soviet missiles from Cuba in exchange for the withdrawal of U.S. Jupiter missiles from Turkey. Moreover, NATO's dense transgovernmental networks partly made up for the lack of official consultation with the Europeans.

One could argue, though, that the evidence of allied influence in the four case studies pertains to, first, British impact on U.S. foreign policy in the context of the "special relationship," and, second, to a particular period of time at the height of the cold war. I take a brief look, therefore, at several NATO decisions regarding nuclear strategy and deployments from the 1960s to the 1980s (chapter 7). The evidence essentially confirms the findings from the in-depth case studies and shows that the empirical results can be generalized to other time periods, issue areas, and to European allies other than the British. Particularly West Germany had a significant impact on American nuclear decisions in the cases of NATO's "flexible response" strategy, the "neutron bomb," and Intermediate-range Nuclear Forces (INF) deployments and arms control.

The concluding chapter 8 starts with a summary of the empirical findings in light of the theoretical expectations. The case studies disconfirm the (structural realist) proposition that the Europeans should not have much impact on U.S. foreign policy, given the condition of bipolarity and the power asymmetry in NATO. I then argue that, on balance, liberal and institutionalist theories focusing on cooperation among democracies, consultation norms, "two-level games," and transnational coalition-building offer a better understanding of the cases than traditional realism including realist bargaining theory.

But there is considerable variation in allied impact on U.S. foreign policy between Britain and Germany, on the one hand, and France, on the other, representing a puzzle for the liberal argument. I maintain that the decreasing French influence on American decisions mainly resulted from a deliberate decision by the Paris government to gradually deinstitutionalize the transatlantic ties. I then propose some avenues for further research. Chapter 8 concludes with a discussion of the study's policy consequences for the transatlantic relationship in the post-cold war environment. The three theoretical approaches evaluated in this book also offer distinct expectations for the future of NATO.

TWO

COOPERATION AMONG ALLIES

POWER, BARGAINING OR DEMOCRATIC COMMUNITY?

THIS CHAPTER provides the theoretical framework of the book and presents the propositions to be evaluated in the case studies. I discuss three conceptual approaches to the study of intra-alliance relations by contrasting two realist explanations with an argument based on liberal and institutionalist theories. First, structural realism in the tradition of Kenneth Waltz represents the "null hypothesis." In a bipolar order, the distribution of power in alliances among unequals should ultimately determine the distribution of influence.

Second, realism in the tradition of Hans Morgenthau and others combining insights from alliance theory, hegemonic stability theory, and bargaining theory comes to different conclusions. Under bipolarity, the two superpowers compete fiercely about the acquisition of client states and, therefore, place some value on maintaining the coalition. Rational alliance leaders, who are interested in the long-term maintenance of their position, are then expected to rule by consent, which implies that small allies can exert at least some leverage on the leader's decisions. Realist bargaining theory spells out the conditions under which small allies influence the great power.

Third, liberal theory following Immanuel Kant argues that it is not the power relationship that determines the influence distribution in alliances among democracies, but the common identities, values, norms, and decision-making procedures that are institutionalized in such alliances and reflect the liberal character of the domestic political structures of the member states. Democracies form "pluralistic security communities" (Karl W. Deutsch); their international institutions are based on norms and decision-making procedures emphasizing timely consultation, compromise, and the equality of the participants. These norms, together with domestic politics as a bargaining resource ("two-level games") and transnational as well as transgovernmental coalition-building provide the tools by which democratic allies are likely to influence each other.

In sum, the three approaches not only posit different outcomes of inter-allied bargaining, but also different processes, how (democratic) allies affect each other's decisions. Thus, differentiating between "outcome" and "process" allows evaluation of the empirical validity of the propositions derived from the three approaches. Structural realism differs from both traditional realism and liberal theory with regard to the outcome of allied influence. Traditional realism and liberalism both expect significant European influence on American foreign policy but assume different processes by which the allies deal with each other.

Prior to a discussion of the various theories, an operational definition of "significant European influence on American foreign policy" is necessary. The concept of "influence" is related to power in the Weberian sense, that is, the ability to get somebody to do something that he or she would not do otherwise.[1] Two problems have to be solved if "influence" is defined in such a way. First, we need to know more about the sources of "influence." This is the realm of the three approaches to be discussed below.

Second, we need measurable indicators of "considerable influence" as opposed to "marginal impact" and the like. There has to be a change in American behavior traced back to allied demands that cannot be explained otherwise. But it cannot be expected that the European allies single-handedly change American preferences and decisions, since many other factors exert influence on U.S. choices. In other words, degrees of "European influence" have to be measured in comparison to these other factors. I only use the notion of "considerable" or "significant" European influence on American decisions if it can be plausibly argued that alternative explanations provide a less convincing account of the particular choices. In the case studies, I regularly discuss alternative accounts emphasizing

the *power structure* of the international system,
domestic politics, and
leadership beliefs.

"European influence on American foreign policy," then, means the following in this study:

• There is an initial disagreement over policies between at least one major European ally and significant U.S. actors in charge of foreign policy decisions.[2]

[1] Since most international relations theorists use the term *power* in the sense of a resource rather than an ability, I will use the term *influence* in the following for the second notion, while *power* will be reserved for the first to avoid confusion. For a discussion of the two concepts of power see Robert O. Keohane, "Realism, Neorealism, and the Study of World Politics," in *Neorealism and Its Critics*, ed. Robert O. Keohane (New York: Columbia University Press, 1986), 1–26, 11. See also David Baldwin, "Power Analysis and World Politics: New Trends versus Old Tendencies," *World Politics* 31, no. 2 (January 1979): 161–94; James G. March, "The Power of Power," in *Varieties of Political Theory*, ed. David Easton (New York: Prentice Hall, 1966), 39–70.

[2] "Initial disagreement" constitutes a precondition for exerting influence. If there is harmony, it is unnecessary to exercise influence, since there is no cooperation problem (see Robert O. Keohane, *After Hegemony* [Princeton, N.J.: Princeton University Press, 1984], 53–54). "Major European allies" are Great Britain, France, and West Germany. "Significant

- European demands are represented in the American foreign policy process, either directly through interallied consultations or indirectly through domestic and/or bureaucratic U.S. actors referring to allied concerns in the internal deliberations.
- Decisions either come close to the initial European demands or represent intra-alliance compromises;
- *and* American decisions cannot be explained more plausibly by alternative accounts.

If European influence on American foreign policy can be found, it should be all the more significant,

- the more the decisions at stake are perceived as *vital* by U.S. actors;
- the more the U.S. definition of *interests* rather than particular choices are involved;
- the greater the *initial disagreement* between U.S. actors and European allies;
- the more an initial U.S. *domestic consensus* on the issue emerges that is opposed to the European views.

Structural Realism: Who Pays the Piper (Ultimately) Calls the Tune

Realism constitutes an obvious point of departure for a discussion of intra-alliance relations among unequals. One could even argue that realism *is* an alliance theory since it is particularly concerned with the balance of power in the international system, that is, with the formation and dissolution of alliances due to changes in the distribution of power.[3] At least two realist perspectives of intra-alliance dynamics, which come to different conclusions concerning the influence of small allies on their leaders, can be distinguished. Both perspectives share fundamental assumptions about the nature of world politics, namely that

(1) states are the dominant and unitary actors in international relations calculating ends and means rationally;
(2) the international system is anarchic, constituting a self-help system; and

---

U.S. actors" are, for example, the president, the State Department, the Pentagon, the military, and congressional committees involved in decisions.

[3] See, for example, Hans J. Morgenthau, *Politics among Nations* (1948), brief ed. (New York: McGraw-Hill, 1993); Kenneth N. Waltz, *Theory of International Politics* (Reading, Mass.: Addison-Wesley, 1979). See also Arnold Wolfers, *Discord and Collaboration* (Baltimore: Johns Hopkins University Press, 1962); George Liska, *Nations in Alliance* (Baltimore: Johns Hopkins University Press, 1962).

(3) rational states calculate their interests in response to the power structure of the international system.[4]

Structural realism or "neorealism" in the tradition of Kenneth Waltz offers a parsimonious systemic theory of international relations.[5] If it is used to generate propositions about foreign policy, the famous statement by Athenian officials to the Melians, as reported by Thucydides, that "the strong do what they can and the weak suffer what they must,"[6] essentially captures the thrust of the argument. The overall power distribution among the units determines the structure of the international system. Bipolarity in the Waltzian sense is characterized by the presence of only two great powers (superpowers) in the system outweighing the resources of all other states. The superpowers do not need allies to secure their own survival, while the smaller states are dependent on them for protection. Defection by one or more allies does not change the overall balance of power (for example, the French withdrawal from the military integration of NATO in 1966 or the Chinese-Soviet split in the early 1960s). As a result, the bargaining leverage of smaller states in alliances under bipolarity is expected to be fairly limited. As Waltz argues, the contributions of smaller states to alliances

> are useful even in a bipolar world, but they are not indispensable. Because they are not, the policies and strategies of alliance leaders are ultimately made according to their own calculations and interests. . . .
>
> Alliance leaders are not free of constraints. The major constraints, however, arise from the main adversary and not from one's own associates.[7]

Smaller states are expected to have little influence on the policies of the

[4] For a discussion of these assumptions see Robert O. Keohane, "Theory of World Politics: Structural Realism and Beyond," in *Neorealism and Its Critics*, 158–203, 164–65.

[5] Strictly speaking, structural realism in the Waltzian sense does not offer a theory of foreign policy. See Waltz, *Theory of International Politics*, chap. 4. It is, therefore, difficult using structural realism to generate hypotheses about the behavior of particular states. The rationality assumption in realist thinking nevertheless provides a link between the systemic structure and state behavior and allows for theorizing about the foreign policy of rational states.

[6] Thucydides, *The History of the Peloponnesian War* (Harmondsworth: Penguin, 1954), book 5, par. 90.

[7] Waltz, *Theory of International Politics*, 169, 170. Glenn H. Snyder applies this thought to the transatlantic alliance: "It is abundantly clear that the European allies will not do the United States' bidding when it is not in their own interest, but it is also clear that they have little positive influence over U.S. policy—when the United States does not wish to be influenced. . . . the word that most accurately describes their behavior is not domination or even bargaining, but unilateralism." Glenn H. Snyder, "Alliance Theory: A Neorealist First Cut," *Journal of International Affairs* 44, no. 1 (Spring 1990): 103–23, 121. For a discussion of the peculiar notion of bipolarity on which this argument relies, see R. Harrison Wagner, "What Was Bipolarity?" *International Organization* 47, no. 1 (Winter 1993): 77–106.

alliance leader under bipolarity. This does not mean that superpowers always coerce their weaker allies into acquiescence; they frequently use persuasion or bribery and also "socialize" their smaller partners to accept the hegemonic system.[8] It is also consistent with the argument that superpowers give in on minor issues to keep their clients happy. But when it comes to vital security interests, alliance leaders are expected to resort to unilateral decisions without paying much attention to the interests of their client states. Only when the power of the alliance leader decreases in comparison to the opposing superpower or when other rival powers emerge would one expect the influence of the smaller partners to increase. In these cases, the structure of the system changes and bipolarity erodes.

The transatlantic security relationship during the 1950s and early 1960s seems to fit Waltzian assumptions about intra-alliance relations under bipolarity. The U.S. economic and military preponderance in NATO was overwhelming. In 1950 the United States was the only nuclear power in the alliance, and its overall military strength (measured in terms of defense spending) was far greater than that of all other NATO allies combined ($17.7 billion versus $8.9 billion). Ten years later, the ratio had actually increased to almost 3:1 ($45.4 billion versus $15.9 billion).[9] The Gross Domestic Product (GDP) of all NATO allies combined reached only 77 percent of the U.S. GDP in 1950; it increased to 91 percent in 1960.[10]

One could even go one step further and argue that the world was not bipolar but unipolar at the time.[11] Militarily, the United States enjoyed nuclear superiority over the Soviet Union, and the USSR's economic wealth reached about 36 percent of the American GDP in 1950 and still less than 50 percent in 1960. As a result, defection of one or two of the European allies would have only marginally affected the global distribution of power.

It could be argued, though, that, in the absence of intercontinental

[8] See G. John Ikenberry and Charles A. Kupchan, "Socialization and Hegemonic Power," *International Organization* 44, no. 2 (Summer 1990): 283–315.

[9] Data in 1960 prices, according to *World Armaments and Disarmament: SIPRI Yearbook 1972*, ed. SIPRI (Stockholm: Almquist & Wiksell, 1972), 82.

[10] The 1950 data include West Germany even though it was not yet a NATO member. Calculated from Robert Summer and Alan Heston, "Improved International Comparisons of Real Product and Its Composition: 1950–1980," *The Review of Income and Wealth*, Series 30, no. 2 (June 1984): 207–62, 220–21, 230, 261.

[11] For critical arguments on the Waltzian notion of bipolarity and its application to the cold war see Richard N. Lebow, "The Long Peace, the End of the Cold War, and the Failure of Realism," *International Organization* 48, no. 2 (Spring 1994): 249–77; Bruce Russett, "The Alleged Role of Nuclear Weapons in Controlling the Soviet-American 'Enduring Rivalry,' and in the Future," in *Nuclear Technology and International Politics*, ed. John Gelstad and Olav Norstad (London: Sage, 1994); Wagner, "What Was Bipolarity?"

ballistic missiles, the United States was dependent on the use of air bases in Europe to fight a war against the Soviet Union.[12] But it did not need these bases to protect its own homeland against a Soviet attack, since the USSR did not possess a meaningful capability to directly threaten American survival at the time. The use of the bases was necessary for *extended deterrence* purposes, that is, to protect the European allies against a Soviet attack. If states are first and foremost concerned about their own survival, as structural realists claim, there was not much the United States had to worry about during the 1950s and early 1960s.

Whether the world was bipolar or unipolar during the 1950s and early 1960s, the European and Canadian allies should have had only limited influence on U.S. foreign policy, if one follows Waltzian assumptions. This should apply even more to cases that did not directly affect European regional security. The case selection in this book favors the assumption of limited allied impact. The 1950–1953 Korean War (chapter 3) was the first military confrontation during the cold war and was fought far away from the European theater. The United States provided most of the United Nations (UN) forces and commanded them. The 1958–1963 test ban negotiations (chapter 5) represented the first attempt at nuclear arms control involving the strategic relationship between the two superpowers. The 1962 Cuban Missile crisis (chapter 6) was the most serious direct confrontation between the United States and the Soviet Union during the cold war. In each of these cases, American decision-makers perceived the country's supreme national interests at stake. With regard to the 1956 Suez crisis (chapter 4) and NATO's nuclear decisions (chapter 7), supreme security interests of the United States were involved to a lesser degree. According to Waltzian realism, one should not expect considerable European influence on U.S. decisions in the first three cases, while the theory appears to be indeterminate concerning the latter two. Nevertheless, whenever U.S. and European interests clash in the time period under consideration, structural realists would expect the alliance leader to prevail.

Traditional Realism: The "Big Influence of Small Allies"

The structural realist argument rests on peculiar assumptions. If one relaxes them, one can still adhere to the fundamental postulates of realism (see above) but posit a greater influence of small states in alliances among unequals. Traditional realists such as Hans Morgenthau, Arnold Wolfers, or George Liska were aware of the possibility that small allies could exert

[12] I thank Robert Jervis for alerting me to this point.

disproportionate influence.[13] Their arguments can be combined with insights from hegemonic stability, public choice, and realist bargaining theories.

First, the Waltzian argument interprets bipolarity as reducing a superpower's dependence on small allies. But while great powers may not need allies under bipolarity to ensure their survival, client states might become an asset in the competition among the two superpowers. After all, bipolarity means that the two great powers in the system have to cope primarily with each other. As "defensive positionalists," they are expected to be concerned about relative gains and losses vis-à-vis each other and to compete fiercely.[14] The more relative gains are important, however, the more significant the acquisition of client states should become. While the loss or defection of one small ally might not be important, superpowers might fear that even small losses might set in motion a chain reaction. As a result, they are likely to believe in "domino theories" or to fear "abandonment" by the allies.[15]

Thus, the condition of bipolarity does not necessarily imply that alliances are irrelevant for superpowers. But if they value client states, they should become concerned about their fate.

There is no question that the United States perceived itself in a fierce competition with the Soviet Union during the 1950s and 1960s, even though the world might still have been unipolar at the time. American decision-makers embarked on a major effort to assemble a global alliance system against the USSR. Among these allies, NATO was the most important U.S. strategic asset. The West European allies were the most powerful of the secondary states aligned with the United States. American concerns about "falling dominoes" first originated with regard to Europe.[16] Thus, as R. Harrison Wagner put it, the peculiar Waltzian notion

[13] See Morgenthau, *Politics among Nations*; Liska, *Nations in Alliances*; Wolfers, *Discord and Collaboration*. See also, Robert O. Keohane, "The Big Influence of Small Allies," *Foreign Policy* 2 (1971): 161–82.

[14] See Waltz, *Theory of International Politics*, 106, 170–73. On "relative gains" in particular, see Joseph M. Grieco, *Cooperation among Nations* (Ithaca, N.Y.: Cornell University Press, 1990), 1–50; Grieco, "Anarchy and the Limits of Cooperation: A Realist Critique of the Newest Liberal Institutionalism," *International Organization* 42, no. 3 (Summer 1988): 485–507. For an argument that relative gains are particularly important under bipolarity see Duncan Snidal, "International Cooperation among Relative Gain Maximizers," *International Studies Quarterly* 35, no. 4 (December 1991): 387–402.

[15] On strategic beliefs about "falling dominoes" see Jack Snyder, "Introduction," and "Conclusion," in *Dominoes and Bandwagons*, ed. Jack Snyder and Robert Jervis (New York: Oxford University Press, 1991): 3–19, 276–90; Robert Jervis, "Domino Beliefs and Strategic Behavior," in *Dominoes and Bandwagons*, 20–50. On fears of "abandonment" see Glenn H. Snyder, "The Security Dilemma in Alliance Politics," *World Politics* 36, no. 4 (July 1984): 461–96. See also Wagner, "What Was Bipolarity?"

[16] See Douglas Macdonald, "The Truman Administration and Global Responsibilities: The Birth of the Falling Domino Principle," in *Dominoes and Bandwagons*, 112–44; Doug-

of bipolarity, "far from explaining U.S. and Soviet behavior during the cold war, makes their behavior inexplicable."[17]

It does not necessarily follow from this line of reasoning that the Europeans should have exerted disproportionate influence on U.S. foreign policy, just because they were important for the American grand strategy. After all, the United States needed NATO only to maintain its superpower *status* in the competition with the Soviet Union, while Western Europe needed the United States to insure its *survival* during the cold war. In other words, there was a fundamental asymmetry in the degree to which both sides of the Atlantic were dependent on each other.

Moreover, great powers can use coercion or consent to rule an alliance among unequals. Only consensual decision-making implies some degree of allied influence on the leader's decisions. Rational choice theorists concerned about hegemonic stability[18] argue that rule by coercion involves lesser costs for the hegemonic power than consensual decision-making in the short run, but might prove harmful to its interests in the long run.[19] Client states that are constantly forced to follow the leader's decisions, will try to defect at the earliest opportunity. The fate of the Warsaw Pact is a case in point. Rule by consent, while constraining the hegemonic power in the short term, might be profitable in the long run. It keeps the small allies happy and might prevent them from defection even when the great power's capabilities are no longer sufficient to provide for their security.

A similar point has been made by critical theorists applying Antonio Gramsci's notion of hegemony to international relations. Hegemonic rule combines material power resources with the spread of cultural values and norms in an "empire by consent."[20] Public choice theory adds that great powers are likely to shoulder a disproportionate share of the burden in

---

las Stuart and William Tow, *The Limits of Alliance* (Baltimore: Johns Hopkins University Press, 1990), 24–46.

[17] Wagner, "What Was Bipolarity?" 89.

[18] See, for example, Charles Kindleberger, *The World in Depression, 1929–1939* (Berkeley: University of California Press, 1973); Kindleberger, "Dominance and Leadership in the International Economy," *International Studies Quarterly* 25, no. 3 (June 1981): 242–54. See also Keohane, *After Hegemony*, particularly chaps. 3, 8; Duncan Snidal, "The Limits of Hegemonic Stability Theory," *International Organization* 39, no 4 (Autumn 1985): 579–614.

[19] For an excellent argument, see Lisa L. Martin, "Interests, Power, and Multilateralism," *International Organization* 46, no. 4 (Autumn 1992), 765–92. See also Stephan Haggard and Beth A. Simmons, "Theories of International Regimes," *International Organization* 41, no. 3 (Summer 1987): 491–517, 502–3.

[20] See, for example, Robert Cox, "Social Forces, States, and World Order: Beyond International Relations Theory," in *Neorealism and Its Critics*, 204–54, 223; Cox, *Production, Power, and World Order* (New York: Columbia University Press, 1987), chap. 7; Geir Lundestad, *The American "Empire"* (Oslo: Norwegian University Press, 1990).

multilateral alliances providing the public good of security, while small states are expected to "free ride" on the alliance leader.[21]

Unfortunately, there is no deductive theory available to decide under which conditions great powers should behave in a farsighted way providing the public good and ruling "by consent," and when they should be oriented toward short-term considerations. Suffice it to claim at this point that, under realist assumptions, (1) bipolarity can well imply that superpowers need alliances to compete with each other; and (2) great powers have at least the option to rule by consent, which presupposes some degree of allied influence on its decisions.

The next step is to specify the conditions under which small states are likely to influence the leader's decisions in alliances among unequals. At this point, we need to relax another assumption of structural realism. In its most parsimonious—Waltzian—form, it is based on a "basic force model" of power in which some well-defined economic and military capabilities by and large translate into the actual exercise of influence.[22] Power resources determine outcomes and the process by which these outcomes are achieved becomes largely irrelevant. However, most realists would probably agree that political influence is rarely directly proportionate to material power capabilities. Waltz himself, for example, includes "competence" among the factors defining a state's capabilities.[23] Hans Morgenthau describes "national morale" and the "quality of diplomacy" as elements of national power. Neither of these are material resources, but process variables that determine how states use their material capabilities to achieve their goals. If process becomes significant, a "force activation model" of power (James March) has to be assumed, explaining which of the available power resources in the system are activated under what conditions in international relations. This is the realm of *realist bargaining theory*, which examines how power is used in negotiations among states.[24] It can be applied to specify the conditions under which small allies are likely to exert significant influence on their leader in situations of conflicting preferences.

[21] The classic argument is Mancur Olson and Richard Zeckhauser, "An Economic Theory of Alliances," *Review of Economics and Statistics* 48 (1966): 266–79. For a more recent argument in this tradition, see Mark A. Boyer, *International Cooperation and Public Goods* (Baltimore: Johns Hopkins University Press, 1993).

[22] See March, "Power of Power."

[23] Waltz, *Theory of International Politics*, 131. For the following see Morgenthau, *Politics among Nations*, chap. 8.

[24] See, for example, William M. Habeeb, *Power and Tactics in International Negotiations* (Baltimore: Johns Hopkins University Press, 1988); Michael Handel, *Weak States in the International System* (London: Frank Cass, 1981); Keohane, "Big Influence of Small Allies"; Robert L. Rothstein, *Alliances and Small Powers* (New York: Columbia University Press, 1968); Jan F. Triska, ed., *Dominant Powers and Subordinate States* (Durham, N.C.: Duke University Press, 1986).

If the superpower places a high value on maintaining the alliance and is farsighted enough to forego short-term gains in bargaining situations with the allies, small states might prevail for any or a combination of five reasons. First, small states can make up for their lack of power vis-à-vis the alliance leader because of more intense motivations. If the survival of the client state is at stake, while the superpower only risks minor setbacks for its status, the former is more likely to drive a harder bargain to achieve its goals than the latter. It is difficult to define empirical indicators for the intensity of preferences without deducing them from actual behavior or from bargaining outcomes.[25] I have, therefore, tried to control for the intensity of preferences by concentrating on cases that did not directly involve European security issues. Only the 1956 Suez crisis and NATO's nuclear decisions represent cases where one can argue that the Europeans were more strongly motivated than the U.S. The Korean War, the test ban, and the Cuban Missile crisis, which constitute the main empirical basis for the argument in this book, involved instances in which the United States perceived its vital interests at stake. Moreover, I particularly look at interallied conflict where both sides appeared to feel equally strong. Thus, differences in the intensity of motivation are unlikely to account for the bargaining outcome in the cases under consideration here.

Second, if both superpowers compete fiercely for relative gains, they should value their alliances highly, fear allied defection, and might believe in domino theories. Under these conditions, small allies can exploit the superpowers' concerns and turn their dependence on assistance into bargaining strength. As Robert Keohane put it, "leaders who believe in domino theories not only have to talk to the 'dominoes,' they have to listen to them and believe them as well."[26]

Client states might threaten to defect or even collapse unless their demands are satisfied by the alliance leader. While the threat to collapse does not apply here, the threat to defect or, more appropriately, to remain neutral in disputes between the United States and the Soviet Union was certainly an option for European states and Canada to increase their bargaining power vis-à-vis Washington. Indeed, there were several instances during the Korean War when Britain and Canada threatened to oppose the United States in the United Nations General Assembly. The test ban case coincided with a time period when France was gradually decreasing its commitment to NATO and when President de Gaulle threatened to "go it alone." Thus, the case studies in this volume allow for an evaluation of the assumption.

Third, the alliance leader could choose not to use the power resources at its disposal because of a high level of threat perception. Since alliances

[25] See Keohane, "Theory of World Politics," 186–87, on this point.

[26] Keohane, "Big Influence of Small Allies," 163.

balance against threats,[27] intra-alliance cooperation might be a function of the perceived level of external danger.[28] The more the alliance leader feels threatened by the opponent, the greater the bargaining power of the small allies.

One would then expect greater allied influence during crises and wars than during periods of relaxed tensions between the superpowers. With regard to the case studies in this volume, greater European impact on American decisions should be found during the Korean War and the Cuban Missile crisis than during the test ban negotiations.

Fourth, client states, while powerless when facing the alliance leader alone, could try to increase their leverage by pooling resources and building a united front against the superpower. In the case of NATO, the combined economic strength of the West European allies almost equaled that of the United States during the 1950s and early 1960s (see above). If they confronted Washington unanimously, they represented a power to be reckoned with. One should then find greater allied influence on U.S. foreign policy when the allies were united as compared to instances when major European governments disagreed among themselves. The former was the case during the Korean War, the Cuban Missile and the Suez crises, while London, Paris, and Bonn disagreed among themselves on the desirability of a test ban treaty and with regard to major nuclear decisions of NATO. Thus, the case selection should allow for an evaluation of this proposition, too.

Fifth, client states can increase their bargaining power if they control issue-specific resources needed by the alliance leader in the particular case. As Hans Morgenthau argued,

> [a] great power has a good chance to have its way with a weak ally as concerns benefits and policies. . . . However, this correlation between benefits, policies, and power is by no means inevitable. A weak nation may well possess an asset which is of such great value for its strong ally as to be irreplaceable. Here the unique benefit the former is able to grant or withhold may give it within the alliance a status completely out of keeping with the actual distribution of material power.[29]

The superpower might be crucially dependent on its client with regard

[27] See Stephen H. Walt, *The Origins of Alliances* (Ithaca, N.Y.: Cornell University Press, 1987).

[28] For a discussion see Ole R. Holsti et al., *Unity and Disintegration in International Alliances* (New York: Wiley, 1973), 16–18.

[29] Morgenthau, *Politics among Nations*, 200–201. For a discussion see Christer Jönssen, "Bargaining Power: Notes on an Elusive Concept," *Cooperation and Conflict* 16, no. 4 (1981): 249–57, 256; Jeffrey L. Hughes, "On Bargaining," in *Dominant Powers and Subordinate States*, 168–99, 178–88.

to a specific resource.[30] In the case of NATO, the allies controlled the rights over the bases in Europe, which the United States needed in a conflict with the Soviet Union. Particularly during the 1950s, the United States could not fight a war against the USSR without the cooperation of its allies, who provided "the real estate from which the war would be launched."[31] This was particularly true for West Germany, which, as the front-line state and the main theater of a potential East-West war, had to permit use of its territory for NATO purposes.[32] I have mostly selected "out-of-area" cases for this study so that allied control over resources in Europe were less likely to matter.

Nevertheless, the case studies should allow for an evaluation of the proposition. During the Korean War, escalation of the conflict into a war against the Soviet Union was a frequent concern among the United States and its allies. Planning for such a contingency required European cooperation. With regard to the test ban case, the United States needed access to a British-owned island in the Pacific in 1961 and 1962 to conduct atmospheric tests. Finally, had the Cuban Missile crisis escalated, the European theater would have been affected almost immediately, a possibility that was very much on the mind of decision-makers in Washington (and in Europe).

In sum, a rationalist argument can be made for the "big influence of small allies" (Keohane), which combines insights from traditional realism, hegemonic stability theory, and realist bargaining assumptions. It disagrees with Waltzian realism and claims that the condition of bipolarity and the ensuing competition among the superpowers over relative gains should induce them to place a high value on the acquisition of allies rather than making the latter irrelevant. If the alliance leader is interested in the long-term preservation of its power status, it is likely to rule "by consent" and to grant the clients some influence on its policies under certain conditions. These conditions are then spelled out by realist bargaining theory. Small allies can increase their bargaining leverage,

- if they hold more intense preferences than the alliance leader;
- if they threaten to defect or to remain neutral in disputes among the superpowers;

[30] Moreover, the client itself—its territory, population, and economic strength—might represent such a resource. Since this list of propositions is predicated upon the assumption that the superpower values the allies highly (why would it otherwise care about them?), the case of an ally as a resource is not included here. The argument would become tautological.

[31] Robert Jervis in a letter of May 3, 1993. Of course, as noted above, the United States did not need these bases to protect its own homeland, which was virtually safe at the time, but to defend the allies themselves.

[32] Given this peculiar position of West Germany, I have avoided looking at German influence on American foreign policy, except for chapter 7, since such impact could be explained in terms of West German control over issue-specific resources needed by the United States.

• if the superpower perceives a high level of threat;
• if the allies pool resources and confront the alliance leader with a unified position;
• if they control material resources that the superpower needs under the circumstances and that cannot be provided otherwise.

These propositions are based on a "force activation model" of power and cannot be evaluated by looking at the outcome of allied influence alone. The process of interallied bargaining has to be examined. Moreover, looking at behavior of the United States and its allies is insufficient to evaluate the propositions. The communications are equally important to find out whether power-based considerations indeed motivated the United States to grant the allies significant influence.

A similar methodology applies to the evaluation of liberal and institutionalist assumptions. They agree with traditional realism as far as the outcome of allied influence is concerned, but posit different processes by which this impact is achieved.

Liberalism: Cooperation among Democracies

The analysis so far shows two weaknesses of realism when applied to intra-alliance relations among unequals. First, the theory is indeterminate with regard to the consequences of bipolarity for the influence distribution in such alliances. Structural realism comes to different conclusions than traditional realism, hegemonic stability theory, or realist bargaining approaches. Second, if we take the latter view, we still cannot infer a "big influence of small allies," *unless* we additionally posit that superpowers are driven by long-term considerations.

Both problems exemplify a well-known shortcoming of realism. It takes state interests for granted and infers them from the power structure of the international system. But rational great powers calculating their interests in terms of these external constraints and opportunities still face choices that cannot be deduced from the theory. To use NATO as an example, there was nothing inevitable about the formation of the Western Alliance, since the U.S. had quite some latitude as to how it defined its interests in Europe.[33] As a Waltzian realist, it could have concluded that the direct confrontation with the USSR was all that mattered, while the fate of the

[33] On this point, see also John S. Duffield, "Explaining the Long Peace in Europe: The Contributions of International Security Institutions" (University of Virginia, November 1992, manuscript); Robert Latham, "Liberalism's Order/Liberalism's Other: A Genealogy of Threat," *Alternatives* 20, no. 1 (Winter 1994); Steve Weber, "Shaping the Postwar Balance of Power: Multilateralism in NATO," *International Organization* 46, no. 3 (Summer 1992): 633–80.

West Europeans would not alter the global balance of power. As a more traditional realist, the United States would have decided—as it actually did—that the Eurasian rim land was geostrategically too significant to leave the West Europeans alone. Both choices are well within the range of legitimate applications of realism.

As a result, we need to "look more closely at *this* particular hegemon" in order to "determine why *this* particular institutional agenda was pursued."[34] In other words, domestic politics and domestic structures have to be considered, that is, the realm of *liberal theories* of international relations.

There are many versions of liberalism in world politics, making it hard to sort out a set of core assumptions. Unlike structural realism, the approach lacks parsimony.[35] In the following, I construct a liberal argument about cooperation among democracies from the core of the theory and deduce propositions which can be evaluated empirically in comparison to realist assumptions.

I reserve the term *liberal theories of international relations* for approaches agreeing that

(1) the fundamental agents in international politics are not states but individuals acting in a social context—whether governments, domestic society, or international institutions;

(2) the interests and preferences of governments have to be analyzed as a result of domestic structures and coalition-building processes responding to social demands as well as to external factors such as the material and social structure of the international system;

(3) international institutions, that is, "persistent and connected sets of rules (formal and informal) that prescribe behavioral roles, constrain activity, and shape expectations,"[36] form the social structure of international politics presenting constraints and opportunities to state actors in a similar way as the international distribution of power.

Liberal theories of international relations emphasize domestic and trans-

[34] John G. Ruggie, "Multilateralism: The Anatomy of an Institution," *International Organization* 46, no. 3 (Summer 1992): 561–98, 592.

[35] For efforts at systematizing a liberal theory of international relations see Ernst-Otto Czempiel, *Friedensstrategien* (Paderborn: Schöningh, 1986), 110–67; Michael Doyle, "Liberalism and World Politics," *American Political Science Review* 80, no. 4 (1986): 1151–69; Robert O. Keohane, "International Liberalism Reconsidered," in *The Economic Limits to Modern Politics*, ed. John Dunn (Cambridge: Cambridge University Press, 1990), 165–94; Andrew Moravcsik, *Liberalism and International Relations Theory*, 2d. ed., Working Paper Series (Cambridge, Mass.: Center for International Affairs, Harvard University, 1993); Bruce Russett, *Grasping the Democratic Peace* (Princeton, N.J.: Princeton University Press, 1993).

[36] Robert O. Keohane, *International Institutions and State Power* (Boulder, Colo.: Westview, 1989), 3.

national groups of individuals affecting state interests and preferences; they also privilege values, norms, and knowledge—*ideas*—as part of the social construction of international relations.[37] It follows that a certain version of regime analysis and cooperation theory that Joseph Grieco called 'neoliberal institutionalism' should *not* be regarded part of the liberal paradigm. This "cooperation under anarchy" perspective shares all realist core assumptions, but disagrees with structural realism on the likelihood of international cooperation among self-interested actors.[38] A liberal approach to international relations as defined above has more in common with social constructivist arguments emphasizing communicative action and the collective identity of actors.[39]

Three prominent strands of modern liberal approaches to international relations—republicanism, institutionalism, and transnationalism—can already be found in the writings of the German philosopher Immanuel Kant, particularly his "Perpetual Peace" (1795).[40] Kant asks which conditions in the relationship among states have to be thought necessary to guarantee freedom and morality of the individual. He deduces the idea of

[37] See, for example, Emanuel Adler, *The Power of Ideology* (Berkeley: University of California Press, 1987); Judith Goldstein and Robert Keohane, eds., *Ideas and Foreign Policy* (Ithaca, N.Y.: Cornell University Press, 1993); Ernst Haas, *When Knowledge Is Power* (Berkeley: University of California Press, 1990); Peter Haas, ed., *Knowledge, Power, and International Policy-Coordination*, special issue of *International Organization*, 46, no. 1 (Winter 1992); David H. Lumsdaine, *Moral Vision in International Politics* (Princeton, N.J.: Princeton University Press, 1993); Joseph S. Nye, Jr., *Bound to Lead* (New York: Basic Books, 1990); Kathryn Sikkink, *Ideas and Institutions* (Ithaca, N.Y.: Cornell University Press, 1991).

[38] As Andrew Moravcsik has argued, this approach should more properly be called "modified structural realism." See Moravcsik, *Liberalism and International Relations Theory*, 34. For the term *neoliberal institutionalism*, see Grieco, "Anarchy and the Limits of Cooperation." Examples include Robert Axelrod, *The Evolution of Cooperation* (New York: Basic Books, 1984); Keohane, *After Hegemony*; Kenneth Oye, ed., *Cooperation under Anarchy* (Princeton, N.J.: Princeton University Press, 1986); Arthur Stein, *Why Nations Cooperate* (Ithaca, N.Y.: Cornell University Press, 1990).

[39] See, for example, Friedrich Kratochwil, *Rules, Norms, and Decisions* (Cambridge: Cambridge University Press, 1989); Harald Müller, "Internationale Beziehungen als kommunikatives Handeln," *Zeitschrift für Internationale Beziehungen* 1, no. 1 (1994): 15-44; Alexander Wendt, "Anarchy Is What States Make of It," *International Organization* 46, no. 2 (1992): 391–425; Wendt, "Collective Identity Formation and the International State," *American Political Science Review* 88, no. 2 (June 1994): 384-96.

[40] See Immanuel Kant, "Zum ewigen Frieden: Ein philosophischer Entwurf" (1795), in *Immanuel Kant: Werke in sechs Bänden*, ed. Wilhelm Weischedel (Frankfurt/M.: Insel-Verlag, 1964), 6:193–251. English translation: "Perpetual Peace: A Philosophical Sketch," in *Kant: Political Writings*, 2d ed., ed. Hans Reiss (Cambridge: Cambridge University Press, 1991), 93–130. In the United States, liberalism in international relations is frequently identified with *Wilsonianism* and Woodrow Wilson's Fourteen Points. See Thomas J. Knock, *To End All Wars: Woodrow Wilson and the Quest for a New World Order* (Oxford: Oxford University Press, 1992).

perpetual peace among states from the concept of morality and the principles of practical reason (*praktische Vernunft*) thereby linking the individual with the international level. Kant's insights help integrating the three components into a coherent liberal theory of foreign policy in order to derive propositions about cooperation in alliances among democracies.

Liberal Republicanism: Democracies Rarely Fight Each Other

According to Kant, the first condition of stable peace among nations defined as the effective elimination of potential causes of war[41] pertains to the republican order of the state. A republican constitution is based on the freedom of the individual, the rule of law, and the equality of the citizens before the law. Democratic republics are likely to keep the peace, because,

> if . . . the consent of the citizens is required to decide whether or not war is to be declared, it is very natural that they will have great hesitation in embarking on so dangerous an enterprise. For this would mean calling down on themselves all the miseries of war, such as doing the fighting themselves, supplying the costs of the war from their own resources, painfully making good the ensuing devastation.[42]

The argument links the domestic structure of the state to its foreign policy—a distinctive feature of a liberal theory of world politics. Kant's postulate that a democratic constitution is a necessary condition for peace has been empirically substantiated. That democracies rarely fight each other is no longer controversial among scholars.[43] The reasons for this finding are less clear; at least two explanations can be distinguished. The first focuses on the *norms* governing democratic decision-making processes and establishing the nonviolent and compromise-oriented resolution of political conflicts, the equality of the citizens, majority rule, tolerance for dissent, and the rights of minorities. Democracies perceive other liberal states as equally governed by these norms:

> Domestically just republics, which rest on consent, then presume foreign republics also to be consensual, just, and therefore deserving of accommodation. . . . At the same time, liberal states assume that non-liberal states, which do not rest on free consent, are not just. Because non-liberal governments are in a state of aggression with their own people, their foreign relations become for liberal governments deeply suspect. In short, fellow

[41] Kant, "Perpetual Peace," 93.

[42] Kant, "Perpetual Peace," 100.

[43] On the state of the art see Russett, *Grasping the Democratic Peace*. For the following see ibid., chap. 2.

> liberals benefit from a presumption of amity; nonliberals suffer from a presumption of enmity.[44]

In other words, the social identity of actors is at least partly derived from the democratic character of the domestic structures. This leads to a collective identification process among actors of democratic states, which also defines the "out-group" as nondemocratic.[45]

A second explanation emphasizes *institutional constraints*. Democratic political systems are characterized by an elaborate set of checks and balances—between the executive and the legislature, between the political system, interest groups, public opinion, and so on. One could then argue that the complexity of the decision-making process makes it unlikely that leaders readily use military force unless they are confident of gathering enough domestic support for a low-cost war. They will perceive leaders of other democracies as equally constrained and, therefore, refrain from violence.[46]

The "institutional constraints" model is theoretically unconvincing. First, the complexity of democratic decision-making procedures is itself partly a function of democratic norms incorporated in the political institutions of liberal systems. It is, therefore, difficult to separate the two explanations. Second, the model cannot explain why democratic leaders sometimes quickly decide to go to war against authoritarian systems, are able to mobilize a lot of societal resources within a short period of time—and get away with it by counting on the "rally 'round the flag" effect.[47] When liberal systems are faced with authoritarian adversaries, the complexity of democratic institutions appears to matter less. Third, institutional constraints—isolated from their normative underpinnings—cannot convincingly explain why rational leaders of democratic systems should not be tempted to exploit equally constrained leaders for a quick and less costly military victory, thereby overcoming their own domestic restrictions.

Thus, the "democratic peace" can be better explained by the norms institutionalized in the decision-making processes of liberal systems. Democracies then perceive other democracies as equally bound by these norms of peaceful conflict resolution as a result of which they do not feel potentially threatened. But it is one thing to account for the "democratic

[44] Doyle, "Liberalism and World Politics," 1161.

[45] For a theoretical argument on this point see Wendt, "Collective Identity Formation and the International State."

[46] For the most recent version of this argument see Bruce Bueno de Mesquita and David Lalman, *War and Reason* (New Haven, Conn.: Yale University Press, 1992), chap. 4.

[47] On this effect see John Mueller, *War, Presidency, and Public Opinion* (New York: Wiley, 1973); Bruce Russett, *Controlling the Sword* (Cambridge, Mass.: Harvard University Press, 1990), chap. 2.

peace." It does not logically follow that liberal states regularly cooperate for common purposes and that the norms governing their cooperation are themselves democratic and allow liberal states equal opportunities to influence each other. Additional assumptions are necessary to carry the argument further.

Liberal Institutionalism: Democracies Form Democratic Communities

Liberal theory does not suggest that democracies live in perpetual harmony with each other and do not face cooperation problems requiring institutional arrangements.[48] Immanuel Kant did not argue that stable peace was the necessary and automatic consequence of the emergence of liberal republics; rather, it has to be "*formally instituted* (*gestiftet*), for a suspension of hostilities is not itself a guarantee of peace. And unless one neighbour gives a guarantee to the other at his request (which can happen only in a *lawful* state), the latter may treat him as an enemy."[49] Kant then postulates a "pacific federation" (*foedus pacificum*) among democratic republics emerging from a formal agreement.

Regime theory argues that a functional demand for formal international institutions exists whenever unilateral and uncoordinated behavior leads to suboptimal outcomes. By pooling resources in international alliances, for example, states balance against external threats more efficiently than by unilateral arms build-ups that might ruin their economies. Regimes reduce transaction costs, provide valuable information for the participants, and stabilize expectations about appropriate behavior.[50]

But a functional need for regimes does not mean that international cooperation will be achieved. Contrary to what "balance of power" theories assume, cooperation even among allies is by no means assured. Allies are

[48] Note again that my use of the term *liberal institutionalism* is different from the conventional usage (see above). *Liberal institutionalism* in this book refers to a line of reasoning that links particular domestic political structures to the likelihood of cooperation and institution-building among states. The notion differs from both "cooperation under anarchy" regime analysis (Grieco's "neoliberal institutionalism") and from "Grotian institutionalism" such as the work of Hedley Bull or Oran Young. On the latter see Bull, *The Anarchical Society* (New York: Columbia University Press, 1977); Young, *International Cooperation* (Ithaca, N.Y.: Cornell University Press, 1989).

[49] Kant, "Perpetual Peace," 98 (German: "Zum ewigen Frieden," 203; emphasis in original).

[50] See Keohane, *International Institutions and State Power*, 101–31; Stephen Krasner, ed., *International Regimes* (Ithaca, N.Y.: Cornell University Press, 1983); Harald Müller, *Die Chance der Kooperation* (Darmstadt: Wissenschaftliche Buchgesellschaft, 1993); Volker Rittberger, ed., *Regime Theory and International Relations* (Oxford: Clarendon Press, 1993); Young, *International Cooperation*.

actually more likely to fight each other than non-allies—except for democratic alliances.[51]

International relations theory has identified various obstacles toward achieving stable cooperation among states, such as fear of cheating, orientation toward relative gains, and uncertainty about each other's (peaceful) motives resulting from the "security dilemma."[52] Each of these hurdles can be overcome among democracies.[53]

Democracies appear to infer external behavior from the values and norms governing the domestic decision-making processes. These norms insure the nonviolent resolution of conflicts. Together with the publicity of the democratic process, they reduce uncertainties about peaceful intentions. Democracies then view each other as peaceful, which substantially reduces the significance of the "security dilemma" among them and, thus, removes a major obstacle to stable security cooperation.

The same is true for the "relative gains" problem, particularly in the security area. In the realist world of anarchy, today's friend can always be tomorrow's enemy; each state has to worry that its ally might gain more from cooperation than itself. But actors of democratic states "know" through the process of social identification described above that they are unlikely to fight each other in the future. They share liberal values pertaining to political life and form what Karl W. Deutsch called a "pluralistic security community" defined as "a group of people which has become 'integrated.' By INTEGRATION we mean the attainment, within a territory, of a 'sense of community' and of institutions and practices strong enough and widespread enough to assure, for a 'long' time, dependable expectations of 'peaceful change' among its population."[54] The commu-

[51] For evidence, see Bruce Bueno de Mesquita, *The War Trap* (New Haven, Conn.: Yale University Press, 1981); Stuart A. Bremer, "Dangerous Dyads: Conditions Affecting the Likelihood of Interstate War, 1816–1965," *Journal of Conflict Resolution* 36, no. 2 (1992): 309–41.

[52] See Grieco, "Anarchy and the Limits of Cooperation;" Krasner, *International Regimes*; Müller, *Chance der Kooperation*; Oye, *Cooperation under Anarchy*; Stein, *Why Nations Cooperate*. On the "security dilemma" see John Herz, *Political Realism and Political Idealism* (Chicago: Chicago University Press, 1951); Robert Jervis, "Cooperation under the Security Dilemma," *World Politics* 30, no. 2 (1978): 167–214.

[53] I do not suggest that interstate cooperation is only possible among democracies, only that obstacles against cooperation can be overcome more easily among liberal systems.

[54] Karl W. Deutsch et al., *Political Community and the North Atlantic Area* (Princeton, N.J.: Princeton University Press, 1957), 5–6. For the following, see ibid., 46–59, 123–33. For work in this tradition see Peter Katzenstein, *Disjoined Partners* (Berkeley: University of California Press, 1976); Richard Merritt, *Symbols of American Community, 1735–1775* (New Haven, Conn.: Yale University Press, 1966); Donald J. Puchala, "Integration Theory and the Study of International Relations," in *From National Development to Global Community*, ed. Richard L. Merritt and Bruce Russett (London: Allen & Unwin, 1981), 145–64; Bruce Russett, *Community and Contention* (Cambridge, Mass.: MIT Press, 1963); and recently

nity of values leads to mutual responsiveness in terms of "mutual sympathy and loyalties; of 'we-feeling,' trust, and consideration; of at least partial identification in terms of self-images and interests; of the ability to predict each other's behavior and ability to act in accordance with that prediction."[55]

While Deutsch's notion of pluralistic security communities was not confined to democracies, it is unlikely that a similar sense of mutual responsiveness could emerge among autocratic leaders. There is nothing in their values that would prescribe mutual sympathy, trust, and consideration. Rather, cooperation among nondemocracies is likely to emerge out of self-interests narrowly defined and to remain fragile.

Most liberal systems not only share democratic values but also a common appreciation of capitalist market economies.[56] Why is it that their community of values is based upon the norms governing their domestic *political* rather than *economic* orders? If the latter were the case, relative gains would matter more, since the norms governing capitalist orders emphasize competition and—albeit regulated—conflict. Fierce economic competition among capitalist states does not contradict the notion of a security community among democracies, though. International competition among capitalists is as much predicated upon a stable and peaceful international order as a domestic capitalist economy requires the state to guarantee property rights and the rule of law. Such a stable international order cannot be built upon capitalist values of competition but requires the mutual recognition of democratic norms of peaceful conflict resolution.

Relative gains are then expected to be less of an obstacle given the content of the shared values. Democracies are free to pursue joint gains by building international institutions for specific purposes. For example, liberal democracies are more likely than authoritarian systems to form alliances against perceived external threats; such alliances also last comparatively longer.[57] At the same time, these institutions strengthen the

---

Emanuel Adler, "Europe's New Security Order: A Pluralistic Security Community," in *The Future of European Security*, ed. Beverly Crawford (Berkeley: Center for German and European Studies, University of California, 1992), 287–326; Adler and Michael Barnett, "Security Communities" (prepared for delivery at the 1994 annual meeting of the American Political Science Association, New York, September 1–4, 1994).

[55] Deutsch, *Political Community*, 129. See also Wendt, "Collective Identity Formation and the International State."

[56] I thank Mark Laffey for alerting me to this point.

[57] See Bueno de Mesquita and Lalman, *War and Reason*, 166–67; Randolph M. Siverson and Juliann Emmons, "Birds of a Feather: Democratic Political Systems and Alliance Choices in the Twentieth Century," *Journal of Conflict Resolution* 35, no. 2 (June 1991): 285–306; Kurt Taylor Gaubatz, "Democratic States and the Duration of International Alliances" (paper presented at the annual meeting of the American Political Science Association, Washington D.C., August 27-September 1, 1991).

sense of common purpose among the members of the community, since the regimes embody its values and norms.

One could then argue that the North Atlantic Alliance represents an institutionalization of the security community among democracies. While the perceived Soviet threat certainly strengthened the sense of common purpose among the allies, it did not create the community in the first place. NATO was preceded by the wartime alliance of the United States, Great Britain, and France, which also closely collaborated to create various postwar regimes in the economic and security areas.[58] From a liberal and social constructivist perspective, one would argue that the sense of community, by delimiting the boundaries of who belonged to "us,"[59] also defined "them," that is, those outside the community who were then perceived as a threat to the common values. In other words, the collective identity led to the threat perception, not the other way round.[60] Of course, Soviet behavior during the immediate postwar years, in particular the Sovietization of Eastern Europe, continuously confirmed the threat perception.

The North Atlantic Treaty contains various allusions to a community of values. The preamble states in an almost Kantian fashion that the treaty partners are "determined to safeguard the freedom, common heritage and civilization of their peoples, founded on the principles of democracy, individual liberty, and the rule of law." Article 2 determines that NATO is not just about preserving its members' external security. The allies pledge to develop peaceful international relations, to strengthen their democratic institutions, and to promote economic cooperation among themselves.[61]

If democracies are likely to overcome obstacles against international cooperation and to enter institutional arrangements for specific purposes,

[58] This argument does not claim to represent a comprehensive and theoretically informed history of NATO, which is not the subject of this book. For evidence, see Richard Best, *"Cooperation with Like-Minded Peoples"* (Westport, Conn.: Greenwood Press, 1986); Don Cook, *Forging the Alliance* (New York: Arbor House/William Morrow, 1989); Sir Nicholas Henderson, *The Birth of NATO* (London: Weidenfeld & Nicolson, 1982); Timothy P. Ireland, *Creating the Entangling Alliance* (Westport, Conn.: Greenwood Press, 1981); Henry B. Ryan, *The Vision of Anglo-America* (Cambridge: Cambridge University Press, 1987); Weber, "Shaping the Postwar Balance of Power;" John W. Young, *France, the Cold War, and the Western Alliance, 1944–49* (New York: St. Martin's Press, 1990).

[59] Of course, NATO did comprise non-democratic states during various time periods. Portugal only became democratic in 1973. Turkey was ruled by authoritarian leaders from 1953 to 1960, 1971 to 1972, and 1980 to 1986. A military junta governed Greece from 1967 to 1973. Note, however, that the Greek participation in NATO's integrated military structure was suspended during that time period.

[60] For a similar interpretation see Latham, "Liberalism's Order/Liberalism's Other."

[61] "The North Atlantic Treaty," in *NATO: Fact and Figures*, 2d. ed. (Brussels: NATO Press Service, 1978), 302–3.

what about the rules and decision-making procedures of these institutions? One would expect that the norms embodied in the regimes reflect the values of the security community. Since values are normative beliefs about what is right or wrong, the norms of these institutions prescribing appropriate behavior[62] should be consistent with the values. Democracies are then likely to form *democratic institutions* whose rules and procedures are oriented toward consensual and compromise-oriented decision-making respecting the equality of the participants. The norms governing the domestic decision-making processes of liberal systems, are also expected to regulate their interactions in international institutions. Democracies externalize their internal norms when cooperating with each other. Power asymmetries should be mediated by norms of democratic decision-making among equals emphasizing persuasion, compromise, and the non-use of force or coercive power. If the norms regulating behavior in international institutions among democracies are themselves democratic, the practices following these norms should enable small allies to influence the decisions of the great powers. Liberal theory posits the "big influence of small allies" resulting from the democratic decision-making norms of alliances among democracies.

In sum, liberal theory argues that democracies do not fight each other because they perceive each other as peaceful. They perceive each other as peaceful because of the democratic norms governing their domestic decision-making processes. For the same reason, they form pluralistic security communities of shared values. Because they perceive each other as peaceful and express a sense of community, they are likely to overcome obstacles against international cooperation and to form international institutions such as alliances. The norms regulating interactions in such institutions are expected to reflect the shared democratic values and to resemble the domestic decision-making norms. These norms provide the tools for small states to influence the great powers in democratic international institutions. Thus, the theory agrees with traditional realism concerning the *outcome* of interallied bargaining, albeit for entirely different reasons.

But liberalism and realist bargaining theory offer diverging propositions regarding the *process* by which state actors influence each other in alliances among unequals. To evaluate the two approaches empirically, it is,

[62] There is considerable confusion in the field surrounding the concept of norms. Following theories of communicative action, I use the term in the sense of "guidance devices" prescribing appropriate behavior that also provide the "means which allow people to pursue goals, share meanings, communicate with each other, criticize assertions, and justify actions" (Kratochwil, *Rules, Norms, and Decisions*, 11). See also Jürgen Habermas, *Theorie des kommunikativen Handelns*, 2 vols. (Frankfurt/M.: Suhrkamp, 1981). For a clarification of the concept of norms in international relations, see Janice Thomson, "Norms in International Relations," *International Journal of Group Tensions* 23, no. 2 (1993): 67–83.

therefore, insufficient to look at the actual behavior or the outcome of bargaining processes and to ignore communicative interactions. Words matter in giving meaning to action. In the following, I deduce liberal propositions about these communicative processes from the overall argument presented above.[63]

Sense of Community and Consultation Norms

If liberal democracies form a community of values, it should affect the identity of the actors and their definition of the national interest. The Western Alliance is expected to alter "American estimates of what can and ought to be done; it may have changed attitudes as to who the 'we' are in whose name the United States may have to act and whose consent has first to be gained."[64] European input should then be considered legitimate even in "out-of-area" cases where supreme American interests are at stake. To a certain degree, decision-makers would no longer distinguish explicitly between U.S. and allied interests. This alteration of the American identity provides the European allies with a "window of opportunity" to influence Washington's decisions. Greater allied influence on U.S. foreign policy is expected, the more allies appeal to the sense of community and/or the more the community consensus is invoked by U.S. actors during the internal discourses.[65]

This proposition implies that the distinction between "interest-driven" and "value- or norm-guided" behavior does not make sense conceptually. Liberal theory argues instead that state interests cannot be taken for granted and that values and norms affect the definition of interests. Only if state interests are treated as fixed and ultimately derived from material power capabilities, can there be a difference between "interests" and norms.

As argued above, the shared values of the democratic security community will be reflected in the rules and decision-making procedures of the institution. Norms of regular consultation, of joint consensus-building, and nonhierarchy should legitimize and enable allied influence. These

[63] While many scholars have worked to spell out realist bargaining theory, a liberal equivalent is still missing. As a result, the following draws on various literatures in a somewhat eclectic way. On the necessity to privilege communicative action in international relations theory see, for example, Friedrich Kratochwil and John G. Ruggie, "International Organization: A State of the Art on an Art of the State," *International Organization* 40, no. 4 (Autumn 1986): 753–75; Kratochwil, *Rules, Norms, and Decisions*; Müller, "Internationale Beziehungen als kommunikatives Handeln."

[64] William R. Fox and Annette B. Fox, *NATO and the Range of American Choice* (New York: Columbia University Press, 1967), 1. For a theoretical argument on identity formation in international politics see Wendt, "Anarchy Is What States Make of It;" Wendt, "Collective Identity Formation and the International State."

[65] However, this process does not guarantee European influence. Actors might pretend to invoke alleged allied concerns in order to further their own goals, thereby exploiting the value consensus for their own purposes.

norms serve as key obligations translating the domestic decision-making rules of democracies onto the international arena. The obligation to regularly consult each other can then be regarded as the functional equivalent to domestic norms regulating the publicity of the political process, its constitutionality, and the equality of the participants. This is not to suggest that consultation norms only exist in alliances among democracies. But consultation should mean *co-determination* when democracies are involved.

Such norms do not need to be explicit. The rules governing the Anglo-American "special relationship," for example, contain primarily informal understandings.[66] Other consultation norms are based on explicit interstate agreements. Article 4 of the North Atlantic Treaty states: "The Parties will consult together whenever, in the opinion of any of them, the territorial integrity, political independence or security of any of the Parties is threatened."[67]

This obligation was later specified by various joint interpretations. In 1951, for example, the NATO "Committee on the North Atlantic Community" demanded a "habit of consultation" to reach "as wide an area of agreement as possible in the formulation of policies."[68] Five years later, the NATO Council established a three-member "Committee on Non-Military Cooperation," which defined consultation as

> more than exchange of information, though that is necessary. . . . It means the discussion of problems collectively, in the early stages of policy formation, and before national positions become fixed. . . . A member government should not, without adequate advance consultation, adopt firm policies or make major political pronouncements on matters which significantly affect the alliance or any of its members, unless circumstances make such prior consultation obviously and demonstrably impossible; in developing their national policies, members should take into consideration the interest and views of other governments, particularly those most directly concerned, as expressed in NATO consultation.

The North Atlantic Council approved this report in December 1956. "Consultation" was meant to provide the allies with the opportunity to co-determine policies. By committing themselves to the consultation norm, the allies were prepared to effectively grant each other influence on foreign policies.

[66] For a discussion see David Reynolds, "A 'special relationship'?" *International Affairs* 62 (1986): 1–20; William Roger Louis and Hedley Bull, eds., *The 'Special Relationship'* (Oxford: Clarendon Press, 1986).

[67] This consultation norm does not contain a territorial limitation such as NATO's military assistance clause, which Article 6 of the treaty confines to the north of the Tropic of Cancer. For the origins of Article 4 and its "out-of-area" context, see Elizabeth Sherwood, *Allies in Crisis* (New Haven, Conn.: Yale University Press, 1990), 14–16.

[68] Quoted from Thomas J. Kennedy, *NATO Politico-Military Consultation* (Washington, D.C.: National Defense University Press, 1984), 8. For the following, see ibid., 9.

The allies also created an elaborate civil and military organizational structure to insure timely consultation.[69] By far the most important forum to coordinate policies is the North Atlantic Council, the highest authority in NATO, which meets twice yearly on the level of foreign and defense ministers. Regular consultations are carried out at the level of ambassadors to NATO (permanent representatives) meeting at least once a week. In addition, there is the military decision-making structure with the Military Committee at the top advising the Council and supervising the integrated military structure. NATO's consultative structure is complemented by institutionalized *bilateral* contacts among the allies.

In addition to the consultation norm codified and institutionalized in various NATO arrangements, specific obligations prescribe consultation procedures in particular circumstances and related to specific issues. During the Korean War, for example, the United States committed itself to consultations with the allies before deciding on the use of nuclear weapons or on military action against the Chinese mainland (chapter 3).

In sum, NATO as an institution is explicitly built around norms of democratic decision-making, that is, nonhierarchy, frequent consultation implying co-determination, and consensus-building. Its institutional rules and procedures are formulated in such a way as to allow the allies to influence each other.

But how are these procedural norms expected to enable allied impact on American policies? First, U.S. decision-makers should either anticipate allied demands or directly consult with the Europeans *before* interests are defined and decisions are taken. U.S. actors should then make a discernible effort to define their preferences in a way compatible with the allied views and to accommodate allied demands. In other words, the consultation norm, while not directly causing specific preferences, should have causally consequential effects.

Second, norms serve as collective understandings of appropriate behavior, which can be invoked by the participants in a discourse to justify their arguments. Consultation norms should then affect the reasoning process by which decision-makers identify their preferences and choices in a similar way as the above-mentioned values. Actors are expected to invoke the norms to back up their respective views and to give weight to their arguments. If there is a collective understanding that allied demands should be accommodated, those who can make a convincing argument that their position is backed by important allies should have an advantage in affecting the final decision.

Third, the cooperation rules and procedures are also expected to influence the bargaining process among the allies. This is fairly obvious with

[69] See the overview in *NATO: Facts and Figures*, 204–27.

regard to consultation. In addition, democratic decision-making procedures deemphasize the use of material power resources in intra-allied bargaining processes, thereby delegitimizing the use of one's superior military or economic power in intra-alliance bargaining.[70] Both the pluralistic security community and specific consultation norms work against the use of coercive power in transatlantic bargaining processes. Instead, inter-allied bargaining among democracies would be characterized by persuasion and socialization. Such "co-optive power"[71] does not necessarily privilege the materially stronger, but should enable smaller states to influence the alliance leader by putting them on a more equal footing. If "empire by consent" is the rule of the game, the ruled can use the consensual norms for their purposes.

But norms can be violated. Norm compliance in human interactions is only to be expected in a probabilistic sense. Instances in which actors violate specific rules and obligations, are of particular interest to the analysis. If norms regulate the interaction, but are breached, one would expect peculiar behavior by both the violator and the victim:

> In deciding whether a particular violation demonstrates the end of a regime, it is important to look to the justification proffered by the violating party(ies). Admission of guilt, apologies, pleas for "understanding the extreme circumstances that forces such an action," etc., are important indicators for the acceptance and validity of the prescriptions and, therefore, for the force of the regime.[72]

I specifically look at cases in which the United States violated specific obligations to consult its allies. If, as liberal theory assumes, these norms legitimize European and Canadian impact on U.S. policies, their violation should reduce such influence considerably. Moreover, I analyze the most important case of U.S.-European confrontation during the 1950s, the 1956 Suez crisis, where Washington coerced its British and French allies to give up their efforts to regain control over the Suez canal.

"Two-Level Games" and Transnational Relations

So far, interallied negotiating processes have been conceptualized as interstate interactions. But core assumptions of liberalism have always challenged the "state-as-unitary-actor" model and emphasized domestic politics and transnational relations.[73] As to domestic politics, it should affect intra-

[70] On this point see also Karen Donfried, "The Political Economy of Alliances" (Ph.D. diss., Fletcher School of Law and Diplomacy, Boston, May 1991).

[71] See Nye, *Bound to Lead*, 31–33, 191–95.

[72] Kratochwil, *Rules, Norms, and Decisions*, 63.

[73] Transnational relations are defined as transboundary interactions that include at least

alliance relations among democracies in much the same way as described by Robert Putnam in his "two-level-game" model.[74] While using material power resources to strengthen one's bargaining position should be considered illegitimate among democracies, references to domestic pressures and constraints are likely to occur frequently. After all, liberal systems have in common that their leaders are constrained by the complexities of democratic political institutions. Since these procedures form the core of the value community among democratic allies, it should be appropriate to use domestic pressures—small domestic "win-sets" in Putnam's terms—to increase one's bargaining leverage. When democratic allies clash over policies, we should expect them to refer frequently to "pressures at home" or to domestic public opinion to strengthen their position. Their influence should increase, the more they can convincingly claim domestic constraints.[75]

Another mechanism by which domestic political processes can affect relations among democratic allies concerns *transnational coalition-building*. Transboundary activities of societal actors largely depend on whether the domestic structures of the states involved enable governments to control these activities. Since democratic systems are based on the separation of state and society, their governments are less able to control the transnational activities of their citizens than authoritarian political systems.[76] Transnational relations are expected to flourish in alliances among democracies.

The same conditions of open political structures and highly institutionalized interstate relations also facilitate the emergence of *transgovernmental coalitions*, defined as transboundary networks among subunits of national governments forming in the absence of central and authoritative national decisions. Without firm instructions, actors in such networks can-

---

one nonstate actor. See Karl Kaiser, "Transnationale Politik," in *Die anachronistische Souveränität*, ed. Ernst-Otto Czempiel (Köln-Opladen: Westdeutscher Verlag, 1969), 80–109; Samuel Huntington, "Transnational Organizations in World Politics," *World Politics* 25 (April 1973): 333–68; Robert O. Keohane and Joseph S. Nye, Jr., eds., *Transnational Relations and World Politics* (Cambridge, Mass.: Harvard University Press, 1972); Keohane and Nye, *Power and Interdependence* (Boston: Little, Brown, 1977); Thomas Risse-Kappen, ed., *Bringing Transnational Relations Back In* (Cambridge: Cambridge University Press, 1995); James N. Rosenau, *Turbulence in World Politics* (Princeton, N.J.: Princeton University Press, 1989).

[74] See Robert Putnam, "Diplomacy and Domestic Politics: The Logic of Two-Level Games," *International Organization* 42, no. 3 (Summer 1988): 427–60; Peter Evans et al., eds., *Double-Edged Diplomacy* (Berkeley: University of California Press, 1993).

[75] This is not to suggest that only democracies play "two-level games." But they should use domestic pressures more frequently than other systems and more successfully when bargaining with each other.

[76] On this point see Risse-Kappen, *Bringing Transnational Relations Back In*; Russett, *Grasping the Democratic Peace*, 25–26.

not be conceptualized as simply representing some unified view of their home states.[77] Strong international institutions such as NATO provide a framework in which informal networks of officials can emerge. The sense of community might further allow for such networks.

But access of nonstate actors to allied political systems does not guarantee influence. As argued above, the community of values leads to the presumption of friendliness among democracies and to decision-making norms in their international dealings that reflect these values. Transnational and transgovernmental coalitions are then likely to become legitimate participants of the domestic political processes. If allied democracies are considered part of "us" in a security community, their representatives should be less distinguishable from other domestic actors in "our" political system. One would expect political and societal actors in allied countries to coalesce with domestic actors in the alliance leader's state. Transnational actors are not peculiar to democracies, of course. But their ability to become legitimate domestic players in the "target state" should be greater within the framework of a democratic security community than in institutions involving other types of political systems.

"Allied influence" would then mean that transnational and transgovernmental coalitions tip the domestic balance toward allied demands. The Europeans are then the more able to affect U.S. foreign policy, the more they succeed in building transnational and transgovernmental alliances with actors inside and outside the American administration.

To summarize this discussion, liberal theory leads to the following propositions about the process by which democratic allies influence each other. Small democratic states are expected to exert a significant impact on a democratic alliance leader,

- the more decision-makers incorporate notions of the value community in their definition of national interests and preferences;
- the more compliance with consultation norms becomes a habitual practice among the allies;
- the more policymakers of small allies use domestic pressures to increase their bargaining leverage;
- the more transnational and transgovernmental coalition-building characterizes interallied interactions.

These propositions differ from the assumptions of realist bargaining theory. The empirical case studies should, therefore, allow for a comparative evaluation of their respective validity.

Table 1 summarizes the theoretical propositions of this study. The em-

[77] See Robert O. Keohane and Joseph S. Nye, Jr., "Transgovernmental Relations and International Organizations," *World Politics* 27 (1974): 39–62; Keohane, *After Hegemony*, 100–101; Keohane, "The International Energy Agency: State Power and Transgovernmental Politics," *International Organization* 32, no. 4 (Autumn 1978): 929–52.

TABLE 1
Expectations about Intra-Alliance Relations among Unequals/Democracies

	Structural Realism	*Traditional Realism*	*Liberalism*
Outcome			
Influence of small allies	marginal	significant	significant
Reasons for outcome	Power distribution under bipolarity	Competition about client states Allied bargaining	Community of democracies Democratic rules of institution
Process	unimportant	Intensity of allied preferences Allied threats to defect Threat perception Unity of small allies Allied control of issue-specific resources	Sense of community Consultation norms "Two-level games" Transnational coalitions

phasis on process rather than outcomes to evaluate the propositions of the various theories faces two difficulties. First, liberals could argue that consultation norms are unlikely to be invoked by the allies, the more consultations have become customary practices. Realists might suggest that small allies do not have to refer explicitly to issue-specific resources and the like when they bargain with the alliance leader, since it will be aware of them anyway. In other words, if one does not find empirical traces of the process variables suggested by the theory, it does not necessarily mean that the theory is falsified.

If taken to the extremes, this problem cannot be solved, since one can always make a counterfactual argument in the absence of data. But careful tracing of the decision-making and interallied bargaining processes should reveal the variables at work. The case studies rely, therefore, on recently declassified material from both the U.S. and the allied countries. I submit that the theory is to be preferred that can be backed by more and better empirical data.

Second, the emphasis on norms and communicative action can be challenged, because political actors tend to lie about and obscure their "real" motives. Again, this problem cannot ultimately be solved, and there is no need to solve it, since individual truthfulness is not subject of this inquiry.

But various clues allow at least for plausibility claims about the degree to which norms and communicative processes are causally consequential:

- Arguments must be consistent, irrespective of the audience. If, for example, U.S. decision-makers refer to norms when dealing with the allies, but to material interests during their internal deliberations, one should be skeptical about the causal significance of the norm.
- As indicated above, justifications, excuses, and so on in cases of norm violation offer particularly important clues about the role of the norm.
- Communicative action and nonverbal behavior must be consistent, at least most of the time. If words and deeds do not match at all, words matter less.

The following chapters evaluate the various theoretical propositions. The Korean War (chapter 3), the test ban negotiations (chapter 5), and the Cuban Missile crisis (chapter 6) serve as the main case studies to assess the assumptions developed in this chapter. The Suez crisis (chapter 4) represents a case of severe norm violation of the allies. Finally, NATO's nuclear decisions (chapter 7) are briefly discussed to demonstrate that the empirical findings of the other chapters also pertain to cases when European security issues were directly involved.

THREE

"OUTPOSTS OF OUR NATIONAL DEFENSE"

CONSULTATION NORMS AND THE MODERATION OF U.S. POLICIES DURING THE KOREAN WAR, 1950–1953

Korea was not a decisive area for us; . . . while the loss of Korea might jeopardize Japan and perhaps bring about its eventual loss, Western Europe was our prime concern and we would rather see that result than lose in Western Europe.

—Robert A. Lovett[1]

WHEN NORTH KOREAN forces attacked South Korea on June 25, 1950, the North Atlantic Treaty was little more than a year old, and NATO's military and political institutions did not even exist. From the very beginning, the Korean War was inextricably linked to European security. The American decision to intervene was itself motivated to a large extent by concerns about Europe and the U.S. credibility vis-à-vis its allies. As President Truman put it, "we considered the Korean situation vital as a symbol of the strength and determination of the West."[2] The president and Secretary of State Acheson were convinced that the American reputation to stand up against communist aggression was at stake. Failure to do so would not only hurt U.S. foreign policy abroad, but, perhaps more important, would significantly diminish the administration's chances of gaining domestic support for its containment efforts in Europe and the military build-up of NATO. Domestic and alliance politics were inextricably linked in the decision to intervene in Ko-

The chapter title is quoted from President Eisenhower during the 144th National Security Council (NSC) Meeting, May 13, 1953, *FRUS 1952–1954*, 15:1016.

[1] Dep. Secretary of Defense Lovett summarizing an interagency meeting of the State Department and the Joint Chiefs of Staff (JCS), Dec. 1, 1950, *FRUS 1950*, 7:1279.

[2] Harry S. Truman, *Years of Trial and Hope*, vol. 2 of *Memoirs* (Garden City, N.Y.: Doubleday, 1956), 339. For a discussion, see Rosemary Foot, *The Wrong War* (Ithaca, N.Y.: Cornell University Press, 1985), 59–60; Richard Whelan, *Drawing the Line* (Boston: Little, Brown, 1990), 112–23.

rea.[3] Within a few days, the Truman administration changed its strategy with regard to East Asia, which until then had excluded South Korea from the "defensive perimeter."[4]

The transformation of the Western Alliance from the North Atlantic Treaty to an international military organization was largely the result of the war. It provided the justification for a large-scale military buildup in Europe and for a major U.S. effort of military assistance in support of its allies.[5]

The European allies and Canada strongly supported the U.S./UN intervention as symbolizing the American commitment to the defense of the "free world" against communist aggression. Six NATO allies contributed troops to Korea—Belgium, Canada, Luxembourg, the Netherlands, the United Kingdom, and the United States (plus Greece and Turkey, which later joined the alliance), with the British providing the largest of the non-U.S. contingents. The British Chiefs of Staff had initially argued against sending troops to Korea, because Britain was already overstretched in Asia. They were overruled, since the Foreign Office argued that British participation would allow London to insist on close consultation with Washington.[6] The British planned to use their military participation as a resource to influence U.S. actions.

Aside from the general support for the UN intervention, the U.S. and its major allies were frequently at odds over most important issues during the war. The British, Canadian, and French governments were concerned that the United States was overcommitting itself in Asia at the expense of European security. As British Foreign Minister Ernest Bevin put it,

> the problem before us is to seek, at a time when the general atmosphere in the United States is least favourable for such a course, to persuade the United States administration not to adopt policies in relation to the Far East which will fail to command general support amongst friendly nations and which will antagonize Asia.[7]

[3] See Thomas Christensen, "Domestic Mobilization and International Conflict" (Ph.D. diss., Columbia University, N.Y. 1993), esp. chap. 5.

[4] On the "defensive perimeter" strategy, see John Lewis Gaddis, *The Long Peace* (New York: Oxford University Press, 1987), 72–103, esp. 94–101. Gaddis argues that the decision to intervene was by no means inevitable and was taken largely on political rather than military-strategic grounds. For details on U.S. policies see Bruce Cummings, ed., *Child of Conflict* (Seattle: University of Washington Press, 1983); Foot, *Wrong War*; Foot, *A Substitute for Victory* (Ithaca, N.Y.: Cornell University Press, 1990); Jon Halliday and Bruce Cummings, *Korea: The Unknown War* (New York: Pantheon, 1988); Whelan, *Drawing the Line*.

[5] For details see Günther Mai, *Westliche Sicherheitspolitik im kalten Krieg* (Boppard: Boldt, 1977).

[6] See M. L. Dockrill, "The Foreign Office, Anglo-American Relations and the Korean War, June 1950-June 1951," *International Affairs* 62 (1986): 459–76, 460.

[7] Memorandum, August 30, 1950, PRO:PREM 8/1171.

The allies were critical of an extension of the war beyond the restoration of the status quo and were adamantly opposed to military activities against China. (The British had recognized the People's Republic in January 1950 against American advice.) The allies also objected to the use of nuclear weapons during the war. From December 1950 on, the British and the Canadian governments used whatever bargaining leverage they could master to convince the United States to open armistice negotiations with the Chinese and, later on, to accept compromises in those talks.[8]

I argue in this chapter that the European and Canadian allies had a moderating impact on U.S. policies throughout the war. While top U.S. decision-makers and the allies shared the overall goal of preventing an escalation of the war into China, they often disagreed over specific courses of action. The allies prevented various military activities that would have risked such an escalation and gained almost veto power over the use of nuclear weapons. The Europeans and Canadians also had a significant impact on the conduct of the armistice negotiations. Allied influence ran against the prevailing domestic pressures in Washington, which pulled in a more confrontational direction.

The allied influence in restraining American policies was not lost on those in the military and the Pentagon who favored more aggressive policies and were frequently overruled, not the least because of allied demands. The military repeatedly complained that particularly the British had disproportionate influence on U.S. policy and that "United States policy in the Far East is being determined in London rather than in Washington."[9]

The Korean War case, therefore, refutes the (structural realist) assump-

[8] On *British* policies, see James Cotton and Ian Neary, eds., *The Korean War in History* (Manchester: Manchester University Press, 1989); Dockrill, "The Foreign Office;" Anthony Farrar-Hockley, *A Distant Obligation*, vol. 1 of *The British Part in the Korean War* (London: HMSO, 1990); Rosemary Foot, "Anglo-American Relations in the Korean Crisis," *Diplomatic History* 10, no. 1 (1986); Peter Lowe, "The Settlement of the Korean War," in *The Foreign Policy of Churchill's Peacetime Administration, 1951–1955*, ed. John W. Young (Leicester: Leicester University Press, 1988), 207–31; Callum A. MacDonald, *Britain and the Korean War* (Oxford: Basil Blackwell, 1990); Ritchie Ovendale, "Britain and the Cold War in Asia," in *The Foreign Policy of the British Labour Governments, 1945–1951*, ed. Ovendale (Leicester: Leicester University Press, 1984), 121–48.

On *Canada*, see Don Munton, "Getting Along and Going Alone: American Policies and Canadian Support in Korea and Cuba" (paper presented to the annual meeting of the International Studies Association, Atlanta, Ga., April 1992); Denis Stairs, *The Diplomacy of Constraint* (Toronto: Toronto University Press, 1974).

On *Australia*, see Robert O'Neill, *Strategy and Diplomacy*, vol. 1 of *Australia in the Korean War, 1950–1953* (Canberra: Australian Government Publication Service, 1981).

[9] "Chief of Mission to the Far East to the Secretary of Defense," July 3, 1954, *FRUS 1952–1954*, 15:1821. For similar complaints see "Memorandum of Department of State-JCS Meeting," February 6, 1952, ibid., 39–40.

tion that small allies only have limited influence on superpowers under bipolarity. But the case does not allow for a clear decision on whether the United States granted its allies disproportionate influence because of strategic considerations, or whether it acted as a liberal alliance leader and member of a security community of democratic nations. On balance, though, liberal arguments about collective identities and consultation norms seem to score slightly better than propositions derived from realist bargaining theory.

Preventing War with China

One of the most important goals of the NATO allies during the Korean War was to prevent an extension of the military conflict into China and to keep the war localized in Korea. Truman and Acheson shared this goal in principle, because the United States was not ready for an escalation that might lead to war in Europe. But the "China lobby," Republicans in Congress, large sections of American public opinion, and part of the U.S. military, in particular U.S./UN Commander MacArthur, exerted heavy pressures on the administration to pursue a more aggressive course against the Chinese Communists.[10] While leading American decision-makers agreed with the allies against the domestic opposition, frequent clashes between Washington and NATO governments occurred with regard to specific courses of military action.

Reluctant Support: The Decision to Cross the 38th Parallel

Given the allied opposition to escalation of the Korean War, it is somewhat ironic that the European governments refrained from weighing in heavily in October 1950, when the decision was taken to cross the 38th parallel. This decision turned out to be the most escalatory Western move of the conflict and led to the entry into war by the People's Republic of China.[11]

General MacArthur strongly recommended crossing the parallel and was supported by the Joint Chiefs of Staff (JCS). The first U.S.-British discussions on the subject took place in late July 1950. U.K. officials stressed that the war should be localized in order to avoid an involvement

[10] On the "China lobby," see Ross Y. Koen, *The China Lobby in American Politics* (New York: Harper & Row, 1974). See also Christensen, "Domestic Mobilization and International Conflict."

[11] Released documents from China strongly suggest that the American crossing of the 38th parallel triggered Mao's decision to dispatch Chinese troops to Korea. See Thomas Christensen, "Threats, Assurances, and the Last Chance for Peace," *International Security* 17, no. 1 (Summer 1992): 122–54.

by the Chinese and the Soviets. The French and the British governments later insisted that a new UN resolution was required to authorize such a military escalation.[12]

The bureaucratic balance of power in Washington gradually shifted in MacArthur's favor. The State Department and others insisted that a decision to cross the 38th parallel could not be taken without consultation with the allies who contributed troops in Korea. NSC, which was approved by Truman on September 11, allowed for military operations north of the 38th parallel provided that Chinese and Soviet forces would not intervene, that the U.S. commander obtained final approval by the president, and that the allies were consulted.[13]

But the Europeans did not use this "window of opportunity" to raise objections. While the Canadian government remained opposed, the British accepted crossing the 38th parallel and drafted a UN resolution that implicitly authorized the operation. Thus, they provided MacArthur's actions with UN legitimacy. The General Assembly adopted a resolution on October 7 that "all appropriate steps be taken to ensure conditions of stability throughout Korea." On the same day, U.S. troops moved into North Korea.[14]

Success: Establishing a Consultation Norm to Prevent "Hot Pursuit"

While the European allies acquiesced in the American decision to move from reestablishing the status quo to a strategy of unifying Korea by force, they consistently held the line with regard to possible attacks against China. On October 6, 1950, the British received assurances that General MacArthur had clear instructions not to attack Manchuria and that a change in his orders would not occur without prior consultations.[15] This obligation to consult the allies became crucial in the following months.

[12] See "Agreed Memorandum, Summary of UK-U.S. Discussions," July 20–24, 1950, *FRUS 1950*, 7:462–65; "Memorandum Regarding Meeting at the State Department," August 25, ibid., 646–48; "Memorandum Regarding NSC Senior Staff Meeting," Aug. 25, ibid., 649–52; "U.S. Delegation Minutes Regarding Preliminary Conversations for September Foreign Ministers' Meeting," Aug. 30, ibid., 667–71.

[13] See Foot, *Wrong War*, 67–74; "Draft Memorandum Prepared by the State Department Regarding U.S. Courses of Action in Korea," Aug. 31, 1950, *FRUS 1950*, 7:671–79; "NSC 81 Draft Report on U.S. Courses of Action with Respect to Korea," Sept. 1, ibid., 685–93; "NSC 81/1, U.S. Courses of Action with Respect to Korea," Sept. 9, ibid., 712–21.

[14] See "UK Draft Resolution on Korea," Sept. 25, 1950, *FRUS 1950*, 7:773–74; "Minutes of Meeting of U.S. Delegation to the UN," Sept. 25, ibid., 768–74; "Draft 8 Power UN Resolution on Korea," Sept. 29, ibid., 826–27. See also Ra Jong-yil, "Political Settlement in Korea: British Views and Policies, Autumn 1950," in *Korean War in History*, ed. Cotton and Neary, 51–65, 56–57; Ovendale, "Britain and the Cold War in Asia," 134–35.

[15] See "Memorandum of Conversation between Dean Rusk [Asst. Secretary of State Far East] and Sir Oliver Franks [UK Ambassador to the U.S.]," Oct. 6, 1950, in *FRUS 1950*, 7:893–96. See also "Ernest Bevin to Sir Oliver Franks," Oct. 11, ibid., 932.

When the Chinese entered the war (as the British Chiefs of Staff had feared all along), General MacArthur asked permission to destroy the Yalu River bridges through which Chinese troops poured into North Korea and to pursue Chinese aircraft into Manchuria ("hot pursuit"). His request was supported by the Pentagon and, subsequently, the CIA. In an interagency meeting on November 6, State Department officials referred to the "commitment with the British not to take action which might involve attacks on the Manchurian side of the River without consultation with them."[16] Because of this commitment, it was decided to postpone a decision, unless the security of U.S. troops was in immediate danger. MacArthur was instructed to bomb the Yalu River bridges from the Korean side only and, "because of necessity for maintaining optimum position with United Nations policy and directives, [to take] extreme care . . . to avoid violation Manchurian territory."[17] The allies remained concerned; the French even suggested a UN resolution to reassure Beijing that Chinese borders would not be violated. On November 16, Dean Acheson repeated the earlier reassurances and pledged to "continue to keep such govts informed, as far as possible in advance of taking such decisions, in order that they may express their views to which full consideration will be given."[18] On the same day, President Truman declared in a press conference that the United States still intended to keep the war localized. Acheson who faced heavy domestic criticism by conservative Republicans, argued constantly that an extension of the war into China would lead to U.S. isolation in the UN at a time when it desperately needed allied support. If there was a general war with China and an armed conflict with the Soviet Union, the United States would soon have to "fight without allies on our side." Acheson also claimed that the Europeans might abandon Washington and cut a deal with Moscow, if the United States did not accommodate their concerns. He stopped short of granting the Europeans a formal veto over U.S. actions when the British Foreign Minister requested it.[19]

But from the time China entered the war, the domestic critics of the Truman administration demanded a tougher policy toward Beijing. Amer-

[16] "Memorandum of Conference between Dean Acheson, Under-secretary of Defense Lovett, and Dean Rusk," Nov. 6, 1950, *FRUS 1950*, 7:1055–57, 1055. See also Foot, *Wrong War*, 89–90, 98.

[17] "JCS to General MacArthur," Nov. 6, 1950, *FRUS 1950*, 7:1075–76. See also "Army Chief of Staff to MacArthur," Nov. 24, ibid., 1222–24.

[18] "Secretary of State to U.S. Mission to the UN," Nov. 16, 1950, *FRUS 1950*, 7:1166. For expressions of allied concerns see ibid., 1151, 1159–61, 1172; Foot, *Wrong War*, 94–95; Truman, *Years of Trial and Hope*, 394.

[19] See "Foreign Office to Sir Franks," Nov. 23, 1950, *FRUS 1950*, 7:1225 n.; "Secretary of State to Sir Franks," Nov. 24, ibid., 1226–27; "Memorandum of Conversation," Dec. 3, ibid., 1323–34 (quote on 1326); "Memorandum of Conversation," Dec. 5, ibid., 1382–86, 1383; "Memorandum," Dec. 5, ibid., 1410. See also Truman, *Years of Trial and Hope*, 387; Foot, *Wrong War*, 99, 103, 106.

ican public opinion increased the pressure on the administration to conduct some decisive military steps in order to end the war quickly.[20] U.S. officials now proposed a UN resolution condemning China as an aggressor, which would authorize further economic and military measures against Beijing. Not surprisingly, France and Britain remained adamantly opposed, arguing that their respective public opinion would not tolerate such a move.[21] A "two-level game" followed in which both sides used their domestic opposition to increase their bargaining position in the interallied talks.

The localization of the war became a major issue during the visit of British Prime Minister Attlee to Washington in December 1950. Internally, the British considered retreating from the policy of unifying Korea by force and examined a cease-fire restoring the status quo at the 38th parallel. The JCS in the United States also recommended a cease-fire given the difficulties of the UN forces on the battlefield. In contrast to the British, however, they suggested declaring China the aggressor followed by a naval blockade and military action against Manchuria, if Beijing rejected the armistice.[22] This proposal was taken up by Dean Acheson in a slightly watered-down version and read to the British during Attlee's visit. The British Chiefs of Staff's reaction captures the mood in London:

> To suggest . . . that we should attack targets in China and then . . . withdraw our forces from Korea is sheer lunacy. . . . we feel that the time has come for us to speak frankly on this subject and insist that some authoritative statement be made. . . . But we are slipping into a position of being made the whipping boy for Allied disaster in Korea. . .[23]

The discussions in Washington showed agreement between the United States and its allies on the overall goal of preventing an escalation of the war into China. But U.S. decision-makers profoundly differed with the British on the appropriate policies toward the People's Republic. Truman and Acheson argued that the regime in Beijing was merely Moscow's pup-

[20] For a discussion of the domestic situation in the United States, see Foot, *Wrong War*, 106–8; Christensen, "Domestic Mobilization and International Conflict," chap. 5.

[21] See, for example, "Memorandum of Conversation between Dean Rusk and Sir Franks," Nov. 29, 1950, *FRUS 1950*, 7:1252–53; "US Mission to the UN to Secretary of State," Nov. 29, ibid., 1255–57; "US Mission to the UN to Secretary of State," Nov. 30, ibid., 1272–75. Acheson thought that the allies were in a "virtual state of panic" and argued that it "is of the greatest importance that we should again bring about unity among our friends." Cf. "Notes on a Meeting between Acheson, the Secretary of Defense, and the JCS," Dec. 1, ibid., 1276–82.

[22] On the British proposal see Ovendale, "Britain and the Cold War in Asia," 137–38. See also "General Brief for the Prime Minister's Visit to Washington," PRO:PREM 8/1200. On the JCS, see "Omar Bradley to Secretary of Defense Marshall," Dec. 4, 1950, *FRUS 1950*, 7:1348.

[23] "Chiefs of Staff to UK Embassy, Washington," Dec. 7, 1950, PRO:FO 371/84164.

pet, while Attlee suggested trying to drive a wedge between the two communist regimes instead of confronting China head-on. The Americans eventually agreed. Both sides repeatedly pointed to their domestic publics to increase the pressures on the ally: "If we surrender in the Far East, especially if this results from the action of our allies, American opinion will be against help in the West to those who had brought about the collapse."[24] Truman and Acheson apparently believed that giving in to allied demands for a more conciliatory policy toward China would jeopardize the domestic support for U.S. assistance to Europe, which American decision-makers considered far more important than the war in the Far East. Attlee seems to have accepted this argument.[25]

The meetings produced a partial agreement with regard to China. The United States reluctantly agreed to pursue a cease-fire resolution in the UN before moving toward condemning Chinese aggression. Washington even accepted a draft text by Asian states. At this point, maintaining allied solidarity and unity in the UN was obviously more important to decision-makers in Washington than giving in to domestic pressures.[26]

To the great relief of the "hawks" in the United States, China rejected the draft cease-fire resolution on December 22. The United States, once again, pushed for a condemnatory resolution and, once again, ran into allied opposition. But the French and the British governments indicated that they might be prepared to condemn Chinese actions at a later stage provided that this would not entail an authorization to conduct military activities against the Chinese mainland. Dean Acheson now applied strong pressure on the British and argued: "As I read the barometer of our public opinion, I am deeply apprehensive that a failure of the UN to recognize this aggression would create a wave of isolationism in this country which would jeopardize all that we are trying to do with and for the Atlantic Pact countries."[27] While he refrained from an explicit threat to withdraw U.S. support from European defense efforts, the domestic politics argument

[24] Dean Acheson to the British in "Memorandum of Conversation," Dec. 4, 1950, *FRUS 1950*, 7:1374–77, 1374. See also the records of the various conversations during the Anglo-American summit. The British records are in PRO:PREM 8/1200; the U.S. records in *FRUS 1950*, 7:1361–74, 1392–1408, 1449–62.

[25] On this point see Christensen, "Domestic Mobilization and International Conflict," 420–34. See also Attlee's personal report to Ernest Bevin about the meetings in Washington ("I think that we have at least shaken the American Service Chiefs by impressing on them the dangers of limited war with China"), Dec. 10, 1950, PRO:PREM 8/1200.

[26] See Foot, *Wrong War*, 109–11; "Dean Acheson to Diplomatic Offices," Dec. 9, 1950, *FRUS 1950*, 7:1486–88; "US Mission UN to Dean Acheson," Dec. 9, ibid., 1496–99; "Acting Secretary of State to U.S. Mission UN," Dec. 20, ibid., 1583–84; "Dean Acheson to U.S. Mission UN," Dec. 28, ibid., 1619–20.

[27] "Dean Acheson to Ernest Bevin," Jan. 5, 1951, *FRUS 1951*, 7:27–28. See also "Dean Acheson to Certain Diplomatic Offices," Jan. 3, ibid., 7–9; "U.S. Mission UN to Dean Acheson," Jan. 3, ibid., 9–12; "Dean Acheson to U.S. Mission UN," Jan. 4, ibid., 25–26.

drove a similar point home. The British government, however, did not budge and continued to oppose a condemnatory resolution. The U.S. ambassador to the UN proposed new language in the American draft resolution to reassure the allies that military activities against China would be subject to a decision by the General Assembly. Dean Acheson explained to the allies that the proposed language did not automatically imply additional measures against China.[28] The president cabled General MacArthur that the most urgent task was to consolidate the majority in the UN, since this majority "is not merely part of the organization but is also the nations whom we would desperately need to count on as allies in the event the Soviet Union moves against us."[29] *Us* in this statement implicitly included Europe, since the USSR did not have the capability to attack the U.S. homeland at the time.

The United States also continued to support efforts by the British, the French, and various Asian states to make the planned UN cease-fire resolution more acceptable to Beijing. On January 13, 1951, the draft resolution was approved in the United Nations, but immediately rejected by the People's Republic. The pressure for stronger action against China became almost unbearable in Washington. On January 19, the House of Representatives adopted a resolution condemning China as aggressor, followed by the Senate four days later. Acheson confided to the British ambassador that he was on "the verge of destruction domestically." He later explained the choice that he faced as "a murderous one, threatening on one side the loss of the Koreans and the fury of Congress and the press and, on the other, the loss of our majority and support in the United Nations."[30] An interallied compromise was needed. The French government declared its support for a condemnatory resolution provided that it did not imply the authorization of military or economic measures against China and that such measures were subject to debate in the General Assembly. On January 20, Acheson delivered the required assurance declaring that the "US does not consider passage this Res wld constitute authorization for extension gen hostilities against Chi mainland by Unified Command, nor wld Res constitute UN permission bomb Chi."[31] This interpretation con-

[28] See "Clement Attlee to Harry Truman," Jan. 8, 1951, *FRUS 1951*, 7:37–39; "Dean Acheson to U.S. Embassy UK," Jan. 9, ibid., 39–40; "U.S. Ambassador UK to Secretary of State," Jan. 11, ibid., 65–66.

[29] "Harry Truman to General MacArthur," Jan. 13, 1951, *FRUS 1951*, 7:77–79, 78. See also "U.S. Mission UN to Secretary of State," Jan. 10, ibid., 51–53; "Dean Acheson to Diplomatic/Consular Offices," Jan. 15, ibid., 83–85; "Draft NSC 101/1," Jan. 15, ibid., 80–81.

[30] The first quote is from "Memorandum of Telephone Conversation Between Dean Acheson and Sir Franks," Jan. 18, 1951, *FRUS 1951*, 7:98–100, 98. The second quote is from Dean Acheson, *Present at the Creation* (New York: Norton, 1969), 513. See also Foot, *Wrong War*, 110–11.

[31] "Dean Acheson to U.S. Mission UN," Jan. 20, 1951, *FRUS 1951*, 7:108–9. For the French approach, see "U.S. Ambassador in Paris to Dean Acheson," Jan. 19, ibid., 107–8.

vinced France and Canada to support the resolution, while the British government continued to oppose it. A cabinet decision urged another UN mediation effort. After some minor U.S. concessions, the foreign secretary and the chancellor of the exchequer convinced their cabinet colleagues that Britain desperately needed American support to deal with its balance-of-payment problems and that, therefore, they had to revise their decision. On February 1, Britain voted with the other allies in support of the condemnatory resolution.[32]

Consultation on Contingencies: Inter-Allied Disputes in 1951 and 1952

The issue of "bombing China" was not over with the condemnatory resolution. In early April 1951, the JCS, responding to the military situation in Korea, requested again to prepare naval and air action against the People's Republic. A majority in American public opinion also favored bombing bases in Manchuria.[33] The State Department asked the allies to authorize in advance retaliatory air strikes against China if the latter attacked UN troops from outside Korea. While consultations were under way, President Truman approved a message that authorized such retaliatory bombardments in Manchuria and elsewhere. It was to be sent to the U.S./UN commander if and when a massive Chinese air attack against UN forces occurred. The allies were annoyed by this unilateral American decision while consultations were under way, and reacted accordingly.[34]

The British strongly objected to the advance authorization of air strikes. The British Ambassador explained:

> Even if the general authorization asked for was granted, his government felt that the effective decision as to the magnitude of the attack must be passed on by his government, and they could not give their agreement in advance of the event. . . . If the U.K. has to go along with everything that follows from the decision, then the U.K. must be in on the decision.[35]

When General MacArthur, whom the allies had distrusted all along, was finally dismissed, they were pleased. But State Department officials

[32] For details, see Dockrill, "The Foreign Office, Anglo-American Relations, and the Korean War," 469–71.

[33] An April 1951 poll is quoted in Foot, *Wrong War*, 139. On the JCS request see "Memorandum by JCS to the Secretary of Defense," April 5, 1951, *FRUS 1951*, 7:295–96.

[34] See "Memorandum by the JCS to the Secretary of Defense," April 6, 1951, *FRUS 1951*, 7:309. On the allied reaction, see "Memorandum of Conversation by the Asst. Secretary of State for UN Affairs," April 6, ibid., 306–7; "Memorandum of Conversation by Paul Nitze," April 13, ibid., 343–44. See also Dockrill, "The Foreign Office, Anglo-American Relations, and the Korean War," 472–73; Foot, *Wrong War*, 144–47.

[35] "Memorandum of conversation between British and U.S. officials," April 12, 1951, *FRUS 1951*, 7:338–42, 339, 341. See also "Memorandum of conversation between British and U.S. officials," April 6, ibid., 307–9.

used the removal to request allied acquiescence to the U.S. demand as a "quid pro quo." They repeatedly referred to adverse consequences for NATO, in the eyes of U.S. public opinion and Congress, if the allies refused to grant the advance authorization to strike targets in China. Internally however, the administration was undecided on how to handle the allied objections. The military opposed the constraint that consultation imposed, while State Department officials emphasized the need to have the allies on board if such escalatory actions were undertaken. Paul Nitze, the director of the Policy Planning Staff, reminded the military that the U.S. needed the British air bases in case of a general war with the Soviet Union. In the end, the United States agreed to consult the British if circumstances permitted and if their consent could be obtained in less than twenty-four hours. When the new commander of the U.S./UN forces, General Ridgway, requested authorization for retaliatory strikes against Manchurian bases on April 27, the JCS granted the request subject to the following provisions:

> However, authority to attack should only be used in the event that in your judgement time and circumstances do not permit reference to the JCS. . . . The consequences of the action authorized may set in chain a course of events making it of the utmost importance to have the support of the other countries and the right to use facilities and bases controlled by them. This support may depend upon consulting or at least informing them of the action prior to its occurrence, if at all possible you should seek JCS advice before taking action.[36]

This paragraph was added to the directive after the State Department had intervened with the president. When the allied ambassadors were informed, they did not raise objections. On May 10, the British government agreed "in principle" to retaliatory air strikes against Manchurian bases, but still insisted that "the decision to authorise retaliatory action must be subject to concurrence by us at the time." London was prepared to grant such permission within a matter of hours after a Chinese attack.[37]

While the allies had to some extent given in to anti-Chinese pressures on the U.S. domestic scene, the conditions attached to the authorization

[36] "JCS to CINCFE Ridgway," April 28, 1951, *FRUS 1951*, 7:386–87. See also "Dean Acheson to the US Embassy in the U.K.," April 17, ibid., 352–53; "Memorandum of discussions at JCS-Department of State meeting," April 18, ibid., 353–62; "JCS to CINCFE Ridgway," May 1, ibid., 394–98.

[37] "Message by Foreign Secretary Morrison to Dean Acheson," May 10, 1951, *FRUS 1951*, 7:427–31, 428. See also "Memorandum by the Dep. Asst. Secretary of State for the Far East," May 2, ibid., 399–400; "Message by Dean Acheson to Foreign Secretary Morrison," April 30, ibid., 390–94; "U.S. Embassy UK to Secretary of State," May 3, ibid., 412–14; "U.S. Embassy UK to Secretary of State," May 4, ibid., 415–16.

were rather strict and essentially required a massive Chinese escalation of the war prior to U.S. attacks against the mainland. NSC 48/5 restated the limited war objectives in May 1951: "to avoid the extension beyond Korea of hostilities with Communist China, particularly without the support of our major allies."[38]

But the issue remained on the interallied agenda. After the armistice negotiations had started in July 1951, the JCS requested that the restrictions concerning bombing the Yalu River installations and "hot pursuit" should be removed and that the allies should be pressured into further sanctions against China, including a naval blockade, if the talks failed. The question of allied consultation again became an issue of contention between the Joint Chiefs and the State Department. The JCS declared their unwillingness "to accept the military risk incident to consultation with the sixteen participating nations preliminary to initiation of countermeasures," while State Department officials maintained that "our action might involve precipitating general war, and we would be in much better shape with our allies if we had taken them into confidence." The disagreement could not be resolved and was taken to the NSC and the president.[39]

In the end, the administration worked out a compromise that was presented to the allies. If the armistice negotiations failed, the Yalu River installations should be bombed, the UN should endorse a naval blockade of China, and—subject to allied approval if circumstances permitted—Chinese air bases should be attacked in retaliation to massive Chinese bombardments of U.S./UN forces inside Korea. State Department officials went to great length to brief the allied foreign ministers about the contingency plans, but Britain, France, and Canada did not raise fundamental objections against bombing the Yalu River installations under the specified conditions. Their main opposition concerned plans of a naval blockade, which the British vehemently refused to consider since it would cut off Hong Kong.[40]

[38] "NSC 48/5," May 17, 1951, *FRUS 1951*, 7:439–42, 439. See also Foot, *Wrong War*, 147–48.

[39] "Memorandum of discussions of JCS-State Department meeting," Aug. 29, 1951, *FRUS 1951*, 7:859–64. See also "JCS to Secretary of Defense," July 13, ibid., 667–68; "Memorandum prepared at the State Department," Aug. 18, ibid., 835–42; "JCS to Secretary of Defense," Aug. 29, ibid., 880–81; "Memorandum by Paul Nitze," Sept. 5, ibid., 883–84. For the following see "Position paper prepared for U.S. delegation to Foreign Ministers' meetings," Sept. 8, ibid., 889–91. See also the discussion in Foot, *Wrong War*, 149–52.

[40] See "U.S. delegation minutes of second U.S.-UK foreign ministers' meeting," Sept. 11, 1951, *FRUS 1951*, 7:890–93; "Memorandum of conversation with members of British delegation," Sept. 11, ibid., 893–900; "Memorandum of conversation with members of British delegation," Sept. 12, ibid., 903–5; "Memorandum of conversation," Sept. 12, ibid., 906; "U.S. delegation minutes of seventh U.S.-UK-French foreign ministers' meeting," Sept. 14, ibid., 916; "Memorandum by Acting Asst. Secretary of State for Far Eastern Affairs," Sept.

The question of bombing Chinese air bases came up again toward the end of 1951 in conjunction with the preparation of NSC 118/2, restating American objectives in Korea. NSC 118/2 reiterated the principle of keeping the war localized but extended the conditions under which unilateral air attacks were allowed against China in case of failed armistice negotiations. Such attacks remained subject to presidential approval, though, thus allowing for allied consultation.[41]

The interagency disputes regarding the conditions under which bombing China should be allowed inextricably linked two issues. First, the State Department and Pentagon were at odds over the extent to which certain military actions were compatible with the goal of keeping the war localized. Second, the agencies profoundly disagreed over the need to consult the allies. The JCS argued: "The United States is now the dominant power in the Western Pacific. Consequently, in any conflict of interest arising between the United States and other Western Powers . . . the United States should in its own interest insist that United States security considerations in that area be over-riding."[42] In other words, the military contested the collective identity of the allied community and favored unilateral policies. The JCS were well aware that abiding by alliance norms would constrain U.S. actions by strengthening the "doves" in Washington, which was precisely how State Department officials used allied arguments in the interagency meetings. Their views carried the day with the president most of the time, partly as a result of Dean Acheson's strong position in the decision-making process.

But there was at least one occasion when U.S. military activities in Korea violated alliance norms. In late June 1952, U.S. aircraft bombed power plants on the North Korean side of the Yalu River for several days without consulting or even informing the allies in advance, which was particularly embarrassing since the British defense minister was in Wash-

---

18, ibid., 919–21; "Memorandum of conversation with the Canadian Ambassador," Oct. 1, ibid., 976–80.

Britain was unable to refuse the American request, since London had just insisted on attacks against Egyptian positions in retaliation to Egyptian attacks on the Suez Canal. The United States had not requested prior consultation. See M. L. Dockrill, "The Foreign Office, Anglo-American Relations and the Korean Truce Negotiations July 1951-July 1953," in *The Korean War in History*, ed. Cotton and Neary, 100–119, 102–3.

[41] "NSC 118/2, U.S. Objectives and Courses of Action in Korea," Dec. 20, 1951, *FRUS 1951*, 7:1382–87, 1386. See "JCS comments on courses of action in Korea," Nov. 6, ibid., 1094–95; "NSC 118, JCS comments," Nov. 9, ibid., 1106–09; "NSC 118/1 Draft Statement on U.S. Courses of Action in Korea," Dec. 7, ibid., 1259–63; Foot, *Wrong War*, 153, 158–160, 169–170.

[42] Quoted from Foot, *Wrong War*, 171. See also Admiral Fechteler's outburst: "I must admit that I get terribly impatient about our concern for the British reactions." Quoted from "Memorandum of Department of State-JCS Meeting," Feb. 6, 1952, *FRUS 1952–1954*, 15:39–40.

ington at the time, while Dean Acheson was visiting London. The British and the Canadian governments concluded that the lack of consultation was no accident, since it precluded the allies from raising objections. Acheson went at great length in London to explain the necessity of bombing the Yalu River plants and was forced by the British foreign minister to apologize for the lack of consultation during a meeting with British parliamentarians. Two months later, when similar decisions were taken to bomb installations close to the Yalu River, the United States abided by the norm, and the British were consulted in due time. They did not raise objections.[43]

Agreement to Disagree: The "Greater Sanctions" Statement

When it came to actual military decisions concerning escalation of the war, the European and Canadian governments could usually count on the State Department and Dean Acheson himself as reliable allies. The transgovernmental coalition succeeded in keeping the war localized. It was far harder for the allies to convince Washington of their viewpoint when faced with a united front of both the Pentagon and the State Department. Such was the case when State Department officials proposed in November 1951 to issue a statement threatening to escalate the war into China if Beijing broke an armistice agreement. They argued that only such a warning would deter a potential violation of an armistice. A memorandum specified that an agreement should be worked out, particularly with the British, and that the war could no longer be localized if the armistice was violated. A complete economic blockade of China should be initiated in this case, a naval blockade agreed upon in principle, and military action against China should be undertaken short of land operations but including bombardments and amphibious assaults.[44]

Not surprisingly, the British and the Canadians were reluctant to agree to such courses of action. Foreign Minister Eden and others argued that, first, U.S. negotiators at the armistice talks should seek tight inspection provisions to verify a cease-fire. In this case, there would be no need for a "greater sanctions" statement. Second, if a statement threatening the extension of hostilities was to be issued, it should be in fairly general terms.

[43] For details see Foot, *Wrong War*, 178–79; Dean Acheson, *The Korean War* [excerpts from Acheson's memoirs, *Present at the Creation*] (New York: W. W. Norton, 1969), 135–36; Dockrill, "Foreign Office, Anglo-American Relations and the Korean Truce Negotiations," 107–8; "Acting Secretary of State to U.S. Embassy in UK," June 24, 1952, *FRUS 1952–1954*, 15:352–54; "Memorandum of JCS–State Department Meeting," June 25, ibid., 356–58.

[44] See "Memorandum by the Office of Northeast Asian Affairs," Nov. 2, 1951, *FRUS 1951*, 7:1081–85, 1084; Foot, *Substitute for Victory*, 77–82; Lowe, "Settlement of the Korean War," 210–11.

The British were not prepared to commit themselves in advance to specific measures. They seemed to be less concerned about air attacks against Manchuria but were adamantly opposed to a naval blockade that would jeopardize Hong Kong.[45]

The U.S. administration took the allied concerns seriously. During an NSC meeting on December 10, there was general agreement that war against China could not be fought without the consent of the allies. President Truman expressed concern about the domestic situation in the United States and feared a wave of isolationism if the Korean situation was not successfully solved. NSC 118/2 (see above) specified that the United States would seek allied agreement on a joint statement threatening the extension of hostilities into China if a cease-fire accord was violated. But it also stated that the United States would unilaterally issue such a statement if the allies did not agree. Acheson then told the British ambassador that the United States insisted on a "Greater Sanctions" statement, but no longer demanded that the allies agree to particular military actions if a cease-fire was violated. Both sides agreed to disagree and not to be bound by the other. As Acheson put it, "This means that UK is not obligated at this time [to] take any particular action and that US is not committed not to take any particular action." He also noted that there was no commitment by the United States "to obtain UK concurrence prior to taking action."[46]

Both sides then argued over the wording of the "Greater Sanctions" statement. The allies succeeded in considerably watering down an American draft that had originally threatened to "bring upon any country" involved in a renewed aggression the "full retribution without geographic limitation." The final "Greater Sanctions" statement, which was approved by all sixteen nations participating in the UN forces, read:

> We affirm, in the interests of world peace, that if there is a renewal of the armed attack, challenging again the principles of the UN, we should again be united and prompt to resist. The consequences of such a breach of the armistice would be so grave that, in all probability, it would not be possible to confine the hostilities within the frontiers of Korea.[47]

[45] See "Memorandum to the Dep. Under-secretary of State," Nov. 21, 1951, *FRUS 1951*, 7:1154–56; "Memorandum of Conversation regarding a meeting with Ambassador Franks," Nov. 21, ibid., 1156–58; "Memorandum of conversation between British and American officials," Nov. 28, ibid., 1189–93; "Anthony Eden to Dean Acheson," Dec. 3, ibid., 1221–23; "Acting Secretary of State Webb to U.S. Embassy in U.K.," Dec. 4, ibid., 1238–39; "U.S. Embassy in UK to Secretary of State," Dec. 12, ibid., 1317–1319.

[46] "Dean Acheson to U.S. Embassy in UK," Dec. 14, 1951, *FRUS 1951*, 7:1332. See also "Record of NSC Meeting," Dec. 10, ibid., 1290–96; "NSC 118/2," ibid., 1385.

[47] Contained in "JCS to CINCFE Ridgway," Jan. 10, 1952, *FRUS 1952–1954*, 15:14. For the various drafts see "Acting Secretary of State to Embassy in UK," Dec. 5, 1951, *FRUS 1951*, 7:1249–50; "Ambassador in UK to Secretary of State," Dec. 8, ibid., 1282; "Ambassador in UK to Secretary of State," Dec. 12, ibid., 1319; "Secretary of State to Embassy in UK," Dec. 18, ibid., 1373; "Secretary of State to Embassy in UK," Dec. 26, ibid., 1453.

When a cease-fire agreement was within reach in the summer of 1953, the allies were reluctant to publish the statement. This time, the Eisenhower administration simply bullied the Europeans into acquiescence, reminding them of their economic dependence on the United States. The statement was issued on August 7, ten days after the conclusion of the armistice.[48]

In sum, the allies consistently tried to prevent the extension of hostilities into China and were largely successful with regard to military actions on the battlefield. The United States fulfilled its obligation to consult most of the time. Since the outcome of such consultations, allied opposition, was known in advance, the norm frequently served to prevent the military from taking action that might have escalated the conflict. Particularly during the Truman administration, allied influence on U.S. policies worked primarily through links to the State Department and to the most important foreign policy player in the administration, Dean Acheson. The secretary of state shared the allied view that an escalation of the war, which might trigger World War III, should be avoided. But his views and those of the allies ran directly counter to the prevailing mood in American domestic public opinion and in Congress.

The allies were less successful with regard to military contingency plans. The "Greater Sanctions" statement, for example, papered over profound differences over what to do if the Chinese or North Koreans renewed their attacks. However, the conditions attached to contingency plans for extending the war into China were extremely restrictive and essentially required a massive and unilateral Chinese escalation of the war in order for U.S. attacks on China to be carried out.

A similar pattern of allied impact through consultation norms and transgovernmental coalition-building with major players in the United States emerged regarding another contingency with which the United States was frequently confronted during the war—the potential use of nuclear weapons.

Preventing the Use of Nuclear Weapons

Since the Korean War represented the first armed conflict during the cold war, it was of utmost importance how U.S. decision-makers dealt with the new nuclear weapons at their disposal. Their non-use set a precedent. There is general consensus in the historical literature that the use of nuclear weapons was considered frequently during the war, not just by subordinate military officials, but high up in the decision-making hierarchy.

[48] See "Memorandum regarding conversation with British officials," June 5, 1953, *FRUS 1952–1954*, 15:1147–48; "152nd NSC Meeting," July 2, ibid., 1300–1312; "Memorandum regarding a Meeting with Allied Ambassadors," July 21, ibid., 1408–11. See also Foot, *Wrong War*, 218–19; Lowe, "Settlement of the Korean War," 227–28.

Deliberations included the NSC and the two presidents, Truman and Eisenhower. Scholars remain divided over how close the world actually came to the use of nuclear weapons.[49] Historians are also not very clear on the reasons why nuclear weapons were not used. The most prominent explanations range from the lack of military targets, the fear of escalation leading to World War III, to sheer luck, since Chinese actions never met the conditions required for the use of nuclear arms. While I do not claim that allied concerns were the only reason for the non-use, allied opposition figured prominently in the deliberations of the decision-makers and became particularly relevant during the Eisenhower administration.

An Obligation to Consult: Deliberations during the Truman Administration

From the beginning of the Korean War, decision-makers envisioned that nuclear weapons might be used at some stage in the conflict. President Truman ordered the preparations of plans for nuclear attacks against Soviet bases in Asia should the USSR enter the fighting. But when asked at news conferences in June and July 1950 whether the U.S. planned to use the atomic bomb in Korea, his answer was consistently negative.

The administration also engaged in an effort at atomic diplomacy and repeated the nuclear bluff of the 1948 Berlin crisis by sending nuclear-configured B-29s without the nuclear cores to Britain. The British who were already concerned about the possible use of nuclear weapons, insisted that a cabinet decision was required if their bases were to be utilized. On July 10, the British cabinet approved the dispatch of the B-29s provided that it was done with as little publicity as possible to avoid overt threats against Moscow.[50] The allied demands undermined the threatening purpose of the deployment to some extent. U.S. strategic planning was heavily dependent on the use of British bases at the time and London used this to increase its leverage over American decisions.[51]

[49] See the accounts in Richard Betts, *Nuclear Blackmail and Nuclear Balance* (Washington D.C.: Brookings, 1987), 31–47; Gaddis, "The Origins of Self-Deterrence: The United States and the Non-Use of Nuclear Weapons, 1945–1958," in Gaddis, *Long Peace*, 104–46; Roger Dingman, "Atomic Diplomacy during the Korean War," *International Security* 13, no. 2 (Winter 1988/89): 50–91; Rosemary J. Foot, "Nuclear Coercion and the Ending of the Korean Conflict," ibid., 92–112; Marc Trachtenberg, "A 'Wasting Asset': American Strategy and the Shifting Nuclear Balance, 1949–54," ibid., 5–49; Mark A. Ryan, *Chinese Attitudes toward Nuclear Weapons* (New York: M. E. Sharpe, 1989). For a comprehensive account see also Nina Tannenwald, "Dogs that Don't Bark" (Ph.D. diss. Cornell University, Ithaca, N.Y., 1995).

[50] For details see Dingman, "Atomic Diplomacy," 57–59; Betts, *Nuclear Blackmail*, 32; Ovendale, "Britain and the Cold War in Asia," 132; Ryan, *Chinese Attitudes*, 25–27.

[51] See Trachtenberg, "A 'Wasting Asset'," 23, on this point. Trachtenberg quotes Acheson as arguing that British views could not be ignored since "we can bring U.S. power into play only with the cooperation of the British" (ibid., n. 70).

Using nuclear weapons in Korea was considered seriously for the first time when Chinese forces crossed the Yalu River in November. The decision was negative, for military and diplomatic reasons. A JCS committee argued that using nuclear weapons was inappropriate "except under the most compelling military circumstances." The State Department maintained that the diplomatic consequences of using the bomb, which had "the status of a peculiar monster conceived by American cunning," would be disastrous with regard to world opinion and to maintaining the support of the European allies.[52] This assessment was confirmed shortly afterward.

On November 30, President Truman declared in a press conference that "there has always been active consideration" to use nuclear weapons and that the United States would take "whatever steps are necessary to meet the military situation" including "every weapon that we have."[53] While the White House tried to clarify the president's remarks immediately, they triggered worldwide protest. British members of Parliament signed a letter to Prime Minister Attlee urging him to go to Washington and, should the bomb be dropped, to withdraw British troops from Korea. To accommodate the domestic debate, Attlee decided to see Truman to urge the Americans that localization of the war was of utmost importance for keeping the UN alliance together (see above). Prior to his visit, he consulted with the French Prime Minister, who also conveyed his opposition to the use of nuclear weapons in Korea.[54] The allied reaction to Truman's ill-conceived remarks served as a reminder to the administration that it would wreck NATO if it decided to use nuclear weapons in Korea.

Attlee received private assurances by the president during his visit in Washington. According to the British records,

> the President said that he had reaffirmed to the Prime Minister that the Governments of the United Kingdom and Canada were partners with the United States in the atomic weapon and that the United States Government would not consider its use without consulting the United Kingdom and Canada. The understanding on this point was clear even though it depended upon no written agreement.

The U.S. records, which did not mention Canada, added that "if a man's

[52] "Memorandum by Bureau of Far Eastern Affairs," Nov. 8, 1950, *FRUS 1950*, 7:1098–1100. See also "Memorandum by Paul Nitze, Policy Planning Staff," Nov. 4, ibid., 1041–42; Foot, *Wrong War*, 116; Ryan, *Chinese Attitudes*, 33–35.

[53] *FRUS 1950*, 7:1261–62. For the following, see "UK Embassy, Washington, to Foreign Office," Nov. 30, PRO:FO 371/84164; "UK Embassy, Washington to Foreign Office," Nov. 30, ibid.; "Notes on a meeting between the Secretary of State, the Secretary of Defense, and the JCS," Dec. 1, *FRUS 1950*, 7:1276–82; "U.S. Mission to the UN to Secretary of State," Dec. 1, ibid., 1300–1301.

[54] On the French attitude see "Foreign Office to Embassy in Washington," Dec. 1, 1950, PRO:PREM 8/1206; "Note for Prime Minister and Foreign Secretary," Dec. 2, ibid.

word wasn't any good it wasn't made any better by writing it down,"[55] giving the commitment the status of a gentleman's agreement characteristic of the Anglo-American "special relationship." The president went considerably beyond the agreed-upon position of the administration by committing the United States to consultations with the allies prior to a decision with regard to nuclear weapons. His commitment was on shaky grounds legally and certain to arise heavy criticism in Congress. When Dean Acheson heard about this, he had, in the words of the British ambassador, "the equivalent of convulsions. . . . Dean began to do what he called 'unachieving' the agreement. It was really the most remarkable exhibition—quite short, absolutely devastating, serious, impassioned—and it was utterly convincing."[56] As a result, the communiqué merely stated that it was the president's desire to keep the British informed about new developments.

Attlee took the president's word as satisfactory for the time being. Subsequent behavior by both sides showed that they were aware of the tacit commitment. They also understood that the written version of the agreement had to be watered down because of domestic problems and legal requirements in the United States.[57]

By traveling to Washington, Attlee did not "prevent" the United States from using nuclear weapons in Korea, since such a decision was not seriously considered at the time. But he established a tacit understanding that Washington should consult its allies whenever decision-makers contemplated the use of nuclear weapons. As Dean Acheson later argued, threatening to employ the atomic bomb would not worry the Soviets too much but amounted to a "political liability" that would "frighten our allies to death."[58]

The Attlee visit did not stop deliberations concerning nuclear weapons in Korea, though. General MacArthur repeatedly requested nuclear

[55] "Memorandum regarding excerpt from Meeting between the President and the Prime Minister," Dec. 7, 1950, *FRUS 1950*, 7:1462. The British records of the meeting are contained in PRO:PREM 8/1200. For the following see "Position Paper prepared for Truman-Attlee Talks," *FRUS 1950*, 7:1464–65.

[56] Sir Franks continues to describe the atmosphere of these Anglo-American "summit meetings": "So the denouement of that was that there were no chairs somehow in the president's office. We had to pull out a sliding panel of his desk, and I had to kneel down beside it to write out a revised communiqué in the light of what had been reachieved. And while I was doing this, the president suddenly turned to me and said, 'How often do you think a British ambassador has knelt before the American president?'" Quoted in James Reston, *Deadline* (New York: Random House, 1991), 148. I thank Susan Brewer for alerting me to this quote. See also "Memorandum for the record," Jan. 16, 1953, *FRUS 1950*, 7:1462–64.

[57] See "Prime Minister to Foreign Secretary," Dec. 10, 1950, PRO:PREM 8/1200; "Prime Minister in Cabinet Meeting," Dec. 12, ibid. For the text of the Anglo-American communiqué, see ibid.

[58] During an NSC meeting on Jan. 25, 1951, quoted from Dingman, "Atomic Diplomacy," 69.

bombs against invasion forces and air fields and even suggested a belt of radioactive cobalt along the Korean/Manchurian border. He was supported by various U.S. senators and congressmen. A majority of American public opinion also continuously supported the use of nuclear weapons against China.[59]

In early April 1951, President Truman authorized the transfer of nuclear bombs from the Atomic Energy Commission (AEC) to the Air Force and sent nuclear-equipped bombers to Guam. But he assured AEC Chairman Dean, who voiced concern regarding the effects of such a decision on allies in Europe and Asia, that no decisions had been made as to the use of these weapons.[60] The B-29s returned to the United States in late June.

The U.S. Army and the JCS remained skeptical about using atomic bombs on the battlefield since no suitable targets were available. At the same time, Dean Acheson reassured London that the United States would not launch nuclear strikes from British bases without British consent. He stopped short of committing the United States to a general consultation norm with regard to other nuclear contingencies. But the British government believed "that as result Attlee discussion last year and subsequent conversations they have firm commitment that bomb will not be delivered from UK bases without prior consultation; that there is qualified commitment to consult on use in F[ar] E[ast]; but that no commitment exists re other use."[61] When Prime Minister Churchill visited Washington in January 1952, the communiqué contained the "understanding that the use of these bases in an emergency would be a matter for joint decision . . . in the light of the circumstances prevailing at the time."[62]

The British had, thus, acquired veto power over an American decision

[59] It was only after the Korean War that American public opinion became firmly opposed to the (first) use of nuclear weapons. See data in Thomas Graham, *American Public Opinion on NATO, Extended Deterrence, and the Use of Nuclear Weapons* (Cambridge, Mass.: Center for Science and International Affairs, Harvard University, 1989). On MacArthur's request for nuclear weapons and other voices in the U.S. domestic debate see Ryan, *Chinese Attitudes*, 38–39, 49–50; Foot, *Wrong War*, 114–15.

[60] Cf. Ryan, *Chinese Attitudes*, 50–51. Roger Dingman has argued that this was the "most serious nuclear action" during the Korean War ("Atomic Diplomacy," 89). He also claims that General Ridgway received a directive giving him "qualified authority to launch atomic strikes in retaliation for a major air attack originating from beyond the Korean peninsula" (76). But the sources quoted by Dingman do not contain a reference to nuclear weapons (*FRUS 1951*, 7:386–87, 394–98). Rather, they contain the above-mentioned authorization to launch retaliatory *air* strikes (rather than atomic strikes) against China under certain conditions. It is unlikely that this directive included the use of nuclear weapons without explicitly mentioning them.

[61] "Ambassador in UK to Department of State," Dec. 28, 1951, *FRUS 1952–1954*, 6:723. See Margaret Gowing, *Policy-Making*, vol. 1 of *Independence and Deterrence* (London: Macmillan, 1974), 316–18.

[62] "Communiqué of Truman-Churchill talks," Jan. 9, 1952, *FRUS 1952–1954*, 6:837–39. See also "Memorandum of Secretary of State," Jan. 6, 1952, ibid., 745; "U.S. minutes of second meeting Truman-Churchill," Jan. 7, ibid., 763–66.

to launch a nuclear attack against the Soviet Union, since the United States needed British bases to reach targets in the USSR at the time. President Truman also reaffirmed the informal commitment given to Attlee that he would consult the allies should he be prepared to authorize the use of nuclear weapons. JCS Chairman Bradley reassured the British prime minister that "it was not our intention to use these bombs" in Korea given the lack of suitable targets.

"Simply Another Weapon in Our Arsenal"? The Eisenhower Administration

In 1950–1951, the United States lacked a large nuclear stockpile. This situation had changed by 1953, when the Eisenhower administration entered office. Lack of nuclear warheads could no longer be considered a reason for restraint in Korea. There is considerable controversy in the literature as to whether the Eisenhower administration changed the skeptical approach of the Truman administration toward nuclear weapons.[63] I argue in the following that a discrepancy between nuclear words and deeds occurred in 1953 and that this discrepancy resulted to a large extent from anticipated allied objections.

Records of NSC meetings in early 1953 indicate that President Eisenhower and Secretary of State Dulles initially pushed for a decision to use tactical nuclear weapons to end the war quickly, if negotiations would not produce an armistice. They also had a broader political objective in mind when they argued that "somehow or other the taboo which surrounds the use of atomic weapons would have to be destroyed."[64] They maintained that there was a false distinction in world public opinion setting atomic weapons apart from all other weapons, which made them practically unusable. Eisenhower and Dulles recognized that a decision to use nuclear weapons to end the Korean War would meet with considerable allied opposition. The president briefly considered starting talks with selected allies but then ruled against it. He asked the Pentagon for a study on the feasibility of a successful military campaign in Korea that included the use of nuclear weapons.[65]

[63] Marc Trachtenberg argues that the JCS began to look more favorably at nuclear employment options because of the huge nuclear build-up. See his "A 'Wasting Asset,' " 28–30. Richard Betts claims that Eisenhower himself pushed for a decision to use nuclear weapons to end the war quickly. See *Nuclear Blackmail and Nuclear Balance*, 37–42. Roger Dingman, however, maintains that there was a difference between nuclear rhetoric and concrete action and that the Eisenhower administration was even more cautious in using the nuclear option than Truman. See "Atomic Diplomacy," 79–89. The above quote is taken from President Eisenhower in an NSC meeting on May 6, 1953, *FRUS 1952–1954*, 15:977.

[64] "NSC Special Meeting," March 31, 1953, *FRUS 1952–1954*, 15:825–27, 826–27. See also "131st NSC Meeting," Feb. 11, ibid., 769–72.

[65] See "Memorandum by National Security Advisor Cutler to Secretary of Defense Wil-

The top military remained reluctant at first. JCS Chairman Bradley and Army Chief of Staff Collins repeatedly voiced their skepticism about the military value of tactical nuclear weapons in Korea.[66] But in the meantime, a JCS committee had reviewed the military options in Korea and passed its study on to the NSC. Three of six possible courses of action involved attacks against China, potentially including nuclear weapons. The study contained a separate section evaluating the political and military advantages and disadvantages of such use. While it considered the constraints posed by U.S. public opinion as essentially unproblematic, the study concluded that extension of the war into China "would severely strain and possibly break the Western alliance and would certainly alienate pro-U.S. feelings in most of Free Asia."[67] Bradley and Collins remained opposed and were supported by the State Department, which pointed to the disruptive effects on NATO. But the president continued to push the issue. Under pressure from both the top (the president) and the bottom (military commanders in the field), the JCS turned around. During an NSC meeting on May 13, Bradley argued that "none of the courses of action which involved operations outside of Korea could really be effectively carried out without the use of atomic weapons." Deputy Secretary of State Smith then mentioned the anticipated allied reaction and maintained that using nuclear weapons against China was "fraught with danger for us from the point of view of the reaction of our allies." NATO would "fall into pieces temporarily." He thought, however, that the Alliance could potentially be repaired if the all-out offensive was quick and successful. The president seemed impressed and stated that the United States desperately needed "to maintain these outposts of our national defense, and we do not wish our allies to desert us. We were already in considerable difficulties with these allies."[68] The JCS were asked to submit their final recommendations to the NSC. They advised that the extension of the war into China required the use of nuclear weapons on a

son," March 21, 1953, *FRUS 1952–1954*, 15:817–18. Eisenhower was well aware of the obligation to consult the allies: "If we decided upon a major, new type of offensive, the present policies would have to be changed and new ones agreed to by our allies. Foremost would be the proposed issue of atomic weapons." He then argued that a U.S. decision to use nuclear weapons "would have created strong and disrupting feelings between ourselves and our allies," but claimed that a successful all-out offensive could repair such rifts. Eisenhower, *White House Years* (Garden City, N.Y.: Doubleday, 1963), 180. Eisenhower's account is consistent with what he stated in NSC meetings at the time.

66 Cf. "131st NSC Meeting," Feb. 11, 1953, *FRUS 1952–1954*, 15:769–72; "Memorandum of JCS-State Department Meeting," March 27, ibid., 817–18.

67 "Report by NSC Planning Board on 'Possible Courses of Action in Korea,'" April 2, 1953, *FRUS 1952–1954*, 15:839–57, 848. For this and the following, see also Dingman, "Atomic Diplomacy," 82–85; Foot, *Wrong War*, 206–11; Ryan, *Chinese Attitudes*, 60–64.

68 "144th NSC Meeting," May 13, 1953, *FRUS 1952–1954*, 15:1014–17, 1016.

massive scale. They cited detrimental effects on NATO among the risks involved, but came out in favor of such a course of action. They also took notice of the obligation to consult the allies and declared that implementation of the plan would be required to obtain the concurrence of as many UN participants in Korea as possible.[69]

On May 20, the NSC reviewed the JCS recommendations. It decided that the JCS plan should be adopted as a "general guide" pending the completion of related studies, including an evaluation by the State Department on political implications. Eisenhower who expressed his support for the plan suggested that "we ought at once to begin infiltrat[ing] these ideas into the minds of our allies."[70] This was the closest the Eisenhower administration came to a decision to employ nuclear weapons in Korea. At this point, the only constraint remaining was anticipated allied opposition. The State Department study concluded that, in the final analysis, the United States would "be faced with choosing directly between Allied and neutral support and the pursuit of the proposed course of action."[71] The NSC document was never implemented, and the matter lost its urgency when an armistice was concluded in July 1953. In late October, the president referred again to the necessary consultations with the allies.[72] He inquired whether such discussions had taken place but did not receive a clear answer. Secretary Dulles later pointed out that a "great deal of 'educational work'" had to be done with the allies on this matter. At an NSC meeting in early December, Dulles clashed with the new JCS chairman, Admiral Radford, who advocated massive nuclear strikes inside and outside Korea. Dulles came out strongly against such action since it involved general war with China and probably with the Soviet Union: "Over and above the cardinal point that the Soviets were almost certain to enter the war, Secretary Dulles predicted that there would be virtually no UN participants with the United States in any general war against China. We would thus be isolated from our allies."[73]

The "educational work" with the allies took place at the Anglo-Franco-American summit in Bermuda in early December 1953. It quickly became clear that the allies had never understood the "Greater Sanctions" statement (see above) as authorizing the use of nuclear weapons. The British were extremely concerned, even though Prime Minister Churchill did not seem to understand the implications at first. During his conversations with Eisenhower, Churchill apparently accepted the president's view that

[69] "JCS to Secretary of Defense Wilson," May 19, 1953, *FRUS 1952–1954*, 15:1059–64.

[70] "145th NSC Meeting," May 20, 1953, *FRUS 1952–1954*, 15:1064–68, 1066.

[71] "Annex to NSC 147," June 4, 1953, *FRUS 1952–1954*, 15:1139–44, 1140.

[72] "168th NSC Meeting," Oct. 29, 1953, *FRUS 1952–1954*, 15:1570–76, 1571. On the lack of implementation of the NSC document see Dingman, "Atomic Diplomacy," 84, 87, 88. For the following see "171st NSC Meeting," Nov. 19, 1953, *FRUS 1952–1954*, 15:1616–20, 1617.

[73] "173rd NSC Meeting," Dec. 3, 1953, *FRUS 1952–1954*, 15:1636–45, 1639.

nuclear weapons should be employed if the Chinese or North Koreans broke the armistice.

But the prime minister later backtracked from his statement; Churchill and Eden succeeded in removing a passage from the president's planned "Atoms for Peace" speech at the United Nations that threatened the use of nuclear weapons in Korea in the event of renewed hostilities. Two days later, Eden and the French Foreign Minister Bidault made it clear to the Americans that they considered the use of nuclear weapons in Korea a new issue that had not yet been discussed and that required further consultation. Eden suggested getting UN approval for such a course of action—an attempt to bury the question. In response, the president implicitly threatened that the American presence in Europe could be jeopardized if the United States had to maintain large numbers of troops both there and in Asia while not being permitted to use the "cheap" nuclear bomb in Korea.[74]

The Bermuda conversations impressed both Eisenhower and Dulles. In subsequent NSC meetings, the president refused any pre-delegation of authority to use nuclear weapons in the Far East and argued that one had to be "a little patient with our allies, who had not as yet fully grasped the import of atomic warfare." Dulles suggested sharing nuclear information with some European allies and "letting some of these fellows in Europe have a few atomic weapons" in order not to alienate them from the United States.[75] The allied objections had left a mark on the secretary of state that partly explains his later views on the nuclear test ban (see chapter 5).[76]

The Korean War established a pattern of allied opposition to the use of nuclear weapons in regional conflicts. The evidence reveals that the administration was well aware of the allied opposition, that it obliged by the consultation norm, and that the alliance argument figured prominently in the internal considerations. But would the United States have used nuclear weapons in Korea in the absence of allied opposition? There are four alternative explanations for the non-use.

First, one could try to explain the non-use on domestic grounds. But U.S. public opinion and the Congress were at best agnostic toward the

[74] For details, see "Eisenhower-Churchill Dinner Meeting," Dec. 5, 1953, *FRUS 1952–1954*, 5:1786; "Second Restricted Tripartite Meeting of the Heads of Government," Dec. 7, ibid., 1808–18. See also the account in Eisenhower, *Mandate for Change*, 248–50. For the Eisenhower-Churchill meetings see "Eisenhower-Churchill Meeting," Dec. 4 and 5, 1953, *FRUS 1952–1954*, 5:1739–40, 1767–1769. For a frank discussion of the British concerns, see the diaries of Eden's private secretary, Evelyn Shuckburgh, *Descent to Suez* (London: Weidenfeld, 1986), 114–15.

[75] "179th NSC Meeting," Jan. 8, 1954, *FRUS 1952–1954*, 15:1704–10, 1708. See also "174th NSC Meeting," Dec. 10, 1953, ibid., 1653–55.

[76] See John L. Gaddis, "The Unexpected John Foster Dulles: Nuclear Weapons, Communism, and the Russians," in *John Foster Dulles and the Diplomacy of the Cold War*, ed. Richard H. Immermann (Princeton, N.J.: Princeton University Press, 1990), 49–58.

issue and at worst sympathetic to employing atomic weapons to end the war quickly. There were not many domestic constraints with regard to nuclear weapons at the time.

Second, the U.S. military leadership was itself opposed to using nuclear weapons given the small stockpile and a lack of suitable targets. This was certainly true for the early years of the war. But by 1952, the U.S. stockpile had significantly increased and the JCS, not to mention the military commanders in Korea, became more favorable toward using the bomb. In 1953, Eisenhower and Dulles pushed the JCS to endorse a massive use of nuclear weapons, if the negotiations failed or the armistice broke down. At that time, anticipated allied opposition remained the only argument against employing atomic weapons.

Third, using nuclear weapons in Korea could have quickly escalated hostilities toward a general war with China and, possibly, the Soviet Union. The non-use was, therefore, in the U.S. national interest quite apart from allied objections. Truman and Acheson shared the allied view that escalation of the Korean War should be avoided. But Eisenhower and Dulles were elected to end the war quickly and, therefore, insisted on exploring the nuclear option. Given the overwhelming U.S. nuclear superiority in 1953, risk of escalation seems to have figured less in their thinking. The fear of losing the allies apparently affected them more.

Finally, allied opposition could have served as a pretext for Eisenhower and Dulles, who might have been opposed to using nuclear weapons all along. It is hard to say what went on in the minds of decision-makers beyond the documentary evidence pointing in a different direction. But even if the two men only pretended to favoring the nuclear use, it is significant that they referred to allied concerns to justify their final decisions. It suggests that they tried to tap into a collective understanding about the value of the Western Alliance.

In sum, the European allies established a consultation norm concerning the use of nuclear weapons during the Truman administration, but were less influential regarding actual employment decisions, which were not seriously considered anyway. The allied impact on actual choices increased considerably during the first year of the Eisenhower administration, when European disapproval became a major argument against using nuclear weapons in Korea. Similar allied influence was noticeable during the armistice negotiations.

Pushing and Pulling the U.S. toward a Cease-Fire

The allies wanted to achieve an early cease-fire agreement, primarily to direct the uncompromising American attention to the European theater.

They were more successful in influencing the substance of the U.S. position than in affecting the timing of an armistice agreement. But the failure to achieve an early cease-fire was not just the result of American intransigence but also of Chinese and Soviet unwillingness to compromise.

Failure: Early Allied Attempts to Reach a Settlement

The European allies lost no time in pursuing a settlement once the war had started. Four days after the outbreak of the fighting, the British embassy in Moscow urged the Soviets to achieve a negotiated solution. The British also hinted that one could trade a return to the status quo in Korea for compromises on the questions of Taiwan and for giving the Chinese UN seat to the People's Republic—two issues already contested between Washington and London. The U.S. reacted strongly against the idea of negotiating with the Chinese at this point. Dean Acheson told the American ambassador in London to leave Ernest Bevin "in no doubt of seriousness with which I view implications of his message and their possible effect on our whole future relationship."[77] When Bevin communicated to Acheson that such threats violated the code of conduct in relations among allies, the secretary of state backed off. But the British did not pursue the substantive question further, either.

The next effort to propose a settlement came immediately after Chinese troops entered North Korea in early November 1950. The Australian government, followed by the British and supported by the French, suggested a demilitarized buffer zone south of the Yalu River which should be administered by both the UN and the Chinese. General MacArthur reacted furiously accusing the British of moving "to appease the Chinese Communists by giving them a strip of Northern Korea [that] finds its historic precedent in the action taken at Munich on 29 Sept 1938."[78] The proposal received lukewarm support at the State Department, but the Pentagon and the military prevailed against the idea. When the British hinted that they were discussing the buffer zone proposal with Canada and India and were also approaching the Chinese, Acheson urged Bevin

[77] "Secretary of State to [U.S.] Embassy in UK," July 10, 1950, *FRUS 1950*, 7:351–52. See also "Foreign Office to [UK] Embassy in U.S.," July 6, ibid., 313; "Secretary of State to [U.S.] Embassy in UK," July 7, ibid., 327; "Foreign Secretary to [UK] Embassy in U.S.," July 7, ibid., 330; "[U.S.] Ambassador in UK to Secretary of State," July 11, ibid., 361; "Meeting between the Secretary of State and the British Ambassador in the U.S.," July 13, ibid., 374. See also Dockrill, "The Foreign Office, Anglo-American relations, and the Korean War," 461; Foot, *Substitute for Victory*, 21–23.

[78] "General MacArthur to JCS," Nov. 9, 1950, *FRUS 1950*, 7:1107–10, 1108. The proposal itself is contained in "Foreign Secretary to Embassy in U.S.," Nov. 13, ibid., 1138–40. See also Peter Farrar, "A Pause for Peace Negotiations: The British Buffer Zone Plan of November 1950," in *The Korean War in History*, ed. Cotton and Neary, 66–79; Foot, *Wrong War*, 92–93; Foot, *Substitute for Victory*, 27–28.

in the strongest terms not to do this. London gave in.[79] But the allies succeeded in establishing a UN cease-fire commission, thereby multilateralizing the negotiating efforts as well as providing allied and other governments with an institutionalized access to the American decision-making process.

The improved military situation on the battlefield gradually softened the U.S. position toward the allied demands. On March 21, 1951, a draft presidential statement was prepared—subject to consultation with the allies—which encouraged a prompt settlement in Korea.[80] The attempt was spoiled by the turmoil following General MacArthur's insubordination and resulting in his dismissal.

Herbert Morrison, Bevin's successor as British foreign secretary, and the French government continued pressing for a political settlement in Korea and for an informal approach to Moscow and Beijing during the Spring of 1951.[81] When the Soviet ambassador to the UN made various conciliatory remarks and then called for an armistice, the allies urged the United States to take him seriously. An interagency meeting decided on June 28 that the U.S./UN commander in Korea should issue an invitation for armistice talks. JCS Chairman Bradley argued, "We could not ignore the effect on the will of our people and other contributing UN member nations to continued support of the hostilities if we in effect turned down what appeared to be an opportunity to end the hostilities."[82] The talks began on July 10, 1951.

"World Opinion" and the Armistice Talks, 1951–1952

UN and allied pressure was indeed needed to prevent the U.S. commander from an uncompromising negotiating position. As Rosemary Foot has pointed out, the decision to leave the talks in the hands of military commanders who had no experience in conducting diplomatic negotiations prevented the United States from seriously exploring various ave-

[79] For details see "Foreign Secretary to [UK] Embassy in U.S.," Nov. 17, 1950, *FRUS 1950*, 7:1173–74; "Secretary of State to [U.S.] Embassy in UK," Nov. 21, ibid., 1212; "Secretary of State to [U.S.] Embassy in UK," Nov. 24, ibid., 1229; "Embassy in UK to Secretary of State," Nov. 25, ibid., 1234–35.

[80] See "Draft of Proposed Presidential Statement on Korea," March 21, 1951, *FRUS 1951*, 7:253–54; Foot, *Substitute for Victory*, 34.

[81] See Ovendale, "Britain and the Cold War in Asia," 138, on the British advances. On the French, see "Memorandum of Conversation between Dean Rusk and the French Ambassador," June 5, 1951, *FRUS 1951*, 7:504–5.

[82] "Department of State—JCS Meeting," June 28, 1951, *FRUS 1951*, 7:566–71, 568. See also "JCS to CINCUNC," June 30, ibid., 598–600. On the allied reactions to the Soviet proposals see, for example, "[U.S.] Ambassador in UK to Secretary of State," June 25, ibid., 552–53; "Memorandum of Conversation Regarding Meeting with French Embassy Officials," June 27, ibid., 7:556–57; Foot, *Substitute for Victory*, 36–37.

nues toward a negotiated settlement.[83] Bargaining through the repeated issuance of ultimatums was not particularly conducive to an agreement. The State Department repeatedly tried mollifying the American negotiating stance by referring to the need to preserve a favorable climate of "world opinion." Less than two weeks after the negotiations had started, the JCS denied Admiral Ridgway's request to go into a recess because of communist intransigence. They argued that the reasons put forward by Ridgway would not "present sufficiently clear and powerful issue before world opinion."[84] Later in the year, similar arguments served to soften Ridgway's negotiating position with regard to the demarcation line.

Prisoners of war (POWs) quickly became the most contentious issue of the armistice talks. As soon as the negotiations had started, U.S. officials considered whether POWs should be repatriated and exchanged irrespective of their personal wishes. Against Dean Acheson's advice, the president strongly supported the principle of voluntary repatriation, which subsequently was introduced at the negotiating table, apparently without prior allied consultation. The British Foreign Office reviewed the new position and found it legally shaky. The Canadian government also voiced concerns. But allied criticism was seriously weakened when the new prime minister, Churchill, came out in favor of Truman's argument in early 1952, overruling his Foreign Office.[85]

In Korea, the policy of nonforcible repatriation led South Koreans to force Chinese POWs to "voluntarily" reject repatriation during initial screenings. The treatment of these POWs and the UN commander's request in May 1952 for breaking off the talks after having issued another ultimatum resulted in strong allied protests. They demanded rescreening of the POWs by a third party. Anthony Eden, the British foreign secretary, who had been in contact with the Chinese through India's Prime Minister Nehru, proposed to break the deadlock in the talks and suggested that an independent body should interview those POWs who did not wish to return home. State Department officials, who sympathized with the British and were concerned about allied and "world opinion," then suggested that India serve as a mediator. During interagency meetings, allied concerns figured most prominently against breaking off the talks. The U.S./UN commander received the following instructions:

> Regardless of logic and reasonableness of our posn on impartial rescreening fol[lowin]g armistice, our principal allies would not now support unilateral

[83] Foot, *Substitute for Victory*, 10–11.

[84] "JCS to CINCFE," July 21, 1951, *FRUS 1951*, 7:716–18, 716. On the general importance of the "world opinion" argument, see Foot, *Substitute for Victory*, 65.

[85] For details see Lowe, "The Settlement of the Korean War," 213–14; Foot, *Substitute for Victory*, 87–94; "Meeting at the White House," Feb. 27, 1952, *FRUS 1952–1954*, 15:68–69.

indefinite suspension of negots, and probably not in any case until after an offer of rescreening prior to armistice has been made in some way and rejected by Communists. . . . Contribute whatever may be possible toward achievement of armistice, and, if negots suspended or Communists break off, make unmistakably clear that issue was principle of non-forcible repatriation rather than entirely subsidiary question of validity of results of UNC screening of method of confirming results.[86]

But the situation changed again three months later. In the U.S. election campaign, the Truman administration was increasingly accused of not being tough enough with the communists. The State Department faced an uphill battle against the military, the Pentagon, an increasing majority in Congress, and public opinion, which all favored breaking off the talks if the communists did not agree to the American position. This time, the argument about the need to preserve allied unity and a favorable "world opinion" lost out against the domestic concerns. The president instructed the U.S./UN negotiator in September 1952 to issue an ultimatum. It was rejected and the negotiations went into unlimited recess.[87]

But the European and Canadian allies did not give up the fight for a more forthcoming American attitude. One of the most serious confrontations with the U.S. followed.

The Clash over the Menon Resolution

To diffuse possible initiatives by other countries, the United States introduced a cease-fire resolution to the UN General Assembly soon after the talks had gone into recess. The Canadian foreign minister suggested that a cease-fire should come into effect after the U.S. resolution had been tabled. Dean Acheson strongly objected to this idea, but was aware of the allied concerns: "It appears to me that our principle job here [at the UN] is to hold our friends and allies together and face a determined Soviet effort to drive a wedge between us."[88] At the same time, the Indian am-

[86] "JCS to CINCFE," June 5, 1952, *FRUS 1952–1954*, 15:310–14, 311–12. See "Memorandum by Dep. Asst. Secretary for Far Eastern Affairs," May 15, ibid., 202–3; "Notes from Secretary of State's Staff Meeting," May 22, ibid., 224; "Memorandum for Secretary of State," May 22, ibid., 227; "Staff Meeting JCS-State Department," May 28, ibid., 256–62. See also Foot, *Substitute for Victory*, 108–29, 132–35, 144–51.

[87] For details see "Staff Meeting JCS–State Department," Sept. 8, 1952, *FRUS 1952–1954*, 15:497; "Meeting JCS–State Department," Sept. 16, ibid., 514–21; "Meeting of Secretary of State, Secretary of Defense, and Members of JCS," Sept. 17, ibid., 522–525; "NSC Meeting with the President," Sept. 24, ibid., 532–38.

[88] Letter to the President, quoted in Acheson, *Korean War*, 140. Acheson's account of the following story can be found ibid., 140–50. For the Canadian initiative, see "Memorandum by Dean Acheson," Oct. 25, 1952, *FRUS 1952–1954*, 15:564; "Memorandum for the Secretary of State," Oct. 27, ibid., 564–66.

bassador to the UN, Krishna Menon, worked on a proposal that took up some ideas that Anthony Eden had suggested earlier (see above). Menon recommended support of the principle of nonforcible repatriation and placement of all POWs into the custody of a commission composed of four "neutral" countries (including Poland, for example), which would take care of their repatriation. Menon kept the specifics deliberately vague in order to make the proposal acceptable to the Chinese. This vagueness, together with the composition of the commission, was precisely what made it difficult for the Americans to digest. The Indian initiative would probably not have gone very far, but it was strongly supported by the British and the Canadian governments, who considered it helpful and thought that they might be able to "manage" Menon in the right direction. The resulting clash over the Menon resolution was not so much between the United States and India as between Washington and its most important allies.[89]

Dean Acheson, who acted against the advice of the JCS, hinted to the allies that the United States might favorably consider the Indian resolution. He emphasized that the principle of nonforcible repatriation had to be spelled out more clearly and that the POW issue had to be solved before an armistice would become effective. The U.S. delegation to the UN was instructed to work along these lines even though the United States would have preferred a different resolution.[90]

Anthony Eden promised to work with Menon to revise the draft. But when the British showed a new draft to Dean Acheson, he declared that "we cld not ask Dept and JCS to accept anything like this draft." The State Department argued that the British proposal "goes so far to meet the Communist point of view as to in fact contemplate the ultimate abandonment of the principle of no forced repatriation."[91] Washington now played hard ball with the allies but was confronted with an almost united front supporting, if not the details, certainly the substance of the Indian proposal. Dean Acheson maintained that allied unity should be preserved at all cost and that, therefore, the allies should turn around. He stated "that

89 See "Meeting Secretary of State—Selwyn Lloyd," Oct. 29, 1952, *FRUS 1952–1954*, 15:566–68; "Memorandum by Ernest Gross, U.S. Mission to the UN," Nov. 1, ibid., 570–72; "Dean Acheson to State Department," Nov. 6, ibid., 583–84; "Acheson to State Department," Nov. 8, ibid., 585–86. See also Lowe, "The Settlement of the Korean War," 220.

90 Cf. "Position Paper for the U.S. Delegation at the UN General Assembly," Nov. 11, 1952, *FRUS 1952–1954*, 15:599–607; "Dean Acheson to State Department," Nov. 9, ibid., 594–95; Shuckburgh, *Descent to Suez*, 48–49; Lowe, "Settlement of the Korean War," 221.

91 "Memorandum to the President," Nov. 13, 1952, *FRUS 1952–1954*, 15:614. This memorandum, which was approved by Truman, asked for authorization for the Secretary of State to oppose strongly the resolution. For the first quote see "Dean Acheson to State Department," Nov. 12, ibid., 611–13. On the British view see Shuckburgh, *Descent to Suez*, 51. See also Foot, *Substitute for Victory*, 155.

British and Canadians, in encouraging Menon, were themselves running very great risks. He [Acheson] asked how they would like it if the US, the USSR, and some Latin Americans voted against a Menon draft resolution with the UK, Canada, and a group of Asians voting in favor of it."[92] NATO would be in jeopardy if the allies did not give in. Acheson also mentioned that the new Republican administration might be far less sympathetic to the allied viewpoint. (When the British contacted Eisenhower, however, he turned out to be favorably inclined toward the Indian resolution.) Secretary of Defense Lovett told the British that the United States would seek a military solution if an honorable armistice could not be achieved. These attempts at coercion violated the informal rules of appropriate behavior among allies and turned out to be counterproductive. Canada, France, and Britain firmly supported the Indian resolution, although the British were prepared to accommodate some of the American demands.[93]

While being tough with the allies, Acheson began to work internally for a compromise position that would amend the Indian resolution in the desired direction. The State Department realized that Washington had to accept the Menon resolution because of the unified allied pressure. But the United States insisted that an umpire should head the repatriation commission and that the POWs who did not want to return home should be released after ninety days. This was communicated to Anthony Eden, who promised to work with Menon in order to accommodate the United States. But the British foreign minister and his Canadian colleague agreed that they would vote in favor of the Indian resolution and against the United States if the American amendments went too far. They were prepared for an open clash with the United States in the UN General Assembly.[94]

At this point the Soviets helped. The Soviet ambassador to the UN launched a vehement attack against the Indian resolution. In response, Dean Acheson gave a speech praising it. As Eden's private secretary com-

[92] "Dean Acheson to State Department," Nov. 15, 1952, *FRUS 1952–1954*, 15:628–33, 629. For the following, see "Memorandum of Meeting between Acheson, Lovett, Bradley, Selwyn Lloyd, Lester Pearson," Nov. 16, ibid., 637–45; Shuckburgh, *Descent to Suez*, 53–54, 57–58.

[93] See "Dean Acheson to State Department," Nov. 17, 1952, *FRUS 1952–1954*, 15:645–47; ibid., 647 [ed. note].

[94] For details see "JCS-State Department Meeting," Nov. 15, 1952, *FRUS 1952–1954*, 15:634–37; "Dean Acheson to State Department," Nov. 19, ibid., 657–59; "Dean Acheson to State Department," Nov. 19, ibid., 659–62; "Dean Acheson to Harry Truman," Nov. 20, ibid., 662–63; "Dean Acheson to the President," Nov. 21, ibid., 663–64; "Acheson to State Department," Nov. 24, ibid., 669–74; "Memorandum for the President," Nov. 24, ibid., 674–75. See also Lowe, "Settlement of the Korean War," 221–22.

mented, "one gets a terrible impression of the United States and Russia as two unwieldy, insensitive prehistoric monsters floundering about in the mud.[95]"

A week later, Committee One of the UN General Assembly voted in favor of the amended Menon resolution, which was then passed by the General Assembly. But China and North Korea rejected it on the grounds that it was too close to the American position. The Menon resolution represented a genuine intra-alliance compromise given the opposite starting positions of both sides. The United States not only accepted the allied and Indian approach in the UN, but also the idea of an independent commission to take care of the POW repatriation after it had agreed earlier to the allied proposal for an impartial screening of the POWs.[96] The allies were essentially united in their views and backed by a large number of UN members, but they faced an equally united bureaucratic and domestic scene in Washington. The allies nevertheless succeeded in moving the United States toward a compromise. The Menon resolution, while rejected by China and the Soviets at the time, foreshadowed the substance of the later armistice agreement.

U.S. officials realized that their problems with the allies were not over with the passing of the Menon resolution: "December 3 res, although sponsored by India, resulted from Brit-Canad-India 'coalition' developed during past few weeks and in final phases supported by Austral, New Zealand and France. We cannot safely assume this 'coalition' has been dissolved nor that it may not again attempt assume further initiative."[97]

Keeping the U.S. on Track: The Conclusion of the Armistice

The allies took further initiatives when the Eisenhower administration entered office. In late March 1953, the Chinese prime minister not only accepted the exchange of sick and wounded POWs but also the principle of nonforcible repatriation, proposing the transfer to a neutral state of those POWs who did not wish to return to their home country. This concession moved China toward acceptance of the Indian resolution. The allies, therefore, urged Washington to resume the negotiations, and the

[95] Shuckburgh, *Descent to Suez*, 59. See "Dean Acheson to State Department," Nov. 24, 1952, *FRUS 1952–1954*, 15:677–79. For the following see "Acheson to State Department," Nov. 25, *FRUS 1952–1954*, 15:680–83; "Acheson to the President," Nov. 26, ibid. 683–86; "Acheson to State Department," Nov. 26, ibid., 689–91.

[96] I disagree, therefore, with Rosemary Foot's assessment that the resolution showed "that the American approach had been imposed on its Western allies, though at some cost to its standing with them" (*Substitute for Victory*, 157).

[97] "U.S. Ambassador to the UN to State Department," Dec. 6, 1952, *FRUS 1952–1954*, 15:706–8, 707.

British foreign secretary suggested that India should become the neutral state. The talks recommenced in late April.[98]

The more the Chinese seemed to accept the terms of the Indian resolution, the more the United States tried to back away from it. On May 13, the American negotiator tabled a new proposal that contained a unanimity rule for the repatriation commission and a provision that POWs from North Korea who did not wish to return home should not be handed over to the repatriation commission at all.

This American attempt to renege on its previous position led to an allied uproar. Like the Truman administration on several occasions before, Eisenhower faced a choice between the support of Congress, U.S. public opinion, and South Korea, on the one hand, and the European and Canadian allies, on the other. The allies won the argument, partly because they were able to count on a transgovernmental coalition with the State Department. During interagency meetings, U.S. officials agonized over the situation, with the State Department referring to allied pressure and the fear of being isolated in the UN. An agreement emerged to essentially go back to the provisions of the Indian resolution but to present it as the final American offer. The acting secretary of state summarized the inter-agency consensus:

> The Korean negotiations are at a crisis. Our position vis-à-vis our Allies is deteriorating daily. We particularly lack support for our position on the immediate release of Korean non-repatriate POWs at the time the armistice comes into effect and for our position that custodial commission act on the basis of unanimity in substantive matters.[99]

After further bargaining, the administration tabled a final proposal containing most of the provisions of the Indian resolution. While Eisenhower had given in to allied pressure, he nevertheless felt it necessary to threaten domestic repercussions in a message to the British prime minister: "I am sure that you will appreciate that any failure on the part of our principal allies fully to support a position so clearly reasonable and fair and going so far to meet the view of those allies, would have most adverse effects upon American public and Congressional opinion at this critical time."[100] A little

[98] See "Memorandum Concerning Conversation with British Embassy Official," April 1, 1953, *FRUS 1952–1954*, 15:831–32; "John Foster Dulles to the President," April 1, ibid., 833; "The President to John Foster Dulles," April 2, ibid., 835; "General Collins to CINCUNC," April 12, ibid., 904–6.

[99] "Memorandum to the President," May 18, 1953, *FRUS 1952–1954*, 15:1046–48, 1046–47. See also "JCS-State Department Meeting," May 18, ibid., 1038–46; "Meeting with Allied Ambassadors," May 19, ibid., 1050–52; Foot, *Substitute for Victory*, 170–75.

[100] "Acting Secretary of State to John Foster Dulles," May 22, 1953, *FRUS 1952–1954*, 15:1079–82, 1080.

more than two weeks later, the POW issue was resolved. Despite a last-minute attempt by Syngman Rhee to torpedo the armistice, the cease-fire agreement was signed on July 27, bringing the Korean War to an end after more than three years of fighting.

The European and Canadian governments would certainly have preferred an earlier cessation of hostilities. Their proposals for a negotiated settlement failed in 1950. When the talks began, they could not prevent their breakdown in October 1952. But the allies ultimately succeeded in pushing and pulling the United States toward an armistice. Their influence was crucial in at least three instances. First, allied pressure in 1951 was instrumental for the start of negotiations and for a positive U.S. response to the Soviet overtures. Second, after the collapse of the talks in the fall of 1952, an allied coalition led by the British and Canadian governments supported the Indian attempt at breaking the logjam over the POW issue. They risked an open confrontation with the U.S. government. Third, the allies forced Washington to return to the provisions of the Indian resolution when it tried to renege on its previous position. This suggests that the allies had a crucial impact on the substance of the cease-fire agreement, less so on its timing.[101]

Conclusions

The European and Canadian allies exerted considerable influence on vital U.S. decisions during the Korean War. They helped prevent specific military actions such as "hot pursuit" and, more important, the use of nuclear weapons, which would have extended the war into China and might have risked escalation into a global conflict. Allied pressure was also significant for the initiation as well as the conduct of the armistice negotiations.

The localization of the war, the (non-)use of nuclear weapons, and the conduct of the armistice negotiations were not marginal items on the American agenda but central to the conduct of the war and to its conclusion. The allies not only affected particular choices but also the definition of U.S. preferences in general. The American decision to intervene, for example, cannot be disentangled from the U.S. position as leader of the transatlantic alliance. Truman and Acheson were convinced that they needed to react against the aggression in Korea in order to maintain the credibility of the U.S. commitment for the defense of Europe.

[101] The analysis emphasizing *American* moves toward a compromise supports the argument that nuclear threats communicated to China in May 1953 were less significant to achieve the ultimate settlement than the previous concessions by both sides. See the excellent discussion in Rosemary Foot, "Nuclear Coercion and the Ending of the Korean Conflict."

Alternative Explanations: National Interest, Domestic Politics, and Leadership Beliefs

Against the above interpretation, one could argue that the various U.S. decisions during the war merely coincided with allied preferences and primarily resulted from a rational calculation of American interests quite apart from considerations about NATO. Escalating the war into China or using nuclear weapons would have made no sense, since the United States would have wasted resources in a part of the world not vital to its strategic interests. At the same time, such escalation risked global hostilities with the Soviet Union for which the United States was not ready, particularly not in 1950–1951. As for the armistice talks, a negotiated settlement was the only rational alternative to escalation in order to end the war quickly. Since escalation was excluded for the above reasons, dragging on a war of attrition in Asia would have continued to waste American resources desperately needed in other parts of the world.

Indeed, most courses of action chosen by the United States during the Korean War made perfect rational sense. But one cannot talk about the American national interest in Korea *without* mentioning the Western Alliance. Why did the Truman and Eisenhower administrations consider a prolonged war in Asia a waste of American resources? Because decision-makers considered Europe as the primary battlefield of the cold war, for which U.S. military resources were more urgently needed than in Asia. Why was escalation of the Korean War risky? Neither China nor even the Soviet Union could have threatened the survival of the U.S. homeland at the time. Escalation was feared because it risked war in Europe, for which the United States and its allies were not prepared. Thus, the survival of the United States was not at stake. At issue were the survival of its NATO allies, and, as a result, the American commitment to Europe.

As for the armistice negotiations, the U.S. desire to achieve a negotiated settlement did not prevent the Truman and Eisenhower administrations from frequently holding non-negotiable and uncompromising positions. As the British ambassador correctly observed, "the United States was seeking a middle way between branding the Chinese as aggressors and negotiating with them. In this policy we end up merely harassing them."[102] Allied input was needed to keep the United States on the negotiating track.

The Korean War case underlines, therefore, that the very notion of "American vital interests" incorporated the need to preserve the Atlantic Alliance and the security of the European allies. One misses the mark to assume that the United States defined its own vital interests first and only then took the interests of its allies into account. American decision-

[102] Sir Oliver Franks during the Truman-Attlee talks in December 1950, quoted from Christensen, "Domestic Mobilization and International Conflict," 433–34.

makers thought in terms of joint interests that also provided an opening for the allies to influence specific choices.

What about domestic politics as an alternative explanation for the various American decisions? Two broad domestic demands pressured U.S. decision-makers:[103]

- to end the war quickly;
- to adopt a firm anti-Chinese policy.

The first demand was compatible with allied preferences, while the second was not. To satisfy both domestic demands at the same time would have required escalating the war against China—the opposite of what the allies wanted. If, as I have argued, the American decisions frequently satisfied allied preferences, domestic politics can hardly be the reason. Many conflicts between the United States and its European allies were actually caused by the need of American leaders to assuage domestic demands. Particularly the Truman administration had to walk a thin line between domestic demands and allied preferences, which explains its reluctance to adopt a more compromising attitude toward Communist China.

This leaves leadership beliefs as an alternative explanation for the outcome. One could argue that Truman and Acheson as well as Eisenhower and Dulles shared the allied interest in keeping the war localized and in achieving an armistice when the war could not be won on the battlefield without escalating it. Indeed, U.S. leaders and the allies agreed on these fundamental goals. But this did not prevent them from frequently clashing over the means. In most instances of disagreement between Washington and the allies over specific courses of action, the Europeans either prevailed or both sides achieved a compromise—from "hot pursuit" to the Menon resolution and the (non-)use of nuclear weapons during the Eisenhower administration. When the allies chose not to raise objections, the more escalatory policy was decided in Washington—as in the case of crossing the 38th parallel.

The beliefs of Truman, Acheson, Eisenhower, and Dulles also included the firm conviction that the preservation of the alliance with Western Europe was more important than the war in Asia, that the United States needed its allies, and that European views had to be accommodated. One could even argue that the attitudes of the U.S. leaders had more in common with the European perspectives on the Korean War than with Congress and American public opinion. Dean Acheson in particular was concerned about a loss of support in the American public for the administration's European strategy, if the U.S. was too soft on communism in

[103] For details see Christensen, "Domestic Mobilization and International Conflict."

Asia.[104] Interallied conflicts during the Korean War occurred not because U.S. leaders needed to be reminded about the significance of Europe for the American strategy in the cold war but because decision-makers in Washington had to accommodate domestic pressures in order to implement this very strategy. For the same reason, the Europeans sometimes gave in to U.S. pressures, since they were aware of the difficult domestic situation faced by the administration.

Thus, leadership beliefs do not represent an alternative explanation to allied influence. Rather, the allied community formed part of the collective identity of top American decision-makers, which in turn enabled the European governments to exert influence on specific courses of action. As a result, the Korean War case disconfirms the structural realist assumption that smaller allies can only marginally affect the decisions of great powers under bipolarity when the latter's supreme interests are at stake (chapter 2). The European allies had a significant impact on crucial U.S. decisions during the war. Alternative explanations for the outcome either do not contradict the claim of allied influence (national interests and leadership beliefs) or appear to be less plausible (domestic politics).

Traditional Realist versus Liberal Explanations

It is less easy to refute a more sophisticated realist argument according to which small allies can exert considerable influence on the great power under specific conditions (see chapter 2). First, the assumption that small states can increase their impact, if they hold more intense preferences on an issue than the great power, applies in this case only to a limited degree. There is no reason to assume that, in general, allied interests were more affected by the Korean War than U.S. preferences. The only point that could be made in this context refers to the greater vulnerability of the allies following a potential escalation of the war, since Soviet retaliation in Europe would have directly affected their national survival. But then, the Unites States also considered its supreme interests at stake in Korea.

Second, the proposition that allied threats to defect or to remain neutral increase their bargaining leverage is only reconcilable with the evidence to some extent. Except for the case of the Menon resolution, the Europeans and Canadians never threatened to publicly disagree with the United States. There was a common understanding that interallied disputes should not surface and weaken allied unity vis-à-vis the Soviets.

The assumption makes sense, though, if American *perceptions* come into play. Top decision-makers frequently feared to be abandoned by the allies or to become isolated in the UN. Both the Truman and Eisenhower

[104] Ibid.

administrations were convinced that they desperately needed the support of the allies—the "outposts of our national defense." If this perception explains European influence on U.S. decisions, it was not well-grounded in reality. The allies had nowhere to go during the Korean War and needed U.S. support to insure their basic security more than the U.S. needed them.

The American fear of isolation from its friends is also to some extent reconcilable with the liberal notion of a security community. If membership in the Western Alliance of democracies prohibiting mutual coercion formed part of the American identity, then the fear of loosing friends if one does not accommodate them makes some sense.

Third, the proposition that allies behave more cooperatively the more they feel threatened by the opponent is only partly confirmed by the evidence. The argument might explain the American desire to keep the European allies aboard. But if alliance cohesion is supposed to be strengthened in times of crisis, one would not expect frequent interallied disputes about central questions of military operations and diplomatic negotiations as occurred during the Korean War.

Fourth, one could argue that the allies had the more influence on American decisions, the stronger they raised their voices and the more they were united. In most instances analyzed above, the Europeans and Canadians held shared concerns. If they stood up to the United States forcefully, as in the cases of the Menon resolution or of the Eisenhower administration's attempt to back away from earlier compromises, the allies succeeded in affecting the American position even though they were confronted with a unified administration acting under strong domestic pressures. Thus, the Korean War case appears to confirm this assumption.

Fifth, realist bargaining theory argues that small allies can increase their leverage if they control issue-specific resources. Given the lack of long-range delivery vehicles for nuclear weapons at the time, the United States would have needed access to military bases in Europe if the war had escalated into global hostilities with the Soviet Union. This problem came up from time to time during NSC meetings and provided the British with additional leverage. In particular, the American willingness to give London an implicit veto over the use of nuclear weapons can be explained by the need to secure access to air bases in Britain.

But the United States did not require those bases to defend its own security, which was not threatened in Europe, but that of its allies. Only if we assume that the America grand strategy pursued joint allied interest does the need of having access to European bases make sense. In other words, the allies gained leverage over the United States by exploiting the sense of collective identity in the transatlantic community.

One could argue, though, that particularly the British and the Canadians controlled another issue-specific resource. Their support for U.S. policies was crucial in the *United Nations* to secure majorities in the General Assembly. In other words, the allies were significant in delivering "world opinion" in favor of U.S. policies.[105]

If control over "world opinion" counts as an issue-specific resource, however, the argument cannot be distinguished from a liberal emphasis on "co-optive power."[106] Realists need additional assumptions to explain why the United States—with all its military and economic might during the early 1950s—was eager to gain UN support for its actions. Liberals referring to the Wilsonian or Kantian visions that partly informed the American worldview after World War II can easily accommodate this point.

In sum, the Korean War case confirms to some degree a sophisticated realist argument about the conditions under which small allies influence great powers. In particular, assumptions about allied unity, threats of defection, and control over issue-specific power seem to hold. The latter two propositions, however, only make sense if Americans perceived a sense of community or if the use of "soft power" is assumed. Realist and liberal interpretations blur at this point.

As to liberal propositions about cooperation among democracies (chapter 2), first, the American fear of being isolated from its friends can be explained in a framework of a democratic "security community" (Karl W. Deutsch) or a "pacific federation" (Immanuel Kant). The same holds true for allied influence as a result of U.S. attempts to secure a favorable climate of "world opinion" in the UN.

Second, obligations to consult shaped both the interallied discourses and the internal deliberations in the U.S. administration to a significant degree. Consultation norms provided the Europeans with crucial opportunities to influence American decisions. U.S. decision-makers understood that consultation meant *codetermination*, that is, allied input in the policy formulation phase, and not just informing the allies *after* decisions had been taken. The obligation to consult also led to the anticipation of allied demands in the U.S. decision-making process, when formal consultations had not taken place. In some instances, particularly involving "hot pursuit" and the non-use of nuclear weapons, the consultation norm resulted in a rejection of certain actions during preliminary considerations, thereby constraining the range of options available to decision-makers. Consultation norms were sometimes violated, as in the case of the attacks against the Yalu River plants. But it was accepted that such violation constituted an aberration from the norm for which one had to apologize.

[105] I thank Robert Keohane for alerting me to this point.

[106] See Joseph S. Nye, Jr., *Bound to Lead* (New York: Basic Books, 1990).

Third, domestic political constraints served as a powerful argument in bargaining processes. Allied leaders regularly played "two-level games." References to the difficult situation at home were far more frequently used to increase one's bargaining leverage than allusions to economic or military power. On the one hand, U.S. decision-makers rarely reminded their European counterparts of their security dependence. But they frequently pointed out—and appeared to genuinely believe—that certain allied behavior could lead to a wave of isolationism in the American public with adverse consequences for the U.S. role in Europe. On the other hand, open allusions to material power resources in interallied bargaining often turned out to be counterproductive.[107] Coercive behavior was considered inappropriate. When the United States violated such norms, it rarely got its way but just provoked more allied stubbornness, as in the case of the Menon resolution.

Fourth, there is some evidence of transgovernmental coalition-building between European governments and State Department officials, including Dean Acheson. An important example concerns the case of "hot pursuit." While Acheson and the allies shared the goal of preventing an escalation of the war, the latter seem to have convinced him that certain courses of action proposed by the military were irreconcilable with this general objective. Acheson then carried the day with the president. Other than that, there were little bureaucratic divisions inside the U.S. administration that the allies could have exploited to advance their cause. The main players, such as Truman and Acheson or Eisenhower and Dulles, not only held shared views most of the time but were prepared to listen regularly to allied concerns.

In conclusion, the Korean War confirms important liberal assumptions about the interaction processes in alliances among democracies. But the evidence is also reconcilable with at least some propositions derived from traditional realism. One should not forget in this context that the transatlantic alliance was just one year old when the Korean War started. Europeans and Americans were still defining their relationship, learning how to deal with each other, and establishing norms of appropriate behavior. Moreover, as the frequent objections of the U.S. military against granting the allies too much influence reveal, the American identity as leader of a democratic community was still contested. The somewhat ambiguous picture emerging from the Korean War might be explained by this historical context. By the time of the test ban negotiations or the Cuban Missile

[107] To quote just one example: When a State Department official told the British during the conflict concerning the Menon resolution that the United Kingdom would suffer much more than the United States from a split between the two countries, Eden's private secretary noted: "It is hard to imagine an argument less likely to move us" (Shuckburgh, *Descent to Suez*, 60).

crisis, the "rules of the alliance game" were established so that a more consistent pattern emerges (compare chapters 5 and 6).

Between the Korean War and the end of the 1950s, the most significant incident of noncooperation among the allies occurred. A book on the transatlantic community cannot ignore the 1956 Suez crisis.

FOUR

"UNWORTHY AND UNRELIABLE" ALLIES

VIOLATION OF ALLIANCE NORMS DURING THE 1956 SUEZ CRISIS

We have now passed the point when we are talking to friends. . . . [W]e are on a hard bargaining basis and we are dealing with an Administration of business executives.
—Lord Caccia[1]

A STUDY that tries to establish the "big influence of small allies" in NATO is challenged by the most significant incident of transatlantic noncooperation during the 1950s—the 1956 Suez crisis. The outcome in this case appears to confirm the structural realist assumption that superpowers are likely to win when they clash with their client states. The United States coerced Britain, France, and Israel through economic pressure to give up their attempts to regain control of the Suez Canal. If the transatlantic relationship constitutes a community of collective identity, it was not very effective during the crisis. Norms of timely consultation and a prohibition of coercive bargaining were all violated during the Suez crisis. In sum, the crisis and its outcome seem to contradict the liberal arguments of this book.

I suggest in the following that, on the contrary, the process leading to the interallied clash cannot be adequately understood without reference to the normative framework of the transatlantic community. First, the outcome of the Suez crisis—U.S. coercion of two major allies—proves to be the exception rather than the rule in the transatlantic relationship, as the other case studies in this book reveal. Second and more important, liberal and institutionalist claims about norms in international relations do not suggest that they are never violated. I argue that the American coercion of its allies resulted from a mutual sense of betrayal of the community

The chapter title quotes President Eisenhower in "Memorandum of Conversation with the President," Oct. 30, 1956, *FRUS 1955–1957*, 16:853–54.

[1] Lord Caccia [UK Ambassador in Washington] to Foreign Office, Nov. 28, 1956, quoted from William Roger Louis, "Dulles, Suez, and the British," in *John Foster Dulles and the Diplomacy of the Cold War*, ed. Richard Immermann (Princeton N.J.: Princeton University Press, 1990), 133–58, 155–56.

leading to the violation of consultation norms and the temporary breakdown of the collective identity.

The British and French governments knew from the beginning that the United States profoundly disagreed on whether force should be used to restore control over the Suez Canal.[2] There was no lack of communication. But officials in London believed in the allied community and concluded that Washington would ultimately "stand by its friends." When they became increasingly frustrated over what they considered as duplicitous American behavior, they embarked on a deception scheme and thus violated norms of consultation. When President Eisenhower and Secretary of State Dulles realized the degree to which they had been deceived, they retaliated. They felt no longer bound by the alliance rules, since Britain and France were behaving in a way inconsistent with the transatlantic community. As a result, superior American power prevailed.

The aftermath of the crisis is also revealing. The Anglo-American "special relationship" was quickly restored. President Eisenhower and the new prime minister, Harold Macmillan, who had been among the most hawkish British officials during the crisis, worked hard to make sure that such a breakdown of the community would never occur again. NATO also worked out new consultation rules.

But the French-American relationship never recovered. While French leaders had already been more sanguine about the interallied conflict than the British, the crisis set in motion a trend of gradually weakening the transatlantic ties between Paris and Washington. This deinstitutionalization culminated in President de Gaulle's 1966 decision to withdraw from the military integration of NATO. The French, thus, learned different lessons from the crisis than the British.

The Origins of the Interallied Conflict: Diverging Interests and Preferences

On July 26, 1956, Egyptian President Gamal Abd'ul Nasser announced the nationalization of the Suez Canal Company, setting in motion events

[2] I essentially agree with Richard Neustadt's earlier analysis of the crisis, which argued that the conflict resulted from the closeness of the transatlantic relationship and not simply from diverging interests. See his *Alliance Politics* (New York: Columbia University Press, 1970). For a similar argument see Elizabeth Sherwood, *Allies in Crisis* (New Haven, Conn.: Yale University Press, 1990), 58–94. For an analysis of the Suez crisis in conventional realist terms, see Douglas Stuart and William Tow, *The Limits of Alliance* (Baltimore: Johns Hopkins University Press, 1990), 58–66. The major analyses of the Suez crisis are David Carlton, *Britain and the Suez Crisis* (Oxford: Basil Blackwell, 1988); Steven Z. Freiberger, *Dawn over Suez* (Chicago: Iven R. Dee, 1992); Keith Kyle, *Suez* (New York: St. Martin's Press, 1991); Diane B. Kunz, *The Economic Diplomacy of the Suez Crisis* (Chapel Hill: University of North Carolina Press, 1991); William Roger Louis and Roger Owen, eds., *Suez 1956* (Oxford: Clarendon Press, 1989).

that led to not only the ill-fated British-French-Israeli attempt to regain control over the canal militarily, but also to a major interallied crisis. The transatlantic clash did not result from diverging interests as such. The United States and its European allies realized from the beginning that they held different views on the issue. Britain and France indicated immediately how seriously they took the Egyptian move and began planning military action. Prime Minister Eden explained to President Eisenhower: "My colleagues and I are convinced that we must be ready, in the last resort, to use force to bring Nasser to his senses. For our part, we are prepared to do so."[3] On July 27, the British cabinet decided not to exclude the military option, even unilateral action without French or U.S. support.

The British and French governments perceived the conflict as not just involving the Suez Canal, but as an attempt by Nasser to alter the power balance in the Middle East and to establish an Egyptian preponderance in the region. The British position was influenced by an arms deal that Nasser had struck with the Soviet Union via Czechoslovakia in September 1955. Officials in London concluded that Nasser had to be removed from power. The French shared this objective, since they held the Egyptian president responsible for assisting the anticolonial rebellion in Algeria. French Foreign Minister Pineau declared: "If Egypt's action remained without a response, it would be useless to pursue the struggle in Algeria."[4]

The U.S. administration shared the allied criticism of Nasser's action, but strongly objected to the planned use of force: "The President said we must let the British know how gravely we view this matter, what an error we think their decision [to drive Nasser out of Egypt militarily] is, and how this course of action would antagonize the American people despite all that could be done by the top officials of the government."[5] This view

[3] "Message Eden to Eisenhower," July 27, *FRUS 1955–1957*, 16:10. For British and French views, see also "US Embassy UK to Dept. of State," July 27, ibid., 3–5; "US Embassy France to Dept. of State," July 27, ibid., 7–9; "US Embassy UK to Dept. of State," July 27, ibid., 13–16; "US Embassy UK to Dept. of State," July 31, ibid., 60–62. For a general overview of British and French attitudes, see Keith Kyle, "Britain and the Crisis, 1955–1956," in *Suez 1956*, ed. Louis and Owen, 103–30; Maurice Vaisse, "France and the Suez Crisis," ibid., 131–43. For the following see Kyle, "Britain and the Crisis," 112–13; Carlton, *Britain and the Suez Crisis*, 36–37.

[4] French Foreign Minister Christian Pineau to his American and British colleagues on July 30, quoted in Vaisse, "France and the Suez Crisis," 137. Pineau went on to say that "France considers it more important to defeat Colonel Nasser's enterprise than to win ten battles in Algeria."

[5] "Memorandum of Conference with the President," July 31, *FRUS 1955–1957*, 16:62–68, 65. See also "Memorandum of Telephone Conversation," July 30, ibid., 46–47; "Dept. of State to Secretary of State," July 28, ibid., 24–25. On the American attitude, see Robert Bowie, "Eisenhower, Dulles, and the Suez Crisis," in *Suez 1956*, ed. Louis and Owen, 189–214; Louis, "Dulles, Suez, and the British." For the following, see "Memorandum by the Joint Chiefs of Staff," Aug. 3, *FRUS 1955–1957*, 16:154–56; "Memorandum of Conversation," Aug. 6, ibid., 151–53.

was communicated to the allies. The reference to domestic opinion as a means to play "two-level games" characterized communications between the United States and the Europeans. The administration remained fairly united throughout the crisis—with the exception of the Joint Chiefs of Staff (JCS), who initially supported the allied preference for military action. While the United States shared the allied concerns about Nasser, the administration did not want to antagonize him for fear of forcing him irrevocably into the Soviet camp. Particularly President Eisenhower left no doubt that he saw no reason to use force against Egypt. As John Foster Dulles explained to the British, the United States could see no justification for military action as long as Egypt did not interfere with the navigation of the canal or did not threaten foreign nationals.[6] U.S. decision-makers saw the conflict in anticolonial terms:

> For many years now the United States has been walking a tightrope between the effort to maintain our old and valued relations with our British and French allies on the one hand, and on the other trying to assure ourselves of the friendship and understanding of the newly independent countries who have escaped from colonialism. . . . Unless we now assert and maintain our leadership, all of these newly independent countries will turn from us to the USSR. We will be looked upon as forever tied to British and French colonialist policies.[7]

The issue of colonialism had long been a question of interallied contention. Given U.S. behavior in Latin America, however, France and Britain viewed Washington's attitude as rather hypocritical.

In sum, from the beginning of the Suez crisis on, the United States and its two major European allies disagreed profoundly on the question of using force. Their respective attitudes were rooted in diverging assessments of the situation in the Middle East, of the larger political context, and of the particular actions by Nasser. The United States made a major effort to restrain its allies from using military force by working for a negotiated settlement and the establishment of an international authority to take control of the Suez Canal. The British and French reluctantly agreed to pursue the diplomatic avenue but viewed it as merely an attempt to buy time, during which they continued their military preparations.

The United States and its allies frequently exchanged their diverging viewpoints through the normal channels of interallied communication, which remained open throughout most of the crisis. Both sides were fully

[6] See the report by the U.K. Ambassador in Washington of a conversation with Dulles, July 30, quoted in Louis, "Dulles, Suez, and the British," 146–47. On the U.S. attitude toward Nasser see Bowie, "Eisenhower, Dulles," 190–91.

[7] Dulles in an NSC Meeting, Nov. 1, quoted from Louis, "Dulles, Suez, and the British," 153.

aware of their conflict. The United States and its allies also knew from the beginning that the British, in particular, were economically dependent on American assistance for the pound sterling and for insuring oil supplies to NATO members in Europe, should the crisis escalate into war.[8] For a conventional, power-based analysis of interallied relations, it might not be surprising that the United States coerced its allies into acquiescence, once the conflict of interests escalated into an open confrontation.

But some puzzles remain. First, why did the British and French, who knew about their economic dependence on the United States and the American disagreement with them, nevertheless go ahead with their military plans and deceive Washington? While France undertook some action to reduce its financial dependence, Britain left itself vulnerable to American economic pressures.[9] How is the miscalculation of the U.S. reaction to be explained? An attempt at seizing military control of the Suez Canal against well-known American opposition should have been too risky to be contemplated in the first place, let alone carried out.

Second, it is not obvious that Washington had to use its overwhelming power to force its allies into giving up their adventure in Egypt. While the U.S. opposition to the allied action was to be expected, the use of coercive power was not. The allies could have agreed to disagree, since no supreme American interests were at stake. The United States could also have confined its opposition to condemnatory action in the UN General Assembly. In other words, U.S. decision-makers had choices about how to react to the allied military action. Their decision to coerce the allies was only one of them.

There is no direct causal link between interallied conflicts of interest and the confrontation experienced during the Suez crisis. To explain both the allied behavior and the American reaction, a closer look at the process leading to the clash is necessary.

Allied Perceptions of American Words and Deeds: Duplicity

The British and French governments knew that military action against Egypt was not possible without at least American neutrality, if not tacit acquiescence. As a result, they agreed to U.S. attempts for a negotiated solution, first through an international conference in London in August 1956 and later through the proposal of a Suez Canal Users' Association

[8] See Diane B. Kunz, "The Importance of Having Money: The Economic Diplomacy of the Suez Crisis," in *Suez 1956*, ed. Louis and Owen, 215–32, 218–219; Kunz, *Economic Diplomacy of the Suez Crisis*.

[9] For details see Kunz, *Economic Diplomacy of the Suez Crisis*, 113–14, 192–93.

(SCUA) in September. But neither Britain nor France were seriously interested in the success of these efforts, since their ultimate goal was not only to secure access to the Suez Canal but also to get rid of Nasser. They endorsed the American efforts to buy time and to create a favorable climate of opinion in the United States and the UN. If Nasser rejected the American-led mediating attempts, as they expected, their preferred military solution would probably meet less international objections, since "all peaceful means" had been exhausted. American support would then be easier to secure.

At the same time, the governments in London and Paris perceived American behavior during the crisis as at best ambiguous, if not deceiving. John Foster Dulles earned himself a reputation of "saying one thing and doing another," as Selwyn Lloyd, the British foreign minister, put it.[10] When the secretary of state met Prime Minister Eden on August 1, for example, he seemed to agree with the aim of cutting Nasser down to size: "A way had to be found to make Nasser disgorge what he was attempting to swallow." Eden was pleased by this apparent agreement between the United States and the British and used the phrase in a later message to Eisenhower.[11] There are some indications that Dulles, unlike the president, who remained staunchly opposed to military force, favored stronger action if Nasser rejected reasonable proposals by the London conference. During a White House meeting on August 12, he supported moral and economic support for the allies if they felt it necessary to act. More than a month later, Dulles discussed a proposal with the British prime minister to set up an Anglo-American working group, which should consider means of weakening Nasser's regime.[12]

While Dulles appeared to agree with the desire to defeat Nasser, meetings between the Egyptian president and the U.S. ambassador to Cairo raised British and French suspicions. Moreover, in discussions with his colleagues from London and Paris, Dulles refused to put any pressure on the Egyptians to accept the terms of the London conference.[13]

[10] Selwyn Lloyd, *Suez 1956: A Personal Account* (London: Jonathan Cape, 1978), 38.

[11] Cf. Eden's message to Eisenhower, August 5, *FRUS 1955–1957*, 16:146–48. The Dulles remark is quoted in Louis, "Dulles, Suez, and the British," 147.

[12] See "Memorandum of Conversation at the White House," August 12, *FRUS 1955–1957*, 16:185–87; also "U.S. Embassy UK to Dept of State," Aug. 2, ibid., 100–102; "Memorandum of 295th NSC Meeting," Aug. 30, ibid., 324–32. "Memorandum of Conversation at British Foreign Office," Sept. 21, ibid., 548–50.

[13] See Vaisse, "France and the Suez Crisis," 140–41. On the Egyptian-American meetings, see "U.S. Embassy Egypt to Dept. of State," July 30, *FRUS 1955–1957*, 16:55–58; "U.S. Embassy Egypt to Dept. of State," Aug. 4, ibid., 133–35. For the following quote see Vaisse, "France and the Suez Crisis," 139. See also "U.S. Embassy France to Dept. of State," Sept. 10, *FRUS 1955–1957*, 16:461–62.

The French government had already concluded in early August that it was better to "act bilaterally [with the British] rather than do nothing trilaterally," since the American election campaign apparently prevented the Eisenhower administration from supporting the allies. In early September, the French foreign minister told the American ambassador that only economic sanctions against Egypt could prevent the Paris government from military action. Paris also reduced its vulnerability to American economic pressure by successfully applying for a standby credit of the International Monetary Fund (IMF) in October.[14]

For the British, however, the sense of betrayal by the Americans increased dramatically as a result of Dulles's handling of his own SCUA proposal. Eden viewed it as a means to corner Nasser further and to use his expected rejection as a pretext for military action. He presented the plan in rather threatening language to the British Parliament on September 12. But in an attempt to dampen the British spin on the proposal and to make it more acceptable to the Egyptians, Dulles declared that "the United States did not intend itself to try to shoot its way through" the Suez Canal. If Nasser should prevent passage, American ships would be sent around the Cape of Good Hope. To make things worse, Dulles argued that there were "no teeth" in the SCUA plan, that is, no enforcement mechanisms to guarantee safe passage. He essentially pulled the rug under what the British viewed as the SCUA's purpose. Feeling betrayed by his ally, Eden concluded on October 8: "We have been misled so often by Dulles' ideas that we cannot afford to risk another misunderstanding. . . . Time is not on our side in this matter."[15] A series of rather angry exchanges over the purpose of the SCUA followed between the British foreign minister and the U.S. secretary of state. These letters made abundantly clear that London viewed the SCUA as an instrument to exert pressure on Egypt, while Washington conceptualized it as a "means of practical working cooperation with the Egyptian authorities."[16] At about the same time, in mid-October, the British government joined the French and Israeli planning of the secret military operation to regain control of the Suez Canal.

The British felt abandoned by the American government, which had violated the community of purpose in their eyes. For two reasons, Lon-

[14] See Kunz, *Economic Diplomacy of the Suez Crisis*, 113–14.

[15] "Eden to Selwyn Lloyd," Oct. 8, quoted in Louis, "Dulles, Suez, and the British," 151. For the Dulles quotes, cf. ibid., 149, 150; Bowie, "Eisenhower, Dulles, and the Suez Crisis," 204–5.

[16] "Dulles to Selwyn Lloyd," Oct. 15, *FRUS 1955–1957*, 16:734–37, 737. Cf. "Lloyd to Dulles," Oct. 15, ibid., 738–40; "Dept. of State to U.S. Embassy UK," Oct. 17, ibid., 744–45.

don chose to deliberately deceive Washington about the military plans in October 1956 without calculating the possible consequences.[17] First, British officials thought that the United States did not want to hear about the military preparations. Selwyn Lloyd argued in a somewhat self-deluding manner that "Eisenhower would have been more offended if we had told him beforehand and then acted in spite of his opposition."[18] In other words, nonconsultation meant that *both* sides retained their freedom, since the United States could have pretended that it was not involved. The British could have thought to get away with military action because of ambiguous statements by, again, John Foster Dulles. In late August, for example, Prime Minister Eden asked Dulles how he should handle a request by the Pentagon for information about British military plans. Eden "said that this was somewhat embarrassing as if they [the United States] told us [the United Kingdom] their plans, we might then feel we had to raise objections or else be a party to what might seem to be an improper use of force." Dulles agreed and suggested that the British should delay their answer to the Pentagon until further notice.[19]

Second and more important, the British government was convinced that the United States would ultimately back it and that allied action would somehow force Washington into line where persuasion had failed. Prime Minister Eden and his foreign minister reckoned that the choice was clear for Washington if it had to take sides between Egypt and its European allies. They convinced themselves that Dulles's ambivalent remarks throughout the crisis supported this assessment. What they perceived as Dulles's duplicity not only created a sense of betrayal leading to the deception in the first place, it also helped to reassure them that the Americans would ultimately support their action.

John Foster Dulles even confirmed that assumption later on. In mid-November, when the American coercion of the British and French to retreat from Suez was in full swing, Dulles asked the British foreign secretary: "Why didn't you go through with it and get Nasser down?" This remark greatly upset Selwyn Lloyd, who saw Dulles as "the man who had led the pack against us, supported the transfer of the matter from the Security Council to the General Assembly and pulled out every stop to defeat us."[20]

[17] See, for example, "U.S. Embassy UK to Dept. of State," Oct. 29, *FRUS 1955–1957*, 16:817–20. Not even the British cabinet was fully informed about the extent of the British-French-Israeli "collusion." For the following see Vaisse, "France and the Suez Crisis," 139; Lloyd, *Suez 1956*, 193, 253; Louis, "Dulles, Suez, and the British," 150.

[18] Lloyd, *Suez 1956*, 193.

[19] "Memorandum of Conversation between Eden and Dulles," Aug. 24, *FRUS 1955–1957*, 16:285–86.

[20] Lloyd, *Suez 1956*, 219. Dulles had made a similar remark during a meeting with the president on Nov. 12, see *FRUS 1955–1957*, 16:1112–14.

The British conviction that the United States would ultimately back it when push came to shove is further confirmed by the fact that, unlike Paris, London did not undertake action to reduce the vulnerability of the pound sterling. The chancellor of the exchequer, Harold Macmillan, one of the most hawkish cabinet ministers during the crisis, was fully aware that the stability of the pound and the British balance of payment were under considerable strain. The British knew that American support for the pound was crucial. But they apparently never contemplated that their behavior could trigger U.S. financial action against their currency.[21]

In sum, the British in particular risked the violation of alliance norms, because they firmly believed in the viability of the North Atlantic partnership. They convinced themselves that the United States was bound by the community and would ultimately value it. This conviction led to wishful thinking, to a "motivated bias," which let them consistently overlook the growing misgivings by the American administration about their allies' behavior.[22] Instead of taking the U.S. objections to the use of force seriously, they relied on reassurances such as the one uttered by Dulles ten days before the invasion of the Suez Canal: "I do not comment on your observations on Anglo-American relations except to say that those relations, from our standpoint, rest on such a firm foundation that misunderstandings of this nature, if there are such, cannot disturb them."[23] The French and the British did not realize that their violation of norms raised doubts in the eyes of American decision-makers about the allied commitment to the community and that this triggered U.S. retaliation in kind.

American Perceptions of Allied Behavior: "Unworthy"

Eisenhower and Dulles—despite all ambiguous statements—never wavered in pursuing two goals, (1) to prevent the use of force, and (2) to reach a negotiated settlement guaranteeing safe passage through the Suez Canal. The administration mediated between its allies and the Egyptians while at the same time trying to restrain the British and French from resorting to military action. Whenever decision-makers succeeded in convincing the allies to continue on the negotiating path, they felt relieved: "I think we have introduced a valuable stopgap into a dangerous situation

[21] For details, see Kunz, "Importance of Having Money," 218–19, 222–23; Kunz, *Economic Diplomacy of the Suez Crisis*.

[22] On the role of "motivated bias" in crises, see Richard N. Lebow, *Between Peace and War* (Baltimore: Johns Hopkins University Press, 1981).

[23] "Dulles to Selwyn Lloyd," Oct. 19, *FRUS 1955–1957*, 16:760.

and while the danger is still there we have perhaps made it more remote and more manageable."[24]

U.S. decision-makers convinced themselves that the allies would come to their senses and follow the American lead toward a settlement. First, the U.S. administration was well aware that the British domestic scene was divided over the issue and that the Labour party opposed the use of force. John Foster Dulles originally thought that this domestic division might weaken the British bargaining position vis-à-vis Nasser as a result of which the chances for a peaceful settlement were diminished. He volunteered to tell the leader of the Labour party that national unity would enhance the chances of a negotiated solution.[25] This line of reasoning only made sense if the British government wanted a peaceful solution to the crisis in the first place. Later, when the United States changed course from persuading to coercing its allies, it counted on the domestic uproar that the Anglo-French-Israeli action created in the House of Commons and which considerably weakened the British government.

Second, the British government was internally divided. Not only did the British defense minister oppose military action, more important and contrary to the picture emerging from his memoirs, Selwyn Lloyd indicated several times to the Americans that he preferred a peaceful settlement. During a conversation with Dulles in late August, for example, the British foreign secretary tried to form a transgovernmental coalition with the secretary of state against his own prime minister. Lloyd expressed concerns about the military plans of his government and argued that Dulles was the only person who could alter Anthony Eden's determination to use force. Lloyd's attempts to achieve a compromise became again apparent in early October, when, according to the UN secretary general, who was present at the meetings, he worked hard in secret negotiations between the British, the French, and the Egyptians to reach an agreement.[26] Only three days later, Prime Minister Eden joined the French and the Israelis in planning the invasion.

In sum, the U.S. administration knew that the British government was weaker than it appeared to be because of the economic situation, internal divisions, and domestic pressures. But this knowledge alone does not ex-

[24] "Dulles to Eisenhower," Aug. 2, *FRUS 1955–1957*, 16:119.

[25] Cf. "Dulles to Eisenhower," Aug. 19, *FRUS 1955–1957*, 16:231–32; "Memorandum of Conversation between Dulles and Eden," Aug. 24, ibid., 285–86. For the following, see Carlton, *Britain and the Suez Crisis*, 72.

[26] See "Memorandum of Conversation between Hammarskjold and Lodge," Oct. 10, *FRUS 1955–1957*, 16:689–92; Bowie, "Eisenhower, Dulles, and the Suez Crisis," 206–7. For Lloyd's plead that Dulles talk to Eden see "Memorandum of Conversation between Dulles and Lloyd," Aug. 23, *FRUS 1955–1957*, 16:281. Compare, however, Lloyd's own recollection of the crisis, *Suez 1956*. On the British defense minister's position see Carlton, *Britain and the Suez Crisis*, 50–51.

plain the American decision to play hardball with the allies. Rather, it was triggered by a series of unilateral allied moves violating norms of consultation, which jeopardized the community of purpose in the eyes of American leaders.

First, the British government decided at the end of August to get the North Atlantic Council involved in the crisis, against the explicit advice of the U.S. government. The allies apparently calculated that the other West Europeans would support their military preparations, while the administration thought that such a move would further complicate discussions at the London conference.[27]

Second, the British government told the United States in late September of its plans to refer the matter to the UN Security Council in order to preempt a likely Soviet move. John Foster Dulles advised against it, since he thought that such action would hinder his attempts to get the SCUA off the ground. The United States was also concerned that the allies might use a Soviet veto in the Security Council as a pretext to go ahead with their military plans. On September 23, the British and French referred the Suez issue to the Security Council anyway. Dulles reacted angrily and stated in a conversation with the French ambassador that "this was an 'extraordinary' performance. We are without information as to the purpose of the British and French approach to the Security Council; we do not know under what Article of the Charter the matter is to be considered; and we have not been informed of the procedure which France and the United Kingdom intend to follow."[28]

By early October, American decision-makers felt a sense of interallied crisis, which was further exacerbated by the controversy over the SCUA: "[Dulles] said that the relations of the United States with France had lately become strained to a degree not paralleled for a very long time past." The U.S. ambassador in London expressed similar feelings with regard to the Anglo-American relationship: "I agree that the Suez problem has strained US-British relations to an extent greater than any of the issues which have disturbed our alliance during my four years here and beyond the limits of divergences which we might regard as generally normal between allies."[29]

American decision-makers increasingly complained that they were left

[27] See "Memorandum for Secretary of State," Aug. 28, *FRUS 1955–1957*, 16:309; "Secretary of State to U.S. Embassy UK," Aug. 30, ibid., 339–40; "Dept. of State to certain diplomatic missions," Aug. 31, ibid., 344–45.

[28] "Memorandum of Conversation," Sept. 25, *FRUS 1955–1957*, 16:574–77, 576. See also "Memorandum of Conversation," Sept. 22, ibid., 564–65; "Memorandum of Conversation," Sept. 25, ibid., 577–79; "Memorandum of Conversation," Sept. 27, ibid., 588–92.

[29] "U.S. Embassy UK to Dept. of State," Oct. 9, *FRUS 1955–1957*, 16:671–73, 671. The first quote is contained in "Memorandum of Discussion at the 299th NSC Meeting," Oct. 4, ibid., 632–34.

in the dark about the British and French plans and that the interallied lines of communications had gradually broken down. Attempts at contacting the allied embassies in Washington did not bring results, since the British and French missions were apparently uninformed of what was going on in Europe. The State Department then asked the U.S. embassies in London and Paris to find out what the two governments were up to. It received reassuring messages, since the American embassies were either deliberately misled by their sources or because they just second-guessed the allied governments. One day before the Anglo-French-Israeli agreement to attack Egypt was signed, the U.S. embassy in Paris cabled Washington that the French government did "not feel it appropriate or desirable to push Franco–United States differences toward showdown prior to election."[30]

On October 26, the U.S. embassy in Israel informed the State Department that there had been a call up of Israeli reservists. Intelligence information gradually came in, reporting Israeli plans to invade Egypt with possible French and British involvement. John Foster Dulles cabled to London that

> there is apparently a deliberate British purpose of keeping us completely in the dark as to their intentions with reference to Middle East matters generally and Egypt in particular. We have had no high-level contact on any of these matters with British Embassy for a week. . . . We have information of major Israeli preparations and suspect there may be French complicity with them and possibly UK complicity with various moves.[31]

In response, the British foreign minister systematically misled the U.S. ambassador; the French ambassador in Washington denied to Dulles that he had reports about military movements.

By the time the Israeli invasion started on October 29, the U.S. administration had sufficient information to suspect that France was involved in the action. But neither Eisenhower nor Dulles wanted to believe that the British government had deceived them, too, until the facts could no longer be denied. The sense of community led to wishful thinking by American decision-makers. During the first meeting in the White House after the start of the invasion, President Eisenhower still assumed that the British were not part of the plot; John Foster Dulles argued that there

[30] "U.S. Embassy France to Dept. of State," Oct. 23, *FRUS 1955–1957*, 16:767. See also "U.S. Embassy UK to Dept. of State," Oct. 19, ibid., 751–53; "Dept. of State to U.S. Embassy France," Oct. 4, ibid., 634–35; "Phone Conversation between John Foster and Allen Dulles," Oct. 18, ibid., 745–46.

[31] "Dept. of State to U.S. Embassy UK," Oct. 26, *FRUS 1955–1957*, 16:790. For a similar cable to France, see "Dept. of State to U.S. Embassy France," Oct. 29, ibid., 815–16. See also "U.S. Embassy Israel to Dept. of State," Oct. 26, ibid., 785. For the following see "Memorandum of Conversation at Dept. of State," Oct. 28, ibid., 803–4; "U.S. Embassy UK to Dept. of State," Oct. 29, ibid., 817–20.

might still be a chance to "unhook" the British and the French from the Israeli action. The United States decided to bring the matter to the UN Security Council but was told by the allies that they would never support a UN move against Israel. Even now, Eisenhower did not believe what he saw. He sent an urgent message to Prime Minister Eden expressing his confusion and demanding "that the UK and the US quickly and clearly lay out their present views and intentions before each other, and that, come what may, we find some way of concerting our ideas and plans so that we may not, in any real crisis, be powerless to act in concert because of our misunderstanding of each other."[32]

Despite the refusal of the British and French to join the United States at the UN, which violated the Tripartite Declaration of 1950, the president still believed in a "misunderstanding." The extent of the Anglo-French-Israeli collusion became clear only a few hours later, when the British and French issued a joint ultimatum demanding that Israel and Egypt withdraw from the Suez Canal to allow for Anglo-French occupation of the canal zone. The plot was immediately apparent, since the Israeli forces had not yet reached the line to which they were supposed to retreat.

Eisenhower only now realized that he had been misled all along and expressed his dismay about the "unworthy and unreliable ally" (see above). Later that day, he declared that he was "inclined to think that those who began this operation should be left to work out their own oil problem—to boil in their own oil, so to speak." He also expected the allies to ask for American help to finance the operation. The next message sent to Eden was addressed to "Dear Mr. Prime Minister" instead of the usual "Dear Anthony," indicating the change in tone. The secretary of state summoned the French ambassador and told him that

> both the British and the French had deliberately kept the United States Government in the dark for the past two weeks, though we had reasons to suspect what was going on. . . . this was the blackest day which has occurred in many years in the relations between England and France and the United States. He asked how the former relationship of trust and confidence could possibly be restored in view of these developments.[33]

Eisenhower and Dulles were not so much upset by the Anglo-French-Israeli use of force itself but by the fact that core allies had deliberately

[32] "Eisenhower to Eden," Oct. 30, *FRUS 1955–1957*, 16:848–50. See also "Memorandum of Conversation at the White House," Oct. 29, ibid., 833–39; editorial note, ibid., 840–42; Bowie, "Eisenhower, Dulles, and the Suez Crisis," 208–9.

[33] "Memorandum of Conversation at the Dept. of State," Oct. 30, *FRUS 1955–1957*, 16:867–68. For the Eisenhower quotes see "Memorandum of Conference with the President," Oct. 30, ibid., 873; "Message from Eisenhower to Eden," Oct. 30, ibid., 866; "Memorandum of Conversation with the President," Oct. 30, ibid., 851–55.

deceived them. The allies had not broken some minor consultation agreements, but had violated fundamental collective understandings constituting the transatlantic community—"trust and confidence." Once the degree of allied deception became obvious, decision-makers in Washington concluded that they were themselves no longer bound by alliance norms. They decided to retaliate in kind and let the allies "boil in their own oil." Now the United States abandoned the community leaving its allies no choice but to back down.

U.S. Coercion and the Restoration of the Transatlantic Relationship

The U.S. administration knew that the allies were under considerable economic and financial strain and that particularly the British pound needed American backing. No longer committed to the norms of the community, the United States used its power immediately and swiftly forced Britain and France to giving up their attempts at the Suez Canal. When the two allies vetoed an American resolution calling for an immediate cease-fire in the Security Council, the matter was transferred to the General Assembly, which voted in favor of an immediate armistice on November 2. By that time, the Bank of England had lost $50 million within two days, and the closing of the Suez Canal constituted a serious problem for the British oil supply. The British treasury requested an immediate standby credit from the International Monetary Fund (IMF). According to Macmillan's memoirs, the U.S., which controlled the IMF almost completely at the time, denied the support as long as Britain had not accepted the cease-fire. The chancellor of the exchequer, who had advocated military action throughout the crisis, now turned around and supported an armistice during the cabinet meeting of November 6. In the Mediterranean, the United States moved its Sixth Fleet into the area where the British operated their naval task force, thereby seriously hampering the British and French military activities.[34] The allies had not much choice but to accept the cease-fire resolution. They were only supported by the United States when the Soviet Union sent threatening letters to Britain, France, and Israel. Washington replied that it would not tolerate Moscow's interference in the crisis.

The interallied crisis was not over with the acceptance of the cease-fire. If the British government had hoped to receive massive IMF support for the pound after having agreed to the armistice, it was mistaken. The U.S.

[34] For details, see Harold Macmillan, *Riding the Storm* (London: Macmillan, 1971), 164; Kunz, "Importance of Having Money," 226–27; Kunz, *Economic Diplomacy of the Suez Crisis*; Carlton, *Britain and the Suez Crisis*, 76–79; Kyle, "Britain and the Crisis," 129.

administration, strengthened by the landslide election victory of President Eisenhower, linked financial support to an allied commitment to withdraw their forces from the Suez Canal, to be replaced by UN peacekeeping troops. The communications between the British and the United States in this context show a certain embarrassment on both sides about the inappropriateness of coercion in their relationship. When Macmillan pleaded for U.S. financial help, he framed it in the following way: "If you can give us a fig leaf to cover our nakedness I believe we can get a majority of the Cabinet to vote for such withdrawal without requiring conditions."[35]

First, the statement implies a recognition of the desperate British situation ("nakedness"). Second, it almost turns the linkage around, as if it was the United States that had to give something to the British rather than London that desperately needed economic support. Macmillan phrased the issue in such a way that it amounted to a balanced deal instead of American coercion of the British. Third, the wording "fig leaf" played down the value of the U.S. assistance to the British. In sum, Macmillan's framing tried to cover up what must have been a most embarrassing moment for his government. In the White House meeting discussing the British request, the notion of a "fig leaf" figured quite prominently, too. Secretary of the Treasury Humphrey declared that the United States was indeed in a position to provide the "fig leaf" of financial support. But the president cut through the rhetoric and stated that

> first, we are ready to talk about help as soon as the pre-condition [French and British initiation of withdrawal] is established; second, on knowing that the British and French forces will comply with a withdrawal undertaking at once, we would talk to the Arabs to obtain the removal of any objections they may have regarding the provision of oil to Western Europe; third, we will then talk about the details of money assistance with the British.[36]

The United States kept the pressure up until it received an unambiguous statement that the British and French would unconditionally withdraw their troops from Egypt. A generous IMF loan of $561 million, a further standby credit of $738 million, and a $500 million credit line by the American Export-Import Bank were then approved immediately.[37]

[35] "U.S. Embassy UK to Dept. of State," Nov. 19, *FRUS 1955–1957*, 16:1163. See also "U.S. Embassy UK to Dept. of State," Nov. 17, ibid., 1142–43; "U.S. Embassy UK to Dept. of State," Nov. 19, ibid., 1150–52. On the entire episode see Kunz, "Importance of Having Money," 227–31.

[36] "Memorandum of Conference with the President," Nov. 20, *FRUS 1955–1957*, 16:1166–69, 1167.

[37] See Kunz, "Importance of Having Money," 231; Kunz, *Economic Diplomacy of the Suez Crisis*. See also "Memorandum of 305th NSC Meeting," Nov. 30, *FRUS 1955–1957*, 16:1218–29; "U.S. Embassy UK to Dept. of State," Dec. 2, ibid., 1232–33; "Memorandum of Phone Conversation between Eisenhower and Dulles," Dec. 3, ibid., 1240.

While the U.S. administration was coercing its allies to withdraw from the Suez Canal, it indicated at the same time that a major effort should be made to restore the transatlantic community. On November 5, in the midst of the interallied crisis and even before the British and French had accepted the cease-fire, a senior State Department official told the French ambassador "that intimate Franco-American relations are in fact a cornerstone of American foreign policy" and asked for his help to "restore the warmth of US-French relations." Two days later, the president called the whole affair a "family spat" in a telephone conversation with Prime Minister Eden. During an NSC meeting on November 8, Eisenhower suggested, in an attempt at "spin control," "not to place all the blame for what had happened on Great Britain and France." JCS Chairman Radford even proposed that the Soviet Union be blamed for what had happened in the Middle East. Eisenhower, whose anger with the allies had apparently disappeared after his election victory, tried to find excuses for the British behavior:

> Returning to the Suez crisis, the President said he now believes that the British had not been in on the Israeli-French planning until the very last stages when they *had no choice* but to come into the operation. He had felt when the British originally denied collusion with the French and the Israelis that they were misleading us, but he had now come to the conclusion that they were telling the truth.[38]

If the British had "no choice," they could not really be blamed for deceiving the United States. The two governments now engaged in almost ritualistic reassurances that their "special relationship" would be restored quickly. During an NSC meeting on November 30, American decision-makers expressed concern about the domestic stability of London's Conservative government. Secretary of Defense Wilson observed that "if the British Government backed down and withdrew their forces from the Canal . . . we should realize how very difficult this decision had been for them and how handsomely they were trying to behave." The decision to massively support the pound once the British withdrew was at least partly motivated by the desire to back the Conservative government in its do-

[38] "Memorandum of Conversation between the President and Dulles" (my emphasis!), Nov. 12, *FRUS 1955–1957*, 16:1112–14. For the preceding quotes see—in the order of their occurence—"Memorandum of Conversation at the State Dept.," Nov. 5, ibid., 1003–7, 1005; "Memorandum of Telephone Conversation between the President and Sir Eden," Nov. 7, ibid., 1040; "Memorandum of Discussions at 313rd NSC Meeting," Nov. 8, ibid., 1070–86, 1085–86. See also "Message from Eden to Eisenhower," Nov. 7, ibid., 1061–62; "Memorandum by the President," Nov. 8, ibid., 1088–89; "Letter from Eisenhower to Mollet," ibid., 1107.

mestic environment.[39] In a later meeting with the British foreign minister, John Foster Dulles almost apologized for the American behavior:

> He wanted Mr. Lloyd to know that the US did not act as it did because "we liked the Egyptians better than we did the British". Nothing . . . could be more fantastic. He said the reason we acted as we did was that we were convinced that there would be little chance of establishing a world order or avoiding World War III if we acquiesced in the British action.[40]

These and other communications show that both sides perceived their clash during the crisis as an aberration not to be repeated. The transatlantic partnership was to be quickly restored.

The Anglo-American "special relationship" was revitalized immediately after the Suez crisis. President Eisenhower and Anthony Eden's successor, Macmillan, worked hard to reestablish the community. The Bermuda summit in March 1957 served to document the restoration of the "special relationship." The long-term impact of the crisis also resulted in a major change in U.S. policies toward nuclear cooperation with the British. In 1958, Congress amended the Atomic Energy Act to allow for the sharing of nuclear information with Britain, which London had requested throughout the decade. As the British influence on U.S. policies during the nuclear test ban negotiations shows (chapter 5), the violation of alliance norms during the Suez crisis reenforced rather than reduced the transatlantic ties.

As to NATO in general, the crisis led to a reform of the consultation procedures. A "Report of the Committee of Three on Non-Military Cooperation in NATO" restated the need for timely consultation among the allies on foreign policy matters in general, not just confined to European security issues (see chapter 2 for details). The North Atlantic Council adopted the report in December 1956.[41]

Conclusions

The Suez crisis was certainly the most important interallied confrontation of the 1950s. The British and French retreated from the attempt to reconquer the Suez Canal by force as a result of American coercive pressure. This outcome appears to confirm the structural realist assumption that superior power wins when alliance leaders and their client states clash in a conflict of interests. But the process leading to the confrontation as well

[39] See "Memorandum of 305th NSC Meeting," Nov. 30, *FRUS 1955–1957*, 16:1218–29 (quote on 1226).

[40] "Memorandum of Conversation," Dec. 10, ibid., 16:1278–1283.

[41] See Sherwood, *Allies in Crisis*, 88–94.

as its aftermath actually confirm liberal and institutionalist expectations about actors' practices when fundamental norms of the relationship are violated.

Alternative Explanations: Power, Domestic Politics, and Leadership Beliefs

One could argue, though, that *power politics* offers a more parsimonious explanation of the crisis than tedious process-tracing and that the mutual accusations of betrayal and norms violations represent nothing but rationalizations of the underlying conflict of interests. There is no question that a serious conflict of interests emerged during the crisis between the United States, on the one hand, and the British and French governments, on the other. But, first, such conflicts occurred before and afterward and were solved more often than not through interallied compromises (see chapters 3, 5, 6, 7). Second, if power politics governed the allied interactions during the crisis, the British behaved irrationally. They were aware of their vulnerability to U.S. financial pressure, but acted as if this handicap did not exist. Third, a power-based account is underdetermining with regard to American behavior during the crisis. It might explain the ultimate outcome but cannot elucidate why the United States continued to mediate between its allies and Egypt for quite some time and despite allied violations of consultation norms and only resorted to coercion when Britain and France started using force. Alternatively, American leaders could have used other means to force the allies to back down without humiliating them in the UN and in world opinion. If, however, the United States faced choices, we need to look at the interaction process to explain the particular decisions.

But what about *domestic politics* as the reason for Eisenhower's decision to coerce the allies? The president was in the midst of an election campaign, and playing to an anticolonialist mood in the American public might have helped him to secure victory. The U.S. opposition to the use of force from the beginning of the crisis on was in part justified by anticolonial statements. Particularly the French government discounted American arguments as motivated by election campaign pressures.

Eisenhower's strong criticism of the use of force and the telecast from the White House on the night of October 31, that is, two days before the election, are certainly consistent with a domestic politics explanation. But this still does not explain the use of coercive power against the British and the French. It only occurred *after* Eisenhower had already won the election. The initial coercion on November 5–6 was not made public and was only revealed in Macmillan's memoirs fifteen years later.[42]

[42] Macmillan, *Riding the Storm*, 164.

Reference to *leadership beliefs* does not represent an alternative explanation to the account offered here, but is actually consistent with it. President Eisenhower and Secretary of State Dulles, the two major players on the U.S. side of the conflict, were firm believers in the allied community. Their efforts to manage the crisis and to mediate between the allies and Egypt as well as the ambivalent signals sent to London and Paris are understandable, if one assumes that they actually experienced their own "conflict of interest" or cognitive dissonance. On the one hand, their collective identity required to maintain the alliance community. It led them to believe that the allies would honor the norms of the community until the deception could no longer be denied. On the other hand, they disagreed profoundly with Britain and France over the particular issues in question. When the allied violation of fundamental rules of the community became obvious, Eisenhower and Dulles felt no longer bound by these rules. Even then did the president state "with emphasis, we do not want the British and French to be branded aggressors."[43] The efforts to restore the transatlantic community after the crisis are also fully reconcilable with the leadership beliefs of Eisenhower and Dulles.

In sum, various alternative explanations for the American behavior during the crisis are either underdetermining with regard to the U.S. turn around toward coercive behavior or compatible with the account presented above. But what does the case study reveal about the validity of sophisticated realist assumptions as compared to liberal explanations?

Realist Bargaining Theory versus Liberal Arguments

If the interaction patterns between the United States and its allies during the Suez crisis are to be compatible with assumptions derived from traditional realism and realist bargaining theory (chapter 2), it has to be demonstrated that the conditions for the "big influence of small allies" posited by the theory were absent in this case. However, these conditions were almost completely present so that the Suez crisis serves to disconfirm sophisticated realism.

First, as to the intensity of allied preferences, there can be no doubt that the British and French governments were at least as strongly motivated as the United States during the crisis. After all, the Egyptian President Nasser had nationalized what they considered their property. The intensity of their preferences might explain to some extent why they chose to deceive the United States and to violate alliance norms. But it certainly did not increase their bargaining leverage against the United States.

[43] "Memorandum of NSC Meeting," Nov. 1, *FRUS 1955–1957*, 16:912–13.

Second, the British and French governments not only threatened to defect—that is, to use military force against the publicly expressed opposition of the alliance leader—they actually carried out the threat. In response, the full power of American coercion hit them.

Third, the interallied conflict over Suez reached its height when Warsaw Pact forces intervened in Hungary, suppressing the uprising. The increase in threat perception should have led to greater alliance cohesion and unity. Instead, U.S. officials implicitly accused the British and French of providing an opportunity for the Soviet Union to act in Hungary while world opinion was distracted by the Suez crisis.[44]

Fourth, allied unity as a condition for allied influence does not work, either. Two core NATO allies, Britain and France, were fairly united in their views. This might explain the American mediation effort at the beginning of the crisis but is inconsistent with the use of coercive power in the end.

Fifth, as far as control over issue-specific resources is concerned, Britain and France depended on U.S. economic and financial support to carry out their military adventure at the Suez Canal, which weakened their bargaining position considerably. While this might explain the ultimate outcome of the interallied conflict, it cannot account for the British and French miscalculation of U.S. behavior.

In sum, with the possible exception of the last factor, the Suez crisis case disconfirms assumptions derived from realist bargaining theory, according to which Britain and France should have been in a better position vis-à-vis the United States than they actually were. This then leaves the *liberal* interpretation presented above.

The confrontation between the United States and its allies developed because each side felt betrayed by the other in fundamental ways. While the French and British violation of consultation norms might be explained by the intensity of their motivations and preferences, the U.S. retaliation in kind cannot. U.S. decision-makers perceived the allied deception as a violation of basic rules, norms, and procedures constituting the transatlantic community. No longer bound by the norms of appropriate behavior, the superior power of the United States prevailed.

Both sides knew that they violated the rules of the "alliance game" and engaged in self-serving rhetoric to cover it up. (Macmillan's "fig leaf" statement was only the most ridiculous example.) More important, the United States and the British worked hard to restore the transatlantic community, suggesting that they did not regard confrontations as experienced during the Suez crisis as appropriate behavior among democratic

[44] See, for example, "Memorandum of Conversation at the State Department," Nov. 5, *FRUS 1955–1957*, 16:1003–7, 1004.

allies. As Eisenhower put it in his memoirs: "Nothing saddens me more than the thought that I and my old friends of years have met a problem concerning which we do not see eye to eye. I shall never be happy until our old time closeness has been restored."[45]

In sum, process-tracing of the crisis in the context of the transatlantic relationship reveals that the "realist outcome" confirms the liberal case. Norm violation challenging the sense of community among the allies provides the key to understanding the interactions leading to the confrontation, the clash, and the restoration of the community.

Variation in Cooperation among Democracies: The Anglo-American versus the Franco-American Relationship

An important puzzle remains, though, for the liberal argument. While the Anglo-American "special relationship" quickly recovered from the crisis, the Franco-American ties never did. The crisis set in motion a gradual trend of deinstitutionalization in the Franco-American relationship, culminating in President de Gaulle's decision to withdraw from the military integration of NATO ten years later. As becomes apparent in the next case study (chapter 5), French influence on American foreign policy steadily decreased.

There are several reasons for this development. First, prior to the Suez crisis, there had already been strains in the Franco-American relationship triggered by what Paris considered U.S. betrayal of the French war effort in Indochina at Dien Bien Phu in 1954.[46] The norms governing the Anglo-American relationship had always been stronger than the rules of the Franco-American alliance. Eisenhower and Dulles were more annoyed by the British deception during the Suez crisis than by the French-Israeli collusion.

Second, to restore the normative underpinnings of a relationship after a major violation of rules requires active efforts on both sides. The U.S. administration pledged repeatedly to the French that it wished to maintain close ties. But the government in Paris drew different lessons from the crisis, as the following bitter comments in the memoirs of the French foreign minister reveal:

> The Americans are victims of a superiority complex. They are not only confident in themselves, but they are confident *only* in themselves. They constitute the only nation in the world to have discovered God and find themselves

[45] Eisenhower's memoirs, quoted from Sherwood, *Allies in Crisis*, 73.

[46] For an overview on French-American relations, see Frank Costigliola, *France and the United States* (New York: Twayne, 1992).

in agreement with him. . . . As a result, they cannot commit an error. If they are nevertheless mistaken, they are all the more surprised that their computers cannot explain how and why they made a mistake.[47]

While the British decided to entangle the Americans further in the transatlantic relationship, the French elite of the Fourth Republic distanced itself as a consequence of the crisis. The colonial war in Algeria, which had motivated much of the French resentment against Nasser during the Suez crisis, increasingly preoccupied the government in Paris and led to the constitutional crisis of the Fourth Republic. When General de Gaulle came into power in 1958 and created the Fifth Republic, he transformed the already existing trend toward the deinstitutionalization of the Franco-American relationship into a coherent foreign policy concept. His quest for "independence" was incompatible with strong ties to the United States.

Thus, the difference in the evolution of the Anglo-American compared to the Franco-American relationship after the Suez crisis resulted from deliberate choices of the respective governments. The variation suggests that liberal assumptions about a "pacific federation" (I. Kant) or a "pluralistic security community" (K. W. Deutsch) of democratic states are insufficient to explain the interaction patterns within the transatlantic alliance. Both Britain and France are liberal democracies. Rather, the liberal account has to be complemented by institutionalist arguments. Norms have to be interpreted, and collective identities are not fixed, but may change over time. Historical events and the lessons drawn from these events vary, and different lessons may lead to variations in institutional behavior. While the British chose to reestablish the "special relationship" with the United States after Suez, the French government decided against it. The consequences became apparent during the test ban negotiations.

[47] Christian Pineau, *1956 Suez* (Paris: Editions Robert Laffont, 1976), 194 (my translation).

FIVE

"A GAME OF GOLF AND A LITTLE TALK"

TRANSNATIONAL COALITIONS AND THE 1958–1963 TEST BAN NEGOTIATIONS

The differences exhibited at the meeting with Macmillan were unfortunate. I said they would have been unfortunate with anybody but Macmillan but that he was practically a member of the family.
—John Foster Dulles[1]

THE 1963 Limited Test Ban Treaty (LTBT) was the first nuclear arms control agreement prohibiting nuclear tests in the atmosphere, in outer space, and underwater. After five years of intensive negotiations, the United States, the Soviet Union, and Great Britain concluded the agreement.[2] I argue in this chapter that British influence on American decisions was crucial in bringing about the test ban treaty. London exerted its impact using transnational and transgovernmental linkages based upon the mutual trust developed in the framework of the Anglo-American "special relationship." These transnational coalitions strengthened the position of test ban supporters in Washington facing an uphill battle with opponents inside and outside the administration. Through their coalition-building efforts, the British almost became a domestic political player in the United States and frequently tipped the balance in Washington in favor of an agreement.

The test ban negotiations allow a comparison of the influence of several

The chapter title quotes British Prime Minister Macmillan during a phone conversation with President Eisenhower, March 21, 1960, PRO:PREM, 11/2994.

[1] John Foster Dulles to Robert Lovett, Aug. 14, 1958, National Archives (NA), Central Decimal Files, 600.0012/8–1458.

[2] The three most comprehensive studies on the test ban negotiations are Robert Divine, *Blowing on the Wind* (New York: Oxford University Press, 1978); Harold K. Jacobson and Eric Stein, *Diplomats, Scientists, and Politicians* (Ann Arbor: University of Michigan Press, 1966); Glenn T. Seaborg, *Kennedy, Khrushchev, and the Test Ban* (Berkeley: University of California Press, 1981). For analyses of the domestic politics of the test ban negotiations see Thomas W. Graham, "The Politics of Failure" (Ph.D. diss., Massachusetts Institute of Technoloy, June 1989), chap. 5; Jeffrey W. Knopf, "Domestic Politics, Citizen Activism, and U.S. Nuclear Arms Control Policy" (Ph.D. diss., Stanford University, June 1991), chaps. 2, 3.

West European allies on U.S. policies, since Great Britain, France, and West Germany disagreed on the issue. While the British government was adamantly opposed to a test prohibition until the summer of 1958, it then turned around completely and became the most stable and most enduring allied supporter of an agreement, which constantly pressured the United States to adopt a more conciliatory negotiating position.[3] The French and West German governments opposed nuclear test limitations throughout the entire period. France viewed them as attempts by the three nuclear powers to prevent it from acquiring nuclear weapons. When President de Gaulle came to power and decided to vigorously continue the French nuclear program, his opposition against a test ban agreement stiffened. France continued to conduct nuclear tests above ground until 1974.[4] In the Federal Republic of Germany, Chancellor Adenauer and his Defense Minister Strauß wanted to keep a German nuclear option open but never embarked on a sustained program. They primarily opposed a test ban agreement for fear that an arms control treaty would freeze the political status quo in Europe and thus hinder the prospects for German reunification.[5]

Compared to Britain, France and Germany did not affect the outcome very much—except for Bonn's successful effort in 1963 to prevent a nonaggression pact as a follow-up to the test ban treaty. I argue that the difference in impact was due to the lack of transnational linkages between treaty opponents in the United States and their counterparts in France and Germany.

The American domestic scene was as split about the desirability of a test ban agreement as the allies.[6] Activist groups and independent scientists

[3] On the development of British arms control policy see J. P. G. Freeman, *Britain's Nuclear Arms Control Policy in the Context of Anglo-American Relations, 1957–1968* (London: Macmillan, 1986). See also John Baylis, *Anglo-American Defence Relations, 1939–1984*, 2d ed. (London: Macmillan, 1984); Timothy Botti, *The Long Wait* (Greenwich, Conn.: Greenwood Press, 1987); A. J. R. Groom, *British Thinking about Nuclear Weapons* (London: Pinter, 1974); Martin S. Navias, *Nuclear Weapons and British Strategic Planning* (Oxford: Clarendon Press, 1991).

[4] On French nuclear policy in general see Wilfried L. Kohl, *French Nuclear Diplomacy* (Princeton, N.J.: Princeton University Press, 1971); L'Université de Franche-Comté et l'Institut Charles-de-Gaulle, *L'Aventure de la Bombe* (Paris: Librairie Plon, 1985); David S. Yost, "France," in *The Allies and Arms Control*, ed. Fen O. Hampson et al. (Baltimore: Johns Hopkins University Press, 1992), 162–88.

[5] See Marc Cioc, *Pax Atomica* (New York: Columbia University Press, 1988); Helga Haftendorn, *Sicherheit und Entspannung* (Baden-Baden: Nomos, 1983), 78–86, 104–22; Christoph Hoppe, *Zwischen Teilhabe und Mitsprache* (Baden-Baden: Nomos, 1993); Catherine M. Kelleher, *Germany and the Politics of Nuclear Weapons* (New York: Columbia University Press, 1975); Hans-Peter Schwarz, "Adenauer und die Kernwaffen," *Vierteljahreshefte für Zeitgeschichte* 37, no. 4 (October 1989), 567–93.

[6] For details on the following see particularly Divine, *Blowing on the Wind*; Knopf, "Domestic Politics, Citizen Activism"; Seaborg, *Kennedy, Khrushchev*.

forced the issue on the public and political agenda and continuously pushed for an agreement. Their efforts were supported in Congress by the Disarmament Subcommittee of the Senate Foreign Relations Committee and its chairman, Hubert Humphrey. Inside the administration, the State Department was the main advocate of an agreement, once Secretary of State Dulles had changed his position in 1957—together with the Presidential Scientific Advisory Committee (PSAC), created under Eisenhower to provide the president with independent scientific advice. Test ban supporters faced stiff opposition throughout the negotiations from the military, particularly the Joint Chiefs of Staff (JCS), the intelligence community including the CIA, scientists from the nuclear weapons laboratories, and the congressional Joint Committee on Atomic Energy (JCAE). The Pentagon and the Atomic Energy Commission (AEC), while joining the opposition during the Eisenhower administration, became more tempered in their criticism under Secretary of Defense McNamara and AEC Chairman Seaborg. Presidents Dwight D. Eisenhower and John F. Kennedy were both personally committed to a nuclear arms control agreement and, from 1958 on, the test ban issue was high on their agenda.[7] However, neither ever showed strong and decisive leadership necessary to overcome the domestic opposition. One has to keep in mind, though, that treaty opponents only needed thirty-four votes in the U.S. Senate to deny ratification, so the opposition could exert far more domestic power than its numerical strength suggested.

Neither U.S. domestic politics nor intra-alliance bargaining as such can explain American negotiating behavior. Rather, the community of democratic values provided a framework in which transnational and transgovernmental links developed, allowing particularly the British to become part of the "family." Domestic and alliance politics interacted. European test ban supporters needed transnational allies in the United States to make a difference in Washington. At the same time, American arms control advocates relied on their allied counterparts to strengthen their domestic position.

Setting the Agenda: Transnational Coalitions among Scientists and Peace Activists

On March 1, 1954, the U.S. hydrogen-bomb test BRAVO accidentally contaminated a Japanese fishing boat, triggering a worldwide debate on the dangers of radioactive fallout from atmospheric nuclear tests. Japan was outraged, but the incident also led to an immediate response on the

[7] On Eisenhower's views on nuclear weapons and arms control see, for example, Stephen E. Ambrose, *Eisenhower* (New York: Touchstone, 1990), 339–41, 403, 486, 543. On Kennedy's views see Seaborg, *Kennedy, Khrushchev*.

other side of the globe. British Prime Minister Churchill appealed to the two superpowers for restraint, and the Labour party demanded a cessation of nuclear tests. Media reports from both Japan and Britain triggered a public debate on nuclear tests in the United States. In April, the British government, following an Indian initiative, suggested a temporary moratorium on H-bomb tests, which the Eisenhower administration rejected on the grounds that the short-term propaganda advantage was not worth restrictions on nuclear weapons development.[8]

But the nuclear testing issue remained on the public agenda, largely due to the pressures of nuclear physicists, biologists, and activist groups. In February 1955, U.S. physicist Ralph Lapp published the first detailed account of the fallout effects of H-bomb tests, followed in March by physicist Joseph Rotblat's paper in the British *Journal of the Atomic Scientists Association*. Shortly afterward, Albert Einstein and the British philosopher Bertrand Russell drafted a public appeal to end the nuclear arms race, which then was signed by scientists from the United States, Britain, France, Germany, and other countries. In the United States, the Federation of American Scientists (FAS) and the journal *Bulletin of the Atomic Scientists* became the major instruments for scientists to support a nuclear test ban and to inform the public about the risks of nuclear fallout. In 1957 the Committee for a Sane Nuclear Policy (SANE) was formed and developed into the main activist group in the United States, lobbying the public and policymakers to support a nuclear test ban.[9]

SANE frequently used transnational contacts to lend international credibility to its demands in the United States. In early 1957, for example, SANE leader Norman Cousins convinced the Swiss physician and Nobel peace laureate Albert Schweitzer to issue a passionate statement calling for a ban on nuclear testing. Schweitzer's appeal in turn inspired Nobel laureate Linus Pauling to initiate a petition campaign supported by thousands of scientists worldwide.

In July 1957 scientists supporting nuclear disarmament founded the Pugwash movement. The Pugwash meetings regularly served as a forum for Eastern and Western scientists, many of whom advised their respec-

[8] For details see Botti, *Long Wait*, 135–38; Divine, *Blowing on the Wind*, 6–32; John Simpson, *The Independent Nuclear State* (London: Macmillan, 1983), 95–96; also: "Memorandum for the Executive Secretary, National Security Council, Subject: Department of State Views on the Proposed Moratorium on Tests," June 23, 1954, Dwight D. Eisenhower Library (DDEL; courtesy of Matt Evangelista). On the lack of seriousness in U.S. disarmament proposals at the time, see Matthew Evangelista, "Cooperation Theory and Disarmament Negotiations in the 1950s," *World Politics* 42, no. 4 (July 1990): 502–28.

[9] For details see Divine, *Blowing On the Wind*, 37–38, 121–23, 127, 161; Freeman, *Britain's Nuclear Arms Control Policy*, 27–28, 33–36; Milton S. Katz, *Ban the Bomb* (Greenwich, Conn.: Greenwood Press, 1986), 14–20; Knopf, "Domestic Politics, Citizen Activism," 117–23, 132–34, 146.

tive governments, to exchange their views. Later, during the Kennedy administration, Pugwash organized various conferences to promote the notion that a comprehensive test ban was verifiable. High-level delegations from the United States, the Soviet Union, Great Britain, and France regularly attended these meetings.[10]

In Great Britain an even stronger peace movement emerged, which succeeded in forming a coalition of prominent scientists, intellectuals, trade unionists, and Labour party officials. In January 1958 and partly in reaction to the British H-bomb tests, the Campaign for Nuclear Disarmament (CND) was founded, which organized the Easter marches to the British nuclear facilities at Aldermaston. In 1960 almost one hundred thousand people participated. CND also moved the Labour party toward unilateral nuclear disarmament. As a result of these alliances between peace groups and traditional leftist organizations, the British Conservative government of Prime Minister Macmillan was faced with a powerful domestic opposition to its nuclear policies.[11]

Thus, scientists and activist groups formed a transnational alliance against nuclear weapons tests. The Japanese government and an increasing number of nonaligned nations, particularly India, joined in the protest, as a result of which pressure on the superpowers to restrict nuclear testing increased dramatically in the UN General Assembly. These activities set the public agenda in both the United States and Great Britain, the two Western nuclear powers at the time. The scientists alerted the world to the risks of radioactive fallout. Activist groups then spread the information to larger audiences and promoted specific political proposals such as a nuclear test ban.[12] Professional organizations such as the U.S. National Academy of Science, the British Medical Research Council, and the British Atomic Scientist Association commissioned reports stud-

[10] See Solly Zuckerman [at the time science adviser to the British Defense Ministry], *Monkeys, Men, and Missiles* (New York: W. W. Norton, 1988), pp. 314–316. See also George Kistiakowsky [presidential science adviser under Eisenhower], *A Scientist at the White House* (Cambridge, Mass.: Harvard University Press, 1976), 423–24. On the history of Pugwash, see Joseph Rotblat, *Scientists in the Quest for Peace* (Cambridge, Mass.: MIT Press, 1972).

[11] See Christopher Driver, *The Disarmers* (London: Hodder & Stoughton, 1964); Richard Taylor, *Against the Bomb* (Oxford: Clarendon Press, 1988); Groom, *British Thinking about Nuclear Weapons*.

[12] Scientists and peace movements interacted in a similar way as reported in research about "epistemic communities" in the environmental issue-area. "Epistemic communities" are expert groups promoting a specific political agenda based on common values and consensual knowledge. See Peter Haas, ed., *Knowledge, Power, and International Policy-Coordination*, special issue of *International Organization*, 46, no. 1 (Winter 1992). However, the "consensuality" of the knowledge had its limits in the test ban case, since scientists at the nuclear weapons laboratories disputed the findings of the scientific advocates of a test ban.

ying the health effects of nuclear testing. The UN General Assembly also established a Scientific Committee on Radiation, following an American proposal. While most of these reports played down the immediate health hazards of radiation from atmospheric tests, they lent credibility to the argument that "safe" nuclear radiation did not exist.[13]

Moreover, the appeals by scientists and activist groups brought the test ban issue on the domestic political agenda in the United States. Encouraged by the scientists, Democratic presidential candidate Adlai Stevenson promoted a test ban during his campaign in 1956.[14] But in the absence of strong public support for a test ban, his advocacy suffered when the Soviet Union seemed to endorse his proposals, which the Republicans exploited immediately in the cold war climate of the 1950s. From then on, though, the test ban issue was on the national agenda. The activities of the peace movements and scientists in conjunction with an increasingly unfavorable climate of "world opinion" against nuclear testing gradually raised the pressure on the administration. President Eisenhower was well aware of the growing protests against nuclear testing: "The President spoke of the rising concern of people everywhere over the effect of radiation from tests, or their reaction each time a test was reported, and their extreme nervousness over the prospective consequences of any nuclear war."[15] Policymakers did not distinguish between pressures originating from domestic constituents, from allies, or from "world opinion" in general. As Eisenhower put it:

> World opinion, even if not well founded, is a fact; world anxiety exists over tests, and causes tension. . . . we need some basis of hope for our own people and for world opinion. . . . it is simply intolerable to remain in a position wherein the United States, seeking peace, and giving loyal partnership to our allies, is unable to achieve an advantageous impact on world opinion.[16]

In other words, antinuclear protests in the United States, transnational activities of scientists, and the growing concerns of allied and nonaligned nations in the UN had a synergistic effect on U.S. decision-makers. Trans-

[13] For details see Divine, *Blowing On the Wind*, 78–79, 123, 221–222; Freeman, *Britain's Nuclear Arms Control Policy*, 30–32.

[14] On the Stevenson campaign, see Divine, *Blowing on the Wind*, 93–112.

[15] "Memorandum of conversation, White House," Sept. 9, 1956, *FRUS 1955–1957*, 20:423–27, 427.

[16] "Memorandum of conference with the President," March 24, 1958, in National Security Archive, Washington D.C., Nuclear Non-Proliferation Collection (NSA:NNP), folder 1958. See also "Memorandum of discussion at the 275th NSC meeting," Feb. 7, 1956, *FRUS 1955–1957*, 20:319–28, 324; "Memorandum of conference with the President," Aug. 9, 1957, NSA:NNP, 1957. See also, "Memorandum of conference with the President," Aug. 16, 1957, ibid.

national and allied demands legitimized and strengthened arguments of activist groups inside the United States. Eisenhower and Kennedy used the external pressures to increase their "domestic win sets" in favor of test ban negotiations, thereby trying to diffuse the opposition.[17]

The domestic and transnational pressures served to change the political priorities of Eisenhower and Dulles. Both had been convinced for quite some time and partly because of allied "education" (see chapter 3) that nuclear war could not be won and that something had to be done to control the escalating nuclear arms race.[18] But given the bureaucratic resistance against restraints on nuclear testing, the issue had been assigned a low priority on Eisenhower's and Dulles's arms control agenda until about 1957. The main impact of the public and transnational protests was to move nuclear testing up the arms control agenda until it became a top concern for decision-makers in 1958. Equally significant, this evolution marks the transition from the nuclear disarmament rhetoric of the 1950s to concrete and specific steps to curb the nuclear arms race, that is, to arms control in the modern sense. Domestic and transnational coalitions forced the United States to concentrate its first practical efforts at nuclear arms control on the test ban issue.

Once the negotiations got under way in 1958, the transnational coalition of scientists in particular served as facilitators for the interstate talks, frequently mediating between the United States and the USSR. For example, Pugwash's most important contribution to the test ban negotiations probably came in the aftermath of the Cuban Missile crisis in 1962, when six U.S. and Soviet scientists signed a public statement suggesting that sealed, automatic seismic recording units—"black boxes"—might offer a way out of the impasse on verifying an agreement. Soviet leader Khrushchev accepted the proposal and incorporated it into Moscow's negotiating position. The momentum was lost, however, during the controversy between Washington and Moscow about the number of on-site inspections required to explore unidentified events (see below).[19]

In sum, transnational coalitions of societal actors and scientists were instrumental in putting the nuclear test ban issue on the public agenda of the nuclear powers, moving it up the political priority list of decision-

[17] I owe this point to David Meyer.

[18] See Ambrose, *Eisenhower*; McGeorge Bundy, *Danger and Survival* (New York: Random House, 1988), 328–34; John Lewis Gaddis, "The Unexpected John Foster Dulles: Nuclear Weapons, Communism, and the Russians," in *John Foster Dulles and the Diplomacy of the Cold War*, ed. Richard H. Immermann (Princeton, N.J.: Princeton University Press, 1990), 47–77. For the following argument, see Knopf, "Domestic Politics, Citizen Activism," chap. 2.

[19] For details see Jacobson and Stein, *Diplomats, Scientists, and Politicians*, 425, 428–430; Knopf, "Domestic Politics, Citizen Activism," 249–50; Seaborg, *Kennedy, Khrushchev*, 177, 183–185.

makers, and facilitating the negotiations. Once the talks between the United States, the USSR, and Great Britain had started, interactions among state actors became more significant in explaining the outcome. As I argue in the following, transgovernmental alliances among British and U.S. senior officials were crucial factors that explain changes in the American negotiating position.

Pushing and Pulling: The British Impact on Eisenhower's Nuclear Testing Policies

From Opposition to Support: The Evolution of British Policy until 1958

From 1954 until 1958, the Conservative governments in London under Prime Ministers Churchill, Eden, and Macmillan faced the following problem. On the one hand, they felt increasing domestic pressures against the British nuclear program and atmospheric tests. They also feared that the United States and the Soviet Union might agree to limitations on nuclear testing on their own terms. On the other hand, the British government was determined to continue its nuclear program, including the development of a hydrogen bomb, which necessitated nuclear tests for several years. As a result, London opposed test limitations until its own H-bomb program had been successful, but shifted gears quite dramatically afterward.

When the Eisenhower administration began to take the suspension of nuclear tests more seriously in the spring of 1957, the National Security Council (NSC) considered a proposal for a partial disarmament agreement, including a fissile material production "cut-off" and a one-year suspension of nuclear tests. To prevent being caught between a rock and a hard place, the British government pursued three strategies. First, it insisted on a firm link between the "cut-off" date and the cessation of nuclear tests, hoping that the Soviet Union would not accept it. Second, it pushed for changes in the American proposal to buy time in the event that a first-step disarmament agreement came sooner rather than later. The British convinced the United States, for example, to push back the expected date for the start of the test moratorium toward November 1958.[20]

Third, and most important, Prime Minister Macmillan demanded revisions in the 1946 U.S. Atomic Energy Act (McMahon Act), which had made nuclear collaboration with foreign powers illegal. London established a linkage between revisions of the McMahon Act and its agreement

[20] For the changes in the U.S. position see "US Position on First Phase of Disarmament," June 11, 1957, modified as of Aug. 13, 1957, NSA:NNP, 1957. For evidence that allied pressure was responsible for the changes see Christian Herter, "Memorandum for the President, Subject: Disarmament," Aug. 13, ibid.

to a test moratorium. Britain was prepared to agree to a moratorium on nuclear tests effective in late 1958, if it acquired data on the design and production of nuclear warheads from the United States. While Eisenhower had been sympathetic to the British demands all along,[21] he faced tough opposition by the military, the Atomic Energy Commission (AEC), and, particularly, the congressional Joint Committee on Atomic Energy (JCAE). But after the Suez crisis, both sides were anxious to repair the "special relationship" (chapter 4) and Macmillan tried to cash in on the new American willingness to accommodate British needs.[22]

The United States apparently committed itself to bilateral talks with Britain on the delivery of nuclear information and material, in the event that Moscow agreed to the first-phase disarmament treaty.[23] In October 1957 the British government exploited the Sputnik shock in the American public. The president now issued a directive to "submit recommended revisions of the Atomic Energy Act of 1954" to facilitate the sharing of nuclear information with "selected allies."[24] Two Anglo-American committees were set up on nuclear cooperation and on weapons development. They quickly achieved agreement.

In early 1958 the president indicated publicly that the McMahon Act would have to be changed before nuclear testing could be restricted, thereby accepting the British position. His statement tried to diffuse domestic pressures for an immediate test ban by reminding his audience of the necessity to accommodate the European allies:

> Here is one very great difficulty about just making a flat agreement for cessation of testing. . . . we belong to an association for which we have great

[21] See, for example, the following quote: "The President closed the discussion with a warm tribute to the kind of scientific and technical cooperation which the British had offered the United States in a whole long period since the beginning of World War II. Our own attitude in response to the British had been foolish and stupid, and we had lost a great deal in all these fields as a result of our 'terrible attitude.'" ("Memorandum of Discussion at the 236th Meeting of the NSC," Feb. 10, 1955, *FRUS 1955–1957*, 20:20–34, 28.)

[22] See, for example, "Message from Prime Minister to President," March 27, 1957, in Public Records Office, London, *Diplomatic Correspondence Files* (PRO:FO), 371/135505: "As you will know, the help we can count on from you under the amended act will largely determine the position we are able to take up on nuclear tests and nuclear disarmament in talks with the Russians." For the following see also Navias, *Nuclear Weapons and British Strategic Planning*, 189–201; Botti, *Long Wait*, 187–90.

[23] See "Department of State, Incoming Telegram from London," Aug. 17, 1957, DDEL; "Dept. of State, Incoming Telegram from London," Aug. 18, DDEL; also Botti, *Long Wait*, 190.

[24] "340th Meeting of the NSC, Box 67, Minutes," Oct. 17, 1957, NA, RG 273, NSC. See also "Memorandum of conference with the President," Oct. 25, 1957, NSA:NNP, 1957; "Memorandum of conference with the President," Oct. 29, ibid.; Harold Macmillan, *Riding the Storm* (London: Macmillan, 1971), 315, 322–23; Navias, *Nuclear Weapons and British Strategic Planning*, 195–96.

> respect, NATO; and some of the nations there are . . . in different states of producing the weapons that require testing and we would have a difficult time, . . . under the present law, to make an agreement with them that would be binding on all of the NATO countries.[25]

Khrushchev's announcement of a unilateral test moratorium on March 31 exacerbated the British anxiety that the two superpowers might stop nuclear tests before its own test series was concluded. In response, the U.S. administration came back to an earlier proposal by British Foreign Minister Selwyn Lloyd and suggested talks among technical experts to study the verification of a test ban.[26] When the Soviets agreed, the Geneva Experts' Conference convened in the summer of 1958 (see below).

The British government was aware that the president was no longer willing to postpone a decision on the cessation of nuclear tests. At a NATO meeting in early May, Foreign Secretary Selwyn Lloyd told John Foster Dulles that the British were prepared to suspend nuclear tests after October 31 (that is, after the completion of their own H-bomb tests) provided that the United States would supply all necessary information to the British after the McMahon Act had been amended. The administration promised to fulfill the British demands.[27]

At the end of June, Congress passed the required amendments freeing the way for increased Anglo-American nuclear cooperation. Eisenhower and Macmillan issued a joint statement on August 22, 1958, to enter test ban negotiations by the end of October and, by that time, to refrain from nuclear testing for one year. From now on, the British government became the most enduring supporter of a test ban agreement—after concluding its own hydrogen bomb tests and insuring Anglo-American nuclear collaboration.

While activist groups, scientists, and "world opinion" in the UN influenced the U.S. administration to accept the temporary cessation of nuclear tests and to enter into negotiations with the Soviet Union, the British government affected the *timing*. London also extracted a major concession from Washington in exchange for agreeing to the suspension of tests. Once the negotiations got under way, however, London wanted an

[25] Eisenhower's press conference, Feb. 26, 1958, quoted in "Dept. of State, to Paris," NA, 600.0012/2–2658. See also "U.S. Embassy, London, to Dept. of State," Feb. 7, NA, 611.41/2–758; Dept. of State, "Memorandum of Conversation," Feb. 28, NA, 600.0012/2–2858.

[26] On the British origins of the proposal see Freeman, *Britain's Nuclear Arms Control Policy*, 77; Michael Wright, *Disarm and Verify* (London: Chatto & Windus, 1964), 134. Sir Wright headed the British delegation to the Geneva test ban negotiations during the Kennedy administration.

[27] See "Memorandum of Conference with the President," May 12, 1958, NSA:NNP, 1958; "Foreign Office telegram to UK Embassy, Washington," May 28, PRO:FO 371/135539; Freeman, *Britain's Nuclear Arms Control Policy*, 88.

agreement more than Washington. The United States had to be pushed and pulled, not Britain.

Coalition among Scientists: The Geneva Conference of Experts

Various transgovernmental alliances among officials working for their respective administrations emerged in the Anglo-American relationship. Members of the U.S. Presidential Scientific Advisory Committee (PSAC) supporting an agreement, for example, closely cooperated with their British colleagues. They found British support particularly helpful. It allowed them to refer to an "international scientific consensus" rather than their own opinion when arguing with test ban opponents in internal meetings.[28]

The most important contribution of scientists toward an agreement consisted of the Geneva Conference of Experts in the summer of 1958, which studied verification options for a test ban. This conference convened as a result of an interstate agreement among Khrushchev, Eisenhower, and Macmillan. It opened the way for formal negotiations by working out an agreed-upon verification scheme.[29] It was one of the first instances that scientists, not professional diplomats, had been assigned the task of solving cooperation problems among states in the gray area between technical and political issues. The U.S. government viewed the conference as purely technical and apparently did not issue specific political instructions to its delegation, headed by PSAC member James Fisk. In contrast, the British team, chaired by Sir William Penney, a scientist working for the British nuclear research facilities, received instructions from the prime minister to work toward an accord—a reflection of the changed U.K. attitude toward a test ban.[30]

Hans Bethe, one of the participants, describes the atmosphere at the Geneva conference as highly professional and oriented toward problem-solving based on consensual scientific knowledge. According to his ac-

[28] Interview with Hans Bethe, Cornell University, Oct. 30, 1990. On PSAC see Robert Gilpin, *American Scientists and Nuclear Weapons Policy* (Princeton, N.J.: Princeton University Press, 1962); James R. Killian, *Sputnik, Scientists, and Eisenhower* (Cambridge, Mass.: MIT Press, 1977); Kistiakowsky, *A Scientist at the White House*. For the British see Zuckerman, *Monkeys, Men, and Missiles*, 307–42.

[29] For the following see Gilpin, *American Scientists and Nuclear Weapons Policy*, 186–94; Jacobson and Stein, *Diplomats, Scientists, and Politicians*, 34–81.

[30] One could argue that the British—and probably Soviet—experts simply carried out the instructions of their governments. This was not the case for the American representatives to the Geneva talks, who had considerably more leeway. As a result, interactions between the Americans and their British and Soviet colleagues cannot be conceptualized as *inter*governmental, but must be regarded as *trans*governmental in the absence of central decisions by the United States. On the Geneva Conference of Experts, see Jacobson and Stein, *Diplomats, Scientists, and Politicians*, 66–67; Killian, *Sputnik, Scientists, and Eisenhower*, 160–61; Zuckerman, *Monkeys, Men, and Missiles*, 308.

count, major contributions came from U.S., British, and Soviet scientists. The main issue was to agree on a system of seismic verification, in particular on the number of control stations to be set up worldwide. When the Soviet scientists proposed a control system of 100–110 stations, U.S. delegation members countered with a system of 650 stations, with more than 100 on Soviet territory. The British offered a compromise of 170 land-based stations and some sea-based posts, which together should have been capable of detecting atmospheric tests down to one kiloton and most underground tests above five kilotons. The proposal was finally accepted by the delegations together with the provision for on-site inspections in the case of unidentified seismic events. This was the first time that Soviet representatives had ever agreed to the principle of on-site verification.[31]

The Geneva agreement constituted the first instance during the test ban talks of state representatives reaching a compromise through transgovernmental interactions. Technical expert consensus opened the door for both the formal interstate test ban negotiations and the Anglo-American decision to cease nuclear testing temporarily.

But the consensus reached in Geneva fell apart only half a year later, when the U.S. weapons laboratories concluded on the basis of underground tests that the Geneva verification scheme would not suffice to monitor a comprehensive test ban. The alleged new evidence became a major stumbling block for the negotiations and could only be removed in 1962, when further findings from seismic research showed that the critique of the Geneva system had been exaggerated.

The 1958 Geneva Conference of Experts proved to be the one and only instance during the talks when scientists were genuinely able to facilitate interstate cooperation. When the governments agreed on "Technical Working Groups" in the fall of 1959 to repeat the experience of the Geneva meeting and to solve political problems via technical expertise, the effort failed. Profound political disagreements among the three powers overshadowed the expert meetings. The failure of the 1959 Technical Working Groups compared to the success of the 1958 Geneva conference shows that scientific impact on interstate cooperation remains dependent on favorable political conditions.[32]

Dropping the Link between Disarmament and a Test Ban

When the test ban negotiations started on October 31, 1958, it quickly became obvious that the U.S. bargaining position contained a major

[31] See details in Divine, *Blowing on the Wind*, 225–27; Jacobson and Stein, *Diplomats, Scientists, and Politicians*, 74–79. Interview with Hans Bethe.

[32] Cf. the comment by the British chief negotiator in Geneva: "If you want evidence to refute the contention that if the politicians would leave the scientists alone, solutions would be at hand, you need look no further than TWGI [Technical Working Group I]" (Freeman, *Britain's Nuclear Arms Control Policy*, 100).

stumbling block by linking the conclusion of a test ban to some unspecified progress in "real disarmament." This link represented the last remnant of the comprehensive disarmament plans of the 1950s, which were used by arms control opponents to prevent agreements. An Anglo-American transgovernmental coalition was responsible for the removal of this linkage from the U.S. position. This coalition included senior officials from the State Department and the British Foreign Office as well as the two negotiating teams in Geneva.

More than two weeks *before* the negotiations started, the British cabinet decided to work toward an early removal of the linkage in the Western bargaining position. The British thought that it would constitute a major defeat for the West in public and world opinion if the talks broke down because of Western insistence on the link. The negotiations should instead concentrate on an adequate verification system.[33]

When Foreign Minister Selwyn Lloyd approached the Secretary of State on October 19, 1958, Dulles replied that he personally understood the British view but was unable to change the U.S. position because of opposition by the Pentagon, the AEC, and the congressional JCAE.[34] The French were also lobbying hard against dropping the link between disarmament and a test ban.

When the talks started, the two negotiating teams in Geneva became the main advocates of dropping the link. On November 20 the U.S. delegation in Geneva urged the administration in Washington to change its position. At the same time, the U.S. team asked its British counterparts to make sure that the U.K. representative in Washington acted quickly in support of the recommendation. Both delegations then lobbied the British prime minister to intervene in Washington on behalf of changing the U.S. instructions.[35]

The State Department, the British embassy in Washington, and the British Foreign Office agreed with the views of the Geneva delegations but opted for a more cautious approach in light of the considerable disagreements inside the U.S. administration. The Pentagon and the Joint Chiefs of Staff (JCS) adamantly opposed dropping the link.[36] State De-

[33] See "Minute by Selwyn Lloyd to Prime Minister," Oct. 14, 1958, PRO:FO 371/132686; "Foreign Office to UK Embassy Washington," Oct. 15, ibid.

[34] Dulles asked Selwyn Lloyd not to mention this conversation to other U.S. officials. Cf. "Foreign Office to Embassy Washington," Oct. 20, 1958, PRO:FO 371/132686; "Embassy Washington to Foreign Office," Oct. 16, ibid.; "Embassy Washington to Foreign Office," Oct. 17, ibid. Dulles sympathized with the British view. A State Department official had indicated to the British ambassador prior to the Selwyn Lloyd-Dulles talks that State would consider British pressure to move the U.S. position as "most helpful." See "Embassy Washington to Foreign Office," Oct. 11, PRO:FO 371/132685.

[35] See the cables by U.K. Delegation Geneva to Foreign Office, Nov. 20, Nov. 21, and Nov. 22, 1958, PRO:FO 371/132692.

[36] At the same time, PSAC did not support the transgovernmental alliance as strongly as

partment officials worked hard to change the U.S. position and constantly referred to the British view to strengthen their arguments internally. Finally, and together with the Foreign Office, they orchestrated a message by Prime Minister Macmillan to President Eisenhower. The State Department advised the British on both the timing and the substance of the letter, which was considered a powerful instrument to influence the American decision-making process.[37]

Macmillan sent his message to President Eisenhower on January 1, 1959. In a meeting considering the reply, Eisenhower overruled the Pentagon and decided to drop the link between progress in disarmament and a test ban agreement.[38] This marks the final transition from the disarmament talks of the 1950s to negotiations on specific arms control measures of the 1960s and beyond.

The British as Mediators: The Quota Proposal for On-Site Inspections

The battle about dropping the link was not over when a new obstacle emerged. Data obtained from underground tests in the summer of 1958 (HARDTACK) convinced the American scientific community (including test ban supporters such as Hans Bethe) that the recommendations of the Geneva Conference of Experts were based on overly optimistic assumptions regarding the detectability of underground tests.[39] While the new data hardened the U.S. position immediately, Macmillan was not convinced. He thought that public opinion might not appreciate the new data as genuine and perceive them as a pretext for blocking agreement.[40]

On-site inspections on Soviet territory then emerged as the major stumbling block toward a test ban, and the British began to work on a compromise solution on this issue. Their outlook on the verification problem was different from the American attitude. While the U.S. admini-

---

was hoped for. See "Memorandum to Dr. Killian regarding PSAC meeting on test suspension," Nov. 21, 1958, NSA:NNP, 1958; "Letter by U.K. Ambassador," Dec. 24, PRO:FO 371/132697.

[37] For details see "Foreign Office to Washington," Nov. 25, 1958, PRO:FO 371/132693; "Embassy Washington to Foreign Office," Nov. 26, ibid.; "Embassy Washington to Foreign Office," Dec. 1, 1958; "Extract of telephone conversation with the Secretary and Christian Herter," Dec. 8, NA, 600.0012/12–858; "Embassy Washington to Foreign Office," Dec. 9, PRO:FO 371/132695.

[38] For Macmillan's message, see his *Riding the Storm*, 569–70. For the U.S. decision-making process, see "Memorandum of conference with the President," Jan. 5, 1959, NSA: NNP, 1959; "Memorandum of conversation with the President," Jan. 12, ibid.; "Letter by President Eisenhower to Prime Minister Macmillan," Jan. 12, ibid.

[39] For details see Jacobson and Stein, *Diplomats, Scientists, and Politicians*, 145–62.

[40] See "Minute about reaction from the Prime Minister on HARDTACK," Dec. 22, 1958, PRO:FO 371/132697.

stration—including many test ban supporters—was primarily concerned about the technical verifiability of an agreement, the British adopted a more political attitude. They argued that adequate, not comprehensive verifiability, was sufficient and that opening up the closed Soviet system to on-site inspections was more important than insuring that a test ban could be verified 100 percent.[41]

In January 1959 the head of the British delegation in Geneva, David Ormsby-Gore, had a private conversation with the chief Soviet scientist, during which the latter indicated that Moscow might be prepared to accept a limited number of on-site inspections.[42] About a week later, Ormsby-Gore proposed a quota on the number of on-site inspections to John Foster Dulles.[43]

At the time, the British prime minister prepared for a visit to the Soviet Union and was determined to achieve some progress in East-West relations. Three days before Macmillan left for Moscow, he sent a message to President Eisenhower in which he suggested the quota proposal. U.S. officials were skeptical. Since test ban supporters faced an uphill battle in the administration because of the new data from the underground tests, they took the British proposal as hard to sell internally. While State Department officials signaled to the British that their suggestion might be acceptable in due time, even the president's science adviser raised objections. Eisenhower wrote back to Macmillan that "we should contemplate no proposals of this type" unless other points had been settled with the Soviets.[44]

[41] The British attitude reflected an approach to arms control emphasizing the political significance of security cooperation and arms control instead of technical solutions. See, for example, Hedley Bull, *The Control of the Arms Race* (London: Weidenfeld & Nicolson, 1961).

[42] See "Memorandum of conversation with Soviets at dinner party," Jan. 28, 1959, PRO:FO 371/140483; "Memorandum by Ormsby-Gore," Feb. 3, PRO:FO 371/140435.

[43] See "Discussions with Mr. Dulles on the nuclear test conference," Feb. 5, 1959, PRO:FO 371/140435. This was apparently the first time that the idea was mentioned to a U.S. official. On February 9, Prime Minister Macmillan approved the proposal. See "Minute by Mr. O'Neill, Foreign Office," Feb. 10, PRO:FO 371/140483. Two days later, a memorandum with the suggestion was handed over to the State Department, PRO:FO 371/140481.

[44] "President Eisenhower to Prime Minister Macmillan," Feb. 23, 1959, PRO:FO 371/140486. See also "Prime Minister Macmillan to President Eisenhower," Feb. 20, PRO:FO 371/140481. For the initial U.S. reactions, see "Embassy Washington to Foreign Office," Feb. 18, PRO:FO 371/140485; "Memorandum of Conference with the President," Feb. 25, NSA:NNP, 1959.

There is some confusion in the literature as to whether the British consulted the United States before Macmillan put forward his proposal to Khrushchev (see Freeman, *Britain's Nuclear Arms Control Policy*, 94). The evidence suggests that, first, U.S. officials including the president knew about the British proposal before Macmillan raised the issue in Moscow. But second, the British did not indicate clearly to American officials whether the proposal would be conveyed to the Soviet Union. Third, when Macmillan arrived in Moscow, the

When the president's letter reached the prime minister in Moscow, it was too late. Macmillan had already conveyed the proposal to Nikita Khrushchev, who reacted favorably. Macmillan even suggested some figures to the Soviet leader to illustrate his proposal ranging from three to twelve obligatory on-site inspections every one to two years. The British prime minister acted completely on his own. The London government had not reached conclusions on possible figures, and no numbers had been discussed with the Americans. Twelve to twenty-four inspections per year were considered internally. Three on-site inspections per year were considerably fewer than were thought possible at the time. No wonder that the British removed the figure from the printed record of the Moscow talks shown to the United States.[45] The Soviets could not know that the British prime minister was merely floating ideas when he mentioned numbers. Three inspections later became part of the Soviet bargaining position and kept haunting the Kennedy administration.[46]

In sum, Macmillan negotiated on his own in Moscow and mediated between the United States and the Soviet Union. Since PSAC opposed the British proposal and the State Department reacted in a lukewarm way, London could not count on a transgovernmental coalition tipping the balance in Washington. While Senator Humphrey made a similar proposal in early March, he did not carry much weight with the Republican administration. When Macmillan visited Washington at the end of March, he was unable to move Eisenhower toward seriously considering the quota proposal.[47]

Khrushchev's public support for the quota proposal on April 23 created new momentum in Washington. Macmillan immediately pushed for a positive American response. This time, the State Department—together

---

British knew about the American objections. In sum, the British played a double-game with the United States and Macmillan's interpretation of Eisenhower's letter as "not altogether discouraging" stretches it a bit (*Riding the Storm*, 601).

[45] "Since this information is so extremely sensitive from the point of view of the Americans and the other allies we are leaving it out of the printed record referred to above." (Letter by Sir Patrick Dean, Foreign Office, to Sir Richard Powell, Ministry of Defense, March 7, 1959, PRO:FO 371/140486). This letter contains details about the numbers Macmillan proposed to the Soviets. Even the Foreign Office thought that the prime minister had gone too far. See also Macmillan's account of his talks in Moscow in *Riding the Storm*, 599–609.

[46] As John McCloy, Kennedy's disarmament adviser, remarked in a meeting, "Prime Minister Macmillan had in a sense pulled the rug out from under us by telling Khrushchev during his visit to Moscow that a lower number of inspections would be acceptable to the West." (Seaborg, *Kennedy, Khrushchev*, 41)

[47] See Macmillan, *Riding the Storm*, 648; "Record of meeting held at Camp David," March 21, 1959, PRO:FO 371/140516; "Record of meeting held at Camp David," March 22, ibid.; "Memorandum for the file by John McCone regarding discussions with Foreign Secretary Selwyn Lloyd," March 23, NSA:NNP, 1959; "Minutes of meeting of interdepartmental working group on disarmament," March 25, ibid.

with the U.S. delegation in Geneva—cautiously supported the British view in the internal meetings, while PSAC continued to join the opposition of the Pentagon, the military, and the AEC. At the final White House meeting, the president indicated his support for the British position that, "by proper locations of stations, we can go a long way toward determining whether a shock is an earthquake or an atomic explosion. . . . we have got to be ready to do something reasonable or we will have great demands put upon us by the public."[48] Eisenhower and Macmillan then responded to Khrushchev and declared their willingness to "explore" the possibility of annual quotas of on-site inspections. London had again succeeded in moving the American position closer to a compromise.

Combining a Threshold Test Ban with a Moratorium on Underground Tests

When the HARDTACK data called into question the Geneva Experts' system, the U.S. Atomic Energy Commission and others began to push for a treaty banning atmospheric tests (ATBT) only. When Eisenhower approached Macmillan in early March 1959, the British were not delighted about giving up the idea of a comprehensive test ban. They proposed that an ATBT should at least be accompanied by a two-year moratorium on underground tests. During that time, scientific research should be carried out to establish a new seismic verification scheme for a comprehensive agreement.[49] Eisenhower indicated his opposition; he was apparently concerned that an uncontrolled moratorium might impede the ratification of an ATBT in the U.S. Senate. The president promised, however, to come back to the British suggestion if the Soviets rejected an ATBT proposal.[50] About a year later, a modified version of the British proposal to combine a limited test ban treaty with a moratorium on underground tests almost led to an agreement.

During the summer of 1959, the Anglo-American transgovernmental coalition comprised of scientists, the two delegations in Geneva, the State Department, and the British Foreign Office reemerged and again influenced the U.S. negotiating position. Secretary of State Christian Herter,

[48] "Memorandum of conference with the President," May 5, 1959, NSA:NNP, 1959. See also Christian Herter, "Memorandum of conversation with the President," May 2, NA 600.0012/5–259; "Message by Prime Minister Macmillan to President Eisenhower," April 29, PRO:FO 371/140438.

[49] For details on the U.S. position, see "Memorandum of Conference with the President," Feb. 17, 1959, NSA:NNP, 1959; "State Dept. to Embassy London" (message from Eisenhower to Macmillan), March 9, ibid. On the British position see "Minute of Meeting at No. 10 Downing Street," March 16, PRO:FO 371/140436; "Memorandum by Secretary of State for Washington Talks," March 17, ibid.

[50] See the letter exchange between President Eisenhower and Prime Minister Macmillan April 6–10, 1959, PRO:FO 371/140437.

John Foster Dulles's successor, indicated to the British that the United States might accept their view at some point and would certainly not object if London declared unilaterally not to conduct underground tests. He also told Selwyn Lloyd that the State Department accepted the British position on quota inspections, while the Pentagon was still opposed. In August U.S. scientists met with their British counterparts in London to discuss the HARDTACK data. The British made clear that they did not agree with the alarmist interpretation of the new data and that there was still room for compromise on a comprehensive test ban.[51] It turned out three years later that they were right.

Toward the end of the year, the differences between the American and the British approaches became more and more obvious. At a State Department meeting in early November, Secretary Herter argued that "it would be difficult for us to proceed on our present course of action if the British would not go along with us." State Department officials used the British demands in the inter-agency meetings to push their own cause in favor of a limited agreement and a continued moratorium. AEC Chairman McCone wondered "whether we were getting ourselves into a position of policy control by the UK."[52]

At about the same time, PSAC scientists and State Department officials began to push for a twenty-kiloton threshold test ban treaty (TTBT) that would apply even to underground tests. George Kistiakowsky, the new science adviser to the president, reported that he had reached an agreement with AEC Chairman McCone in favor of a treaty linking the level of the threshold to the number of inspections accepted by the Soviets. By early January 1960, PSAC recommended a threshold agreement with a limit at about twenty kilotons.[53]

[51] On the Anglo-American discussions among scientists, see Killian, *Sputnik, Scientists, and Eisenhower*, 168; Kistiakowsky, *A Scientist at the White House*, 38; interview with Hans Bethe. On the talks involving Herter and Selwyn Lloyd, see "Record of conversation between the Secretary of State and Mr. Herter," June 20, 1959, PRO:FO 371/140517; "Record of conversation at Mr. Herter's villa in Geneva," July 23, ibid.; "U.K. Delegation to Foreign Minister's meeting to Foreign Office concerning conversation with Mr. Herter," Aug. 1, PRO:FO 371/140518.

[52] "Memorandum of meeting with the Vice President," Dec. 11, 1959, NSA:NNP, 1959. The first quote is taken from "Memorandum of conversation, subject: Meeting of the Secretary's disarmament advisors," Nov. 3, NA 600.0012/11–359. See also Macmillan, *Pointing the Way* (London: Macmillan, 1972), 100–109.

[53] On Kistiakowsky's and PSAC's activities, see Kistiakowsky, *A Scientist at the White House*, 198, 211, 222–23. Cf. also Philip Farley, "Memorandum for Secretary regarding 'course of action in nuclear test negotiations,' " Dec. 26, 1959, NA 751.5611/12–2659; "Memorandum of conference with the President," Dec. 29, NSA:NNP, 1959. The British were well informed about the deliberations inside the administration. See, for example, "Letter by C. D. Wiggin, Embassy Washington, to H. C. Hainworth, Foreign Office," Dec. 30, PRO:FO 371/149269.

Test ban supporters in the United States repeatedly asked the British to put pressure on the American decision-makers. In early January, for example, an aide to Senator Humphrey told a British official that the senator "had lost hope in any initiative from the president and he therefore looked to the prime minister." Dr. Killian, Eisenhower's former science adviser, asked the British to "continue to press these views upon the United States administration." In early March the U.S. chief negotiator in Geneva argued that "an intervention from our [the British] side, perhaps at the highest level, would carry more weight than his own representation."[54] These and other conversations indicate the conviction of test ban supporters in the United States that domestic pressure alone was insufficient to change the American position.

The British mounted a major effort to convince the United States that a threshold treaty was only negotiable if combined with a moratorium on *all* underground tests. On January 14, Selwyn Lloyd wrote to Secretary Herter:

> If we were to insist on a treaty which left open the possibility of underground testing below a specified magnitude I think that the Russians would break off the negotiations. . . . I am afraid the odium of failure to reach an agreement would thus fall on the West. Unjust though this would be, I do not think that in the present state of world opinion . . . we can afford to allow this to happen.

The accompanying cable instructed the British ambassador in Washington to leave Herter "in no doubt about the strength of our feeling."[55] When Herter's response did not satisfy the Foreign Office, Selwyn Lloyd wrote another, rather angry letter indicating the profound differences between the U.S. and the British views. He also told Herter confidentially that he was suggesting that Macmillan should write to the president. As a result, Herter proposed tabling the threshold test ban treaty in Geneva while keeping the moratorium question open, since it would not be part of a treaty anyway.

At the same time, Herter tried to blackmail the British, arguing "that any open split between us on the nuclear testing issue might have repercussions on our defence cooperation in the nuclear field." He particularly pointed to the unpredictability of the JCS. As a result, the British foreign secretary backed off temporarily. In the meantime, Macmillan had already decided against a message to Eisenhower, since he did "not want to

[54] "Delegation Geneva to Foreign Office," March 4, 1960, PRO:FO 371/149282. For the other quotes see David Ormsby-Gore's memorandum of conversation, Feb. 4, PRO:FO 371/149276; Ormsby-Gore's memorandum of conversation, Jan. 5, PRO:FO 371/149269.

[55] "Foreign Office to Embassy Washington," Jan. 16, 1960, PRO:FO 371/149272. The first quote is taken from "Foreign Office to Embassy Washington," Jan. 14, PRO:FO 371/149273.

come up against a blank wall with the President. He has evidently taken a position on this and now that it has become public it would be difficult for him to retreat from it at once."[56] In this instance, the United States used its power to prevent further interventions by the British. At the same time, an informal norm of the transatlantic alliance not to embarrass each other in public worked *against* allied influence on American policies. But when Eisenhower was asked during a press conference whether the United States would resume testing, he answered that such a decision had to be decided with the allies, indirectly allowing the British a veto on the issue.[57]

When the U.S. negotiator tabled the new proposal on February 12, stating that the United States would feel free to test below the threshold, the British negotiator reserved the position of his government on the issue. He went as far as he could in such talks without revealing the extent of the Anglo-American split. As the British had predicted, the Soviets concentrated their attacks on the possibility of renewed U.S. nuclear tests. At the same time, they indicated that they might accept a TTBT that included a moratorium on all underground tests.[58]

Throughout February, the negotiations made some progress regarding both the threshold and the quota proposals; test ban supporters in the administration gained ground. In light of these developments, the British went so far as to suggest to the Soviets not to make further concessions, because they might be counterproductive given developments in Washington. When the Soviet negotiator Tsarapkin suggested to David Ormsby-Gore that Moscow could accept a moratorium outside a formal treaty, the British advised strongly against tabling such a proposal, because "if there is a danger of such a compromise being turned down coming from the British, then the danger would be infinitely greater when it came from the Soviet Union."[59] Shortly afterward, the Soviets tabled their accep-

[56] "Memorandum by the Prime Minister to Selwyn Lloyd," Jan. 29, 1960, PRO:FO 371/149276. On the exchange between Selwyn Lloyd and Herter see "Foreign Office to Embassy Washington," Jan. 27, ibid.; "Christian Herter to Selwyn Lloyd," Feb. 2, ibid.; "Embassy Washington to Foreign Office," Feb. 4, ibid.; "Foreign Office to Embassy Washington," Feb. 5, ibid.

[57] In both cases, the norms governing the allied relationship served as convenient excuses for both statesmen. Macmillan might have given up on the idea of influencing Eisenhower and used the norm to justify his behavior. For Eisenhower, blaming allied insistence for a decision not to resume testing was a convenient way to overcome domestic pressures in favor of testing.

[58] For details see the cables by the U.K. delegation Geneva to the Foreign Office, Feb. 11, 1960, PRO:FO 371/149278; Feb. 12, 1960, PRO:FO 371/149279; Feb. 16, ibid. See also "Memorandum by Selwyn Lloyd to the Prime Minister," Feb. 23, PRO:FO 371/149280. For a general discussion of this phase of the Geneva negotiations see Jacobson and Stein, *Diplomats, Scientists, and Politicians*, 238–46.

[59] David Ormsby-Gore, "Letter to Selwyn Lloyd," March 18, 1960, PRO:FO 371/149284. See also cables by the U.K. delegation Geneva to the Foreign Office, March 2, and March 4, PRO:FO 371/149282.

tance of the TTBT coupled with a moratorium below the threshold as part of the agreement.

Now the British went for the homestretch and increased their pressure on Washington. Macmillan called Eisenhower and essentially invited himself to Washington:

> **Eisenhower**: In the meantime, we are looking at the thing [the moratorium] very sympathetically and it looks like we have made a little mileage. . . .
> **Macmillan**: It would be wonderful if it could be tied up by you. I want you to do this job [conclude a test ban treaty]. . . . I would slip over and see you, if you liked, on Saturday or Sunday. We could have a game of golf and a little talk.[60]

These and other telephone conversations had the desired effect. The British demands for high-level talks in Washington tipped the balance in their favor inside the administration. On March 24, the president overruled the Pentagon and the AEC and decided to offer a one-to-two-year moratorium outside a treaty. This was one year less than the British had asked for, but the U.S. accepted in essence London's long-held position.[61] When Macmillan visited Eisenhower at Camp David, the issue was basically settled and the two heads of government announced their agreement "to institute a voluntary moratorium of agreed duration on nuclear weapons tests below that threshold, to be accomplished by unilateral declaration of each of the three powers," as soon as the threshold test ban agreement was signed.[62]

This was the closest the Eisenhower administration came to the conclusion of a test ban agreement. The Anglo-American proposals were taken to the Paris four-power summit in May 1960 in order to conclude the agreement with Khrushchev. But then the Soviets shot down a U-2 reconnaissance plane, resulting in renewed confrontation between the superpowers and the cancellation of the summit by Khrushchev. Arms control opponents in Washington used the incident to renew their attacks on a test ban.

[60] "Record of telephone conversation between the Prime Minister and the President," March 21, 1960, PRO:PREM 11/2994. In another example of transgovernmental networking, Secretary of State Herter had suggested to Macmillan that he phone the president. See Macmillan, *Pointing the Way*, 186.

[61] For accounts of the meetings in Washington, see Kistiakowsky, *A Scientist at the White House*, 279–82. See also Macmillan, *Pointing the Way*, 188–89; "Aide Mémoire by U.S. Government to Her Majesty's Government," March 28, 1960, PRO:FO 371/149284.

[62] "Joint Declaration about Nuclear Tests," March 29, 1960, PRO:PREM 11/2994. See also Macmillan, *Pointing the Way*, 190–91; Kistiakowsky, *A Scientist at the White House*, 286–87; "Meeting of the President with the Prime Minister," March 29, NSA:NNP, January–August 1960.

Keeping the Pressure Up: British Efforts during the Kennedy Administration

The stalemate inside the U.S. government gave way to a slightly more positive attitude toward a test ban when the Kennedy administration entered office. Robert McNamara, the new secretary of defense, and Glenn Seaborg, the new AEC chairman, were more inclined to look favorably at an agreement than their predecessors. The creation of the Arms Control and Disarmament Agency (ACDA) gave arms control supporters a bureaucratic foothold in the administration. However, test ban opponents continued to lobby Congress and, given the requirements for treaty ratification, continued to have powerful tools at their disposal to block progress toward an agreement.

The British continued to push. Kennedy and Macmillan developed an even closer personal relationship than was the case under Eisenhower. Kennedy's science adviser, Jerome Wiesner, was a close friend of Solly Zuckerman, his British counterpart.[63] Most important, David Ormsby-Gore, the new British ambassador in Washington, had not only been London's chief negotiator at the Geneva talks, but was also a long-term friend of the new president. At least part of Kennedy's personal views of a test ban resulted from Ormsby-Gore's influence when Kennedy was still in the Senate. The British ambassador then became a truly transgovernmental actor in the sense that he remained one of Kennedy's close advisers and, at the same time, the representative of his government in Washington. Ormsby-Gore's identification with the United States went so far that he once promised Kennedy to "heed your parting advice about arguing our [the British] nuclear matters in terms of *our* interests, not yours."[64]

After the conclusion of a comprehensive policy review in Washington, the Unites States and the United Kingdom tabled a complete draft treaty at the Geneva negotiations in April 1961, which came considerably closer to the British position than Eisenhower's latest proposals. The two states suggested a threshold test ban and a three-year moratorium on underground tests below the threshold. The verification scheme included nineteen internationally staffed seismic detection stations inside the Soviet

[63] Zuckerman reports the following episode in his memoirs: "One day Jerry [Wiesner] telephoned to say that his man was 'getting cold', and would I get mine (i.e., Macmillan) to give him a shove. The code was somewhat obscure, but the message clear enough." Zuckerman, *Monkeys, Men, and Missiles*, 323.

[64] Quoted in Michael Beschloss, *The Crisis Years* (New York: Edward Burlingame Books, 1991), 493 [emphasis in original]. On Ormsby-Gore's earlier advice to Kennedy, see ibid., 84. On Anglo-American relations during the Kennedy years, see David Nunnerly, *President Kennedy and Britain* (London: Bodley Head, 1972).

Union and a maximum of twenty annual on-site inspections for each of the three nuclear powers. However, the Soviets rejected this as well as subsequent concessions.[65]

During the Vienna summit in June 1961, Khrushchev accepted three on-site inspections per year, even though a Soviet official had hinted before that the USSR might agree to the Anglo-American figure. After the U.S.-Soviet confrontation in Vienna, however, pressure in Congress and by the military increased to resume nuclear tests. The British embarked upon a major campaign to prevent such a U.S. move. An inquiry at U.S. embassies also indicated that Washington would face a grave setback in world opinion, if it decided to resume testing first. A PSAC panel concluded that there was no immediate military need for testing. The State Department argued that "the dominant factors to be considered in determining U.S. policy on this question in the immediate future are those relating to the over-all posture of the United States as regards our allies, world opinion, and the USSR."[66] Kennedy wrote a letter to Macmillan in early August stating that he had decided to make one more effort at the Geneva talks and not to resume testing in 1961 unless the Soviets did so, but that he probably could not wait much longer.

Christmas Island and the Resumption of U.S. Atmospheric Tests

The Soviet resumption of atmospheric tests on September 1 dealt a severe blow to efforts to prevent U.S. nuclear tests. The pressure on the president to respond in kind became insurmountable. In mid-September, the United States resumed underground nuclear tests. The main controversy now centered around whether to recommence atmospheric tests. The following instance represents an example of issue-specific power, "two-level games," and alliance norms in Anglo-American bargaining.

In late October, Prime Minister Macmillan proposed announcing a six-month moratorium on atmospheric testing. Kennedy's national security adviser, McGeorge Bundy, interpreted this as an attempt "to get hooked to an agreement not to test without his consent. This is dirty pool." He also doubted that the British Foreign Office and the U.K. ambassador

[65] Cf. details in Seaborg, *Kennedy, Khrushchev*, 41–60. For the following see Beschloss, *Crisis Years*, 213; "Extract from transcript of Vienna talks between President Kennedy and Chairman Khrushchev," June 4, 1961, in Library of Congress, W. A. Harriman-Papers (WAH), Box 560, TBT-Background 1.

[66] George Ball, "Memorandum for the President, subject: report of panel on nuclear testing," Aug. 4, 1961, NSA:NNP, 1961. See the PSAC panel report, ibid. On the British pressures and the inquiry with U.S. embassies, see Seaborg, *Kennedy, Khrushchev*, 65, 66–68. For the following, see John F. Kennedy, "Letter to Macmillan," Aug. 3, NSA:NNP, 1961.

supported Macmillan's view.[67] The proposal was turned down but did not prevent London from further approaches.

While the British firmly opposed the resumption of atmospheric testing, they requested permission to detonate their own nuclear device at the U.S. underground test site in Nevada. At the same time, the U.S. government wanted to retain the option of conducting atmospheric tests at the British-owned Christmas Island in the Pacific. Knowing the British objections to atmospheric testing, the U.S. found it necessary to attempt issue linkage and to "pool this request [use of Nevada test site] into the Christmas Island issue for whatever bargaining power it might hold."[68] Kennedy granted the British request for underground tests in Nevada and, at the same time, asked "for early assurance" that the United States could use Christmas Island. He did not formally link the two issues, but created a moral obligation for the British to reciprocate.

Neither the power asymmetry between the two states nor the norms of the Anglo-American relationship would have allowed the British to pocket the American concession and deny the request for Christmas Island.[69] Instead, the British replied to the American moral issue linkage with a similar attempt of their own by connecting their consent to the American use of Christmas Island to a new attempt at negotiations. At first, Macmillan asked for more information on the purpose of the planned tests and suggested that he should meet Kennedy to discuss the issue. As a result, work at the island could not begin right away, as the United States had planned. Officials then learned that the British wanted to know very specific details about the tests; the president decided to grant them this request. American officials became quite concerned that the British would assume a veto position over the U.S. testing program and recommended that "we make it clear to the British that the U.S. decision whether or not to test in the atmosphere was independent of whether they granted the use of Christmas island; we had to retain control of our own test program."[70] The British attempt at issue linkage was rejected.

[67] See McGeorge Bundy, "Memorandum for the President, subject: talk with Macmillan," Oct. 27, 1961, NSA:NNP, 1961. The memorandum contains the quote. See also Seaborg, *Kennedy, Khrushchev*, 108–9, 113–14.

[68] McGeorge Bundy to Seaborg, according to Seaborg, *Kennedy, Khrushchev*, 117. For the British request to use the Nevada test site, see Macmillan's message to Kennedy, Nov. 3, 1961, PRO:PREM 11/3706. For the following see Kennedy's message to Macmillan, Nov. 11, ibid.; Seaborg, *Kennedy, Khrushchev*, 117–18.

[69] As Macmillan told Solly Zuckerman: "I've been reading all these minutes of yours about Christmas Island, and I want you to know that I agree completely with you. Yet there are reasons which make it impossible for me to say 'no' to the President. But I also know that I shall live to regret what I have to do" (Zuckerman, *Monkeys, Men, and Missiles*, 320).

[70] Seaborg, *Kennedy, Khrushchev*, 125. For the following, see ibid., 126–30; Freeman, *Britain's Nuclear Arms Control Policy*, 111–13; Alistair Horne, *Macmillan, 1957–1986* (London: Macmillan, 1989), 321–26; Zuckerman, *Monkeys, Men, and Missiles*, 320–22.

During the Bermuda summit between the president and the prime minister in December 1961, Macmillan pushed Kennedy hard toward a new arms control effort. The president made it privately clear to Macmillan that he felt close to the British view but faced tough domestic constraints, particularly in the Senate. The prime minister replied with his own "two-level game" and insisted that he needed cabinet approval to permit the U.S. preparations for tests at Christmas Island.

In early January 1962, Macmillan wrote a long letter to Kennedy, which an American official called a "hysterical document" practicing "emotional blackmail." The prime minister agreed to make Christmas Island available to the United States but expected full consultation prior to a decision for atmospheric tests and a new arms control initiative. He suggested a foreign ministers meeting of the nuclear powers prior to the opening of the Geneva 18 Nation Disarmament Committee (ENDC), scheduled for March.[71] While Macmillan did not make his agreement to grant the Christ mas Island facilities conditional upon U.S. approval of a new initiative, he told Kennedy through Ormsby-Gore that he would need another cabinet meeting if the president refused to agree to his proposal.

The president replied that he was in favor of a new arms control initiative, but made it quite clear that he did not accept issue linkage:

> I would hope very much that the Cabinet would not intend a coupling of this sort. . . . I am sure from our previous talks that you understand the requirement on me, as President, to retain freedom to prepare to test, and freedom to test, on the basis of the whole situation and the best judgement available at the time. . . . In particular it would seem wrong, at this stage, to make any definite link between the timing of tests and the progress of new efforts toward disarmament.[72]

While the British had successfully moved the United States toward a new arms control appeal to Khrushchev, they gave in on this last point. They insisted on "full consultation" regarding the start of the new test series but agreed to make Christmas Island available to the United States without attaching further conditions. In early February, Macmillan and Kennedy

[71] Macmillan's letter to Kennedy, Jan. 5, 1962, quoted from Macmillan, *At the End of the Day* (London: Macmillan, 1973), 154–62. The quotes from an American State Department official are taken from Beschloss, *Crisis Years*, 363. For the following see Macmillan's message to Ormsby-Gore, Jan. 5, PRO:PREM 11/4041; Ormsby-Gore's message to the prime minister, Jan. 10, ibid.

[72] "John F. Kennedy to Macmillan," Jan. 13, 1962, PRO:PREM 11/4041. See also "Ormsby-Gore to Macmillan," Jan. 13, ibid.; Freeman, *Britain's Nuclear Arms Control Policy*, 114. For the following see "Prime Minister to the President," Jan. 16, PRO:PREM 11/4041; "Prime Minister to Ormsby-Gore," Jan. 16, ibid.; "Ormsby-Gore to Prime Minister," Jan. 18, ibid.; "Prime Minister to Ormsby-Gore," Jan. 18, ibid.; "Embassy Washington to Foreign Office," Jan. 20, ibid. See also Macmillan, *End of the Day*, 153–68.

issued a joint appeal to Khrushchev that the ENDC should be started at the foreign minister level. After some bickering the Soviet leader agreed. On March 2 Kennedy announced that the United States would resume atmospheric testing at the end of April unless the Soviet Union would sign a test ban treaty before that. Both the ultimate timing of the tests and the wording of the announcement had been proposed by the British.[73]

In sum, the British succeeded insofar as the new joint initiative was concerned. They were unable to prevent the resumption of U.S. atmospheric tests, though, since both the Pentagon and the State Department, not to mention the AEC and the military, supported resumption.[74] Thus, London lacked allies inside the administration. Both sides attempted power bargaining on the issue. The United States tried to link the British tests at the Nevada side to the Christmas Island issue, while London coupled the latter to a new arms control initiative. Since attempts at issue linkage to increase bargaining leverage were incompatible with appropriate behavior in the Anglo-American relationship, London and Washington went to great lengths to phrase their respective undertakings in non-threatening language. In this particular case, reference to norms covered old-fashioned power bargaining.

Toward a New Negotiating Proposal

While the United States was now prepared to undertake a new arms control initiative in parallel to its resumption of atmospheric tests, the president had not yet decided on the content of a proposal. Throughout the spring and summer of 1962, a transgovernmental coalition including State Department officials, PSAC, the Geneva delegations, and their British counterparts gradually moved the United States position closer to a compromise, against opposition by the AEC, the military, and the JCAE.

Beginning in late January 1962, the British lobbied hard for further American concessions with regard to

- transforming the 1961 draft treaty from a threshold test ban into a *comprehensive* test stop agreement;
- reducing the number of control posts and on-site inspections in the Soviet Union.

[73] See "President to Prime Minister," Feb. 27, 1962, PRO:PREM 11/4042; "Ormsby-Gore to Prime Minister," Feb. 28, ibid.; "Prime Minister to President," Feb. 28, ibid.; "Prime Minister to Ormsby-Gore," March 1, PRO:PREM 11/4043; Seaborg, *Kennedy, Khrushchev*, 136–39.

[74] See Robert McNamara, "Memorandum to the President," Feb. 1, 1962, NSA:NNP, January–May 1962; Dean Rusk, "Memorandum for the President," Feb. 20, ibid.

In early March, Ormsby-Gore suggested three on-site inspections plus additional ones in case of suspicious events.[75] He, thus, came back to Macmillan's suggestion to Khrushchev in 1959. Ormsby-Gore's proposal became the official British position and was presented to the United States, which reacted with utmost caution at first. During various White House meetings, the president indicated that he personally supported moving toward the British position and that "it was most important that we avoid a split" with London on this.[76] But he was unable to move the administration in light of sharp opposition by the military, the AEC, and even Secretary of State Rusk. Ormsby-Gore then succeeded in lobbying Jerome Wiesner, McGeorge Bundy, and the American chief negotiator, Arthur Dean, toward the British view. When the ENDC opened in mid-March, the United States and the United Kingdom proposed a comprehensive test ban with the same verification requirements as the threshold draft treaty of April 1961 and some other concessions. But Soviet Foreign Minister Gromyko rejected any controls on Soviet territory, thus reneging on Khrushchev's own proposal at the Vienna summit.

In the meantime, the British science advisers had concluded from new scientific data that control posts inside the USSR were no longer necessary to monitor a test ban treaty and that national monitoring devices in conjunction with occasional on-site inspections would suffice. When Macmillan suggested this to Kennedy, Ormsby-Gore advised his government that, given the congressional opposition, "the President's room for manoeuvre is . . . strictly limited unless he can present an overwhelming scientific case for any change in the United States position."[77] British scientists were sent to Washington to convince their American colleagues but failed miserably. Their efforts resulted in a confirmation of the previous U.S. position, even though Jerome Wiesner pushed hard for aban-

[75] For this and the following see "Ormsby-Gore to Foreign Office," Jan. 26, 1962, PRO:PREM 11/4041; "Ormsby-Gore to Foreign Office," March 2, PRO:PREM 11/4043; "Foreign Office to Embassy Washington," March 5, ibid.; "Embassy Washington to Foreign Office," March 7, ibid.; "Ormsby-Gore to Foreign Office," March 9, ibid.; Seaborg, *Kennedy, Khrushchev*, 140–43.

[76] In a White House meeting on March 7, quoted from Freeman, *Britain's Nuclear Arms Control Policy*, 118–19.

[77] "Ormsby-Gore to Foreign Office," March 10, 1962, PRO:PREM 11/4043. For this and the following see also "Foreign Office to Embassy Washington," March 7, ibid.; "Memorandum by Solly Zuckerman," March 7, ibid.; "Prime Minister to President," March 10, ibid.; "President to Prime Minister," March 10, ibid.; "Ormsby-Gore to Foreign Office," March 13, ibid.; "Sir Penney to Sir Roger Makins," March 18, PRO:PREM 11/4044; "Ormsby-Gore to Prime Minister," March 19, ibid.; "Zuckerman and Penney to the Prime Minister," March 21, ibid.; "Geneva delegation to Foreign Office," March 26, ibid.; "Foreign Office to Embassy Washington," March 29, ibid.; Macmillan, *End of the Day*, 171–77; Seaborg, *Kennedy, Khrushchev*, 145–49.

doning the insistence on seismic control posts inside the Soviet Union. Shortly afterward, the Swedish and other neutral states tabled in Geneva what the British called a "poor edition" of their proposal.[78]

The joint efforts by test ban supporters inside the administration, the British, and the neutrals to move the United States toward more of a compromise position slowly gained ground because of two developments. First, the resumption of atmospheric tests softened up test ban opponents in the administration and in Congress, at least to some extent. The president told Macmillan that the two governments should work on a new offer for Geneva.[79] Second, findings from the Pentagon's seismic research program VELA showed that verification of a test ban was possible with fewer control posts in the Soviet Union and with less on-site inspections than was previously thought necessary. The results vindicated the British scientists who had suggested exactly that to their American counterparts several months earlier. On July 14 Arthur Dean publicly declared that international detection posts inside the USSR might actually not be needed. His remarks created a stir in Washington, since there was no agreement on a modified U.S. position.[80]

Following Kennedy's suggestion, the U.S. Arms Control Agency, the two Geneva delegations, and the British Foreign Office worked on two draft treaties, one proposing an atmospheric test ban, the other suggesting a comprehensive agreement. The British saw the U.S. draft even before it was cleared with the Pentagon and the AEC.[81] They immediately started to put pressure on the United States, and Ormsby-Gore told the president of "the very difficult situation we would find ourselves in should Congressional opposition prevent the Americans putting forward reasonable control proposals based on the latest scientific assessment."[82] Following various interagency meetings, Kennedy told Macmillan that the United States was now prepared to lower the number of control posts inside the Soviet Union to about five, but also asked to retain the Christmas Island facilities on a standby basis. Macmillan agreed to this request and renewed his appeal for a test ban: "As you know, my own view is that all nuclear tests should be abolished and . . . I do not believe that we should be worse off if this were to happen. Whatever your and our scien-

78 "Foreign Office to Geneva delegation," April 1, 1962, PRO:PREM 11/4045.

79 See "Extract from Record of Meeting held at the White House," April 28, 1962, PRO:PREM 11/4045; "Prime Minister to Secretary of State," May 3, PRO:PREM 11/4046.

80 See Seaborg, *Kennedy, Khrushchev*, 162–64; "Embassy Washington to Foreign Office," July 6, 1962, PRO:PREM 11/4046; "Memorandum for the Prime Minister," July 6, ibid.; "Embassy Washington to Foreign Office," July 7, ibid.

81 For details see "Secretary of State to Prime Minister," May 11, 1962, PRO:PREM 11/4046; "Embassy Washington to Foreign Office," June 12, ibid.; "Embassy Washington to Foreign Office," July 6, ibid.

82 "Ormsby-Gore to Foreign Office," July 25, 1962, PRO:PREM 11/4046.

tists may say, I believe that we could really detect any significant series of Soviet tests if they tried to cheat."[83] The president replied that he could not now give up the idea of control posts on Soviet territory because of domestic opposition but hinted that he might do so if Moscow accepted the principle of on-site inspections. With regard to the latter, the British were now prepared to go below eight to ten inspections. In fact, Foreign Secretary Home had told Gromyko in July that "a very small amount of inspection was essential. It would be only a few people for a few hours."[84]

On August 27, 1962, the United States and the United Kingdom tabled two draft treaties, one containing an atmospheric test ban, the other envisioning a comprehensive agreement that left the number of control posts and on-site inspections open. The Soviets were told privately that it would be considerably lower than those contained in the previous draft. The transgovernmental coalition had moved the American negotiating position considerably toward a compromise. Moscow rejected both drafts immediately.

The Cuban Missile crisis in October 1962 added momentum to the negotiations. In the immediate aftermath of the crisis, the three states came very close to the conclusion of a comprehensive test ban. Right after the crisis, two crucial conversations took place. First, Ambassador Dean apparently told a Soviet official that the United States might be prepared to accept three to four on-site inspections. Second, Jerome Wiesner suggested to a leading Soviet scientist that, if Moscow proposed three to four on-site inspections, the U.S. would probably suggest seven to eight, as a result of which one could settle for five. Since these numbers essentially corresponded to what Macmillan had mentioned to the Soviets in March 1959 and what the British had signaled to them ever since, Khrushchev could well assume that the Americans were signaling a deal. On December 19, Khrushchev declared the Soviet preparedness to accept two to three on-site inspections together with three "black boxes" on Soviet territory.

While the British would have accepted the Soviet position, Kennedy still feared that he might lack the majority in the Senate needed for treaty ratification. In his reply, the president suggested eight to ten annual inspections. He was prepared to accept six. However, the limits of Khrushchev's own domestic base of support had apparently been reached at this

[83] "Prime Minister to the President," Aug. 1, 1962, PRO:PREM 11/4046. See also "President to Prime Minister," July 27, ibid.; "Geneva delegation to Foreign Office," Aug. 1, ibid. On the interagency meetings in the United States, see Seaborg, *Kennedy, Khrushchev*, 164–68. For the following, see "President to Prime Minister," Aug. 3, PRO:PREM 11/4046.

[84] "Record of conversation between Foreign Secretary and Soviet Foreign Minister," July 23, 1962, PRO:PREM 11/4046. See also "Foreign Office to Embassy Washington," Aug. 5, ibid.

point.[85] The incident represents *the* major lost opportunity for the Kennedy administration to achieve a comprehensive test ban. It is somewhat mysterious that the British apparently did not mount a major effort to pressure both sides toward a compromise, as they did in early 1960 when Macmillan invited himself to Washington to push for an agreement. The most likely reason for the British restraint is that the Anglo-American agenda at the time was overloaded with the crisis following the unilateral cancellation of the Skybolt missile by the United States.

In mid-March 1963, when the Geneva negotiations were still deadlocked over the disagreement concerning the number of on-site inspections, Prime Minister Macmillan pushed again for an agreement. In a letter to Kennedy, he suggested five on-site inspections for a comprehensive test ban[86] and, at the same time, proposed to concentrate on an atmospheric test prohibition. His initiative and a visit by SANE leader Norman Cousins to Khrushchev paved the way for the Harriman mission, which concluded the Limited Test Ban Treaty in July 1963.[87] Five years of constant pushing and pulling had finally led to the first nuclear arms control treaty.

U.S. Attempts at Bribery: Dealing with French and German Opposition

Test ban supporters in the United States advocated the cessation of nuclear tests as a nonproliferation measure, directed in particular against attempts by France, Germany, and the People's Republic of China to acquire the bomb.[88] The French government made no secret of its desire to go nuclear and opposed a test ban agreement as a result.

[85] For details see Beschloss, *Crisis Years*, 572–73, 577; Seaborg, *Kennedy, Khrushchev*, 177–81; Jacobson and Stein, *Diplomats, Scientists, and Politicians*, 430–32; "Letter by Khrushchev to Kennedy," Dec. 19, 1962, in National Security Archive, Washington D.C., The Cuban Missile Crisis, 1962 (NSA:CMC), Microfiche collection (Washington: Chadwyck-Healey, 1990), Doc. 02772; "Letter by Kennedy to Khrushchev," Dec. 28, ibid., Doc. 02790; Interview with Raymond Garthoff, Brookings Institution, December 1990.

[86] See Freeman, *Britain's Nuclear Arms Control Policy*, 139–41; Seaborg, *Kennedy, Khrushchev*, 208. At about the same time, a Soviet scientist asked George Kistiakowsky to convey a message from Khrushchev to the White House that the Soviets would compromise on five on-site inspections. When he communicated this to the administration, no action was taken, to his surprise. See Kistiakowsky, *Scientist at the White House*, 423–24.

[87] See Horne, *Macmillan*, 506–608. On the Cousins mission, see Beschloss, *Crisis Years*, 586–88; Knopf, "Domestic Politics, Citizen Activism," 255–57. The British contribution to the Moscow negotiations was fairly limited, since Macmillan trusted Averell Harriman and instructed the British team to fully support the American negotiator.

[88] See, for example, "Memorandum of conference with the President," April 23, 1957, NSA:NNP, 1957; Robert McNamara's speech at the NATO Council, May 5, 1962, NSA: CMC, Doc. 00213; Secretary of Defense, "Memorandum for the President, subject: The

Germany had renounced its intent to produce nuclear weapons in October 1954 as a precondition to its entry into NATO. In 1957 and 1958, however, the Bonn government was involved in a joint French-German-Italian arms cooperation effort that included nuclear weapons. The project was finally stopped by President de Gaulle.[89] The Bonn government's desire to keep the nuclear option open might have motivated its opposition to the test ban. Equally important, Chancellor Adenauer was convinced at the time that attempts at East-West détente should include, if not be preceded by, progress with regard to German reunification.

Neither France nor West Germany influenced the negotiations in a manner comparable to Britain. But both the Eisenhower and Kennedy administrations attempted to at least insure the acquiescence of the two allies by offering side payments and bribes.

Agreement to Disagree: The French

The test ban issue in Franco-American relations was linked to whether Washington should grant Paris nuclear collaboration similar to what London had received. In October 1957, the United States adopted NSC 5721, establishing American opposition to the French nuclear program. At the same time, though, NSC 5707/8 allowed the United States to provide nuclear weapons systems to allies under what became known as "dual-key" arrangements. On various occasions in 1958 and 1959, U.S. officials offered to deliver nuclear-capable weapons to France or to assist in the development of nuclear-powered submarines. But when the French asked to receive information "comparable to that given the UK" under the revised McMahon Act, U.S. officials never gave a clear response, since the AEC was firmly opposed.[90]

Diffusion of Nuclear Weapons with and without a Test Ban Agreement," July 1962, NSA: NNP, June–December 1962. This memorandum estimated the French motivation to continue its nuclear program as "high," while assigning a "moderate" desire to West Germany and a four- to five-year period until Germany could carry out a first test.

[89] For details see Schwarz, "Adenauer und die Kernwaffen;" Colette Barbier, "Les négociations franco-germano-italiennes en vue de l'établissement d'une coopération militaire nucléaire au cours des années 1956–1958," *Revue d'histoire diplomatique* 104, no. 12 (1990): 81–113; Eckart Conze, "La coopération franco-germano-italienne dans le domaine nucléaire dans les années 1957–1958: Un point de vue allemand," ibid., 115–32.

[90] For details, see "340th Meeting of the National Security Council," Oct. 17, 1957, NA, RG273, NSC, Box 67, Minutes; "Memorandum of conversation at the State Department with the French Ambassador," June 25, 1958, NA 711.5611/6–2558; "Memorandum for the President, subject: Offer of Nuclear-Capable Weapons to France," July 1, 1959, NSA:NNP, 1959; "Briefing Note for the NSC meeting," Aug. 18, 1959, NA, NSC, 417 Mtg., Box 80; "State Dept. outgoing telegram to U.S. Embassy Paris," Aug. 19, 1959, NSA:NNP, 1959.

After France had conducted its first nuclear tests, the NSC established that the country

In contrast to the British, French officials rarely explored the extent to which the Americans were prepared to assist them in the nuclear field. They hardly tried to form transgovernmental alliances that the British used so effectively to influence American policies. They could have aligned with the Joint Chiefs of Staff, for example, who supported an independent French nuclear force as an addition to the Western deterrence capability. Charles de Gaulle went full speed ahead with the French nuclear program and made it clear that he did not want to get entangled in interallied nuclear cooperation efforts that might hinder French independence.

The French government consistently refused to become involved in the test ban negotiations. Washington and Paris agreed to disagree with regard to nuclear arms control. But the American and British governments tried to accommodate Paris on several occasions during the negotiations. The British made sure, for example, that France was included in the 1958 Geneva Conference of Experts (see above). Originally, the United States had planned to exclude Canadian and French scientists from the meeting.[91] During the fall of 1959, when France came under heavy pressure from African and Asian states in the UN General Assembly to abandon its planned tests in the Sahara, the United States sided with Paris even though its UN delegate had strongly recommended against it.[92] In February 1962 the British government tried to get France involved in the foreign minister meeting at the opening of the Geneva 18 Nations Disarmament Committee. Macmillan received a classic "agree to disagree" reply from President de Gaulle:

> We French are determined to pursue our own tests as far as our means allow and however limited these means may be at the moment. . . . Obviously, if it was only a question of preventing any nuclear tests in the future while permitting the enormous armaments accumulated to continue to exist, France would not subscribe as far as she is concerned . . . without, however,

did not meet the requirements for nuclear collaboration under the amended Atomic Energy Act. See "Memo for the NSC, 'Increased Nuclear Sharing with the Allies,' Annex B," Aug. 23, 1960, NA, MILL 224. These policy statements did not prevent low-level nuclear cooperation between the United States and the French.

[91] See "Embassy Washington to Foreign Office," May 15, 1958, PRO:FO 371/135539; "Foreign Office to Embassy Washington," May 17, ibid.; "Embassy Washington to Foreign Office," May 18, ibid.

[92] See "US UN to State Department," Oct. 23, 1959, NA 751.5611/10–2359; "State Dept. to US UN," Oct. 24, NA 751.5611/10–2459; "US UN to State Dept.," Nov. 5, NA, 751.5611/11–359; "State Dept. to US UN," Nov. 6, NA 751.5611/11–559; "Memorandum of conversation with the French Ambassador," Nov. 6, NA 751.5611/11–659; "Memorandum for the Secretary," Nov. 10, NA 751.5611/11–1059.

making any objection to the Three Powers . . . undertaking in future to abstain from new explosions.[93]

Most important, the Kennedy administration tried to bribe France into accepting the Limited Test Ban Treaty in July 1963. Kennedy indicated to the British that he was prepared to grant France similar access to nuclear information as the British enjoyed, if Paris signed the LTBT. The U.S. ambassador in Paris approached the French foreign minister on the issue, and Averell Harriman was instructed in Moscow to make sure that no treaty provisions prohibited such cooperation.[94] Kennedy wrote de Gaulle on July 24 asking him not to take a firm position against the LTBT. While he recognized that adherence to the agreement would deprive France of significant information regarding nuclear weapons, the United States was prepared to explore ways that could make French tests unnecessary. Kennedy recognized the political and technical problems involved, but was hopeful that they could be overcome in a mutually beneficial way.[95]

This was the most explicit offer of nuclear collaboration the United States had ever made to the French. If de Gaulle had decided to play the issue in a similar way as Macmillan in 1958, France might have been placed on an equal footing with Britain concerning nuclear cooperation with the United States. But the French president turned the American offer down and told Kennedy that France could not receive the help of another state under conditions that limited its right to dispose of these weapons and interfered with its sovereignty.[96] At a press conference three days later, de Gaulle declared that the treaty was of little practical importance unless it would lead to other steps and that France would proceed with its own efforts. Obviously annoyed, Kennedy declared that the United States had made "some suggestions recently as to how cooperation could be more satisfactorily developed if there were a test ban, but we have received no response from the French Government, other than the remarks of General de Gaulle at his press conference."[97] But the presi-

[93] "President de Gaulle to Prime Minister," Feb. 6, 1962, PRO:PREM 11/4041. Two years earlier, Macmillan had received an almost identical response before he traveled to Washington to convince Eisenhower of a test ban. See Macmillan, *Pointing the Way*, 187.

[94] For evidence see Beschloss, *Crisis Years*, 626; Horne, *Macmillan*, 519–20; "State Dept. to Moscow," July 17, 1963, WAH, Container 561, TBT 11.

[95] For details see Daniel Colard and Jean-Francois Guilhaudis, "L'option nucléaire, le problème des essais et la position de la France sur le désarmement," in *L'Aventure de la Bombe*, 281–308, 285. The account is based on notes from Bertrand Goldschmidt, director of the French Commissariat à l'Energie Atomique at the time. See also Beschloss, *Crisis Years*, 626.

[96] According to Colard and Guilhaudis, "L'option nucléaire," 284–85; also Beschloss, *Crisis Years*, 626.

[97] "Press Conference No. 59 of the President of the United States," Aug. 1, 1963, WAH,

dent left the door open and answered affirmatively when asked whether he was prepared to recognize France as a nuclear power in the terms of the Atomic Energy Act.

The incident shows that the Kennedy administration was prepared to grant France nuclear assistance in order to get de Gaulle's signature under the test ban agreement. Kennedy's offer resembles the Eisenhower administration's efforts five years earlier to get British support for the negotiations. President de Gaulle refused, since Franco-American nuclear cooperation would have jeopardized his quest for independence.

Preventing a Nonaggression Pact: The Germans and the Test Ban Agreement

The German government only raised its voice when Harriman negotiated the LTBT in Moscow. Bonn was concerned about two issues. First, a treaty open to any country could be signed by the German Democratic Republic (GDR), as a result of which the international community would implicitly recognize East Germany as a sovereign state. Fortunately, the Soviet Union had a similar problem with the possible accession of Taiwan to the treaty. It was agreed in Moscow through an oral understanding that none of the three depository governments was required to accept ratification documents by a regime that it did not recognize, but that these documents could be deposited with any of the three in order to constitute accession to the treaty. Chancellor Adenauer was not satisfied. He forced Secretary of State Rusk to make a statement before the Senate Foreign Relations Committee that East German subscription to the LTBT did not constitute recognition of the GDR by the United States.[98]

Second and more important, the German government prevented the United States from seriously pursuing a *nonaggression pact* between NATO and the Warsaw Treaty Organization as a follow-up to the LTBT. During the Moscow negotiations, the major issue of contention between the United States and the Soviet Union was not so much the test ban

---

Container 562, TBT 14. Two weeks later, Secretary of State Rusk declared that "I don't want to get into what might be permitted under the treaty itself. I think that if all countries sign the treaty and there were clearly no prohibited explosions, then these issues [of nuclear assistance] would move into another field in terms of nuclear policy, alliance policy, and the rest of it." (ibid.)

[98] For details, see handwritten note by (probably) Adrian Fisher regarding "deposit by unrecognized regimes," Aug. 2, 1963, WAH, Box 562, TBT 15; "Moscow to State Department," July 23, WAH, Box 561, TBT 7; "State Dept. to Moscow," July 24, ibid., TBT 9; Seaborg, *Kennedy, Khrushchev*, 249–50; Hans Jörg Grabbe, *Unionsparteien, Sozialdemokratie und Vereinigte Staaten von Amerika* (Düsseldorf: Droste, 1983), 345–48.

agreement itself; it essentially followed the Anglo-American draft treaty of August 1962. Rather, the issue of a nonaggression agreement came up quickly.

Nikita Khrushchev had established a link in early July 1963 between an atmospheric test prohibition and the conclusion of a nonaggression pact, which had been a long-standing Soviet demand. Both sides had already exchanged papers pertaining to the issue in March 1962. The U.S. position, cleared with the German foreign minister, stated that "force should not be used to change existing frontiers and demarcation lines in Europe or for any other aggressive purpose," explicitly mentioning the intra-German border.[99]

But later on, the Adenauer government strongly rejected the idea of a nonaggression pact and argued that such an agreement would implicitly recognize the political and territorial status quo in Europe, in particular East Germany. The State Department then instructed Harriman to explore the possibility of a nonaggression pact with the Soviets but to reject a linkage and to insist that the issue had to be discussed with NATO before the United States could commit itself.[100]

It quickly became clear in Moscow that the Soviets were serious about Khrushchev's linkage. Harriman asked Washington to approve a draft communiqué that mentioned the Soviet proposal in a positive manner and contained an agreement by both sides to consult with the allies on the desirability of a nonaggression pact. The State Department held a firm line of not committing the United States to anything without allied consultation. After lengthy negotiations—both among the two Western delegations and with the Soviets—a complicated communiqué was adopted: "The heads of the three delegations discussed the Soviet proposal relating to a pact of non-aggression. . . . The three Governments have agreed fully to inform their respective allies . . . and to consult with them about continuing discussions on this question with the purpose of achieving agreement satisfactory to all participants."[101] The Bonn government made

[99] Quoted from George Ball, "Memorandum for the President, 'Analysis of Language of Khrushchev Speech . . .', Annex A," July 2, 1963, WAH, Container 560, TBT-Background. See also "Chronology of Proposed NATO–Warsaw Pact Non-Aggression Pact," undated, ibid., TBT-Background 2. For the following, see the documents ibid.

[100] See Carl Kaysen, "Draft Instructions for Averell Harriman," July 8, 1963, WAH, Container 560, TBT-Background 3. At the same time, Carl Kaysen, McGeorge Bundy's deputy, explored the possibility of a nonaggression pact with West Berlin's mayor Willy Brandt. See his letter to Brandt, July 5, ibid., TBT-Background 1.

[101] "Agreed Communiqué," released on July 25, 1963. See also "Moscow to State Dept.," July 15, WAH, Container 561, TBT 5; "Moscow to State Dept.," July 18, ibid., TBT 6; "Moscow to State Dept.," July 23, ibid., TBT 7; "Moscow to State Dept.," ibid.; "State Dept. to Moscow," July 23, ibid., TBT 9. The British were in favor of a nonaggression

sure that this commitment to further talks led nowhere. Unlike Foreign Minister Schröder, who supported a West German signature of the LTBT, Chancellor Adenauer and many Christian Democrats in Bonn opposed the Moscow agreement. Secretary of State Rusk had to come to Bonn to convince Adenauer to sign the treaty. In exchange, the chancellor apparently received assurances that Washington would not pursue the idea of a nonaggression pact further. The proposal died a gradual death both in the U.S. administration and in NATO. Harriman later complained that the State Department, by giving in to the German demands, was "letting the president down unbelievably," because it did not pursue the consultations promised to the Soviets.[102]

The incident shows the influence of the German government on U.S. foreign policy once Bonn decided to get involved. Bonn's impact is all the more notable, since West Germany had practically no choice with regard to the LTBT. Had it refused to sign the agreement, it would have raised suspicions that it was prepared to go nuclear. Such suspicions would have damaged the German diplomatic position in Europe and with the United States.

Conclusions

This chapter demonstrates that the European allies, in particular the British, continuously influenced U.S. policy during the test ban negotiations. As Glenn Seaborg, Kennedy's AEC chairman, put it: "Considering their relative unimportance as a military force, particularly in nuclear weapons, it is remarkable to consider how much influence the British had over U.S. arms and arms control policies."[103] The insistence to drop the link between disarmament and a test ban in 1958, the quota proposal for on-site inspections in 1959, the suggestion to combine a threshold test ban agreement with a moratorium on underground tests in 1960, the pledge not to resume atmospheric tests without a new arms control initiative in 1962, and the pressures to lower the number of on-site inspections during the

agreement, but the State Department strongly rejected their draft. See "Suggested Language on Nonaggression Pact, handed to Carl Kaysen/William Tyler by Duncan Wilson," July 21, ibid., TBT 8; "State Dept. to Moscow," July 22, ibid., TBT 9.

[102] W. Averell Harriman, "Oral History Interview, 5: Kennedy Period," Feb. 27, 1970, WAH, Container 638, Kennedy School. On the German reaction see Grabbe, *Unionsparteien, Sozialdemokratie*, 345–48; Hoppe, *Zwischen Teilhabe und Mitsprache*, 144–51. See also Henry Owen, "Memorandum to Members of Tuesday Planning Group," Aug. 23, 1963, WAH, Container 561, TBT 12; State Dept., Policy Planning Council, "Steps in a Process Toward Détente," Aug. 23, 1963, ibid., Container 518, USSR General 1963; William Tyler, "Memorandum to the Secretary" [undated], ibid., Container 457, East-West Relations.

[103] Seaborg, *Kennedy, Khrushchev*, 113.

same year: these initiatives originated in London and eventually became the American negotiating position. Moreover, the United States did not pursue a nonaggression pact with the Soviets in order to secure Germany's signature to the treaty. The French unwillingness to influence the American negotiating position only confirms the point. Kennedy attempted to bribe President de Gaulle into signing the LTBT by offering him nuclear collaboration.

European influence on U.S. nuclear testing policies did not concern marginal issues. Each of the proposals and initiatives mentioned above were heavily contested inside the administration and subject to fierce bureaucratic and domestic battles. The test ban case disconfirms the (structural realist) "null hypothesis" of this book, that small allies are unlikely to exert much influence on superpowers when the latter's vital interests are at stake. But what about alternative explanations to account for the outcome?

The Limits of Alternative Explanations: Cooperation Problems, Domestic Politics, and Leadership Beliefs

The LTBT represented a very modest arms control agreement and a far cry from what the British would have preferred, namely a comprehensive test ban. The treaty did little to curb nuclear testing, let alone the U.S.-Soviet arms race in general. One could, therefore, argue that the case essentially confirms realist arguments about the limits of international cooperation, particularly in the security realm. Mutual fears of cheating and concerns that an agreement might favor the other side are frequently cited as obstacles to security cooperation.[104] Indeed, test ban opponents in the United States constantly made these arguments.

Approaches emphasizing the limits of security cooperation, particularly when it comes to fierce hegemonic rivalries such as the cold war, might explain the failure to achieve a comprehensive test ban. But they cannot account for the *success* of the LTBT and the fact that some agreement was reached despite all the obstacles. The focus on cooperation problems in an anarchic international environment appears to be indeterminate with regard to modest arms control achievements. One has to bear in mind in this context that the LTBT was not so much significant because it constrained arms, but because it represented the first in a series of nuclear arms control agreements leading to the Non-Proliferation Treaty,

[104] See, for example, Joseph M. Grieco, "Anarchy and the Limits of Cooperation: A Realist Critique of the Newest Liberal Institutionalism," *International Organization* 42, no. 3 (Summer 1988): 485–507; Robert Jervis, "From Balance to Concert: A Study of International Security Cooperation," in *Cooperation under Anarchy*, ed. Kenneth Oye (Princeton, N.J.: Princeton University Press, 1986), 58–79.

to SALT, and, more generally, to a relaxation of tensions in the East-West conflict, culminating in the European détente of the 1970s. It is, therefore, an important finding that the first nuclear arms control treaty would probably not have been possible without constant pressures by the British.

This is not to suggest that London single-handedly manipulated U.S. foreign policy in the desired direction. Test ban supporters inside and outside the administration constantly demanded an agreement. Presidents Eisenhower and Kennedy both wanted an arms control success. But neither domestic or bureaucratic politics nor leadership beliefs provide a sufficient explanation for the LTBT.

As for domestic politics, test ban advocates consisted of peace activists and public interest groups, independent scientists, the Senate Subcommittee on Disarmament, arms control officials in the State Department, and the Presidential Scientific Advisory Committee. They faced strong opposition from the military, the AEC, the weapons laboratories, and the congressional Joint Committee on Atomic Energy. The latter was particularly significant, since it controlled crucial votes in the Senate, given the two-thirds majority requirement for treaty ratification. This institutional condition provided treaty opponents with a powerful opportunity to block the negotiations and forced Presidents Eisenhower and Kennedy into compromises. The domestic situation in the United States produced a stalemate that could only be overcome when outside actors entered the scene.

This is what allied influence adds to an account focusing on domestic politics. The outcome is hard to explain if domestic and alliance politics are treated separately. The British did not so much change the preferences of the two presidents and other U.S. actors (with the possible exception of Ormsby-Gore's role advising Kennedy when he was a senator). But they frequently introduced new ideas to overcome the U.S.-Soviet deadlock and, more important, added considerable weight to the arguments of domestic test ban supporters. Transgovernmental alliances between administration officials and the British repeatedly tipped the bureaucratic balance in Washington in favor of new negotiating concessions. Transnational coalitions among peace activists and scientists increased the domestic power of test ban supporters in the United States by lending international legitimacy to their arguments. Even the two presidents frequently referred to British pressure and the need to avoid allied tension when they wanted to move the administration toward more forthcoming positions. In sum, the main impact of transnational and transgovernmental coalitions was to increase the "domestic win set" supporting a test ban in the United States.

In the few instances when the British did not weigh in heavily, arms control advocates inside the administration often lost the argument. This was the case in late 1963 when Washington and Moscow were less than five on-site inspections apart from achieving a comprehensive test ban. Macmillan apparently did not mount a major effort to pressure the United States. The administration changed its position only marginally and the opportunity was lost.

But it is also true that the British did not accomplish their goals when they lacked coalition partners in the United States. Examples include the initial American reluctance to accept the quota proposal for on-site inspections or to combine a threshold test ban with a moratorium on underground tests in 1959, as well as the British failure to prevent the resumption of atmospheric tests in 1962. In these instances, test ban supporters in the U.S. bureaucracy either disagreed with London or were reluctant to join the cause for fear of domestic opposition.

As for leadership beliefs, the two presidents wanted an agreement. Eisenhower considered it his greatest failure not to have achieved an arms control treaty with the Soviets.[105] Kennedy called the "failure to get an agreement on the cessation of nuclear testing" his greatest disappointment of his first year in office.[106] But during the five years of negotiations, neither president ever exercised decisive leadership on the issue despite the personal convictions of both. They always worked for compromises among the competing bureaucratic factions and hesitated to overrule the military or the AEC. Judging from the documents, Kennedy does not come across as a strong leader in the test ban case, in contrast, for example, to his performance during the Cuban Missile crisis (see chapter 6). It should be noted, though, that even strong presidential leadership would not have guaranteed a successful arms control treaty, since only thirty-four votes in the Senate could block it.

In sum, alternative explanations focusing on cooperation problems, domestic politics, and leadership beliefs appear to be insufficient to explain the achievement of the test ban treaty in 1963. Emphasizing allied influence alone would be equally misleading. Rather, a picture emerges combining leadership beliefs and domestic politics with allied influence, which together overcame the cooperation problems. The allies, particularly the British, weighed in as part of the "family," thereby creating a "winning domestic coalition" in the United States.

Realist versus Liberal Expectations about Process

If allied influence was causally consequential to achieve the test ban agreement, we still have to evaluate how realist propositions about process score in comparison with liberal approaches (chapter 2). Some in-

[105] See Ambrose, *Eisenhower*, 543.

[106] Kennedy's press conference, Jan. 15, 1962, quoted from Seaborg, *Kennedy, Khrushchev*, 134.

stances of allied influence on American policies appear to confirm realist bargaining theory. For example, the German successes in preventing an implicit recognition of the GDR through specific provisions concerning the deposition of ratification documents and, more important, in thwarting a nonaggression agreement between NATO and the Warsaw Pact can be accounted for by differences in the intensity of preferences. While the United States did not seem to care much about the issues, the Adenauer government appeared to be very upset about them. The same holds true for the French success in preventing a U.S. vote in the UN General Assembly that condemned the French tests in the Sahara.

What about allied threats to defect as a means to increase their bargaining leverage? One could argue that the British "defected" at least once during the negotiations, when Macmillan proposed the quota for on-site inspections to Khrushchev against Eisenhower's advice in 1959. But this "defection" had no discernible impact on U.S. decisions. The prime minister's visit to Washington immediately following his visit to Moscow did not change Eisenhower's position. Only when the State Department began to support the British four weeks later was London able to influence U.S. policies. Transgovernmental coalition-building rather than British "defection" was responsible for the change.

The test ban case also disconfirms two other propositions derived from realist bargaining theory. First, if allied influence is a function of increased levels of threat perception, we should not see much allied impact on U.S. decisions in arms control and détente cases such as the test ban. Second, the proposition that allied unity increases allied influence is also disconfirmed in this case, given the profound disagreements between the British, on the one hand, and the French and Germans, on the other, on the desirability of a test ban.

As for allied control over issue-specific resources,. three instances come to mind. First, the United States needed British participation in the negotiations given its nuclear power status. London gained U.S. concessions with regard to the Atomic Energy Act and Anglo-American nuclear collaboration in exchange for its joining the test moratorium in 1958. Second, the Kennedy administration needed access to the British-owned Christmas Island in 1962 to conduct atmospheric tests. Macmillan successfully used the American dependence to bargain for a new arms control initiative. Third, Kennedy would have provided France with increased nuclear information to get President de Gaulle's signature to the LTBT. But the latter refused to use his issue-dependent power to gain concessions. Moreover, the French decision to go nuclear did not increase the nation's bargaining leverage over the United States during the negotiations.

One might also argue that the consistent British influence on the American negotiating position resulted from the country's nuclear power status.

It is certainly true that the United States needed British consent to get an agreement. But this consent was never a problem once London joined the negotiations in 1958. Rather, it was the United States that had to be convinced that a test ban was in its interests. Under these circumstances, a British threat not to sign an agreement was no viable option to push the United States in the desired direction. In addition, Britain was crucially dependent on U.S. assistance for its own nuclear program, as the Skybolt crisis dramatically showed. In other words, the U.S. administration had at least as much control over issue-specific resources in this particular case as its British ally.

In sum, there were some instances during the five years of negotiations during which the European allies engaged in power bargaining with the United States to further their demands. But realist bargaining theory can explain neither the variation in impact between the British and the French nor the variation in London's influence itself. Most important, assumptions derived from traditional realism fail to account for the most significant finding of this case study, the consistent and continuous British influence on U.S. nuclear testing policies. The same holds true for the agenda-setting effects of transnational coalitions among activists and scientists as well as for their facilitating role during the negotiations.

I have argued above that the allied influence on the American negotiating behavior can be explained by the interacting effects of domestic and alliance politics, in particular transnational and transgovernmental coalition-building. This, of course, is the realm of liberal arguments about international relations. If one assumes an allied community of values, it can easily be explained why the British were treated almost as any other domestic player in the United States and why constant consultation on all levels of government was a habitual practice during the negotiations.

The presence or absence of such transnational and transgovernmental coalitions also accounts for the considerable difference in impact between the British and the French. Paris almost never made an effort at coalition-building with test ban opponents in Washington in order to gain influence on U.S. decisions. Instead, de Gaulle relied mainly on traditional diplomatic contacts. Yet, the German government successfully built transgovernmental coalitions with the State Department, in particular Dean Rusk, to prevent the United States from pursuing a nonaggression pact.

In conclusion, the test ban case—like the Korean War case—confirms that NATO allies influenced U.S. foreign policy considerably. On balance, liberal propositions about cooperation among democracies, allied community, and transnational coalition-building offer a better explanation for the process of alliance interactions than assumptions derived from traditional realism and realist bargaining theory. The same holds true for the Cuban Missile crisis.

SIX

A "STRIKE ON CUBA WHICH MAY LOSE BERLIN"

THE EUROPEANS AND THE 1962 CUBAN MISSILE CRISIS

[The United States is] so . . . involved with 42 allies and confrontation in many places, that any action we take . . . will greatly increase the risks of direct action involving . . . our other alliances.
—Dean Rusk[1]

THE CUBAN MISSILE crisis was the most serious U.S.-Soviet confrontation of the cold war. While we know today that neither side was prepared to risk nuclear war over the Soviet missiles in Cuba, President John F. Kennedy and General Secretary Nikita Khrushchev each was afraid that the other would escalate the conflict in ways that could get out of control.[2] Decision-makers in Washington were convinced that the supreme national interests of the United States were at stake and that America could not allow the Soviets to put offensive missiles into Cuba. Why care about allies when national security is endangered?

I argue in this chapter that the fate of the Western Alliance was the most important foreign policy concern for U.S. decision-makers apart from the direct confrontation with Moscow and Cuba. They constantly worried how West Europeans might react to possible courses of action and

The chapter title is quoted from John F. Kennedy, in "October 27, 1962: Transcripts of the Meetings of the ExComm," *International Security* 12, no. 3 (Winter 1987/88): 30–92, 55.

[1] Dean Rusk in "ExComm Transcript," Oct. 16, 1962, in National Security Archive, *The Cuban Missile Crisis, 1962*, Microfiche Collection (Washington, D.C.: Chadwyck-Healey, 1990) [NSA:CMC], Doc. 00622.

[2] For details, see Richard N. Lebow and Janice G. Stein, *We All Lost the Cold War* (Princeton, N.J.: Princeton University Press, 1994), 19–145. See also Michael Beschloss, *The Crisis Years* (New York: Edward Burlingame Books, 1991), 431–575; James Blight, *The Shattered Crystal Ball* (Savage, Md.: Rowman & Littlefield, 1990); Blight and David Welch, *On the Brink* (New York: Hill & Wang, 1989); McGeorge Bundy, *Danger and Survival* (New York: Random House, 1988), chap. 9; Laurence Chang and Peter Kornbluh, eds., *The Cuban Missile Crisis, 1962* (New York: New Press, 1992); Raymond Garthoff, *Reflections on the Cuban Missile Crisis*, rev. ed. (Washington, D.C.: Brookings, 1989); Maurice Vaisse, ed., *L'Europe et la Crise de Cuba* (Paris: Armand Colin, 1993).

what Moscow might do against Europe in response to American moves. As Walt W. Rostow, then head of the Policy Planning Council in the State Department, put it later, "what really reduced our freedom of action was not the Turkish bases—it was that we lead an Alliance."[3] Concerns about Europe influenced the two most important American choices during the crisis. First, the decision in favor of a blockade as opposed to an air strike against the missile installations in Cuba was taken in part to avoid Soviet retaliation against Europe, in particular Berlin. This course of action was also considered most likely to ensure continued support by the NATO allies. Second, the deal leading to the withdrawal of the Soviet missiles from Cuba, which involved the secret U.S. assurance that it planned to remove the Jupiter missiles from Turkey, was intrinsically linked to alliance considerations. U.S. credentials in the Western Alliance were at stake, which explains why the removal of militarily obsolete weapons became such a problem for the administration.

It is a widespread myth that the NATO allies suffered from a lack of consultation during the Cuban Missile crisis. The myth was partly perpetuated by members of the U.S. administration, such as Roger Hilsman, Director of Intelligence in the State Department: "If you had the French Government and the British Government with all their hangups and De Gaulle's hangups we would never have done it, it's as simple as that."[4] It is true that the allies were not consulted during the first week of the crisis. Outside the inner circle of Kennedy's advisers, nobody was. During the second week of the crisis, however, the European governments had ample opportunities to influence Washington's choices. The British participated almost directly in the U.S. decision-making process. Moreover, an important source of allied influence during the Cuban Missile crisis ensued from anticipatory behavior by U.S. decision-makers. They acted *as if* they had thoroughly consulted with European governments and set the U.S. diplomatic machinery in motion to find out how key allies would react to possible courses of action. Since the American diplomats in Europe were part of NATO's transgovernmental networks, the consequence was that allied governments knew fairly well what was going on in Washington. Finally, the discourses in Kennedy's Executive Committee (ExComm) showed the collective belief of decision-makers that they had to act on behalf of the allied community. They made virtually no distinction between U.S. and allied interests. Since membership in the allied community was part of their collective identity, pursuing unilateral as opposed to joint interests was not an option available to them.

[3] "Oral History Interview with W. W. Rostow," April 25, 1981, NSA:CMC, Doc. 03301.

[4] "Interview with David Nunnerly," NSA:CMC, Doc. 03251. See also Frank Costigliola, "Kennedy, the European Allies, and the Failure to Consult," *Political Science Quarterly*, forthcoming.

Allied Consultation during the Crisis

Cuba is located south of the Tropic of Cancer and even the adjacent waters do not belong to the territory covered by the North Atlantic Treaty. The assistance clause in Article 5 of the treaty did, therefore, not apply. But Article 4 of the treaty stipulates a general commitment to consult whenever an ally feels a threat to its national security. U.S. decisions during the crisis also had immediate repercussions for allied security.

Whether to consult the allies was discussed during the very first ExComm meeting on October 16. Secretary of State Rusk argued strongly in favor of consultation and maintained that unilateral U.S. actions would put the allies at risk, in particular if the United States decided in favor of a quick air strike. National Security Adviser McGeorge Bundy disagreed and pointed to "the amount of noise we would get from our allies saying that . . . they can live with Soviet MRBMs, why can't we; . . . the division in the alliance; the certainty that the Germans would feel that we were jeopardizing Berlin because of our concern over Cuba."[5] The president stated that warning the allies would mean "warning everybody" (that is, the Soviets). McGeorge Bundy then proposed that key allies should be informed shortly before the planned U.S. action, a suggestion that seemed to express the ExComm consensus during these first meetings.

Most recent interallied conflicts over relations with Cuba influenced the reluctance of U.S. decision-makers to fully consult. First, the European reaction to the Bay of Pigs invasion had been as disastrous for the United States as the invasion itself.[6] Second, immediately prior to the crisis, Washington made a hitherto unsuccessful effort at convincing European governments to join an economic embargo of Cuba, since the Soviet Union used ships under British, Norwegian, and Greek flags to deliver goods to the island. On October 3, the United States presented its cause at a NATO council meeting and failed. One day later, the president signed an executive order to be effective after two weeks, closing U.S. ports to any ships engaged in trade with Cuba. Congress also voted to withhold economic and military assistance from countries engaged in trade with Cuba.[7]

[5] Quoted from "White House Tapes and Minutes of the Cuban Missile Crisis," *International Security* 10, no. 1 (Summer 1985): 164–203, 179. For the following see ibid. and NSA:CMC, Doc. 00622.

[6] As Dean Acheson commented: "[The allies] were watching a gifted young amateur practice with a boomerang, when they saw, to their horror, that he knocked himself out" ("Oral History with Dean Acheson," April 27, 1964, NSA:CMC, Doc. 03194).

[7] The State Department tried to fight off this legislation and, at the same time, to alleviate protests by the allies. See "National Security Action Memorandum No. 181," Aug. 23, 1962, NSA:CMC, Doc. 00252; "Congressional Testimony by Dean Rusk," Sept. 5, ibid.,

This was the background against which the administration decided not to consult the allies during the first week of the crisis. But lack of consultation did not free decision-makers from concerns about the Europeans. There was unanimous consensus that U.S. inaction with regard to the Soviet missile deployment in Cuba would be disastrous for the U.S. credibility vis-à-vis its allies. As Robert McNamara put it later, "For all kinds of reasons, especially to preserve unity in the alliance, we had to indicate to the Soviets that we weren't going to accept the presence of offensive missiles in Cuba."[8] The reputation of the U.S. government was perceived to be at stake, particularly in light of Kennedy's September 13 statement that "this country will do whatever must by done to protect its own security and that of its allies," if Cuba should become an offensive military base for the Soviet Union.[9] The argument about reputation involved domestic and alliance politics; both aspects became indistinguishable.

The decision not to consult key allies during the first week strengthened the position of the "doves" in the ExComm. They argued that an air strike and military action against the Soviet installations in Cuba without prior consultation would wreck NATO. Dean Rusk set the tone during an ExComm meeting on October 16. He argued that a strike against Cuba could lead to Soviet retaliation elsewhere in the world. If the United States took such an action without letting its allies know about it, "we could find ourselves . . . isolated and the alliance crumbling, very much as it did for a period during the Suez affair, but at a moment of much greater danger . . . for the alliance."[10] It was then agreed to assess the potential political and military consequences of various courses of action. The position paper on the political implications of military action confirmed Rusk's point.

Lack of allied consultation was not the most important argument in favor of the blockade. Fear of losing control by escalating the crisis into a

---

Doc. 00348; "J. F. Kennedy's News Conference," Sept. 13, ibid., Doc. 00408; "State Department on West European Shipments to Cuba," Sept. 25, ibid., Doc. 00454; "Dean Rusk to Amb. Finletter," Oct. 2, ibid., Doc. 00487; "Finletter to Dean Rusk," Oct. 3, ibid., Doc. 00511; "George Ball to Chairman, Select Committee on Export Control," Oct. 8, ibid., Doc. 00546; "Dean Rusk, Circular Cable," Oct. 11, ibid., Doc. 00575.

[8] Robert S. McNamara in Blight and Welch, *On the Brink*, 188. See also "Memorandum by Theodore Sorensen Reviewing the Interagency Agreement/Disagreement Regarding Courses of Action in Cuba," Oct. 17, 1962, NSA:CMC, Doc. 00649.

[9] Quoted from Chang and Kornbluh, *Cuban Missile Crisis*, 356. See also Lebow and Stein, *We All Lost the Cold War*, 99.

[10] "ExComm Transcript, 6:30–7:55 pm," Oct. 16, NSA:CMC, Doc. 00623. For similar arguments see "Adlai Stevenson to the President," Oct. 17, ibid., Doc. 00652; "Charles Bohlen to Dean Rusk," Oct. 17, ibid., Doc. 00645; "State Department, Internal Paper Regarding 'UN Aspects of Cuban Situation I,' " Oct. 19, ibid., Doc. 00693. For the following see "Possible World Consequences of Military Action," Oct. 19, NSA:CMC, Doc. 00679.

military confrontation was more significant. But it is noteworthy that the decision not to consult the allies during the first week of the crisis did not accomplish its goal, namely to preserve the freedom of U.S. action against "hang-ups" from Europe. Belonging to the community of democracies formed a part of the American identity, as a result of which decision-makers continued to define U.S. preferences in terms of joint interests rather than narrow self-interest. Nonconsultation constrained U.S. choices, since it precluded certain courses of (military) action because of repercussions for NATO. The U.S. violation of consultation norms during the first week of the Cuban Missile crisis had, therefore, different consequences than the interallied deception during the Suez crisis (chapter 4).

Once the president had decided to institute the quarantine, the State Department worked around the clock to inform the allies. The procedure is worth describing, since it reveals a hierarchy among the allies. While all major European allies were notified prior to congressional leaders, certain countries were more equal than others in the eyes of the U.S. administration. Great Britain was in a league of its own. London was to be informed first, long before the president's speech announcing the quarantine. An intelligence briefing was also planned for the Canadians and the British. Next in the hierarchy came France's President de Gaulle, followed by Germany, Canada, Italy, and Turkey as well as the North Atlantic Council as a whole. The State Department sent special emissaries and intelligence officers to Ottawa, London, Paris, and Bonn to insure the support of these allies. In de Gaulle's case, his reaction was considered potentially so troublesome that President Kennedy asked former Secretary of State Dean Acheson to brief the French President. Selected NATO allies including the mayor of West Berlin, Willy Brandt, received personal letters from the president. All other allies including those in Latin America were informed just one hour before the speech.[11]

Decision-makers in Washington attached considerable importance to the timely notification of major European allies. The treatment of the Organization of American States (OAS) was significantly different. While the Europeans were pampered with intelligence briefings and carefully worded letters by the president, the Latin Americans were simply pressured into supporting U.S. actions. Dean Rusk instructed the U.S. ambassadors "to use whatever pressure tactics you think will be most effective in securing prompt support in Organ of Consultation [of the OAS] . . . except offer of new AID money, keeping in mind strong US governmental

[11] See Alexis Johnson and Paul Nitze, "Fourth Draft of Timetable regarding the Imposition of Quarantine and President's Speech," Oct. 20, NSA:CMC, Doc. 00719. See also State Department, "Summary of Activities. Midnight October 20 to midnight October 22, 1962," ibid., Doc. 01887; Dino A. Brugioni, *Eyeball to Eyeball* (New York: Random House, 1991), 319–44.

and public feelings which will exist about any country which does not support Hemisphere solidarity on this issue."[12] This was all the more significant since OAS support—in contrast to NATO's—was deemed crucial to make a legal case at the United Nations. The differential treatment shows the weight that U.S. decision-makers attributed to its European allies as compared to those in the OAS. There was no correlation between the degree to which the United States consulted with an ally and its potential bargaining leverage over the United States.[13]

It is a myth that nonconsultation of the allies continued through the second week of the crisis. From October 22 on, the Europeans were not only regularly informed about the U.S. deliberations but had ample opportunities to influence American thinking through a variety of bilateral and multilateral channels. Among the key allies, only the British chose to do so (see below). As I argue later in this chapter, the Turks and the British apparently knew about the key decision involving NATO during the second week of the crisis, that is, the secret deal to remove the Jupiter missiles from Turkey in exchange for the withdrawal of the Soviet missiles from Cuba.

The most important multilateral forum to discuss the Cuban Missile crisis with Europeans and Canadians was the North Atlantic Council, whose permanent representatives met repeatedly from October 23 on. During the first meeting, most allied ambassadors expressed sympathy with the U.S. position but complained about the lack of prior consultation.[14] The most dramatic North Atlantic Council meeting took place on the morning of October 28. Without knowing Khrushchev's decision to withdraw the missiles, the NATO ambassadors were briefed that "the US Government may find it necessary within a very short period of time in its own interest and that of its fellow nations in the Western hemisphere to take whatever military action may be necessary to remove this growing threat to the hemisphere."[15] Confronted with this imminent danger of military escalation, the permanent representatives almost unanimously raised their concerns, and some urged the United States to continue on the diplomatic track. The issue of the Jupiter missiles in Turkey was also discussed (see below).

[12] "Dean Rusk to U.S. Ambassadors in Latin America," Oct. 21, NSA:CMC, Doc. 00743.

[13] I owe this point to Robert Jervis.

[14] See "NATO-Ambassador Finletter to State Department," Oct. 23, NSA:CMC, Doc. 00953; "Embassy NATO to Foreign Office," Oct. 23, Public Records Office, London, Diplomatic Correspondence Files (PRO:FO) 371/162375.

[15] Ambassador Finletter's brief for the NATO Council, Oct. 27, which was handed over to the British, PRO:FO 371/162392. On this and the following see "Rusk to Finletter," Oct. 28, NSA:CMC, Doc. 01580; "Finletter to State Department," Oct. 28, ibid., Doc. 01602; "Gordey, France-Soir, Letter to Richard Estabrook," ibid., Doc. 01860; "[U.K.] Embassy NATO to Foreign Office," Oct. 28, PRO:FO 371/162382.

Apart from the multilateral setting of the North Atlantic Council, key allies kept in close touch with Washington through bilateral channels. Their impact varied greatly.

The British Response: Support for a "Deal"

The mechanisms of the "special relationship" provided the British with information about the crisis two days before London was officially notified. British, Australian, and Canadian officials were attending an intelligence conference at the Pentagon when British experts noticed that their American colleagues were barely seen at the meetings. They alerted the British ambassador, David Ormsby-Gore, on October 17 and concluded that an international crisis was in the making, probably involving Cuba. Ormsby-Gore informed Prime Minister Macmillan on October 19, while the head of the British intelligence service was briefed by his American counterparts.[16] This was the first time that an American ally heard about the crisis. As always, the transnational Anglo-American intelligence community worked.

One day before the president's televised speech, but after the decision in favor of the quarantine had been made, Kennedy met with the British ambassador, the first encounter between the president and an allied official during the crisis. Kennedy sounded out Ormsby-Gore on the choice between the quarantine and an air strike without indicating his own decision. The British ambassador did not believe that the missiles deployed in Cuba constituted a serious military threat to the U.S. and strongly favored the blockade. An air strike, he argued, could well result in Soviet action against Berlin. Kennedy confirmed that he had decided in favor of the quarantine.[17]

Later on October 21, the British prime minister received a personal message from the president, who justified his lack of consultation and promised to be "in the closest touch" from now on.[18] No other ally enjoyed as many contacts with the president during the second week of the crisis. Kennedy conducted almost daily telephone conversations with Macmillan. The British ambassador saw the president four times and had numerous phone conversations with him. Ormsby-Gore was also present

[16] For details see Brugioni, *Eyeball to Eyeball*, 189, 219–220, 327; Elie Abel, *The Cuban Missile Crisis* (New York: Lippincott, 1966), 66, 74; Harold Macmillan, *At the End of the Day* (London: Macmillan, 1973), 180; Alistair Horne, *Macmillan 1957–1986* (London: Macmillan, 1989), 362–85.

[17] For details see Macmillan, *End of the Day*, 190–94; Horne, *Macmillan*, 363–64, 369.

[18] Macmillan, *End of the Day*, 182–84. For the following see ibid., 184–94; Horne, *Macmillan*, 367; Letter by Ormsby-Gore to Foreign Secretary Home, Nov. 9, 1962, PRO:FO 371/162401.

on October 23 when Robert Kennedy briefed his brother about the first meeting with the Soviet Ambassador Dobrynin.[19]

As Ormsby-Gore's advice indicated, the British became the most "dovish" of the major allies including the Canadians.[20] When Macmillan was briefed about the crisis, he remarked at first that "now the Americans will realize what we in England have lived through for the past many years." In his reply to Kennedy, he assured the president that Britain would support the United States but mentioned again that Europeans had lived under the threat of Soviet nuclear weapons for quite some time. He demanded that the United States made a good legal case in favor of the quarantine, since the interruption of the freedom of the seas was "difficult to defend in peace time." He then wondered about possible Soviet reactions against the blockade including attempts at trading American bases in Europe or even West Berlin for the withdrawal of the missiles from Cuba. Macmillan urged close consultation "to steer things within the alliance and elsewhere."[21] Kennedy perceived Macmillan's message as the "best argument for taking no action."

Internally, the British had concluded that the quarantine violated international law. The lord chancellor urged that this view should be conveyed to the Americans, but the Foreign Office and Macmillan himself decided that this was not the time for a confrontation with Washington on the interpretation of international law. The United States was to be told that "Her Majesty's Government are not satisfied as to the legality of the blockade in international law."[22] Macmillan suggested to the American ambassador that British ships should not be stopped and searched if London provided Washington with information about their location and their cargo.

More important, the British prime minister was as concerned as President Kennedy that the crisis might get out of control, and he favored a *cooperative solution*. On October 24, he told Ormsby-Gore:

[19] See Robert Kennedy, *Thirteen Days* (New York: W. W. Norton, 1968), 44.

[20] On the Canadian reaction to the crisis see Don Munton, "Getting Along and Going Alone: American Policies and Canadian Support in Korea and Cuba" (paper presented to the annual meeting of the International Studies Association, Atlanta, Ga., April 1992). Canada was particularly annoyed that the United States had raised the alert status of the North American Air Defense system (NORAD) without bothering to consult with Ottawa as Washington was obliged under a U.S.-Canadian agreement. Compared to the British impact, the Canadian input was apparently negligible.

[21] Macmillan, *End of the Day*, 184–90. See also Horne, *Macmillan*, 364–66. For the following quote see "507th NSC Meeting," Oct. 22, NSA:CMC, Doc. 00840.

[22] "Foreign Office to Embassy Washington," Oct. 25, PRO:FO 371/162375. See also "Memorandum by Lord Chancellor," Oct. 25, PRO, Cabinet Files (PRO:CAB), 129/111, C.(62)170; "Memorandum to Secretary of State," Oct. 25, PRO:FO 371/162380; "Foreign Office to UK Mission UN," Oct. 23, PRO:FO 371/162375. For the following see "Foreign Office to Embassy Washington," Oct. 24, PRO:FO 371/162377.

> If I am right in assuming that the President's mind is moving in the direction of negotiations before the crisis worsens, I think that the most fruitful course for you to pursue at the present might be to try to elicit from him on what lines he may be contemplating a conference. . . . I suppose that the starting point for any such proposal would be the recognition of the plain duty of responsible Governments to confer without delay about all possible methods of retreating from the brink of nuclear war.[23]

He suggested that the U.S. should raise the blockade if the Soviets refrained from putting more missiles into Cuba. Disarmament issues should become the subject of a summit meeting, he argued, while a "straight bargain" about bases (Europe versus Cuba) would spell trouble within NATO.

Ormsby-Gore conveyed Macmillan's ideas to McGeorge Bundy but urged that the president should make it very clear to Macmillan that ending the blockade without withdrawal of the Soviet missiles from Cuba was no viable option. The British ambassador thus sided with the United States and effectively undercut the suggestion of his prime minister, which was similar to an appeal by UN Secretary General U Thant. Macmillan's proposal of a summit meeting was taken up and endorsed by the State Department's Policy Planning Staff.[24]

When Macmillan phoned Kennedy later on October 24, he refrained from suggesting an end to the quarantine in exchange for a Soviet pledge not to put more missiles into Cuba. But he urged the president that nothing should be done in a hurry. Kennedy agreed. Macmillan then asked: "Do you think we ought to try and do a deal, have a meeting with him, or not?"[25] The president asked Macmillan's advice regarding a possible invasion of Cuba. The prime minister responded in a message on October 25 and strongly recommended against such a course of action: "Events have gone too far. . . . we are now all in a phase where you must try to obtain your objectives by other means."[26] He also suggested that Kennedy should respond favorably to U Thant's proposal provided that a UN inspection system was in place when the blockade was called off. Macmillan did not support the U.S. demand that the missiles had to be removed before the quarantine would be raised.

One day later, Kennedy discussed with Macmillan the possibility of an

[23] "Foreign Office to Embassy Washington," Oct. 24, PRO:FO 371/162378.

[24] See W. W. Rostow, "Memorandum for Dean Rusk, How the US Should Respond to Summit Proposal," Oct. 25, NSA:CMC, Doc. 01340. On Ormsby-Gore's conversation with the National Security Adviser, see "McGeorge Bundy to J. F. Kennedy Regarding Conversation with Ormsby-Gore," Oct. 24, NSA:CMC, Doc. 01193.

[25] Macmillan, *End of the Day*, 198–203, 202–203. See also Lebow and Stein, *We All Lost the Cold War*, 121.

[26] Macmillan, *End of the Day*, 204.

international guarantee not to invade Cuba in exchange for the removal of the Soviet missiles. This suggestion had come up at the UN and was to become part of the deal leading to the solution of the crisis. The British prime minister strongly endorsed the proposal and recommended that the UN secretary general should go to Cuba to verify the inoperability of the Soviet missiles and to stop further work. The president committed himself to further consultation with Macmillan before any military action would be taken.[27]

On October 27, when the crisis reached its climax, the British considered an initiative of their own along the lines discussed between Kennedy and Macmillan. The London government told the UN and the United States that it was prepared for a public appeal containing a request to U Thant to go to Cuba, the suspension of quarantine measures during that visit, and the noninvasion pledge.[28] Since Khrushchev agreed to remove the missiles from Cuba the next day, the British initiative was no longer necessary.

In sum, London supported Kennedy throughout the crisis but urged him "to find a middle course" avoiding nuclear war and allowing some face-saving solution for Khrushchev.[29] Whether the British proposals for deescalation made a difference in the U.S. decision-making process is unclear. But it is probably safe to argue that the close contact between Kennedy, Macmillan, and Ormsby-Gore during the second week of the crisis strengthened the president's view that, whatever happened, he "would *not* go to war."[30] Given Kennedy's own convictions about the importance of the Western Alliance that he expressed time and again during the crisis, it was significant that a key ally whom he trusted fully endorsed his search for a "deal."

In addition, the British government influenced three minor American decisions directly. First, the Defense Department favored raising the alert status of all U.S. forces including those in Europe on similar levels ("Defense Conditions 3 and 2," respectively). When NATO Supreme Allied Commander Europe (SACEUR) Norstad paid his farewell visit to London (he was then ordered to remain at his post for the duration of the

[27] For details see Macmillan, *End of the Day*, 209–11; "Message by Macmillan to the President," PRO, Prime Minister Files (PRO:PREM), 11/4051.

[28] For details see "Memorandum by Secretary of State Caccia," Oct. 27, PRO:FO 371/162384; "Message by Macmillan to the President," Oct. 27, PRO:PREM 11/4052; "Foreign Office to UK Embassy UN," Oct. 27, PRO:FO 371/162387; "Foreign Office to Embassy Washington," Oct. 27, ibid. See also Macmillan's message to Khrushchev, Oct. 28, ibid. 371/162382.

[29] Macmillan in a British cabinet meeting, Oct. 25, PRO:CAB 128/36, C.C.(62) 62d Conclusions.

[30] James Blight's comment in "October 27, 1962 ExComm Transcripts," 85 (emphasis in text).

crisis), Macmillan strongly urged him not to mobilize NATO forces and to refrain from anything that might be considered provocative. Norstad requested and got permission to exempt the U.S. forces in Europe from raising their alert status to DEFCON 3. They were the only U.S. forces excluded from the worldwide alert.[31]

The U.S. Air Force was not pleased. Certain precautionary measures were taken, such as the transfer of contingency nuclear strike targets from squadrons in Germany to units in Britain in order to free the former for conventional operations in Berlin. Ninety-four U.S. aircraft returned to European bases from training in Libya, and nuclear weapons were loaded on U.S. bombers on Quick Reaction Alert status (QRA). Finally, the commander of the U.S. Navy base at Holy Loch, Great Britain, decided unilaterally to move several Polaris submarines out at sea—a precautionary measure that nevertheless could have been perceived as highly escalatory by the Soviets.[32]

The second case of British impact concerned the radius of the interception line. When Ambassador Ormsby-Gore met Kennedy on October 23, he learned that the interception line for the quarantine had been extended to eight hundred miles so that the Navy ships would remain outside the range of MIG fighters stationed in Cuba. Ormsby-Gore proposed that the line should be shortened to 500 miles to give the Soviets more time to reconsider their position. The president agreed and issued the appropriate order.[33]

Third, Prime Minister Macmillan urged the United States to make the best possible case for its actions before world opinion, particularly in the UN, and strongly recommended that the photographs showing the Soviet missile sites in Cuba be released to the media. Ormsby-Gore finally convinced the president to publish the pictures on October 23 and helped him selecting the most dramatic photographs. Their publication in Great Britain, the U.S. media, and at the UN achieved the desired effect.[34]

[31] For details see Macmillan, *End of the Day*, 188–90, 195; "JCS to Dean Rusk," Oct. 22, NSA:CMC, Doc. 00833; "JCS Chronology of Decisions Concerning Cuban Missile Crisis," ibid., Doc. 02780; "Finletter to Dean Rusk," Oct. 22, ibid., Doc. 00836.

[32] For details, see Garthoff, *Reflections*, 60; "U.S. Air Force Response to the Cuban Missile Crisis," NSA:CMC, Doc. 02811; "Oral History, Interview with Vice Admiral Beshany," ibid., Doc. 03275.

[33] For details, see Kennedy, *Thirteen Days*, 45; Arthur Schlesinger, *A Thousand Days* (Boston: Houghton Mifflin, 1965), 817–18; Macmillan, *End of the Day*, 195–97. The practical consequences of this decison are unclear. According to Scott Sagan, the quarantine line had already been established five hundred miles away from the eastern tip of Cuba, even though this was not explicitly ordered by the president. See Scott Sagan, "Nuclear Alerts and Crisis Management," *International Security* 9 (Spring 1985): 99–139, 110.

[34] For details on this episode see Beschloss, *Crisis Years*, 494; Horne, *Macmillan*, 365–66, 369; Macmillan, *End of the Day*, 196–97.

The French and German Reactions: Support

Since the 1956 Suez crisis (chapter 4), the Franco-American relationship had gradually deteriorated. President de Gaulle's vision of Europe and of the transatlantic relationship was decidedly different from the American approach. When the Kennedy administration took a critical view of the French independent nuclear program, the Franco-American relationship was further strained. It is, therefore, not surprising that Washington was nervous about the French and particularly de Gaulle's reaction to the Cuban Missile crisis. The administration believed that the French president might criticize the United States, endanger allied unity, and damage the U.S. position. As a result, the French received special treatment, and Kennedy asked Dean Acheson to brief General de Gaulle.

Washington was in for a surprise. France turned out to be the most supportive among the major allies. Unlike Macmillan, who asked for further evidence and originally did not share the American concern over the missile deployment, de Gaulle first refused to look at the photographs arguing that "a great nation like yours would not act if there were any doubt about the evidence, and, therefore, I accept what you tell me as a fact without any proof of any sort needed." After Acheson's briefing, he declared in another grandiose gesture: "You may tell your President that France will support him in every way in this crisis."[35] On October 27, he went a step further and told the U.S. ambassador, Charles Bohlen, that France "with its limited means" would be at the American side, if the crisis escalated into war.

But de Gaulle was well aware that the United States had not consulted its allies in advance. Before Acheson even started his briefing, the French president asked whether he had come to inform or to consult with him. Acheson confirmed the former. De Gaulle then told Bohlen several days later that the Cuban Missile crisis was U.S. business. He could not resist adding "that the French for centuries had lived with threats and menaces, first from the Germans and now from Russia, but he understood the US had not had a comparable experience."[36] When the crisis was over, de Gaulle wrote to the British prime minister complaining about the lack of consultation: "It is true that neither you nor we have been consulted by the United States at the occasion. Given the nature of this matter and the consequences it could have had, I believe that it should have been other-

[35] According to "Oral History with Dean Acheson," April 27, 1964, NSA:CMC, Doc. 03197. See Kennedy's personal letter to de Gaulle, ibid., Doc. 00797; "US Embassy Paris to Secretary of State," Oct. 23, 1962, ibid., Doc. 01024. For the following see "Ambassador Bohlen, Paris, to Secretary of State," Oct. 27, NSA:CMC, Doc. 01557.

[36] "Ambassador Bohlen, Paris, to Secretary of State," Oct. 27, NSA:CMC, Doc. 01557.

wise."[37] The French foreign minister, Couve de Murville, disagreed with this analysis. He felt that the United States was quite justified in not consulting the allies and that one should not conclude that the Americans would act on their own if, for example, Berlin were involved. But he also declared that the Soviet missiles in Cuba did not alter the military balance.

The French government nevertheless firmly supported the United States during the crisis and the French representative in the North Atlantic Council worked hard to insure allied support for American actions. The American concern over French backing had been unnecessary.

At the same time and continuing a pattern that was also discernible during the test ban negotiations (chapter 5), the French president made no attempt to influence American decisions during the second week of the crisis. Unlike Macmillan, who immediately became active when he heard about the crisis, de Gaulle merely registered the information given to him and indicated his support for President Kennedy.

While the United States was concerned about the potential unpredictability of General de Gaulle, it worried about the West German reaction for different reasons. First, unlike France, German territory was directly affected by American decisions as the theater of possible Soviet military responses. Washington feared a move against the "Achilles heel" of the Western Alliance, Berlin (see below). Second, U.S.-German governmental relations were somewhat tense at the time, since the Kennedy administration's sympathies appeared to belong to the Social Democratic opposition in Bonn, in particular to its leader, Willy Brandt. Chancellor Adenauer was widely considered to be out of touch with reality.[38]

Adenauer turned out to be one of the most hawkish allies. When the American ambassador briefed him, he declared that he was not surprised by the Soviet action. When he met Dean Acheson, he urged the United States to do more to create unrest in Cuba and argued that "we should consider all possible actions for elimination of Castro regime and Soviet influence in Cuba, including rapid tightening of quarantine restrictions."[39] This was the opposite of what the British government had recom-

[37] "Il est vrai que ni vous, ni nous, n'avons été en l'occurence consultés par les Etats-Unis. Etant donné la nature de cette affaire et les suites qu'elle aurait pu avoir, je crois qu'il aurait dû en être autrement" ("Message de Gaulle to Prime Minister," Nov. 6, PRO:FO 371/162402; my translation). For the following see "Embassy Paris to Foreign Office," Nov. 2, PRO:FO 371/162392; "Embassy Paris to Foreign Office," Nov. 3, ibid. 371/162394.

[38] For details see Hans Jörg Grabbe, *Unionsparteien, Sozialdemokratie und Vereinigte Staaten von Amerika* (Düsseldorf: Droste, 1983).

[39] "US Embassy Bonn to Secretary of State," Oct. 24, NSA:CMC, Doc. 01224. See also "US Embassy Bonn to Secretary of State," Oct. 22, ibid., Doc. 00863. For the following see "US Embassy Bonn to Secretary of State," Oct. 23, ibid., Doc. 01025; "US Mission Berlin to Secretary of State," Oct. 23, ibid., Doc. 00950.

mended. Adenauer's attitude was particularly interesting, since he did not seem to care about what could happen to his own country and to Berlin if Soviet influence in Cuba was "eliminated" by the United States. The Kennedy administration worried more about Berlin than the German chancellor.

While the German government and all political parties supported the United States during the crisis, Adenauer asked Washington to publish the photographs to make a convincing case to world public opinion. The mayor of West Berlin also endorsed the American actions but was less hawkish than the chancellor. Even Brandt did not seem to be too concerned about what might happen to his city. There was also no indication that the citizens of West Berlin panicked during the height of the crisis. While there was some hoarding of food, the city remained comparatively calm despite the gravity of the situation.[40] The Berliners had been through many crises during recent years to get too excited over the Cuban Missile crisis.

Symbol of Allied Community I: Berlin

In contrast to the attitudes of the Bonn government and the Berliners themselves, the U.S. administration was extremely concerned about the fate of the city. Since the late 1950s, the Soviet Union had issued one ultimatum on Berlin after another and had threatened to conclude a separate peace treaty with East Germany, thereby jeopardizing the security of and free access to West Berlin.[41] Prior to the Cuban Missile crisis, there were some indications that Moscow was prepared to tighten the situation in Berlin again. On June 18, 1962, for example, Khrushchev conveyed another threat against Berlin to Kennedy, and on September 11, he indicated to the German ambassador that he would proceed with a peace treaty shortly after the American elections. A few days later, the Soviet leader told the Austrian vice chancellor that the USSR would retaliate in Berlin if the United States invaded Cuba.[42]

[40] See "CIA Memorandum, The Crisis USSR/Cuba," Oct. 24, NSA:CMC, Doc. 01123; "US Mission Berlin to State Department," Oct. 24, ibid., Doc. 01171.

[41] For details see, for example, Marc Trachtenberg, *History and Strategy* (Princeton, N.J.: Princeton University Press, 1991), 169–234.

[42] For details, see "US National Indications Center, the Soviet Bloc Armed Forces and the Cuban Crisis," June 18, 1963, NSA:CMC, Doc. 03130; Arthur Schlesinger, *Robert Kennedy and His Times* (Boston: Houghton Mifflin, 1978), 512. Soviet officials deny that the missile deployment in Cuba had anything to do with Berlin, citing instead the threat of an American invasion and attempts to redress the strategic balance. See Blight and Welch, *On the Brink*, 267–68; Garthoff, *Reflections*, 21–22; Lebow and Stein, *We All Lost the Cold War*, 23–24.

It is therefore not surprising that the Berlin issue came up during the first ExComm meeting on October 16. Dean Rusk speculated that Khrushchev might have deployed the missiles in Cuba to increase his bargaining leverage over Berlin. Concerns about Berlin influenced the internal deliberations in two ways. First, the American commitment to Berlin was one more reason to preclude inaction against the Soviet missiles in Cuba. As the president put it during the second ExComm meeting, if the Soviets put missiles in Cuba without an American response, Moscow would build more bases and then squeeze the West in Berlin.[43] Decision-makers believed that they needed to react strongly in Cuba so as to deter Moscow from actions against Berlin.

Second, concerns about Berlin also served as another restraining factor on U.S. decisions. The city's exposure inside the Soviet bloc made it an easy target of retaliatory action against American moves in Cuba. State Department officials even argued that the contemplated quarantine of Cuba might lead to a Soviet counterblockade of Berlin, which could trigger a direct military confrontation between the two superpowers.[44]

Kennedy worried about Berlin almost constantly. Fear of Soviet action against the essentially defenseless city was one reason for his decision in favor of the blockade and against more forceful military action. As the president told Macmillan, possible reprisals against Berlin were "really why we have not done more than we have done up till now."[45] Kennedy's personal and emotional commitment to Berlin was again apparent during the crucial ExComm meeting on October 27, when he was faced with the choice between an air strike and a "missile swap" (see below):

> What we're going to be faced with is—because we wouldn't take the missiles out of Turkey, then maybe we'll have to invade or make a massive strike on Cuba which may lose Berlin. . . . we all know how quickly everybody's courage goes when the blood starts to flow, and that's what's going to happen in NATO . . .—we start these things and they grab Berlin, and everybody's going to say, "Well that was a pretty good proposition."[46]

In a nutshell, the Berlin issue symbolized the role of the North Atlantic

[43] "White House Tapes," 185. See also Dean Rusk in Blight and Welch, *On the Brink*, 177; State Department, "Internal Paper," Oct. 17, NSA:CMC, Doc. 00643; Lebow and Stein, *We All Lost the Cold War*, 103.

[44] See State Department, "Internal Paper on Blockade," Oct. 18, NSA:CMC, Doc. 00664. See also T. Sorensen, "Memorandum Reviewing Interagency Agreement/Disagreement," Oct. 17, ibid., Doc. 00649; "Possible World Consequences of Military Action," Oct. 19, ibid., Doc. 00679; "Tentative Agenda for NSC Meeting," Oct. 21, ibid., Doc. 00761.

[45] Telephone conversation Macmillan-Kennedy, Oct. 26, in Macmillan, *End of the Day*, 209–11.

[46] "October 27, 1962: ExComm Transcripts," 55, 58.

Alliance in the minds of U.S. decision-makers throughout the crisis—precluding both inaction and a rush into escalation. Concerns about the city and the fate of Europe in general were causally consequential not by determining specific choices but by constraining the range of options available to decision-makers.

Given the limited strategic value of Berlin, it is remarkable that there was no discussion of whether the American commitment to Berlin was worth risking a nuclear confrontation with the Soviets. President Kennedy and other ExComm members almost treated Berlin as if it was another American city for which American soldiers were supposed to die. It did not seem to make a difference whether the fate of Berlin or New York was at stake. Berlin symbolized the allied community and the values for which the cold war was fought. It was probably the city's very vulnerability to Soviet pressures that made it such a significant symbol for the U.S. commitment to the defense of Europe.

Of course, U.S. concerns about Berlin were also a question of American reputation and credibility of commitment. But the discourses about the city in the ExComm and particularly Kennedy's own statements went further than just reputational worries. U.S. decision-makers identified with Berlin as they did with no other place in the world during the crisis. If concerns about Berlin had just been motivated by reputational considerations, they should have calmed down when the Germans themselves were less alarmed.[47]

Rather, U.S. decision-makers took various precautionary measures. First, the ExComm instituted a subcommittee on Berlin chaired by Paul Nitze. It coordinated U.S. planning with regard to the city and analyzed the effects of a possible blockade of Berlin in response to the American quarantine of Cuba.[48]

Second, Kennedy tried to deter the Soviet Union from actions against Berlin in his television address on October 22, declaring, "Any hostile action anywhere in the world against the safety and freedom of peoples to whom we are committed—including the brave people of West Berlin—will be met by whatever action is needed."[49] Berlin was the only part of the world besides the Soviet Union and Cuba specifically mentioned in the speech.

[47] Kennedy's personal identification with Berlin was apparent during his triumphant visit to the city on June 26, 1963. During a speech in front of city hall he talked about Berlin as *the* symbol of freedom and democracy during the cold war and then exclaimed "Ich bin ein Berliner" [I am a Berliner]. See Willy Brandt's description of the episode in his memoirs, *Begegnungen und Einsichten* (München: Droemer, Knaur, 1978), 72–74.

[48] See Bundy, "ExComm Meeting 2, Record of Action," Oct. 23, NSA:CMC, Doc. 00965; "Record of Berlin Subcommittee Meeting," Oct. 24, ibid., Doc. 01190; Bundy, "ExComm Record of Action," Oct. 24, ibid., Doc. 01188.

[49] Kennedy's TV address, Oct. 22, NSA:CMC, Doc. 00847.

Third, administration officials explored a diplomatic track to stabilize the situation once the crisis was over. Partly in response to the British proposal for a summit meeting, the State Department began to explore possible topics including a "modus vivendi" with regard to Germany and nonaggression declarations between NATO and the Warsaw Pact. With regard to Berlin, the Policy Planning Staff even proposed "to put matter on ice" and to allow East Germany to substitute for the Soviet Union in access functions.[50] Many administration officials including the president thought that the aftermath of the Cuban Missile crisis provided an opportunity to work for an agreement with the Soviets on Berlin.[51] Kennedy complained to the British ambassador about the German (and French) resistance:

> He said that he personally would dearly like to get at least a temporary settlement of the Berlin question in the near future but he recognized that the attitude of France and West Germany might still make this impossible. He only hoped that the Germans and the French would not forget too soon the terrible fears that must have gripped all sane men during the last critical week.[52]

Whether or not the Germans forgot their fears, the Bonn government succeeded in resisting any settlement of the Berlin question. When Chancellor Adenauer visited Washington in November, the State Department issued a statement that no new Berlin initiative was planned. Only when Chancellor Brandt started the new German *Ostpolitik* in 1969–1970 was it possible to conclude the Four-Powers Agreement, which stabilized the Berlin situation.

Symbol of Allied Community II: The Jupiter Missiles

Berlin was an important concern of U.S. decision-makers during the crisis. But Berlin was peripheral to its *solution*. The Jupiter medium-range ballistic missiles (MRBMs) deployed under NATO arrangements in

[50] "W. W. Rostow to Dean Rusk Re How US Should Respond to Summit Proposal," Oct. 25, NSA:CMC, Doc. 01340. The ExComm's Planning Subcommittee endorsed this view. See "Memorandum by Planning Subcommittee to Rusk re Negotiations," Oct. 26, NSA:CMC, Doc. 01446.

[51] As a State Department official put it, "Now is the time to beat up Adenauer . . . and offer the Soviets a deal." ("Robert Komer to McGeorge Bundy concerning Memorandum by Raymond Garthoff," Oct. 29, NSA:CMC, Doc. 01651)

[52] "Embassy Washington to Foreign Office," Oct. 29, PRO:FO 371/162386. For the following see "Transcript of State Department Press Briefing on Adenauer's Visit to Washington," Nov. 14, NSA:CMC, Doc. 02303.

Turkey and Italy, however, became part and parcel of the crisis settlement.

Obsolete, but Symbols of the Alliance: The Jupiter Missiles

In December 1957 the U.S. urged the NATO council to decide on the deployment of MRBMs in Europe, since long-range ballistic missiles were not yet available to cover targets in the Soviet Union. Several European governments including West Germany refused to accept missiles on their soil, partly because they did not want to provoke the Soviet Union. Washington then pressured its southern European allies to accept the missiles and, finally, Italy and Turkey agreed to host the Jupiter MRBMs under dual-key arrangements (that is, allied possession of the missiles and U.S. control of the warheads), while Great Britain received Thor MRBMs.[53]

Less than two years later, the United States began to have second thoughts. In June 1959, President Eisenhower expressed his reservations about the deployments: "If Cuba or Mexico were to become Communist inclined, and the Soviets were to send arms and equipment, what would we feel we had to do then. He thought we would feel that we would have to intervene, militarily if necessary."[54] Eisenhower invoked an analogy that would become reality three years later. Khrushchev told Vice President Nixon shortly afterward that the Soviet Union felt indeed provoked by the planned missile deployment at its periphery.[55]

But Italy and Turkey made it clear to the United States that they had only reluctantly agreed to deploy the missiles, that their governments had spent a lot of political capital to convince their domestic constituencies, and that they were not prepared to give up the MRBMs. Turkey, which had always felt neglected by NATO and the United States, turned the issue into a symbol for the American commitment to defend the country.

U.S. officials became increasingly doubtful about the military value of the missiles. In the fall of 1960, the chairman of the Atomic Energy Commission, John McCone, visited the bases in Europe and returned convinced "that these Jupiter missiles should be removed and replaced with Polaris submarines. . . . I made a very strong recommendation to Presi-

[53] On the controversy surrounding the Jupiter missiles see Catherine Kelleher, *Germany and the Politics of Nuclear Weapons* (New York: Columbia University Press, 1975); David N. Schwartz, *NATO's Nuclear Dilemmas* (Washington, D.C.: Brookings, 1983), 62–81.

[54] "Memorandum of Conference with the President," June 17, 1959, NSA:CMC, Doc. 00011. See also "Memorandum of Conference with the President," June 19, 1959, ibid., Doc. 00012; "Memorandum of Conversation with the President," Jan. 17, 1961, ibid., Doc. 00031; Lebow and Stein, *We All Lost the Cold War*, 43–44.

[55] See "Memorandum of Conversation Nixon-Khrushchev," July 26, 1959, NSA:CMC, Doc. 00013.

dent Eisenhower in that regard, and it was seriously considered."[56] The subsequent report emphasized the vulnerability of the missiles.

When the Kennedy administration assumed office, the president directed an interagency committee to review the Jupiter deployment. Dean Rusk and State Department Counselor McGhee approached the Turkish foreign minister in April 1961 and ran into fierce opposition. The minister argued that the costs for the missiles had just been approved by the Turkish Parliament and that Turkey regarded the issue as a test case for the American alliance commitment. SACEUR Norstad strongly supported the Turkish view. It is noteworthy in this context that the country had just returned to democracy and that the U.S. was committed to strengthening the Turkish democratic institutions. McGhee recommended to the president that no action should be taken.[57]

Preparations for the deployment then proceeded as planned even though nobody in the upper echelons of the Kennedy administration believed in the military value of the missiles. In August 1962 the president asked again what could be done "to get Jupiter missiles out of Turkey," but received no formal reply.[58] By coincidence, the first Jupiter missiles were handed over to the Turkish armed forces on October 22, 1962—the day of Kennedy's announcement of the quarantine. While the upper echelons of the U.S. administration were not aware of this, Moscow's intelligence certainly did not miss it.[59]

In sum, by the time of the Cuban Missile crisis, the Jupiter missiles had become a *political symbol* of alliance cohesion and of the U.S. commitment to NATO and Turkey. Most American officials thought that the systems were militarily obsolete and dangerously vulnerable; Kennedy would have preferred their withdrawal long before.

The Emerging Cuba—Turkey Link

Not surprisingly, the Jupiter MRBMs became immediately linked to the Soviet missile deployment in Cuba. The Soviet Union connected the two issues during the Spring of 1962, that is, at the time when the decision to

[56] John McCone in "Testimony before the U.S. Senate Committee on Foreign Relations," Jan. 25, 1963, NSC-CMC, Doc. 02883. For the following, see Robert McNamara, "Testimony at the U.S. House Armed Services Committee, Hearing on Military Posture," Jan. 30, 1963, ibid., Doc. 02887.

[57] "Memorandum by Counsellor McGhee to McGeorge Bundy," June 22, 1961, NSA: CMC, Doc. 00093. See also "National Security Action Memorandum No. 35," April 6, 1961, ibid., Doc. 00043; "Oral History Interview with George McGhee," Aug. 13, 1964, ibid., Doc. 03211; "Letter by Dean Rusk to James Blight," Feb. 25, 1987, ibid., Doc. 03322.

[58] See "National Security Action Memorandum No. 181," Aug. 23, 1962, NSA:CMC, Doc. 00252; Bundy, *Danger and Survival*, 428; Kennedy, *Thirteen Days*, 72–73. Robert Kennedy's version of the story is only partly correct, since the book represents a sanitized version of his diaries.

[59] See Garthoff, *Reflections*, 71, fn.; Blight and Welch, *On the Brink*, 75, 171.

place offensive missiles in Cuba was made in the Kremlin.[60] In early September 1962, the Soviet news agency TASS issued a statement complaining that the United States was surrounding the USSR with military bases while not allowing Moscow to put defensive weapons into Cuba.

The link then became part of the domestic debate in the United States. Conservative senators demanded that the administration reject any connection between Cuba and American bases on the periphery of the Soviet Union. On October 2, the president publicly declared: "The United States' commitments around the world are to assist in the defense of these countries. The Communist effort in Cuba, of course, is to provide a springboard for an attack upon this entire hemisphere."[61] Dean Rusk committed the administration not to trade bases. Domestic politics during an election year and alliance considerations coincided at this point. The senators who pressured the administration in rejecting the linkage argued that the United States had to live up to its alliance commitments.

The issue of the Jupiter missiles came up during the first ExComm meeting on October 16. Dean Rusk speculated that the Soviet motive for the Cuban missile deployment might be to balance the Jupiter missiles in Turkey. Kennedy trapped himself in an argument that implicitly justified the Soviet action by suggesting that the threat posed by the American missiles in Turkey could indeed be equated with the Cuban situation:

> **Kennedy**: . . . but what is the advantage of that? It's just as if we suddenly began to put a major number of MRBMs in Turkey. Now that'd be goddam dangerous, I would think.
> **Bundy?**: Well, we *did*, Mr. President.
> **Kennedy**: Yeah, but that was five years ago.[62]

The idea of a "missile swap" came up the next day when a State Department paper speculated that a "possible constructive outcome of this crisis" could be "a trade-off of Cuban missile installations against Turkish and Italian JUPITERS, to be substituted for promptly by an accelerated European MRBM force."[63] Adlai Stevenson, the ambassador to the UN, proposed that the United States should announce the negotiability of all nuclear missile bases, if the Soviets removed the missiles from Cuba.

60 For details see Garthoff, *Reflections*, 12, 15; Blight and Welch, *On the Brink*, 295–96.

61 Kennedy Speech at a Luncheon for Latin American Foreign Ministers, Oct. 2, NSA: CMC, Doc. 00496. For the whole episode, see TASS Statement, Sept. 11, ibid., Doc. 00396; "Memorandum by W. W. Rostow to the President," Sept. 3, ibid., Doc. 00335; "U.S. Senate, Congressional Record," Oct. 2, ibid., Doc. 00483. For the following see "Dean Rusk on ABC," Sept. 29, ibid., Doc. 00471.

62 ExComm Transcript, Oct. 16, in "White House Tapes," 190. For Rusk's argument, see ibid., 177.

63 "What Course of Action Should We Follow if Construction on Missile Sites Continues?" Oct. 17, NSA:CMC, Doc. 00643. For the following see "Adlai Stevenson to John F. Kennedy," Oct. 17, ibid., Doc. 00652.

The idea was discussed at ExComm meetings during the first week of the crisis. Robert McNamara argued strongly in favor of a "missile swap" as a minimum price the United States would have to pay to get the Soviet missiles out of Cuba. Abram Chayes, the State Department's legal adviser, apparently polled members of the ExComm on the issue; nobody thought that the U.S. could resolve the crisis without trading the Jupiters. But the president ruled against bargains over bases in Turkey and Italy for the time being, while he was willing to discuss the issue with the Soviets in the future.[64]

Throughout the crisis, the administration was fairly divided over a "missile swap." The split cut across divisions between departments and even led to differences of opinion inside specific agencies. In the State Department, for example, the Bureau for European Affairs, the Policy Planning staff, and the Politico-Military Affairs staff were originally opposed to any attempt to equate the Jupiter missiles in Turkey with the Soviet missiles in Cuba. Walt W. Rostow argued: "If the idea should spread, justifiably or unjustifiably, that the US was considering a Cuba-for-Turkey deal, or a grand mutual withdrawal around the globe, growing doubts would be raised about the dependability of US commitments."[65]

In the Pentagon, members of the Office of International Security Affairs expressed opposition to trading away the Jupiter missiles. Among the military, SACEUR Norstad became the most significant guardian of the Jupiter missiles.

Supporters of a "missile swap" included the Arms Control and Disarmament Agency, the offices of International Organization Affairs and the Legal Adviser at the State Department as well as the U.S. mission to the UN. They used the issue to promote nuclear-free zones and a general U.S.-Soviet agreement for the removal of nuclear missiles from foreign

[64] For evidence, see State Department, "The Cuban Crisis, 1962," entries of Oct. 17, 18, 20, NSA:CMC, Doc. 03154; Theodore Sorensen, "Draft of Letter by the President to Khrushchev," Oct. 18, ibid., Doc. 00676; "Possible World Consequences of Military Action," Oct. 19, ibid., Doc. 00679; "Draft Speech for the President to Announce Imposition of Blockade," Oct. 19, ibid., Doc. 00681; Schlesinger, *Robert F. Kennedy*, 515–16; "Minutes of ExComm Meeting," Oct. 19, NSA:CMC, Doc. 00699; Blight and Welch, *On the Brink*, 102–3.

[65] "Walt Rostow to McGeorge Bundy," Oct. 24, NSA:CMC, Doc. 01164. For the Policy Planning staff see also various papers by Raymond Garthoff in his *Reflections*, 197–201. On the Bureau for European Affairs, see "Attempts to Equate Soviet Missile Bases in Cuba with NATO Jupiter Bases in Italy and Turkey," Oct. 22, NSA:CMC, Doc. 00570. See also "Memorandum by William Brubeck to McGeorge Bundy," Oct. 22, ibid., Doc. 00822. Note, however, that Rostow and the undersecretary for European affairs, William Tyler, worked out a face-saving proposal on October 25 (see below). For the following, see "Internal DOD, International Security Affairs Paper," ibid., Oct. 26, Doc. 01398; "US Embassy Paris to State Department," Nov. 11, ibid., Doc. 02246; "SACEUR Norstad to President Kennedy," Oct. 27, ibid., Doc. 01486.

bases.[66] In the Pentagon, the civilian leadership including Defense Secretary McNamara was favorably inclined toward a "missile swap" and emphasized the military obsolescence of the Jupiters.

During the second week of the crisis, the idea of trading the Soviet missiles in Cuba for the Jupiter missiles in Italy and Turkey was also discussed in public. On October 25 Walter Lippmann advocated such a deal in the *Washington Post*, while the Austrian foreign minister suggested that both superpowers could abandon military bases in the vicinity of each other's territory. To reassure Turkey, Dean Rusk sent a cable confirming the American commitment to the country's security.[67]

Transgovernmental Discussions about Potential Solutions

In the meantime, the Turkish Jupiter bases had come up in various interallied discussions. While the United States did not conduct formal consultations on the issue, the density of the transatlantic networks provided enough opportunities to hear out each other's views.

A "missile swap" was apparently discussed in the British government. Prime Minister Macmillan, for example, wrote in his diary of October 22 that Kennedy "may *never* get rid of Cuban rockets except by trading them for Turkish, Italian, or other bases."[68] SACEUR Norstad reported that, during his visit to London on October 23, a high-ranking British official inquired about the desirability of a missile trade, Turkey against Cuba. A Foreign Office paper suggested a "freeze" of certain existing bases on either side, mentioning Cuba and Turkey.[69]

But London remained opposed to an explicit missile trade throughout the crisis. Macmillan argued that a "straight bargain about bases . . . might strike the neutrals as cynical and involve us in serious difficulties with some N.A.T.O. countries, quite apart from Berlin."[70] Nevertheless, the British did favor a "deal" (see above). On October 26, the prime minis-

[66] For details see "W. Averell Harriman to George Ball," Oct. 22, NSA:CMC, Doc. 00816; "USACDA on Nuclear Free Zones," Oct. 24, ibid., Doc. 01119; "Harlan Cleveland to Rusk/Ball on UN Role," Oct. 24, ibid., Doc. 01159.

[67] See Walter Lippmann, "Today and Tomorrow," *Washington Post*, Oct. 25, 1962; "Embassy Vienna to State Department," Oct. 25, NSA:CMC, Doc. 01458; "Dean Rusk to Embassy Ankara: Message for Turkish Foreign Minister," Oct. 25, ibid., Doc. 01298. Turkey received similar reassurances from the British. See "Embassy Ankara to Foreign Office," Oct. 25, PRO:FO 371/162380.

[68] Macmillan, *End of the Day*, 187.

[69] See "US Embassy Paris to State Department," Nov. 11, NSA:CMC, Doc. 02246; "David Bruce, US Ambassador to Britain, Diary," entry of Oct. 25, ibid., Doc. 01281; "Memorandum by Foreign Office official," Oct. 25, PRO:FO 371/162388.

[70] "Foreign Office (Macmillan) to Embassy Washington," Oct. 24, PRO:FO 371/162378. See also "McGeorge Bundy to the President Regarding a Conversation with David Ormsby-Gore," Oct. 24, NSA:CMC, Doc. 01193.

ter suggested to Kennedy that he immobilize the Thor MRBMs on British soil for a period of time, during which the crisis would be resolved. He might not have recalled that his own government had announced in August that the Thors were to be phased out by the end of the year.[71] His remarks suggest that the British views coincided with those held in the U.S. administration by proponents of a face-saving deal with the Soviets. The Kennedy administration could be pretty certain that a key ally would endorse a "missile swap" if it was done in such a way as not to jeopardize the American commitment to Europe.[72]

At the same time, the Turkish government began to raise concerns over a potential "missile swap," particularly when the Soviet ambassador in Ankara began to argue that Moscow regarded the Jupiter missiles as its "Cuba." The Turkish representative raised the issue in the North Atlantic Council. While Dean Rusk publicly denied any connection between the Cuban Missile crisis and the situation anywhere else in the world, he also hinted that, in the long run, disarmament negotiations could deal with the location of weapons.[73]

Rusk alluded to one possible option for a face-saving deal discussed inside the U.S. administration and in transgovernmental networks including NATO representatives and officials from various governments, particularly in Britain and Turkey. Removing U.S. missiles from Europe in the context of *disarmament negotiations* following the withdrawal of the Soviet missiles from Cuba was supported by ACDA, the U.S. mission to the UN, and the British government.

The administration also considered speeding up plans for the Multilateral Force (MLF), a sea-based nuclear force of American, British, and French systems under a joint NATO command, which had been originally proposed by the Eisenhower administration. State Department officials suggested to "urge the Turkish and Italian governments . . . to record what we take to be their intent: i.e., their desire to phase out IRBM's when it is clear that the multilateral force will come into being—especially

[71] For details, see Macmillan, *End of the Day*, 210; Garthoff, *Reflections*, 71, fn. The Thor missiles were removed from Britain by December 1962.

[72] A close reading of Macmillan's memoirs reveals an ambivalance on the Jupiter issue. On the one hand, the prime minister writes that he "should never have consented, in spite of the argument which might be urged about the obsolescence of the missile base in Turkey, to this as a permanent deal" (*End of the Day*, 212). On the other hand, his diary entry of November 4 states that a "Turkey-Cuba deal would of course have been greatly to the advantage of the U.S. The Turkey base is useful, but not vital. Cuba was vital." (*ibid.*, 217)

[73] For details see "[U.S.] Ambassador Hare, Ankara, to State Dept.," Oct. 23, NSA:CMC, Doc. 01080; "Hare to State Dept.," Oct. 24, ibid., Doc. 01260; "Rusk, Circular Cable," Oct. 24, ibid., Doc. 01140; "Rusk to US Embassies, West Europe," Oct. 25, ibid., Doc. 01294; "Rusk to US Embassy, Ankara," Oct. 25, ibid., Doc. 01298.

since Polaris and other US external forces will provide needed coverage in the meantime."[74]

The United States set its diplomatic machinery in motion to anticipate allied reaction to the withdrawal of the Jupiter missiles in such a context. Dean Rusk told the U.S. ambassadors to NATO, Turkey, and Italy that a negotiated solution to the Cuban Missile crisis might involve the removal of the Jupiters: "Therefore need prepare carefully for such contingency in order not repeat not harm our relations with this important ally."

He then asked the ambassadors to assess the consequences of a Jupiter removal under various scenarios including an open deal and military compensation in terms of Polaris submarines or the MLF. He told the ambassadors not to discuss this "with any foreigners."[75]

The U.S. ambassador to NATO, Finletter, responded along the lines already discussed in the State Department. He argued that Turkey regarded the Jupiter missiles as a symbol of the alliance commitment to its defense and that no arrangement should be made without the approval of the Turkish government. While he thought that Norway, Denmark, and the British might accept a "missile swap," Finletter strongly advised against any open deal. He then proposed a "small southern command multilateral seaborne force on a 'pilot basis'" utilizing Polaris submarines and manned by mixed U.S., Turkish, and Italian crews. Such an arrangement could allow the United States to offer the withdrawal of the Jupiters to the Soviets.[76] The ambassador to Italy essentially concurred with Finletter's assessment, arguing that the government in Rome would probably agree to the Jupiter withdrawal if Italian security was not affected.

U.S. Ambassador Hare cabled a gloomy assessment from Ankara: "Turks deeply resent any coupling of Turkey and Cuba on ground that situations completely different and that suggestions to that effect, especially when coming from Western sources, are both inexcusable and seriously damaging."[77] But Hare went on to discuss possible solutions, among

[74] "William Tyler, Walt Rostow, and Philip Talbot to Dean Rusk," Oct. 25, NSA:CMC, Doc. 01306. See also "Internal Memorandum," Oct. 23, ibid., Doc. 00886; State Dept., "Internal Paper, Scenario for Multilateral Southern MRBM Command," Oct. 26, ibid., Doc. 01412; "W. W. Rostow to the Secretary, Subject: Alliance Missiles," Oct. 26, ibid., Doc. 01448. Removal of the Jupiters when Polaris submarines would become available in early 1963 had apparently been discussed between Secretary of State Rusk and his Turkish colleague back in April 1961. See Lebow and Stein, *We All Lost the Cold War*, 44.

[75] "Dean Rusk to US Embassies to NATO and to Turkey," Oct. 24, NSA:CMC, Doc. 01138.

[76] "Finletter to State Dept.," Oct. 25, NSA:CMC, Doc. 01328. For the following see "US Embassy Rome to State Dept.," Oct. 26, ibid., Doc. 01463.

[77] "Hare to State Dept.," (section one) Oct. 26, NSA:CMC, Doc. 01470. For the following see "Hare to State Dept.," (sections two and three) Oct. 26, NSA, Nuclear History Documents.

them a strictly secret deal with the Soviets. Turkey should receive some compensation in terms of a sea-borne nuclear force as well as "military hardware" for the country itself. Under these conditions, even Hare thought that a "missile swap" was possible. These cables, together with an assessment by General Norstad, who remained adamantly opposed to any deal,[78] were discussed in the ExComm meetings on October 27 and influenced the president's decisions.

There are various indications that both Finletter and Hare talked to "foreigners" about a secret "missile swap" despite Rusk's directive and that their advice to the ExComm was based on these discussions. The ideas put forward by British officials have already been mentioned. There was also some discussion at NATO in Paris. Finletter reported later that the idea for a face-saving pilot MLF arrangement had been suggested to him by another permanent representative.[79]

Most important, the Turkish government, at least its foreign ministry, indicated to the American and the British ambassadors that it was not completely opposed to a removal of the Jupiters: "We have evidence that thinking in the Ministry of Foreign Affairs is firmly on the lines that there can be no individual bargaining of the Turkish and Cuban situations; and that Turkish bases could only be discussed after a suitable lapse of time and in a general NATO context."[80] This is exactly what happened. The Turkish view was all the more significant, since the U.S. had apparently discussed the MLF idea with the Turkish ambassador in Washington already.[81]

Finally, the president involved the British ambassador in his deliberations. Ormsby-Gore met Kennedy on Saturday morning, October 27, after Khrushchev's publicly broadcast demand of a "missile swap" had reached the U.S. The president made similar points as during the ExComm meetings on that day, indicating "that from many points of view the removal of missiles from Turkey and Cuba to the accompaniment of guarantees of the integrity of the two countries had considerable merit."[82] Kennedy then mentioned to Ormsby-Gore that Ambassador Hare had been asked for his views on the

[78] See "General Norstad to the President," Oct. 27, NSA:CMC, Doc. 01486.

[79] See "Finletter to State Dept.," Oct. 28, NSA:CMC, Doc. 01602. Finletter cabled that the representative (identity excised in the declassified document) had actually "volunteered" this suggestion. In other words, Finletter did not violate Rusk's order.

[80] "[U.K.] Embassy Ankara to Foreign Office," Oct. 28, PRO:FO 371/162382. See also "Embassy Ankara to Foreign Office," Oct. 28, ibid. 371/162381. The British ambassador reports his conversations with Turkish officials and with his American colleague Hare in these cables. This strongly suggests that both ambassadors had contact with the Turkish foreign ministry on the matter. The Turkish government most probably knew what was going on in Washington.

[81] According to "W. W. Rostow to the Secretary, Subject: Alliance Missiles," Oct. 26, NSA:CMC, Doc. 01448.

[82] According to "[U.K.] Embassy Washington to Foreign Office," Oct. 27, PRO:FO 371/162382.

matter and "he thought it might be helpful if our Ambassador to Turkey [that is, the British ambassador] could also give his opinion." The British Ambassador in Ankara came to the same conclusions as his U.S. colleague.

In sum, when the crisis reached its climax on October 27, a solution had emerged in discussions that included the State Department, the Pentagon, U.S. diplomats in Europe, NATO representatives in Paris, and various allied governments, at least the British and the Turks. The solution entailed a strictly secret deal between Washington and Moscow, which included the removal of the Jupiter missiles from Turkey in exchange for military compensation for the ally, after the Soviets had withdrawn their missiles from Cuba. While the United States did not formally consult the allies on these plans, transgovernmental networking provided sufficient information indicating that Turkey and other allies could live with such a deal. At least the British knew about the president's views on the subject on October 27.

The Secret Deal

The ExComm meetings on October 27 devoted most of their time to the options of an air strike against Cuba versus a "missile swap."[83] U.S. membership in the allied community and the ensuing obligations did not *cause* the final choice. But the sense of allied community among ExComm members served as a frame of reference in which the various courses of action were discussed. Both sides in the debate referred to the need of preserving NATO to strengthen their case. Supporters of an air strike argued that a missile trade would lead to the denuclearization of NATO and indicate that the United States was prepared to tamper with the indivisibility of allied security for selfish reasons. This latter point found widespread support among uncommitted ExComm members. As McGeorge Bundy put it: "In their [the Turkish] own terms it would already be clear that we were trying to sell our allies for our interests. That would be the view in all of NATO. It's irrational, and it's crazy, but it's a terribly powerful fact." Supporters of the missile trade, such as George Ball, countered: "I don't think NATO is going to be wrecked, and if NATO isn't any better than that, it isn't good to us."[84] The president seemed to be opposed to an air strike and steered a middle course during this discussion. He was primarily concerned that the Soviet public

[83] The significance of the October 27 meetings has recently become doubtful because of revelations by the former Soviet ambassador to the United States, Anatoly Dobrynin, that he discussed a "missile swap" during a secret meeting with Robert Kennedy on Friday, Oct. 26. But no documentation was found in Moscow archives backing the account, and Dobrynin now agrees that the crucial meeting with the president's brother took place Saturday night, Oct. 27 (personal communication by Richard N. Lebow). On Dobrynin's erroneous account, see Bruce Allyn et al., "Essence of Revision: Moscow, Havana, and the Cuban Missile Crisis," *International Security* 14, no. 3 (Winter 1989/90): 136–72, 158–59.

[84] Both quotes are in "October 27, 1962: ExComm Transcripts," 39, 77.

demand might provoke a public counterresponse by the Turkish government that would jeopardize a secret solution to the crisis. He argued that the United States faced a terrible dilemma. On the one hand, the U.S. commitment to its allies was at stake. On the other hand, many alliance members around the world (he particularly mentioned Britain) might regard a missile trade as a reasonable deal and would not understand if the U.S. rejected it and instead started military escalation with the potential of global warfare:

> But we are now in the position of risking war in Cuba and in Berlin over missiles in Turkey which are of little military value. From the political point of view, it would be hard to get support on an air strike against Cuba because many would think that we would make a good trade if we offered to take the missiles out of Turkey in the event the Russians would agree to remove the missiles from Cuba. We are in a bad position if we appear to be attacking Cuba for the purpose of keeping useless missiles in Turkey. We cannot propose to withdraw the missiles from Turkey, but the Turks could offer to do so.[85]

Kennedy also maintained that the Turkish government and the NATO allies in general might not be aware of the danger of military escalation and that the implications of the air strike option had not been fully explained to them. It was then decided to convene a NATO council meeting and to inform the allies that the U.S. was considering an air strike. The issue of the Jupiter missiles should not be brought up.

In the end, a secret deal with the Soviets together with some military compensation for the allies was endorsed by Robert Kennedy, Dean Rusk, Robert McNamara, and CIA head John McCone. The proposal also carried the day with the president. It was agreed that the Jupiter missiles could not be removed without Turkish approval and that, therefore, the United States would have to persuade the government in Ankara.

After the ExComm meeting, a small group of Kennedy's advisers assembled and discussed an oral message to be transmitted to Dobrynin by Robert Kennedy. Dean Rusk then proposed that the attorney general should simply tell Dobrynin that the U.S. was determined to get the Jupiter missiles out of Turkey as soon as the crisis was over. The group also agreed to keep absolute secrecy about this. Robert McNamara later argued: "It was important to frame it exactly as it was framed because don't forget we were dealing not with a military problem but with a political problem. And if we had not framed the withdrawal of the missiles from

[85] Bromley Smith, "Summary Record of ExComm Meeting," Oct. 27, NSA:CMC, Doc. 01541. For the following see "October 27, 1962: ExComm Transcripts"; McGeorge Bundy, "ExComm Record of Action," Oct. 27, NSA:CMC, Doc. 01539; Bromley Smith, "Summary Record of ExComm Meeting," Oct. 27, ibid., Doc. 01541.

Turkey as we did, we would have created another political problem. We would have divided the Alliance."[86]

Shortly after the meeting of Kennedy's advisers, the president's brother met with Ambassador Dobrynin. According to Dobrynin's cable to Moscow, Robert Kennedy told him in rather dramatic terms that the crisis was quickly escalating and that the United States might soon bomb the missile bases in Cuba, which could lead to war in Europe. The president's brother repeated the noninvasion pledge and told Dobrynin when asked about Turkey:

> If that is the only obstacle to achieving the regulation . . . then the President doesn't see any unsurmountable difficulties in resolving this issue. . . . The greatest difficulty for the President is the public discussion of the issue of Turkey. Formally the deployment of missile bases in Turkey was done by a special decision of the NATO Council. To announce now a unilateral decision by the President of the USA to withdraw missile bases from Turkey—this would damage the entire structure of NATO. . . . In short, if such a decision were announced now it would seriously tear apart NATO. . . . I think that in order to withdraw these bases from Turkey . . . we need 4–5 months. . . . However, the President can't say anything public in this regard about Turkey. . . . R. Kennedy then warned that his comments about Turkey are extremely confidential; besides him and his brother, only 2–3 people know about it in Washington.[87]

Robert Kennedy told Dobrynin with surprising clarity and frankness the true reasons for the American desire to keep the "missile swap" a secret. U.S. concerns about NATO cohesion were apparently so significant that Kennedy tried to involve even the Soviets in the cover-up. When Dobrynin brought a letter from Khrushchev on October 29 in which he spelled out the agreement concerning the Jupiter missiles, the United States did not accept it and told the Soviets that the deal would be off if Moscow publicized it.[88]

President Kennedy was not prepared to risk war with the Soviet Union over obsolete missiles in Turkey. If Khrushchev had not agreed to Kennedy's proposals of October 27, a contingency plan existed under which UN Secretary General U Thant would have issued a call for removal of the missiles both from Cuba and from Turkey. Kennedy could

[86] McNamara in "Transcript of Discussion about Cuban Missile Crisis (Sloan Foundation Interview)," NSA:CMC, Doc. 03307. See also McNamara in Blight and Welch, *On the Brink*, 190–92. On the small group meeting on Oct. 27, see Bundy, *Danger and Survival*, 432–34; "Letter by Dean Rusk to James Blight," Feb. 25, 1987, NSA:CMC, Doc. 03322.

[87] "A. F. Dobrynin's Telegram to MID USSR," Oct. 27, in Lebow and Stein, *We All Lost the Cold War*, 524–26, 525. For Robert Kennedy's account of the meeting, see Beschloss, *Crisis Years*, 536.

[88] Cf. Beschloss, *Crisis Years*, 546–47; Garthoff, *Reflections*, 95 fn.

have accepted such an appeal more readily than a public demand from Khrushchev.[89]

While Washington waited for Khrushchev's response, Ambassador Finletter was instructed to convey the seriousness of the situation to the North Atlantic Council. A message was also sent to NATO governments that the United States might undertake military action against Cuba, which could provoke Soviet retaliation against the missiles in Turkey. The allies were told that the United States was prepared to render the Jupiter missiles inoperable and to inform the USSR about it. Washington then offered to position Polaris submarines in the Mediterranean to cover the targets that had been assigned to the Jupiters. The allied governments were asked to consult and to report back their views immediately.[90]

If the purpose of these messages was to scare the allies, it succeeded. At the North Atlantic Council meeting on October 28, a consensus against military action emerged. At the same time, most council members were opposed to trading away the Jupiter missiles, while some wished to keep the door open for later negotiations on the issue.

Getting the Jupiter Missiles out of Turkey

Once Khrushchev had accepted the president's proposal, the next step for the U.S. government was to remove the Jupiter missiles from Turkey without raising suspicions of a "missile trade." On October 30, Walt W. Rostow of the State Department's Policy Planning Staff outlined the pathway to remove the Jupiter missiles from Turkey and to follow up on the idea to institute a pilot "Southern Command multilateral sea-based force." While arrangements for the pilot MLF would be worked out, Polaris submarines would be stationed in the Mediterranean. Once these agreements were in place, Rostow argued that "it would probably not be difficult to move the Turkish and Italian governments to indicate . . . that they would wish to phase out IRBM's at an appropriate time.[91]

These plans coincided with a directive by Robert McNamara that followed the president's order and stipulated that the Jupiter missiles should be removed from Turkey and Italy by May 1963. NATO and the govern-

[89] See "Letter by Dean Rusk to James Blight."

[90] See "Message to North Atlantic Council and Governments of All NATO Countries," Oct. 27, NSA:CMC, Doc. 01476. See also "Secretary of State to Ambassador Finletter," Oct. 28, ibid., Doc. 01580. Finletter's briefing paper was handed over to the British. See PRO:FO 371/162392. For the following see "Finletter to State Department," Oct. 28, NSA:CMC, Doc. 01602; "Report by Gordey, France-Soir, to Richard Estabrook," ibid., Doc. 01860; "UK Embassy NATO Paris to Foreign Office," Oct. 28, PRO:FO 371/162382.

[91] W. W. Rostow, "Memorandum, Subject: Turkish IRBM's," Oct. 30, NSA:CMC, Doc. 01726. See also Henry Owen, "Memorandum to McGeorge Bundy," Oct. 29, ibid., Doc. 01654; "Memorandum to Alexis Johnson," Oct. 30, ibid., Doc. 01714.

ments in Ankara and Rome should be approached. Officials in the State Department and the Pentagon, who were unaware of the missile deal, raised concerns. Even Dean Rusk, who had suggested the deal on October 27 in the meeting of Kennedy's closest advisers, now sent a memorandum to the president objecting to the removal of the Jupiters "in the near future."[92]

The administration used a mix of pressure, persuasion, and bribery to solicit Ankara's agreement to remove the missiles only months after they had become operational. In January 1963, Turkey announced that the Jupiter missiles were to be withdrawn and replaced by modern Polaris submarines. In March, McNamara's envoy General Wood visited the Turkish defense minister and offered new military assistance including tanks, aircraft, helicopters, and naval vessels to maintain "confidence and morale GOT [Government of Turkey]" and "obviating possible GOT stalling on Jupiter dismantling."[93]

The first Polaris submarine was on station in the Mediterranean in early April and the dismantling of the Jupiter missiles began. On April 25, 1963, the last Jupiter missile was removed.[94] The United States had fulfilled its commitment to the Soviet Union.

At the same time, the cover-up of the "missile swap" continued. Right after the crisis, Dean Rusk reassured the Turkish government that "no deal of any kind was made with USSR involving Turkey." The administration stuck to this line. Both Dean Rusk and Robert McNamara lied to Congress:

> **Sen. Hickenlooper**: May I just ask the Secretary, your statement is then that the removal of the missiles from Turkey . . . was in no way, shape of form, directly or indirectly, connected with the settlement, the discussions or the manipulation of the Cuban situation?
>
> **Rusk**: That is correct, Sir.
>
> . . .
>
> **McNamara**: There is absolutely no connection whatsoever between the

[92] Dean Rusk, "Memorandum for the President," Nov. 9, *John F. Kennedy Library* (courtesy of Don Munton). See also "William Tyler to the Secretary," Nov. 9, ibid.; "Jeffrey Kitchen to Robert Komer, State Dept.," Nov. 10, NSA:CMC, Doc. 02219; "General Norstad to the President," Nov. 1, ibid., Doc. 01798; "Robert Komer, NSC, to McGeorge Bundy," Nov. 12, ibid., Doc. 02260.

[93] "Dean Rusk to US Embassy Ankara," March 7, 1963, Kennedy Library (courtesy of Don Munton). See also "USAFE Logistics Group Turkey, Historical Data Record 7/1–12/31/1962," NSA:CMC, Doc. 02817; "USAFE Operations in the Mediterranean, 1945–1970," ibid., Doc. 03373; "President's Press Conference," Jan. 24, 1963, ibid., Doc. 02882; "Oral History, Raymond Hare," Sept. 9, 1969, ibid., Doc. 03249; "FBIS, Western Europe," March 13, 1963, ibid., Doc. 02995.

[94] See "Handwritten Note by Robert McNamara to the President," Apr. 25, 1963, NSA:CMC, Doc. 03081.

> forced removal by the U.S. military pressure upon Cuba of the Soviet missiles introduced in Cuba on the one hand and not the removal but the modernization—of the missiles in Turkey and Italy.[95]

For domestic and alliance reasons, the administration projected the appearance that the Cuban Missile crisis had been resolved solely through American toughness. Admitting that there was a secret trade between missiles in Cuba and missiles in Turkey would not only have confirmed fears of abandonment by the allies, it would have counteracted the image conveyed by the Kennedy administration after the crisis, namely that its firmness had forced the Soviets to blink.[96]

Conclusions

American decision-makers were more concerned about the country's vital interests and survival during the Cuban Missile crisis than in all other cases analyzed in this book. It appears, therefore, to be counterintuitive that alliance considerations should play a significant role under these circumstances. But American decision-makers not only worried constantly about European reactions to their preferred courses of action. The choices were significantly influenced by anticipated allied demands and—albeit to a lesser degree—direct allied input. The two most important American decisions during the crisis—the installation of the blockade and the offer of a secret "missile deal"—cannot be explained without taking the alliance factor into account.

U.S. membership in an alliance of democratic states shaped the process by which decision-makers struggled over the definition of American interests and preferences during the crisis:

- The Soviet missiles had to get out of Cuba—to some extent, because the American reputation vis-à-vis its allies was at stake.
- Escalatory actions such as an invasion of Cuba were to be avoided—partly because the Soviet Union might retaliate against Europe.
- A public "missile swap" had to be prevented—because of the necessity to maintain alliance cohesion.

U.S. membership in the Western Alliance not only influenced specific choices but also the process by which American preferences were identified. But what about alternative explanations? As in the preceding chap-

[95] "Testimony at the US House Armed Services Committee," Jan. 30, 1963, NSA:CMC, Doc. 02887. The quote from Dean Rusk is taken from "Testimony before US Senate Committee on Foreign Relations," Jan. 25, 1963, ibid., Doc. 02883. For Rusk's reassurance to the Turkish government see "Secretary of State to US Embassy Ankara," Oct. 29, 1962, ibid., Doc. 01641.

[96] In fact, both Kennedy and Khrushchev blinked. See Lebow and Stein, *We All Lost the Cold War*, 144, on this point.

ters, I first discuss the possibility that the outcome of the Cuban Missile crisis can be explained without referring to the alliance factor. I then proceed to evaluate the validity of traditional realist versus liberal propositions with regard to the case.

Alternative Explanations: Power, Domestic Politics, and Leadership Beliefs

One could argue that the American decisions during the Cuban Missile crisis were perfectly rational given the risks and opportunities at stake. The decision in favor of the blockade rather than an immediate air strike during the first week of the crisis made good sense if a potentially uncontrollable escalation was to be avoided. The noninvasion pledge in conjunction with the "missile swap" represented minor concessions on the American part. As the Bay of Pigs incident had shown, an invasion of Cuba entailed military risks and could have resulted in another public relations disaster. "Swapping" the real and operational Soviet missiles in Cuba for the militarily obsolete Jupiter MRBMs in Turkey was a good deal for the United States. The secrecy of the deal also insured that the president could portray himself as the "tough guy" who had successfully stood up to Soviet adventurism. This image helped considerably during the congressional elections in November 1962.

Such an account is not wrong. The blockade, the noninvasion pledge, and the secret "missile swap" were perfectly rational decisions. But a rational choice account proves to be indeterminate, *unless* alliance considerations come into play. The opposite arguments in favor of escalating the crisis through an air strike or even an invasion were as rational as those in support of the blockade or the "missile deal." Supporters of an air strike correctly argued that the risks of escalation were minimal given the overwhelming U.S. superiority, both locally in the region and on the global nuclear level.[97] Only if Soviet retaliation against Europe was considered a problem, could one make a rational argument against the air strike and other escalatory steps. Berlin was the American Achilles heel during the crisis, not New York City.

The question remains whether domestic political considerations serve as a better explanation for the decisions of the Kennedy administration during the crisis.[98] The Democrats faced tough congressional elections in November. Prior to the crisis, Republicans in Congress had accused the

[97] This argument was made by the Joint Chiefs of Staff and is repeated until today. See, for example, Ray S. Cline, "Commentary: The Cuban Missile Crisis," *Foreign Affairs* 68, no. 4 (Fall 1989): 190–96.

[98] For a discussion see Richard N. Lebow, "Domestic Politics and the Cuban Missile Crisis: The Traditional and Revisionist Interpretations Reconsidered," *Diplomatic History* 14, no. 4 (Fall 1990): 471–92. See also Lebow and Stein, *We All Lost the Cold War*, 96–102.

administration of being soft toward both Moscow and Havana. Partly in response to these pressures, President Kennedy had publicly committed himself in September 1962 not to accept offensive weapons in Cuba.

There are two reasons why a domestic political account alone does not seem to present a sufficient explanation for U.S. decisions during the crisis. First, domestic pressures predominantly worked in one direction, toward a quick and tough American response to the installation of Soviet missiles in Cuba. The Republicans demanded this all along. The administration was well aware that public support and the "rally 'round the flag" effect would erode quickly if the president was unable to remove the perceived threat within a short period of time.[99] There was not much domestic counterpressure in favor of deescalation to give Moscow time to back down, or even toward a cooperative solution. The alliance factor, on the other hand, worked in both directions—a "carrot and stick" approach that was firm but left room for compromise.

Second, domestic and alliance politics cannot be disentangled during the Cuban Missile crisis. Both exerted a synergistic influence. The conservative critics of the Kennedy administration, for example, used the alliance argument in the domestic dispute and argued that U.S. "dovishness" toward Cuba and the Soviet Union seriously endangered the North Atlantic Alliance.[100] Moreover, U.S. decision-makers did not perceive domestic politics and alliance considerations as two separate questions. In those few instances in which domestic political arguments came up in the ExComm, they were almost always connected to alliance arguments. The following comment by Robert McNamara on Kennedy's fear of impeachment if he did not act forcefully, serves as a typical example: "What he conveyed by that statement about being impeached was his recognition of the political consequences of not appearing to be firm—consequences not so much to him personally but rather to the nation, to the alliance, to the risks of future conflict with the Soviets."[101] McNamara interprets the statement about impeachment as involving the allies—as if the Europeans could have removed Kennedy from office.

A final alternative explanation points to the strong leadership by John F. Kennedy during the crisis. Indeed and in contrast to the test ban negotiations (chapter 5), the president's personality and preferences were extremely significant during the crisis, and he was "fully on the job," as McGeorge Bundy put it.[102] While he carefully listened to advice, the

[99] See, for example, Walt W. Rostow, "Memorandum to McGeorge Bundy," Oct. 24, 1962, NSA:CMC, Doc. 01164.

[100] See, for example, "US Senate, Congressional Record," Oct. 2, NSA:CMC, Doc. 00483.

[101] McNamara in Blight and Welch, *On the Brink*, 190–91.

[102] McGeorge Bundy, "Transcriber's Note," in "October 27, 1962: ExComm Transcripts," 31.

decisions were his. If the president's preferences explain U.S. choices during the crisis, do we need the alliance factor?

First, John F. Kennedy identified himself strongly with the community of allied democracies; this identity shaped his preferences. He valued NATO highly and was extremely concerned about possible Soviet actions against the European allies, particularly Berlin. Second, this appreciation of the allied community enabled actors such as the British ambassador and Prime Minister Macmillan to serve as valued counsels whose arguments the president took as much into account as those of his closest advisers. During the second week of the crisis, the British participated in the U.S. decision-making process.

In sum, alternative accounts emphasizing power and rational action, domestic politics, or presidential leadership are actually consistent or at least compatible with an argument emphasizing allied influence. American behavior during the Cuban Missile crisis cannot be fully understood if one ignores U.S. membership in the North Atlantic Alliance.

The Allied Influence: Traditional Realism versus Liberalism

If the Cuban Missile crisis serves as another example of the "big influence of small allies," how do the two theoretical approaches (chapter 2) that assume that lesser powers can indeed influence alliance leaders score?

A realist arguing in the tradition of Hans Morgenthau might not be surprised by the degree of allied impact during the Cuban Missile crisis. If the United States valued NATO at all, it should be concerned about maintaining allied unity during the crisis and should try to uphold the reputation of protecting allied interests. While this general point cannot be denied, realist thinking conceptualizes interallied relations in terms of power-based bargaining. The empirical evidence can only partly be reconciled with these assumptions about process.

First, allied influence could result from *stronger preferences* on the part of the small states as compared to the alliance leader. This argument does not apply in this case, since the United States perceived its supreme national interests at stake. American decision-makers were apparently even more concerned about the fate of the allies than were some European governments, particularly with regard to Berlin.

Second, the United States might have feared *allied defection* or neutrality during the crisis and, thus, may have given in to the demands of the Europeans. The decision to institute a blockade rather than to carry out an air strike was at least partly motivated by the fear of losing allied support in the absence of thorough consultation on the issue. Such arguments were frequently made during the first week of the crisis. The same motivation could explain the decision in favor of a secret "missile swap."

But this reasoning only holds true for the first week of the crisis, as long as decision-makers in Washington did not know the European reaction. Once the NATO allies were informed about the situation, they overwhelmingly supported the United States. As a result, fear of allied defection should not have concerned the United States during the second week of the crisis. No European ally ever threatened to remain neutral during the crisis in an attempt to increase its bargaining power. The British, for example, who were both the most closely consulted among the allies and the most critical to specific courses of actions, offered frequent advice but never wavered in their support for the president.

Third, one could argue that the high degree of U.S. *threat perception* enabled the Europeans to affect the decisions in Washington. Indeed, this point could explain why ExComm members went to such great lengths to anticipate European reactions to possible courses of action and to take them into consideration.

Fourth, *allied unity* as a potential cause for allied influence does not apply in this case. The Europeans were united, but in favor of U.S. policies, even though they were concerned about specific courses of action.

Finally, the United States would have needed *allied resources* to carry out a war against the Soviet Union if the crisis had escalated; this should have increased allied bargaining leverage vis-à-vis Washington. This argument only holds true, however, if that escalation had taken place in Europe. In other words, the United States would have needed European bases primarily to protect its allies rather than its own homeland.

Moreover, nothing indicates that U.S. decision-makers took (anticipated) allied views into account because they were afraid of being denied the use of military bases in Europe. The two European locations most frequently mentioned in the ExComm, Berlin and the Turkish Jupiter bases, did not represent European assets to increase allied bargaining power but rather liabilities with little value from a strategic point of view.[103] If the United States was desperate about its survival, why should decision-makers worry about Berlin (which NATO could not militarily defend anyway) and about some obsolete missile bases?

Thus, realist assumptions about power-based bargaining among allies appear to be confirmed only to some extent. In general, however, the Cuban Missile crisis reinforces the results from the preceding case studies that realist bargaining theory is not of much help to understand interallied relations in NATO.

[103] As Raymond Garthoff put it in a memorandum for Alexis Johnson on Oct. 27: "The Jupiters are not important as a military-strategic asset—but then, neither is Berlin. Yet both have elemental significance as symbols of the integrity of the Alliance and especially of our commitment to stand by the interests of each of its members" (quoted from Garthoff, *Reflections*, 201).

What about liberal arguments about cooperation among democracies? That U.S. decision-makers did not particularly distinguish between domestic and European concerns, that they worried as much about the fate of Berlin as about New York City, and that they regarded obsolete Jupiter missiles in Turkey as major obstacles to the solution of the crisis—these puzzles make sense if one assumes a security community of democratic nations on behalf of which the Kennedy administration acted. Membership in the Western Alliance affected the identity of American actors in the sense that the "we" in whose name the president decided incorporated the European allies. The alliance community as part of the American identity explains the lack of distinction between domestic and alliance politics as well as the sense of commitment that U.S. decision-makers felt with regard to their allies. Those who invoked potential allied concerns in the internal discourses added weight to their arguments by referring to the collectively shared value of the community.

But the Cuban Missile crisis also poses problems for a liberal argument about democratic alliances. The lack of allied consultation during the first week violated, if not the letter, then at least the spirit of the North Atlantic Treaty, which asks for consultation if the security of one of the parties is threatened (Article 4). Moreover, if consultation norms are supposed to enable allied influence, institutionalists should be puzzled by the fact that the lack of consultation did *not* result in lesser allied impact during the first week of the crisis. The contrast to the Suez crisis is striking (chapter 4). In 1956, Britain, France, and the United States temporarily stepped out of the normative framework of the Western Alliance. This resulted in power bargaining and the United States prevailed. But during the Cuban Missile crisis, the lack of consultation did not lead to U.S. unilateralism. In fact, the memory of the Suez crisis partly let U.S. decision-makers act "as if" they had fully consulted the allies. U.S. leaders did not escape the normative framework of the Western Alliance by choosing not to listen to European input. The lack of consultation did not achieve its intended goal of freeing the president and his advisers from worries about the allies.

But the U.S. did resume its obligations under the NATO treaty during the second week of the crisis. From October 21 on, the British government in particular enjoyed the "special relationship" and advised the president by using its transgovernmental linkages with the U.S. administration. Ormsby-Gore and Macmillan were almost treated by the president as if they were members of the ExComm. When the issue of trading the Soviet missiles in Cuba for the Jupiter missiles in Turkey came up, the informal transatlantic networks of the allied community worked again. The idea of a secret deal partly originated in these networks, and the Turkish government seems to have unofficially agreed.

In sum, the Cuban Missile crisis strongly underscores the finding of this book that the European allies exerted disproportionate influence on American foreign policy at a time when the power distribution in NATO was overwhelmingly in favor of the United States and when America's supreme security interests were at stake. Traditional realists would have expected some European impact during the crisis, since the American reputation to protect its allies was at stake. But power-based assumptions about bargaining among allies are confirmed only to a limited degree.

As to liberal and institutionalist theory, the case is fully consistent with the argument that a pluralistic security community of democracies shapes the identity of the actors. The Cuban Missile crisis also underscores the assumption that transgovernmental networks and coalitions are primary transmitters of allied influence in highly institutionalized relationships among democracies. But the case also challenges the institutionalist argument about consultation norms, since the American violation of the norm during the first week of the crisis did not appear to be causally consequential.

SEVEN

BLOWING UP NEW YORK TO SAVE BERLIN?

NORMS, TRANSNATIONAL RELATIONS, AND NATO'S NUCLEAR DECISIONS

SKEPTICS could argue that the findings of this study pertain to a particular time-period, the 1950s and early 1960s; to specific European actors, namely the British; and to special cases outside the direct realm of European security. While another set of detailed case studies is beyond the scope of this book, substantial empirical evidence suggests that the European influence on American foreign policy continued in later periods of time; included NATO decisions regarding military strategy and weapon deployments in Europe; was not confined to the Anglo-American "special relationship"; and can be accounted for by liberal and institutionalist assumptions.

Decisions on nuclear strategy and deployments preoccupied NATO throughout the cold war. They involved the survival interests of both the United States and the Europeans, leading to similarly intense preferences. For Europeans,[1] especially nonnuclear countries such as West Germany, the prevention of war in densely populated Central Europe was the most important security objective during the cold war. This goal was to be realized through (nuclear) deterrence and—from the 1970s on—through détente with the Soviet Union and Eastern Europe. Since a military conflict in Central Europe would most probably have resulted in the destruction of what was supposed to be defended, most Europeans were primarily interested in confronting the Soviet Union with a high risk of nuclear escalation in the event of any military conflict in Europe, thereby emphasizing a deterrence strategy based on punishment rather than denial.[2] For the United States, things were more complicated. On the one hand, America was the major provider of (nuclear) security for Western Europe and had committed itself to its defense, thereby risking its own

[1] The following is highly simplistic. *The* European view on nuclear issues did not exist as there was no unified American perspective. The transatlantic strategy debate has always been transnational, even though nuclear warfighting and counterforce strategies were never as popular in Europe as they were in parts of the American strategy community.

[2] On these distinctions, see Glenn H. Snyder, *Deterrence and Defense* (Princeton, N.J.: Princeton University Press, 1961).

survival. On the other hand, it made neither political nor moral sense to blow up the world in response to a military conflict confined to Europe.

While the nuclear debate in NATO was mainly framed in terms of deterrence strategy and theory, it was ultimately about the meaning and the limits of the mutual commitment to the transatlantic community. How indivisible was the security of the NATO area? For the United States, the ultimate question was whether Berlin was part of "us" to the extent that there was no difference between an attack on the city and an attack on New York. For Western Europe, the question was to what extent the allies could trust American commitments and normative obligations to risk the survival of New York for the defense of Berlin. European governments then set an important criterion for the credibility of the American commitment: whether Washington was willing to let West Europeans codetermine NATO's nuclear posture. (For the United States, burden-sharing assumed a similar role of testing the European commitment to the common defense.)

I briefly discuss three cases: the debate about the NATO strategy of "flexible response" in the 1960s, the "neutron bomb" decision, and intermediate-range nuclear forces (INF) deployment and arms control in the late 1970s.

The Debate about "Flexible Response"

The NATO strategy of "flexible response"[3] had two origins, one in the United States and one at NATO headquarters in Europe. But the strategy advocated by the Kennedy administration in 1962 and the doctrine MC 14/3 adopted by NATO in 1967 were different. In the United States, the strategic community had become increasingly worried during the late 1950s about the credibility of "massive retaliation." It began advocating nuclear options emphasizing counterforce and countervalue rather than countercity targeting. At about the same time, Supreme Allied Commander Europe (SACEUR) Norstad started lobbying for a change in NATO's strategy toward greater emphasis on direct, conventional defense. When the Kennedy administration entered office in 1961, it under-took a comprehensive review of strategic planning and essentially adopted both proposals.

[3] For excellent analyses of the "flexible response" debate, see Ivo Daalder, *The Nature and Practice of Flexible Response* (New York: Columbia University Press, 1991); Helga Haftendorn, *Kernwaffen und die Glaubwürdigkeit der Allianz* (Baden-Baden: Nomos, 1994), 31-105; Jane E. Stromseth, *The Origins of Flexible Response* (New York: St. Martin's Press, 1988). See also Paul Buteux, *The Politics of Nuclear Consultation in NATO* (Cambridge: Cambridge University Press, 1980); David N. Schwartz, *NATO's Nuclear Dilemmas* (Washington, D.C.: Brookings, 1983), chap. 6.

In May 1962 Secretary of Defense McNamara presented the American proposal for flexible response to his NATO colleagues.[4] He argued in favor of the counterforce orientation and promoted a new NATO strategy based on the idea of controlled nuclear escalation. Advocating centralized nuclear control and planning, he argued strongly against small nuclear forces targeted against Soviet cities. While he did not renege on the American pledge to use nuclear weapons in Europe first,[5] he strongly promoted strengthening NATO's conventional posture in order to raise the so-called nuclear threshold.

The European responded to McNamara's proposals in an extremely reluctant way, to say the least. The French, whose attempts to create an independent nuclear force were directly attacked by the American secretary of defense, reacted with open hostility.[6] Paris stuck to the concept of finite nuclear deterrence and argued that a "flexible nuclear response" strategy was impossible to carry out. More important, the French government perceived the McNamara strategy as another proof that the United States was about to withdraw from its alliance commitment. In 1963 the French military representative at NATO vetoed the first planning document (MC 100/1) to convert McNamara's proposal into an alliance strategy. As a result of the French opposition, MC 14/3 could only be adopted *after* France had left NATO's military integration in March 1966. But the veto and the public opposition reduced French influence on studies conducted at NATO headquarters and among allied governments with the purpose of finding an interallied compromise.

While France presented the U.S. with a unified position against flexible response, the Federal Republic of Germany was split.[7] There was not much support for the emphasis on escalation control in nuclear strategy for fear that this might weaken the U.S. nuclear guarantee. German Chancellor Konrad Adenauer and Defense Minister Franz Joseph Strauß opposed "flexible response" as strongly as their French colleagues. When Chancellor Erhard replaced Adenauer in 1963, the attitude of the Bonn government became more favorable toward the U.S. proposals and, in 1964, the German government tried to mediate between the French and the United States. On the one hand, West Germany was the only NATO

4 See Schwartz, *NATO's Nuclear Dilemmas*, 156–65.

5 In private, McNamara advocated a no-first-use policy, see Stromseth, *Origins of Flexible Response*, 56. Since most West European governments considered such a pledge an American withdrawal from its commitment to the common defense, it never became official U.S. policy.

6 For the following see Haftendorn, *Kernwaffen*, 47–51; Stromseth, *Origins of Flexible Response*, 52–55, 96–120.

7 For details see Haftendorn, *Kernwaffen*, 31–105; Stromseth, *Origins of Flexible Response*, 121–50. See also Catherine M. Kelleher, *Germany and the Politics of Nuclear Weapons* (New York: Columbia University Press, 1975).

ally to substantially increase its conventional forces during the 1960s. On the other hand and in contrast to McNamara's views, Bonn never accepted the notion that a viable conventional defense could somehow replace nuclear deterrence in Europe.

At the same time, both the German Army and leaders of the Social Democratic opposition (SPD) in Bonn expressed sympathy for the Kennedy administration's emphasis on a strong conventional defense. Helmut Schmidt, the SPD's defense spokesman at the time, published a book introducing the new ideas of the American strategic community to the German debate. His efforts exemplify the strong transnational ties developing between the German SPD and the Kennedy administration during the early 1960s.[8]

The British position changed considerably when the Labour party took over in 1964.[9] The Macmillan government shared the French view and objected to the American criticism of independent nuclear forces. But it never used the French approach of public opposition and relied instead on the private diplomacy of the "special relationship" to moderate the American position. The Labour party, however, particularly the new defense secretary, Denis Healey, shared the views of the German SPD that there should be a strong conventional defense in Europe. Economic problems prevented the British Labour government from following through with this emphasis when entering office.

By 1965 the United States was confronted with two distinct European transnational coalitions with regard to flexible response. The European conservatives led by the French government were adamantly opposed to both the concept of nuclear escalation control and the renewed emphasis on conventional defense. The European Social Democrats supported the latter concept but remained opposed to the idea that nuclear escalation could somehow be controlled. Both groups formed their own transnational ties into the United States, the conservatives mainly with the JCS, who were skeptical of McNamara's plans, the Social Democrats with the civilian leadership of the Kennedy administration.

The transatlantic coalition-building resulted in the NATO strategy of flexible response of 1967. The most important compromises were hammered out in an informal, transgovernmental working group that included U.S., British, and German representatives. MC 14/3 represented an alliance compromise of the different viewpoints and left important details

[8] See Helmut Schmidt, *Verteidigung oder Vergeltung* (Stuttgart-Degerloch: Seewald, 1961) (trans. to English as *Defense or Retaliation* [New York: Praeger, 1962]). On the transnational ties between the SPD and the Kennedy administration, see Hans Jörg Grabbe, *Unionsparteien, Sozialdemokratie und Vereinigte Staaten von Amerika, 1945–1966* (Düsseldorf: Droste, 1983).

[9] For details see Stromseth, *Origins of Flexible Response*, 151–74.

deliberately vague.[10] First, MC 14/3 stressed direct defense on the level of a (supposedly conventional) attack chosen by an aggressor. This emphasis was a far cry from McNamara's original ideas about a viable conventional defense option, which should have eventually eliminated the need to use nuclear weapons first. Second, the strategy contained the option of deliberate escalation into nuclear war, thereby combining the idea of escalation risk favored by many European governments with efforts at escalation control supported by American strategists. This part of flexible response was rather ambiguously phrased and remained contested throughout the 1970s. In 1969, however, NATO adopted political guidelines for the initial use of nuclear weapons based on an Anglo-German draft emphasizing the political rather than the military character of nuclear first use. It was agreed that the purpose of a nuclear first use was to send a political signal to an attacker rather than to achieve military objectives on the battlefield. The guidelines thus implemented a view of flexible response close to the initial European preferences emphasizing the risk of escalation into nuclear war.[11]

The "Neutron Bomb" Controversy

While NATO's "flexible response" strategy came about through Anglo-German-American coalition-building across the Atlantic, the "neutron-bomb" (Enhanced Radiation Weapon or ERW) controversy[12] mainly involved Bonn and Washington. It essentially centered around the meaning of the transatlantic community with regard to risk-sharing and the norms governing the relationship.

A nuclear warhead with increased radiation and reduced yield had been worked on in the United States since the 1950s. NATO's Nuclear Planning Group discussed the issue since the early 1970s in connection with its evaluation of new technologies to implement the flexible response doctrine with regard to theater nuclear forces. In June 1977 the "neutron bomb" became subject of a public controversy on both sides of the Atlantic when the German Social Democrats used American newspaper reports to initiate the first domestic debate on nuclear issues since the late 1950s.

[10] See Haftendorn, *Kernwaffen*, 57–97; Stromseth, *Origins of Flexible Response*, 175–94.

[11] It was agreed, though, that even a political signal required more than just a nuclear warning shot. Cf. details in Daalder, *Nature and Practice of Flexible Response*, 72–79; J. Michael Legge, *Theater Nuclear Weapons and the NATO Strategy of Flexible Response* (Santa Monica: RAND Corporation, 1983).

[12] For the following see Daalder, *Nature and Practice of Flexible Response*, 137–58; Thomas Risse-Kappen, *The Zero Option* (Boulder, Colo.: Westview, 1988), 26–31; Sherri L. Wassermann, *The Neutron Bomb Controversy* (New York: Praeger, 1983).

German Chancellor Helmut Schmidt came under heavy and conflicting pressures from the Carter administration and the left wing of his own party, the SPD. The United States used an emerging consensus in NATO's Nuclear Planning Group in favor of the "neutron bomb" to urge Germany to accept deployment on their territory *prior* to an American decision to produce the weapon. For Carter, the issue was nuclear risk-sharing in the alliance. At the same time, a growing antinuclear movement in the German SPD asked for "conditions rendering deployment of the neutron bomb on West German soil unnecessary," as a party congress put it.[13]

Given such conflicting pressures, the German government decided in January 1978 to accept the deployment of the "neutron bomb" conditionally, *if and when* arms control talks about the weapon had failed and the warheads would not be solely deployed in West Germany. The Germans wanted a NATO "dual-track" decision on deployment and arms control. In February and March, a consensus along these lines was worked out in the North Atlantic Council and between Bonn and Washington. On April 7, 1978, days before the Council was to take the final decision, President Carter, who judged that the German commitment to deployment was too vague, deferred production of the "neutron bomb." This unilateral cancellation of a NATO decision created an uproar in Western Europe, particularly in Bonn. Chancellor Schmidt, who personally did not favor the "neutron bomb," had spent a lot of domestic capital and played a "two-level game" to move his party toward the U.S. position. He felt personally betrayed by Carter, which only confirmed his negative image of the U.S. president. Carter's unilateralism not only destroyed the delicate balance between domestic and alliance demands that motivated the German desire for a NATO "dual-track" decision, it also violated the norms, rules, and decision-making procedures in NATO. The alliance leader reneged unilaterally from a pending contractual obligation, which the United States had supported all the way to the final decision stage; alliance cohesion was shattered.

But the "neutron bomb" case had important consequences for the U.S. approach to a far more significant issue, NATO's 1979 "dual-track decision" on INF.

INF, the "Dual-Track" Decision and the Zero Option

The NATO decision-making process leading to the "dual-track decision" and the zero option[14] on INF resembles the way in which flexible re-

[13] SPD Parteitag Hamburg, November 15–19, 1977, *Dokumente Frieden*, 7 (my translation).

[14] On the following see Jeffrey Boutwell, *The German Nuclear Dilemma* (Ithaca, N.Y.: Cornell University Press, 1990); Daalder, *Nature and Practice of Flexible Response*, 159–226; Ernst-Christoph Meier, *Deutsch-amerikanische Sicherheitsbeziehungen und der NATO-*

sponse came about. Strong and conflicting transnational and transgovernmental coalitions developed across the Atlantic, each with its own agenda and preferences.

Efforts to modernize NATO's long-range INF posture originated from a coalition including

- high-ranking military at NATO's headquarters in Brussels, who argued that the implementation of "flexible response" required such deployments;
- center-right civilian strategists on both sides of the Atlantic with links to the anti-SALT coalition in the United States, who claimed that the strategic parity codified by the Strategic Arms Limitation Talks (SALT) agreements threatened the credibility of U.S. extended deterrence for Europe; and
- the U.S. military looking for deployment options of newly available cruise missiles.

These groups were initially not concerned about the Soviet build-up of SS-20 missiles; their demands resulted mainly from rather arcane deterrence considerations. But the SS-20 was crucial for European leaders such as German Chancellor Helmut Schmidt and British Prime Minister James Callaghan, for whom the Soviet build-up constituted a new threat to European security and symbolized a violation of the European détente spirit and of German *Ostpolitik* in particular. Schmidt decided to push the INF issue on NATO's political agenda during a speech in London in October 1977. From the beginning, he emphasized the connection between INF modernization and arms control.

The Carter administration reacted reluctantly to the European demands. The president, Secretary of State Vance, and Secretary of Defense Brown neither believed in the strategic requirements for new NATO INF nor considered the SS-20 a new threat. They nevertheless agreed in the spring of 1978 to give in to the European demands. First, the Carter administration had to make up for the "neutron bomb" disaster and its violation of alliance norms. It was argued in Washington that NATO would not survive another blow like that. American behavior in the aftermath of the ERW controversy resembles the Eisenhower administration's at-

---

Doppelbeschluß (Rheinfelden: Schäuble-Verlag, 1986); Susanne Peters, *The Germans and INF Missiles* (Baden-Baden: Nomos, 1990); Risse-Kappen, *Zero Option*. Detailed documentation of the following argument can be found in these works. For theoretical interpretations of the INF case that closely resemble the following line of argument, see Richard Eichenberg, "Dual Track and Double Trouble: The Two-level Politics of INF," in *Double-Edged Diplomacy*, ed. Peter Evans et al. (Berkeley: University of California Press, 1993), 45–76; Jeffrey Knopf, "Beyond Two-level Games: Domestic-International Interactions in the Intermediate-range Nuclear Forces Negotiations," *International Organization* 47, no. 4 (Autumn 1993): 599–628.

tempts to repair the transatlantic relationship following the Suez crisis (chapter 4). Second, domestic and alliance considerations coincided. The emerging anti-SALT coalition in the United States threatened to jeopardize the ratification of the upcoming SALT II agreements in the Senate. U.S. decision-makers calculated that they could bargain European support for SALT II in exchange for American backing of INF modernization. Alliance support for SALT II would then be used in the ratification debate to shift the domestic balance of power in favor of the agreement.[15] Carter tried to use NATO for his domestic coalition-building efforts and to exploit the American sense of allied community for his purposes.

The arms control component of NATO's 1979 decision also originated in Europe. Leaders such as Schmidt and Callaghan preferred to solve the SS-20 problem through an arms control agreement. They viewed INF modernization as a potential bargaining chip in U.S.-Soviet negotiations. Moreover, the "neutron bomb" debate had sensitized the left wing of Social Democratic and Labour parties throughout Europe. Since these parties were in power in the most important INF deployment countries (Germany, Great Britain, and the Netherlands), there was no domestic "winning coalition" for INF deployment unless the NATO decision linked modernization to serious arms control efforts. As with the deployment option, the U.S. administration gave in to European demands.

In December 1979 the North Atlantic Council adopted the "dual-track" decision to deploy 572 American Pershing II and ground-launched cruise missiles in Western Europe and, at the same time, to offer arms control negotiations to the Soviet Union.

Two years later, when the INF negotiations began, the East-West climate had profoundly changed. After the Soviet intervention in Afghanistan and the turnaround in American defense policy, the two superpowers had embarked upon renewed confrontation, while the European governments tried to preserve their regional détente. The Reagan administration brought adamant opponents of arms control into office, but was nevertheless back at the negotiating table in late 1981, due to coinciding and mutually reinforcing domestic and allied pressures.[16]

The origins of the INF "zero option," which became Reagan's bargaining proposal in 1981 and was ultimately accepted by Mikhail Gorbachev in the 1987 INF treaty, represents another example of European influence on American nuclear policies through transgovernmental coalition-

[15] The Soviet intervention in Afghanistan at the end of 1979 changed the domestic equation again. The considerations reported here refer to the situation in 1978, when the Carter administration shifted course in favor of INF modernization.

[16] For details see, for example, Michael Krepon, *Arms Control in the Reagan Administration* (Washington, D.C.: University Press of America, 1989); Bernd W. Kubbig, *Amerikanische Rüstungskontrollpolitik* (Frankfurt/M.: Campus, 1988); David Meyer, *A Winter of Discontent* (New York: Praeger, 1990).

building.[17] The idea that NATO could forego deployment of the Pershing II and cruise missiles if the Soviets accepted significant reductions of their SS-20 originated in the left wing of various European Social Democratic parties back in 1979. On Helmut Schmidt's insistence, the possibility of a "zero option" had been included in the classified version of the 1979 INF decision at the very last minute.

Two years later, the peace movements in Europe were in full swing. But only in Germany were they able to influence policies directly through the left wing of the SPD which, unlike Britain's Labour party, was still in power. Ronald Reagan's global "zero solution" (zero U.S. INF in exchange for zero SS-20) was brought about by a rather strange transatlantic coalition. On the West European side, it comprised the Schmidt government reacting to heavy domestic pressure. While Schmidt did not believe that the Soviets would accept the zero option, he considered it a viable starting point for the talks from which to move quickly toward more negotiable formulas.[18]

Inside the U.S. administration, the zero option was supported by opponents of arms control such as Richard Perle, who did not believe in the strategic rationale of the INF deployment anyway and favored a blunt Western arms control proposal that could be used to hammer away at the Soviet Union, thereby blocking an agreement indefinitely. Thus, the "zero option" coalition comprised enthusiastic arms control supporters in Europe and equally passionate arms control opponents in the United States who joined forces for completely different reasons.

There was also a transnational alliance against the "zero option." On the one hand, it consisted of the above-mentioned "modernization coalition" of NATO military and strategic analysts who insisted that some INF deployment was necessary irrespective of the SS-20. On the other hand, the coalition comprised officials from various foreign ministries in Europe and the U.S. State Department who were convinced that the "zero option" was nonnegotiable. Of course, this transgovernmental coalition had almost no chance, since it was pitched against the most important European leader at the time, Chancellor Schmidt, and a U.S. president who liked simple ideas that could be easily communicated to the public.

Conclusions

This sketchy overview of nuclear decision-making in NATO serves to underline various arguments of this book. First, it shows again the significant European influence on U.S. foreign policy and confirms that the

[17] The best historical account of the U.S. decision-making process leading to the "zero option" is Strobe Talbott, *Deadly Gambits* (New York: A. Knopf, 1984). For the European side, see Risse-Kappen, *Zero Option*, 78–85.

[18] Author's interview with Helmut Schmidt, June 1985.

overall conclusion of this study also applies to cases other than the Korean War, the test ban, and the Cuban Missile crisis. One could argue, of course, that the "neutron bomb" and 572 INF were too insignificant in the U.S. nuclear arsenals for American administrations to care much about. This is precisely why I selected the Korean War, the Suez crisis, the test ban negotiations, and the Cuban Missile crisis as the main case studies in this book and why NATO's nuclear decisions are only used in an auxiliary fashion.

Second, NATO's nuclear decision-making processes show that European influence on American foreign policies was neither confined to the 1950s and early 1960s nor limited to the British government. In the three instances discussed above, nonnuclear Germany was a major player in alliance decisions, particularly during the 1970s.[19] With regard to the "neutron bomb" and INF, the German government became the most important counterpart of the U.S. in shaping alliance decisions. One could argue, though, that this is not too surprising, since Germany as the main nuclear deployment country held the most intense preferences and the United States needed Bonn's agreement to station nuclear weapons in the country. It nevertheless confirms the findings of this book that Germany used similar mechanisms as the British to influence Washington's policies, namely alliance norms and transgovernmental coalition-building. The Franco-American relationship of the late 1950s and early 1960s then appears to present the exception to the rule of how allies deal with each other in NATO, while the dynamics of the Anglo-American and German-American relationships resemble each other.

This leads to a third point referring to the process of allied interaction. Unlike the four cases investigated in the main studies of this book, NATO's nuclear decisions as such cannot be used to evaluate liberal propositions about process against realist bargaining theory. It has already been mentioned that the allies probably held more intense preferences than the U.S. regarding nuclear deployments in Europe. Washington also needed European agreement on nuclear issues, since the allies controlled U.S. access to military bases. This might have added to their bargaining leverage. Finally, deterrence considerations such as the credibility of the U.S. commitment to the European defense added to allied influence on NATO decisions. Open disagreements among the allies would have undermined the U.S. need to reassure the Europeans and, at the same time, to impress upon the Soviet Union that, indeed, Americans were prepared to risk New York for Berlin.[20] In sum, traditional realism and

[19] For further evidence of this point, see Haftendorn, *Kernwaffen*.

[20] I thank Robert Jervis for alerting me to this point. For a theoretical argument on the interaction between intra-alliance relations and relations with the opponent, see Glenn H. Snyder, "The Security Dilemma in Alliance Politics," *World Politics* 36, no. 4 (July 1984): 461–96.

realist bargaining theory can well explain the considerable European influence on NATO's nuclear decisions.

But the similarity between NATO's nuclear decision-making processes and the way in which the allies influenced the United States during the Korean War or the test ban negotiations is nevertheless remarkable. Transnational politics was significant with regard to both the "flexible response" and the INF decisions, while the latter and the "neutron bomb" cases involved various "two-level games" with domestic and alliance politics on both sides of the Atlantic interacting with each other.[21] Transgovernmental coalition-building and "two-level games" appeared to be even more important with regard to NATO's nuclear decisions than in the out-of-area cases where consultation norms were particularly significant.

The variation is not surprising, because the institutional provisions for treating "out-of-area" issues in NATO are regulated differently as compared to decisions involving military strategy and weapons deployments in Europe. The consultation norms that proved to be so important to explain allied influence on the United States during the Korean War and the Cuban Missile crisis are institutionalized in Article 4 of the North Atlantic Treaty. They do not apply when strategy and deployment decisions are involved that require not just consultation, but *joint decisions* by the organization, that is, the North Atlantic Council. NATO as an institution plays a more important role in nuclear decisions than in "out-of-area" cases. Studies of international organizations and regimes have shown that transnational and transgovernmental relations flourish inside such institutions.[22] This explains why transnational politics was even more significant to account for allied influence on NATO's nuclear decisions than in the "out-of-area" cases.

In sum, the brief look at nuclear decision-making in NATO confirms the finding that Europeans had a consistent and significant influence on American policies throughout the history of the alliance and that this impact was not confined to the British and their "special relationship" with the United States. From the Korean War to INF, a pattern of allied interactions based on a sense of community, normative regulations (consultation rules as well as joint decision-making procedures), and transnational politics can be observed.

[21] For similar analyses see Eichenberg, "Dual Track and Double Trouble;" Knopf, "Beyond Two-level Games."

[22] See, for example, Robert Keohane and Joseph Nye, "Transgovernmental Relations and International Organizations," *World Politics* 27 (1974): 39–62; Keohane, "The International Energy Agency: State Power and Transgovernmental Politics," *International Organization* 32, no. 4 (Autumn 1978), 929–52.

EIGHT

CONCLUSIONS

THE TRANSATLANTIC COMMUNITY AND THE EUROPEAN IMPACT ON AMERICAN FOREIGN POLICY

THIS CHAPTER starts with a summary of the empirical case studies in light of the theoretical assumptions presented in chapter 2. Three in-depth case studies relying on primary sources (chapters 3, 5, 6) show significant European influence on American foreign policy during the 1950s and early 1960s. A brief literature survey of NATO's nuclear decisions from the early 1960s to the mid-1980s (chapter 7) confirms the findings with regard to later time periods and allies other than the British and the French. The 1956 Suez crisis (chapter 4) represents the exception to the rule, a case of U.S. coercion of major European allies.

The findings of this book challenge, therefore, the *structural realist* proposition that small states should have less influence on the alliance leader, the greater the power asymmetry in alliances under bipolarity. The outcome of significant European influence on U.S. policies is consistent with *traditional realism*, on the one hand, and *liberal* propositions, on the other. The former argues that the great power's interest in maintaining the alliance provides smaller states with considerable bargaining leverage under certain specified conditions. The latter approaches suggest that democratic states develop a collective identity and a community of values leading to and strengthened by cooperative institutions. Since traditional realism and liberalism expect similar outcomes of allied influence on great powers, we must look at the interaction processes to evaluate the respective validity of the different approaches. Realist bargaining theory assumes that small allies use various power resources to exert influence, while liberalism emphasizes a sense of community, norms of consultation, "two-level games," and transnational coalition-building. The findings of the case studies suggest, on balance, that the process by which the Europeans influenced U.S. decisions can be better explained by liberal accounts than by traditional realism.

But not all allies had the same impact on American decisions. There is considerable variation in allied impact on U.S. foreign policy between

Britain and Germany, on the one hand, and France, on the other, representing a puzzle for the liberal case. I argue that the French government under President de Gaulle decided in the late 1950s to gradually reduce its institutional ties to Washington. This decision resulted in a decreasing French influence on American decisions.

The case studies do not provide a thorough empirical answer to the question of whether alliances among democracies are indeed special. To evaluate the argument further, systematic comparisons with alliances among nondemocracies are needed, which is beyond the scope of this book. One would also need to look more closely at the origins and the evolution of the collective identity than was possible in this study, which concentrated on the communicative and behavioral consequences of identities and norms. I suggest avenues for further research on these questions.

Finally, I draw policy conclusions for the future of the transatlantic relationship in a post–cold war environment. If the Western Alliance is based primarily on shared values, norms, and a collective identity rather than on the perception of a common threat, one should expect the transatlantic security community to persist in one institutional form or another. Maintaining the institutionalized community is in the European interest, because it prevents potential American unilateralism in a post–cold war environment. Intact transatlantic institutions also provide the United States with a legitimate say in European affairs despite decreasing security dependence of the allies and declining American power.

Summary of the Findings: Collective Identity, Norms, and the Big Influence of the European Allies

The Outcome: European Impact on U.S. Foreign Policy

According to Kenneth Waltz's version of realism,[1] small states are not expected to exert much influence on the policies of the alliance leader given the uneven distribution of power in bipolar systems, as a result of which the superpower does not need allies for its own security. To evaluate this proposition, the case selection was biased in favor of Waltz's argument, since it concerned a time period—the 1950s and early 1960s—during which the power asymmetry between the U.S. and the Europeans was overwhelming. The case selection also involved instances when U.S. decision-makers perceived the American supreme national interest to be at stake.

With the exception of the Suez crisis, the empirical findings challenge the structural realist argument. The Europeans and Canadians influenced crucial U.S. decisions during the Korean War, the test ban negotiations,

[1] See Kenneth Waltz, *Theory of International Politics* (Reading, Mass.: Addison-Wesley, 1979), esp. 168–70.

the Cuban Missile crisis, and concerning nuclear strategy and deployments in Europe. In each of these cases, at least one major European ally disagreed firmly with Washington's approach to the issues at stake. The allied views came up in direct consultations with the United States and were represented or anticipated by participants in the American decision-making process. Most U.S. decisions and resulting actions came either close to the initial European demands or constituted intra-alliance compromises. The allies affected how American policymakers defined the country's national interest as well as specific policy choices.

During the 1950–1953 Korean War (chapter 3), the escalation of the war and its extension into China, the use of nuclear weapons, and the armistice negotiations were among the most critical issues faced by decision-makers. Truman and Acheson as well as Eisenhower and Dulles acted under heavy domestic and sometimes military pressures usually pointing toward tougher policies against North Korea and Communist China. The European and Canadian allies pulled strongly in the opposite direction, against escalation and in favor of negotiations. They did not succeed in every instance, but they consistently strengthened the position of those opposing escalation. When the allies chose *not* to object, the war escalated, as was the case with the crossing of the 38th parallel in the fall of 1950. In the case of the Korean War, the NATO allies affected general U.S. preferences such as the decision to intervene in the first place as well as specific choices.

During the 1958–1963 test ban negotiations (chapter 5), the British government consistently pushed for an agreement with the Soviet Union. London succeeded in moving Washington's bargaining position toward

- dropping the link between disarmament and a test moratorium (1958);
- putting quotas on the numbers of on-site inspections (1959);
- combining a threshold test ban with a moratorium on underground tests (1960);
- combining the resumption of atmospheric tests with new arms control initiatives (1962); and
- lowering the number of required on-site inspections (1962).

Compared to the British, the French and the German governments, which opposed a test ban, were less influential. Bonn managed to convince the Kennedy administration not to pursue a nonaggression pact as a follow-up to the test ban in exchange for the German signature of the agreement.

The 1962 Cuban Missile crisis (chapter 6) represents another case of allied influence, even though consultations with the allies, particularly the British, only took place during the second week of the crisis. But the Kennedy administration worried constantly about potential European reactions to its actions and set its diplomatic machinery in motion to anticipate potential allied demands. Alliance considerations influenced both American preferences—to get the Soviet missiles out of Cuba, for example—as well as the range of particular choices. The two most important U.S. decisions—a blockade of Soviet ships en route to Cuba and a secret deal to withdraw the Soviet missiles from Cuba in exchange for removal of U.S. Jupiter missiles from Turkey—cannot be explained without taking the alliance factor into account.

As for NATO's nuclear decisions (chapter 7), the "flexible response" strategy of 1967 constituted an intra-alliance compromise between the original U.S. proposals and the European reaction. The deployment and arms control decisions on intermediate-range nuclear forces (INF) in the late 1970s and early 1980s were also heavily influenced by allied, particularly German, preferences.

The 1956 Suez crisis (chapter 4) represents the only case in which the outcome conforms to the expectations of structural realism. The United States used its superior economic power and coerced the British and French allies to abandon their efforts of regaining control over the Suez Canal.

National Interests, Leadership Beliefs, Domestic Politics: Complementary rather than Alternative Explanations

The empirical case studies present sufficient evidence to challenge the proposition that small allies have only limited influence on their leaders in a bipolar system, if the latter's vital interests are at stake. The findings do not suggest that giving in to allied demands ran counter to American interests. The decisions of refraining from an escalation of the Korean War, of agreeing to a test ban treaty with the Soviet Union, of installing a blockade and accepting a secret missile deal during the Cuban Missile crisis, and so on—these choices made perfect rational sense given the risks and opportunities at hand.

The problem is that the opposite decisions would not have been completely irrational, either. Given the U.S. nuclear superiority during the Korean War, there was not much that the Soviets could have done against American security in retaliation for a massive U.S. attack on China. A similar case can be made for the Cuban Missile crisis, given the continuing U.S. nuclear superiority and its conventional superiority in the region. In fact, such arguments were made supporting escalatory courses of action during both the Korean War and the Cuban Missile crisis. They failed to carry the day—not because Presidents Truman, Eisenhower, or Kennedy thought that those holding different views were stupid.

Rather, alliance considerations became part and parcel of the way in which decision-makers defined the American national interest. Escalating the Korean War or the Cuban Missile crisis was considered dangerous, because the Soviet Union could have retaliated against the NATO allies, involving the U.S. in another European war. Decision-makers took it for granted that taking care of European interests was also in the U.S. national interest. Decision-makers made virtually no distinction between the joint allied and the U.S. self-interest.

In sum, a power-based rational actor analysis of the various cases can hardly explain the outcome, *unless* alliance considerations are included in what the U.S. defined as its national interest. The evidence points to similar conclusions with regard to leadership beliefs and domestic politics as alternative explanations for the American decisions. During the Korean War and the Cuban Missile crisis, Truman and Acheson, Eisenhower and Dulles, as well as Kennedy and Rusk held strong convictions and exerted powerful leadership. Their value systems included the conviction that preserving the transatlantic relationship was in the supreme interest of the United States. This in turn provided the Europeans with an opportunity to influence decisions, since the American leaders were prepared to listen to those about whose fate they cared. Thus, leadership beliefs do not provide an alternative explanation for the outcome, but actually enabled allied influence in the first place.

Leadership beliefs played a somewhat different role during the test ban negotiations and with regard to NATO's nuclear decisions. While Presidents Eisenhower and Kennedy privately seemed to share the British view in favor of a test ban, they never exerted strong leadership to overcome domestic and bureaucratic opposition as they did during the Korean War or the Cuban Missile crisis. In the cases of "flexible response," the "neutron bomb," and INF, Presidents Kennedy, Johnson, Carter, and Reagan rarely held strong preferences or exerted significant leadership, either. But they were prepared to listen to allied advise and to take it into account. Given the lack of presidential attention, bureaucratic politics prevailed inside the administration. The European allies—the British in the test ban case and the Germans in the case of NATO's nuclear decisions—then used transnational and transgovernmental coalitions to influence American decisions.

With regard to domestic politics, U.S. decision-makers faced strong pressures in favor of confrontational and escalatory policies during the Korean War, while the domestic scene was essentially split during the test ban negotiations. Disputes between the U.S. and its allies occurred in both cases, because decision-makers in Washington had to reconcile domestic and allied demands in a "two-level game." Truman and Acheson frequently used the allied demands to win the domestic debate, arguing that escalation would isolate the United States among its friends. Allied concerns then strengthened their position vis-à-vis the domestic audience. During the test ban negotiations, the British changed the domestic and bureaucratic balance of power in Washington. Given the two-thirds majority requirement for treaty ratification in the U.S. Senate, test ban opponents were in a powerful position to block an agreement. British officials successfully formed "winning" transnational and transgovernmental coalitions with domestic and bureaucratic players in Washington, moving the administration's negotiating position toward compromises with the Soviet Union. When London failed to intervene in Washington, test ban opponents frequently blocked agreements. The allies, thus, affected the domestic balance of power in both cases, more indirectly during the Korean War, more directly during the test ban negotiations.

U.S. domestic politics were less important during the Cuban Missile crisis and concerning NATO's nuclear decisions. In the latter case, Congress and public opinion did not care much. During the Cuban Missile crisis, domestic politics and alliance considerations cannot be disentangled. On the one hand, it was necessary to take action against the Soviet missile deployment in Cuba in order to avoid the appearance of being "soft" on communism in the eyes of the U.S. public, partly *because* such "softness" would have jeopardized the alliance. On the other hand, a quick military escalation of the crisis, which might have led to Soviet actions against Europe, would also have eroded Kennedy's domestic support.

In sum, the case studies not only show significant European influence on American foreign policy, thereby challenging the assumptions of structural realism, they also indicate that alternative explanations are either indeterminate with regard to the decisions in question or complement the account presented here.

The Process according to Traditional Realism: Power-Based Bargaining among Allies?

Strong European influence on U.S. foreign policy is consistent with various theoretical explanations (chapter 2). Traditional realism as well as hegemonic stability theory would argue that the U.S. needed its European allies as the most important asset in the global power rivalry with the Soviet Union. Accommodating allied demands under certain conditions was then in the long-term American interest to preserve its power status. The evidence equally confirms liberal arguments that the U.S. and its allies formed a "pacific federation" (Immanuel Kant) or a "pluralistic security community" (Karl W. Deutsch) of democratic nations. This common identity and feeling of closeness committed the allies to joint decision-making in institutions such as NATO and enabled them to affect each other's preferences and choices.

Since the *outcome* of considerable European influence on American foreign policy is consistent with sophisticated realist as well as liberal thinking, we need to look at the *process* of interallied interaction and bargaining to evaluate the explanatory power of the two approaches.

Realist bargaining theory argues, first, that states can overcome an inferior power position in negotiating situations if they hold more intense preferences than the great power. It is impossible to determine whether the United States or its allies were more intensely motivated during the interallied conflicts of the Korean War, the test ban negotiations,[2] or the Cuban Missile crisis. The United States saw its supreme national interests at stake in each of these cases. The Suez crisis disconfirms the proposition, since the British and French arguably held more intense preferences than the United States, but had to give in to American coercion. Only in the case of NATO's nuclear decisions could one argue that the allies were more strongly motivated than the United States, since their immediate security was at stake.

A second proposition holds that small allies can exploit the superpower's need to preserve the relationship by threatening to defect, thereby increasing their bargaining leverage. The strong version of the argument does not apply, since none of the allies threatened to leave NATO in the cases considered here. On the contrary, if the French gradual disengagement from NATO starting in the late 1950s is considered the "exit" option, the assumption would be disconfirmed. De Gaulle's intransigence did not increase his bargaining leverage in the test ban case or during NATO's decision-making process on "flexible response."

A weaker variant could refer to allied threats to pursue unilateral policies, thereby jeopardizing alliance cohesion and/or playing to American *fears* of allied defection. During the Korean War, the case of the Menon resolution comes to mind. Britain and Canada warned that they would vote differently from the United States in the UN General Assembly. Moreover, U.S. decision-makers frequently argued that "we do not wish our allies to desert us"[3] in order to justify giving in to European demands vis-à-vis a critical domestic audience. With regard to the Cuban Missile crisis, the United States might have feared allied neutrality during the first week of the crisis, when it had not yet consulted them. Such fears did

[2] An exception is the German success in preventing a nonaggression pact between the two blocs as a follow-up to the test ban treaty. The Germans were probably more strongly motivated than the Kennedy administration.

[3] President Eisenhower in "144th NSC Meeting," May 13, 1953, *FRUS 1952–1954*, 15: 1014–17, 1016.

not make much sense in the second week of the crisis, though, since the allies supported the United States in general, while expressing concern about particular choices.

During the test ban negotiations and NATO's nuclear decisions, U.S. decision-makers rarely expressed fears of allied defection—except for Carter's decision to push NATO's dual-track decision on INF in the aftermath of the "neutron bomb" debacle. The case of the Suez crisis also disconfirms the assumption. When Britain and France not only threatened to pursue unilateral policies, but actually carried out their threat, the American economic power struck them. Except for the Korean War then, allied threats to pursue unilateral policies or U.S. fears of European neutrality can only explain isolated incidents.

Third, allied influence on the alliance leader might increase, the higher the perceived level of outside threat leading to mutual fears of abandonment. This proposition might explain the high degree of alliance cohesion during the Cuban Missile crisis, but is disconfirmed in all other cases. No correlation exists between the perceived level of threat on both sides of the Atlantic and the degree of alliance cohesion or allied influence on U.S. policies. On the one hand, the U.S.-Soviet confrontation during the Korean War should have led to less interallied disputes. The confrontation among the allies during the Suez crisis should not have occurred at all given its coincidence with the Hungarian crisis. On the other hand, European influence on Washington's policies should have decreased during the test ban negotiations, since it concerned arms control and détente, that is, a relaxation of tensions between the superpowers. The consistent pattern of interallied conflicts and European impact on American policies with regard to NATO's nuclear issues also bears no connection to the ups and downs of the East-West relationship in the 1960s, 1970s, and 1980s.[4]

Fourth, the unity of small allies vis-à-vis the superpower might increase their bargaining leverage. There are indeed some instances in which the U.S. modified its position when confronted with a unified allied position, particularly during the Korean War. But allied unity is not a necessary condition for allied influence. During the Suez crisis, Anglo-French harmony did not help at all, while Anglo-French disagreement during the test ban negotiations did not prevent London from exerting considerable impact on Washington's decisions. The Cuban Missile crisis case does not confirm the proposition, either. The allies were united, but in support of the U.S. approach to the crisis.

A fifth proposition derived from realist bargaining theory holds that small allies can use issue-specific resources to increase their bargaining leverage. For example, the United States needed access to European

[4] For similar findings, see Fred Chernoff, *After Bipolarity* (Ann Arbor: University of Michigan Press, 1994).

bases in order to fight a nuclear war against the Soviet Union before intercontinental ballistic missiles were available. It is not clear, though, why this condition should have helped increase the European influence on American policies unless one assumes that the United States planned a preventive war against the USSR.[5] The United States needed the bases primarily to *protect its allies* rather than the American homeland and to carry out nuclear strikes against the USSR in response to an attack against the allies. But then, it was also in the supreme allied interest to give the United States access to the bases, as a result of which this permission should not have increased European bargaining leverage.

This line of thinking applies even more to the case of NATO's nuclear decisions, since the advent of intercontinental ballistic missiles (ICBMs) rendered the European bases less important for the American military strategy. If granting access to European bases increased the allied bargaining leverage vis-à-vis the United States, we need to assume that American decision-makers did not distinguish between European security interests and their own. This argument, though, coincides with liberal claims about a transatlantic security community.[6]

There were some instances, though, where European allies used issue-specific capabilities to increase their influence on U.S. decisions. The German impact on NATO's nuclear decisions, for example, could be explained by the country's significance for the American cold war strategy. During the Korean War, Britain and Canada were quite significant in securing a favorable climate of "world opinion" in the UN General Assembly, which U.S. decision-makers deemed crucial. But control over "world opinion" only qualifies as issue-specific power if immaterial resources are taken seriously and the United States was concerned about legitimizing its policies through multilateral institutions.[7] Realist and liberal arguments blur at this point.

The Suez crisis case could be explained on the basis of issue-specific capabilities, but on the part of the United States, since Washington controlled the British access to economic and financial resources. Apart from these cases and other isolated instances, though, there is no consistent allied use of issue-specific power to explain the pattern of European influence on U.S. foreign policy.

In sum, while traditional realism or hegemonic stability theory are consistent with the outcome of allied influence on American foreign policy,

[5] Some officials in the American bureaucracy indeed thought about "preventive war" during the early 1950s. But there was no coherent U.S. policy planning for such a strategy. See Marc Trachtenberg, *History and Strategy* (Princeton, N.J.: Princeton University Press, 1991), chap. 3.

[6] I owe this point to Robert Jervis.

[7] See Joseph S. Nye, Jr., *Bound to Lead* (New York: Basic Books, 1990), 191–95.

TABLE 2
Congruence between Theoretical Expectation and Empirical Evidence

	Korean War	*Suez Crisis*	*Test Ban*	*Cuban Crisis*	*Nuclear Decisions*
Structural Realism					
Outcome	−	+	−	−	−
Traditional Realism					
Outcome	+	−	+	+	+
Process					
Intensity of preferences	n/a	−	n/a	n/a	+
Threat of defection	+	−	−	+/−	+/−
Threat perception	−	−	−	+	−
Allied unity	+	−	−	n/a	−
Issue-specific resources	+/−	+	−	−	+
Liberalism/Institutionalism					
Outcome	+	−	+	+	+
Process					
Value community	+	+	+	+	+
Consultation norms	+	+	+/−	+/−	+
"Two-level games"	+	+	+	n/a	+
Transnational coalitions	n/a	n/a	+	+	+

\+ = Outcome/process confirms expectation of theory
− = Outcome/process disconfirms expectation of theory
+/− = Outcome/process confirms expectation of theory to limited degree
n/a = theoretical expectation does not apply

realist bargaining theory provides only limited insights into the process of transatlantic interactions. As Table 2 reveals, none of the propositions derived from realist bargaining theory is systematically linked to the pattern of allied influence.

First, power-based bargaining assumptions did not apply in many cases in which the Europeans successfully affected Washington's decisions. Second, none of the propositions is fully confirmed more than once—except for the use of issue-specific resources. Most assumptions are disconfirmed more often than validated. Third, the two assumptions from realist bargaining theory that score best—fear of allied defection and allied issue-specific power—complement rather than challenge liberal propositions. The empirical evidence supporting these propositions can equally well be explained by assuming a security community. Finally, traditional realist assumptions obtain the best results for the cases of the

Korean War and NATO's nuclear decisions. Concerning the former, the Western Alliance was just one year old and the allies were only beginning to get used to the norms governing the relationship. As to NATO's nuclear decisions, sophisticated realism and liberalism co-vary, which is why I have not selected the case as primary supporting evidence for this book. We have to look at liberal expectations to get a fuller understanding of the intra-alliance dynamics at work.

The Process according to Liberalism: Collective Identity, Norms, and the Interplay of Domestic Politics and Transnational Relations

Several claims can be reconstructed from liberal approaches to explain the process of cooperation among democracies (chapter 2). Following Kantian thinking about a "pacific federation" and Karl W. Deutsch's concept of a "pluralistic security community," one would expect a collective identity to emerge when democracies interact in an institutionalized setting such as an alliance.[8] While Americans do not cease to remain Americans, and Europeans remain Europeans (or British, German, and French), they nevertheless identify with each other and care about each other's fate. Liberal theory assumes that the *content* of this collective identity refers to shared values such as human rights, the rule of law, and democratic governance. Democratic values and norms are then expected to inform the principles, rules, and decision-making procedures of the international institutions in which democracies cooperate. In short, *democratic allies form democratic alliances.*

Statements by American decision-makers expressing a sense of community permeate the case studies, such as

- Truman reassuring Attlee that Britain and Canada "were *partners* with the United States in the atomic weapon;"
- Eisenhower calling the allies "outposts of *our* national defense";
- Dulles referring to Macmillan as "a member of the *family*";
- Kennedy exclaiming that "the Soviets had *us* either way; if *we* did nothing, they had *us*, and if *we* reacted, *we* were left exposed in Turkey or in Berlin."[9]

The *we* in these statements made virtually no distinction between the United States and its allies. The discourses in the National Security Council

[8] For a conceptualization of collective identity, see Alexander Wendt, "Collective Identity Formation and the International State," *American Political Science Review* 88, no. 2 (June 1994): 384-96.

[9] My emphasis. The quotes are taken from (in the order of their appearance) "Meeting between the President and the Prime Minister," Dec. 7, 1950, PRO:PREM 8/1200; "144th NSC Meeting," May 13, 1953, *FRUS 1952–1954*, 15:1016; "John Foster Dulles to Robert Lovett," Aug. 14, 1958, National Archives (NA), 600.0012/8–1458; Milton Leitenberg, "Chronology of the Cuban Missile Crisis," Oslo, 1989, manuscript, 110.

and in other meeting groups reveal that membership in the transatlantic community constituted part of the collective identity among decision-makers. The community was understood as the "free world," that is, liberal democracies, placed against "them," the communist states.[10] American decision-makers saw themselves as leading the community of democracies and as acting on their behalf without making distinctions between U.S. interests and those of its allies. They tried to pursue "joint gains."[11]

One could dismiss such references to a community of purpose as rhetoric to cover traditional and self-interested behavior for domestic or allied consumption. Even then would it be significant that U.S. decision-makers thought it necessary to frame their preferences in community rhetoric rather than to refer to unilaterally defined strategic interests. But the references to the value community among democracies were causally consequential for both the decisions themselves and the interactions with the allies. First, it led to a habit in which giving in to European demands was not considered "concessions" but appropriate behavior by a "good" alliance leader.

Second, those referring to the allied community during the internal debates added significant weight to their arguments. They invoked the transatlantic community in the political discourses and frequently persuaded decision-makers that specific courses of action were indeed in the best interest of the United States. The references were persuasive and "tipped the balance," because they reminded decision-makers of their collective identity as part of the community.

This does not imply that the collective identity was never contested. During and after the Korean War, for example, the U.S. military frequently complained that the European allies exerted disproportionate influence on American policies and that "United States policy in the Far East is being determined in London rather than in Washington."[12] Such complaints rarely carried the day and were frequently counterproductive for the purpose of those who raised them.

[10] The intensity with which the United States fought and perpetuated the cold war is consistent with such an interpretation of liberal theory. The Soviet Union was perceived not only as outside the community but as an existential threat to its core values. The liberal rules of the community not only did not apply to U.S.-Soviet relations, but the East-West conflict was defined by U.S. decision-makers in such a way that hostility and confrontation prevailed, particularly during the 1950s. On U.S.-Soviet interactions perpetuating the cold war, see Richard N. Lebow and Janice G. Stein, *We All Lost the Cold War* (Princeton, N.J.: Princeton University Press, 1994).

[11] See Arthur Stein, *Why Nations Cooperate* (Ithaca, N.Y.: Cornell University Press, 1990), chap. 6, for a rational choice conceptualization of joint interests. For an argument on American multilateralism in NATO, see also Steve Weber, "Shaping the Postwar Balance of Power: Multilateralism in NATO," *International Organization* 46, no. 3 (Summer 1992): 633–80.

[12] "Chief of Mission to the Far East to the Secretary of Defense," July 3, 1954, *FRUS 1952–1954*, 15:1821.

Causally consequential references to a community of values alone do not challenge a sophisticated realist argument, though. Invoking a liberal community might simply cover the power-based interest of the United States in maintaining the alliance. The strategic literature on the indivisibility of alliance commitments makes this point. The empirical literature on alliances has shown, however, that alliance commitments are certainly divisible and that cooperation among allies is actually quite rare—except for democratic alliances.[13]

But references to the allied community not only served as powerful arguments in the political discourses tipping the domestic and bureaucratic balance of power in favor of allied demands, they also provided European and Canadian governments with a "window of opportunity" to influence U.S. policies. If community arguments were just liberal rhetoric or the "icing on the cake" of traditional power interests, decision-makers were at least caught by their own words.

The second liberal claim pertaining to democratic alliances holds that the community of purpose is institutionalized in both diffuse and specific *norms of interallied consultation.* American decision-makers shared the understanding with the allies that consultation meant codetermination and not just listening to each other's views. This understanding explains why consultation norms became hotly contested during the Korean War debates about "hot pursuit" or the use of nuclear weapons as well as during the first week of the Cuban Missile crisis. The Pentagon and the military during the Korean War as well as some "hawks" during the Cuban Missile crisis argued that there was no need to consult with the Europeans. They knew that they were likely to lose the debate when the allies were brought in.

Consultation norms enabled European allies to directly influence American decisions and to sometimes gain almost veto power over U.S. actions. Prominent examples include "hot pursuit," the non-use of nuclear weapons, and the armistice negotiations during the Korean War as well as the moderating influence of the British government during the second week of the Cuban Missile crisis. In the case of NATO's nuclear strategy and deployments, the joint decision-making process in Brussels represented the functional equivalent of consultation norms.

The norms affected U.S. decisions even when the Europeans were not directly involved. Three cases can be distinguished. First, policymakers

[13] For details see Bruce Bueno de Mesquita, *The War Trap* (New Haven, Conn.: Yale University Press, 1981); Stuart A. Bremer, "Dangerous Dyads: Conditions Affecting the Likelihood of Interstate War, 1816–1965," *Journal of Conflict Resolution* 36, no. 2 (1992): 309–41. For the strategic literature on alliance commitments, see, for example, Ole R. Holsti et al., *Unity and Disintegration in International Alliances* (New York: Wiley, 1973); George Liska, *Nations in Alliance* (Baltimore: Johns Hopkins University Press, 1962); Arnold Wolfers, *Discord and Collaboration* (Baltimore: Johns Hopkins University Press, 1962).

sometimes chose not to consult, because they knew the European position from previous occasions. These instances did not violate the norm, since consultations had been carried out earlier and the results were known. The European view entered the decision-making process "as if" there had been full consultation—and with a similar outcome of allied influence. Examples include several occasions during the Korean War as well as during the second week of the Cuban Missile crisis.

Second, the first week of the Cuban Missile crisis represents an anomaly insofar as the United States deliberately violated the norm to consult the allies but nevertheless remained influenced by anticipated allied demands. The fate of Europe, particularly of Berlin, became part and parcel of the deliberations in the ExComm. Nonconsultation actually strengthened the position of the "doves." Certain courses of action were excluded *because* the allies had not been consulted. U.S. decision-makers decided to violate a specific rule of interallied conduct but could not liberate themselves from the normative framework of the Western Alliance.

Third, the violation of consultation norms sometimes resulted in a lack of allied influence. The most significant case was the Suez crisis (chapter 4). The coercive U.S. reaction to the Anglo-French-Israeli military efforts to recapture the Suez Canal cannot be explained by American opposition to the use of force alone. From the beginning of the crisis, the United States and its allies held divergent views on the issue at stake, but Washington tried accommodating the British and French and mediated the conflict for a long period of time. On the one hand, the British and French governments felt increasingly betrayed by the United States and then embarked on a scheme to deceive Washington. Eisenhower and Dulles, on the other hand, could not imagine that the Europeans would violate fundamental norms of the alliance. When they did just that, the United States retaliated and no longer played by the rules of the alliance. They switched to coercive bargaining and won, as Waltzian realists would expect. The British and Americans, however, worked extremely hard after the crisis to restore the normative foundation of their "special relationship."

A similar pattern occurred when the Carter administration violated important alliance rules by unilaterally canceling the production of the "neutron bomb" after it had successfully urged its allies, particularly the Germans, to accept the deployment of the weapon. Norm violation in this case also led to increased efforts to restore the transatlantic relationship.

Apologies, justifications, and attempts at restoring the relationship are to be expected when norms are violated. Such behavior offers important indications that the norms effectively govern the relationship and that the actors recognize their validity.[14] Actors also interpret norm-consistent behavior as validating and reenforcing the sense of community. Severe norm

[14] On this point, see Friedrich Kratochwil, *Rules, Norms, and Decisions* (Cambridge: Cambridge University Press, 1989), 63.

violations such as those experienced during the Suez crisis then challenge their collective identity. Ritualistic behavior to restore the relationship serves to rebuild and to regain the sense of community.

A third liberal proposition confirmed by the evidence of the case studies relates to "*two-level games*."[15] While material power capabilities were rarely used to strengthen one's position vis-à-vis the allies, U.S. and European leaders frequently alluded to domestic pressures when they were driving a hard bargain with each other. During the Korean War, for example, Truman and Acheson told the British on various occasions to back off, since continued allied pressure would hurt the European cause with the American public, leading to a wave of isolationism. During the Korean armistice negotiations and the test ban talks, the British government often argued successfully that the uncompromising American attitude would lead to increased domestic protests and to a wave of anti-Americanism. In the INF case, the Bonn government argued both in 1979 and in 1981 that a serious legitimacy crisis of NATO was to be prevented in Germany. The United States should, therefore, accept the arms control track of the NATO decision and agree to the "zero solution."

In other words, the U.S. and its allies pointed to a small domestic "win-set" in order to increase their bargaining leverage vis-à-vis each other. The allied governments could easily verify such claims given the publicity of the political processes in democratic systems. Playing "two-level games" proved to be far more successful than coercive bargaining backed by material resources. The latter was considered inappropriate behavior among democratic allies, while the former was regarded as entirely legitimate. After all, democratic governance requires insuring sufficient domestic support.

A fourth liberal proposition argues that the community of purpose enables the flourishing of *transnational and transgovernmental coalitions*. If there is a strong sense of community institutionalized in norms prescribing frequent consultation, one would expect transnational politics to affect outcomes, because the boundaries between the domestic and the international realm start blurring.[16] Highly institutionalized alliances among democracies can no longer be conceptualized as interstate relations, but as networks among like-minded actors across national boundaries.

Indeed, the story of this book is to a large extent about transnational

[15] See Robert Putnam, "Diplomacy and domestic politics: The logic of two-level games," *International Organization* 42, no. 3 (1988): 427–60; Peter Evans et al., eds., *Double-Edged Diplomacy* (Berkeley: University of California Press, 1993).

[16] See Thomas Risse-Kappen, "Introduction," in *Bringing Transnational Relations Back In*, ed. Thomas Risse-Kappen (Cambridge: Cambridge University Press, 1995). On transgovernmental relations in particular, see Robert O. Keohane and Joseph S. Nye, Jr., "Transgovernmental Relations and International Organizations," *World Politics* 27 (1974): 39–62.

and particularly transgovernmental coalition-building. In the test ban case, transnational social movements as well as expert communities brought the issue to the interstate agenda in the first place. During the negotiations, British officials regularly participated in the internal bureaucratic as well as domestic deliberations in Washington. Changes in the U.S. negotiating position frequently resulted from transgovernmental coalitions including the two allied negotiating teams in Geneva, the British foreign office, and the U.S. State Department. During the Cuban Missile crisis, the transgovernmental networks inside the alliance institutions partly made up for the lack of official consultation. The proposal for a secret "missile swap," for example, appears to have originated in these networks. With regard to NATO's nuclear decisions, it is impossible to describe the transatlantic interactions as interstate negotiations. Transnational and transgovernmental coalitions centered around specific policy proposals and often held competing views. These proposals became causally consequential when the coalitions managed to convince powerful NATO governments.

Allied officials such as the British Ambassador Ormsby-Gore during the Kennedy administration were often treated and behaved as if they were part of the American domestic scene or legitimate bureaucratic players. The transgovernmental networks produced "winning coalitions" in the administration as well as in domestic politics. Allied failure to align with like-minded American actors frequently resulted in their losing the argument.[17] While transnational politics is not confined to relations among democracies, their frequency, regularity, and impact on the transatlantic relationship appear to be peculiar. This is particularly true for transgovernmental coalition-building. Informal networks among senior officials and government bureaucrats often worked out common policies on issues of transatlantic contention and then "sold" these compromises to their national governments. Decision-making in NATO seems to consist mainly of transgovernmental networking and can only be compared to processes inside the European Union. Similar findings have also been reported with regard to the U.S.-Japanese security relationship—another highly institutionalized alliance among democracies.[18]

[17] This process is different from "two-level games," according to which national decision-makers can use international pressure and agreements to increase their domestic "win-sets." In the test ban case and concerning NATO's nuclear decisions, the European allies influenced the size of domestic and/or bureaucratic "winning coalitions" by participating in the policymaking processes themselves, that is, by affecting the 'domestic game' directly.

[18] On transgovernmental relations inside the European Union, see David Cameron, "Transnational Relations and the Development of the European Economic and Monetary Union," in *Bringing Transnational Relations Back In*, ed. Risse-Kappen; on the U.S.-Japanese security relationship, see Peter Katzenstein and Yutaka Tsujinaka, "'Bullying,' 'Buying,' and 'Binding': US-Japanese Transnational Relations and Domestic Structures," ibid.

Consultation norms, "two-level games," and transnational coalition-building represent different but not mutually exclusive pathways by which democratic allies influence each other. Transgovernmental coalitions prevailed in cases when the policymaking process in Washington was characterized by strong bureaucratic divisions (test ban negotiations, the Cuban Missile crisis to some extent, and most of NATO's nuclear decisions). Transgovernmentalism then represents the intra-alliance variant of bureaucratic politics. The Korean War shows that the Europeans emphasize consultation norms as a tool to influence policies when faced with a rather united administration in Washington. There were less bureaucratic divisions in this case and Presidents Truman and Eisenhower exerted strong leadership.

In sum, this study not only challenges the proposition that the European allies should not have much impact on U.S. foreign policy when vital American interests are at stake. As Table 2 reveals, liberal insights explain the *outcome* as well as the interaction *processes* in the transatlantic security community better than even sophisticated realism.

This does not imply that liberalism accounts for the entire empirical variation. Two important puzzles remain for that perspective. First, a liberal perspective can only partly account for the anxiety of American decision-makers about being abandoned by their allies during both the Korean War and the Cuban Missile crisis. On the one hand, U.S. leaders might have feared that their arguments lacked persuasiveness and were, therefore, insufficient to keep the allies aboard. On the other hand, leaders who sincerely believe in the democratic security community should worry less about the reliability of their allies. Even France's President de Gaulle supported the United States during the Cuban Missile crisis. Neither realist nor liberal theories can convincingly explain the American "fear of abandonment."[19] The second puzzle concerns the variation in allied influence on U.S. foreign policy.

Variation in Allied Influence: The British and Germans versus the French

Not every European government had the same impact on Washington's decisions. Most significant, there is a striking difference in the British and German as compared to the French influence on U.S. policies. In the cases of the Korean War, the test ban negotiations, and the Cuban Missile

[19] For a realist argument that "fear of abandonment" is unlikely among allies under bipolarity, see Glenn H. Snyder, "The Security Dilemma in Alliance Politics," *World Politics* 36, no. 4 (July 1984): 461–96.

crisis, the story of "allied" influence is to a large degree about British impact in the Anglo-American "special relationship." As far as NATO's nuclear decisions are concerned, the Federal Republic of Germany weighed in heavily on Washington's decisions. Compared to that, the French influence on U.S. policies was less important and decreased gradually from the Suez crisis on. How can this variation in impact be explained?

The finding poses problems for both realist and liberal accounts. Britain, France, and Germany were the dominant powers in Western Europe during the cold war and thus should have had similar effects on U.S. policies. If the British nuclear status during the 1950s made the difference, France should have increased its influence during the late 1950s and early 1960s, that is, after Paris had decided to go nuclear. If realist bargaining arguments hold true, President de Gaulle's open threats to leave the alliance (at least its military integration) should have increased the French leverage vis-à-vis Washington. As to nonnuclear Germany, it should have had a lesser impact on U.S. decisions than both nuclear powers. Alternatively, one could argue that the German front-line status during the cold war provided Bonn with unique issue-specific resources to increase its bargaining leverage.

The empirical evidence challenges these expectations. If one compares the Korean War with the test ban negotiations and the Cuban Missile crisis, the French impact decreased rather than increased in comparison to the British. The French opposition to test limitations did not influence Washington, at least less so than the last-minute effort by the Germans. The French impact on the evolution of NATO's flexible response strategy also pales in comparison to Bonn's.

The difference in influence is also hard to reconcile with liberal arguments about a democratic alliance. All three countries were democratic and enjoyed cooperative relationships with one another and in NATO, at least until France left the military integration in December 1966.

The evidence reveals, however, that the British, German, and French foreign policies used the institutional opportunities provided by the transatlantic relationship rather differently. Throughout the 1950s, London continuously nurtured its "special relationship" with Washington, based on informal, but highly effective norms and understandings. After the Suez crisis, the British doubled their efforts and quickly restored the relationship. London used the American sense of community and the commitment to consult the allies to the fullest, thereby gaining enormous influence on U.S. foreign policy. The British were also masters in building transgovernmental coalitions with players inside the U.S. administration. As Henry Kissinger commented in his memoirs, the "special relationship"

> involved a pattern of consultation so matter-of-factly intimate that it became psychologically impossible to ignore British views. They evolved a habit of meetings so regular that autonomous American action somehow came to seem to violate club rules. . . . It was an extraordinary relationship because it rested on no legal claim; it was formalized by no document; it was carried forward by succeeding British governments as if no alternative was conceivable. British influence was great precisely because it never insisted on it; the "special relationship" demonstrated the value of intangibles.[20]

The informal nature of the Anglo-American relationship challenges the assumption of most regime analysts that international institutions are more effective when based on formal interstate agreements in conjunction with compliance mechanisms. The "special relationship" does not pass the "explicit rules" test of regime theory, but it nevertheless achieves "prescriptive status in the sense that actors refer regularly to the rules" and gives "rise to a measure of rule-consistent behavior."[21] The communications in the Anglo-American relationship show that the actors held a joint understanding of desirable and appropriate behavior and that this understanding enabled them to exert influence on each other. The intersubjective meaning of what constituted the mutual commitment to the allied community was causally consequential for the behavior rather than explicit rules incorporated in formal agreements.

The informal habit of consultation in the transatlantic relationship was not confined to the Anglo-American ties, even though there seem to be some special features resulting from a common culture and a common language. The Germans—and the Canadians, one should add—created their own "special relationship" with Washington. Konrad Adenauer's close ties to Dean Acheson, President Eisenhower, and particularly John Foster Dulles; Willy Brandt's connection to the Kennedy administration; Helmut Schmidt's personal friendship with Gerald Ford, Henry Kissinger, and Cyrus Vance; and, finally, Helmut Kohl's relations with the Reagan, Bush, and Clinton administrations are just examples on the top level of decision-makers. On the working levels of governments, the German-American relationship is characterized by informal transgovernmental coalitions among senior officials similar to the Anglo-American case. The German political parties also developed close transnational links with var-

[20] Henry Kissinger, *White House Years* (New York: Weidenfeld & Nicolson, 1979), 90.

[21] For these definitions of international regimes, see Volker Rittberger, "Research on International Regimes in Germany," in *Regime Theory and International Relations*, ed. Rittberger (Oxford: Oxford University Press, 1993), 3–22, 10–11. See also Robert Keohane, "The Analysis of International Regimes," ibid., 23–45, 26–29; Keohane, *International Institutions and State Power* (Boulder, Colo.: Westview, 1989), 3–4.

ious administrations and important players in Congress. The Germans concentrated their efforts on shaping American policies toward Europe, while until most recently they kept their distance with regard to "out-of-area" issues. Hence their less significant impact in the cases analyzed here, except for NATO's nuclear decisions![22]

The differences between the Anglo-American and the German-American alliances, on the one hand, and the Franco-American relationship, on the other, are striking. The Paris government drew the opposite conclusion from the Suez crisis than the British. Frustrated by previous disappointments about American policies, the French government of the Fourth Republic decided to gradually reduce its ties to Washington and the transatlantic alliance.[23] When President de Gaulle entered the scene in 1958, he continued that course and developed a comprehensive rationale of French independence, which was partly motivated by the need to provide the institutions of the Fifth Republic with a distinctive foreign policy legitimacy. The requirements of "independence" demanded that the French government openly opposed Washington's policies. Influence was sometimes not even desired, since it would have disconfirmed the image of the United States conveyed and nurtured with an eye toward the French domestic audience. This might explain the lack of French influence on American policies during the test ban negotiations even though the Paris government could have formed transnational coalitions with test ban opponents in the U.S. military and Congress. But the French never attempted to do so, retreating instead to a policy of "agreeing to disagree." The need to show independence might also explain why President de Gaulle wholeheartedly supported President Kennedy during the Cuban Missile crisis but later complained about the lack of consultation.[24]

The French government deliberately decided to deinstitutionalize its relationship with Washington and as a result gradually lost influence.[25] But when the Franco-American ties were reduced to traditional interstate relations, the lack of French impact in Washington only confirmed de

[22] For details see, for example, Hans Jörg Grabbe, *Unionsparteien, Sozialdemokratie und Vereinigte Staaten von Amerika, 1945–1966* (Düsseldorf: Droste, 1983); Helga Haftendorn, *Kernwaffen und die Glaubwürdigkeit der Allianz* (Baden-Baden: Nomos, 1994); Wolfram Hanrieder, *Germany, America, Europe* (New Haven, Conn.: Yale University Press, 1989); Thomas Schwarz, *America's Germany* (Cambridge, Mass.: Harvard University Press, 1991).

[23] For an excellent history of that time period, see Frank Costigliola, *France and the United States: The Cold Alliance since World War II* (New York: Twayne, 1992), 79–117.

[24] This is particularly ironic, since the British government was more critical of U.S. actions during the crisis than the French, but did not complain about a lack of consultation.

[25] Paris was, of course, not soley responsible for the gradual deterioration of the relationship. The Eisenhower and, even more so, the Kennedy administration, did a lot to confirm the French perception that "les Anglo-Saxons" did not care much about them.

Gaulle's conviction that France should go it alone. French policy toward the United States became a self-fulfilling prophecy.[26]

In sum, the variation in impact on U.S. foreign policy among the three European countries appears to result from a difference in the degree of (informal) institutionalization of the bilateral ties. While Britain and Germany combined "loyalty" and "voice" to effectively influence Washington, France used the "exit" option.[27] It should be noted, though, that the deinstitutionalization of the Franco-American relationship represents the exception to the general findings of this book.

The different degrees of influence on American foreign policies has implications for the theoretical argument. The liberal claim that these countries were democracies and formed a "pluralistic security community" with a collective identity is obviously insufficient to explain the variation in impact on American foreign policy. Institutionalist claims about the role of norms and collective understandings of appropriate behavior add explanatory value to the argument. The practices of the actors give meaning to these norms. Norm compliance becomes a measure by which actors reassure themselves and their interaction partners about the collective identity of the community. By the same token, decreasing norm compliance gradually deinstitutionalizes the relationship and also reduces the sense of community. The norms are not static but subject to change by the practices of actors.[28]

Institutionalism that does not leave room for agency is equally insufficient to account for the variation in impact. Traditional regime analysis, for example, emphasizes explicit rules, employs a rather static approach to norms, and neglects communicative action as well as the process by which actors give meaning to the norms through their practices.[29] NATO's consultation norms and rules applied to all alliance members, not just to the British and Germans. Informal intersubjective understandings and interpretations of the actors on both sides of the Atlantic about what these norms and rules meant and what the transatlantic community implied

[26] This trend has been reversed recently by the Mitterrand government, which developed rather close relations to the U.S. governments from Reagan to Clinton.

[27] See Albert Hirschman, *Exit, Voice, and Loyalty* (Cambridge, Mass.: Harvard University Press, 1970).

[28] This point resembles closely arguments by social constructivists on the mutual constitutiveness of intersubjective structures and agency. See, for example, Alexander Wendt, "The Agent-Structure Problem in International Relations Theory," *International Organization* 41 (1987): 335–70. For an argument stressing the significance of communicative action, see Harald Müller, "Internationale Beziehungen als kommunikatives Handeln: Zur Kritik der utilitaristischen Handlungstheorie," *Zeitschrift für Internationale Beziehungen* 1, no. 1 (1994): 15–44.

[29] On this point, see Friedrich Kratochwil and John Ruggie, "International Organization: A State of the Art on an Art of the State," *International Organization* 40, no. 4 (Autumn 1986): 753–75; Kratochwil, *Rules, Norms, and Decisions*.

do the explanatory work, accounting for the variation in impact. Here, the differences between the Anglo-American, Canadian-American, and German-American ties, on the one hand, and the Franco-American relations, on the other, are striking.

Suggestions for Further Research

This book combines liberal and institutionalist insights to show that democracies not only do not fight each other but are likely to develop a collective identity facilitating the emergence of cooperative institutions for specific purposes. These institutions are characterized by democratic norms and decision-making rules that liberal states tend to externalize when dealing with each other. The enactment of these norms and rules reinforces and strengthens the sense of community and the collective identity of the democracies. Domestic features of liberal democracies enable the community in the first place. But the institutionalization of the community exerts independent effects on the interactions. In the final analysis then, democratic domestic structures and international institutions do the explanatory work together.

The empirical evaluation of this argument against the dominating approaches in the field of alliance theory—that is, several versions of realism—represents only a first step toward a systematic empirical assessment. Further research is needed in at least three areas.

First, it needs to be shown whether the findings pertaining to the North Atlantic Alliance hold up with regard to other alliances and cooperative institutions among democracies as well. Some initial work has been done with regard to the European Union. David Cameron's findings about the transnational and transgovernmental origins of the European Economic and Monetary Union confirm the argument about the significance of transnational relations in highly institutionalized settings. Harald Müller comes to similar conclusions with regard to the evolution of a common European nonproliferation policy. Peter Katzenstein and Yutaka Tsujinaka show the significance of transgovernmental coalitions in the U.S.-Japanese security alliance.[30] However, more research is necessary on the interaction of collective identities, norms, and behavioral patterns in these relations. Does the U.S.-Japanese security alliance exhibit a similar sense of community as NATO, and how does this affect the Japanese

[30] See Cameron, "Transnational Relations and the Development of the European Economic and Monetary Union;" Harald Müller, ed., *A European Non-Proliferation Policy* (Oxford: Clarendon Press, 1987); Müller, ed., *How Western European Nuclear Policy Is Made* (London: Macmillan, 1991); Katzenstein and Tsujinaka, "'Bullying,' 'Buying,' and 'Binding.'"

influence on U.S. foreign policy? What about the U.S.-Israeli relationship? Does the undisputed influence of Israel on American policies toward the Middle East reflect a collective identity based on common democratic values or is it rather based on transnational religious ties? Does it make a difference for the impact on American foreign policy that these are bilateral alliances as opposed to the multilateral NATO? Do the findings of this study point to a general conclusion that the collective understandings about the meaning of explicit rules and not so much the norms themselves have causal consequences for the interaction patterns among the allies?

The inquiry also needs to be extended to alliances among nondemocracies. The most important shortcoming of this book is probably that it does not compare its empirical findings to interallied relations involving authoritarian systems. Some sketchy evidence nevertheless suggests that the interaction patterns in nondemocratic alliances are different and confirm closely to realist expectations, particularly realist bargaining theory.

Concerning the Middle East, for example, Stephen Walt has argued that common ideology played only a limited role in the formation of alliances among Arab states. While Michael Barnett disagrees, pointing to the significance of pan-Arabism, he also concurs that this collective identity has been weaker than the sense of community among democratic allies such as the United States and Israel.[31] Work on the U.S.–Saudi Arabian relationship suggests that this alliance has been based on narrowly defined self-interests and that the Saudi influence on American foreign policy has been limited.[32]

A study comparing U.S. relations with Latin America and interaction patterns within the former Warsaw Pact concludes that these relations can well be analyzed within the framework of public choice and realist bargaining theories.[33] The case study on the Cuban Missile crisis in this book (chapter 6) also reveals that the impact of the Organization of American States (OAS) on U.S. decisions was negligible compared to that of NATO.

[31] See Stephen Walt, *The Origins of Alliances* (Ithaca, N.Y.: Cornell University Press, 1987); Michael Barnett, "Institutions, Roles, and Disorder: The Case of the Arab States System," *International Studies Quarterly* 37, no. 3 (September 1993): 271–96; Barnett, "Identity Politics and Security Communities in the Middle East," prepared for Peter Katzenstein, ed., *Norms and International Security*, forthcoming.

[32] See, for example, Benson Lee Grayson, *Saudi-American Relations* (Washington, D.C.: University Press of America, 1982); David E. Long, *The United States and Saudi Arabia* (Boulder, Colo.: Westview, 1985).

[33] See Jan F. Triska, ed., *Dominant Powers and Subordinate States* (Durham, N.C.: Duke University Press, 1986). However, this study did not compare its findings with institutionalist expectations. For a proposal for the study of security communities in general, see Emanuel Adler and Michael Barnett, "Security Communities" (paper prepared for delivery at the 1994 annual meeting of the American Political Science Association, New York, Sept. 1–4).

But a systematic study applying the assumptions put forward in this book to alliances among authoritarian regimes or between the former and democratic systems does not exist. One could, for example, compare the interaction patterns in NATO with other American-led alliances such as the OAS or SEATO as well as with bilateral arrangements between the U.S. and various Asian states during the cold war. Studying the former Warsaw Pact and comparing it to NATO appears to be problematic, since Soviet relations with Eastern Europe constituted an informal empire rather than an alliance among sovereign states.[34]

A second area where further research is warranted concerns the origins of the collective identity and the norms examined in this book. This and other inquiries in the role of norms in international relations primarily demonstrate that ideas and communicative action are causally consequential in world politics and that they provide a better understanding of the dynamics at work than traditional approaches focusing on behavior alone.[35] Far less attention has been devoted to the processes by which these norms and collective understandings came about. We need to know more about the processes by which the transatlantic community originated during the 1940s. Historical evidence suggests, for example, that the Anglo-American alliance of World War II was of primary significance for the emergence of the post-1945 community.[36] But little systematic research has been done on the relationship between the liberal international order promoted by the United States, Great Britain, and France after the war, on the one hand, and the origins of the cold war, on the other.[37] How did the collective liberal identity of the transatlantic community affect the perception of an increasing Soviet threat? And how did the perceived threat and the emerging image of the Soviet Union as the "other" influence the sense of community itself, leading to its institutionalization in the North Atlantic Alliance?

A third area for further research concerns the role and impact of ideas

[34] See, for example, David Holloway and Jane M. O. Sharp, eds., *The Warsaw Pact* (Ithaca, N.Y.: Cornell University Press, 1984); Stephan Tiedtke, *Die Warschauer Vertrags-Organisation* (München: Oldenbourg, 1978).

[35] See, for example, Katzenstein, *Norms and International Security*; Elizabeth Kier, *Images of War* (Princeton, N.J.: Princeton University Press, 1995); Audie Klotz, *Protesting Prejudice* (Ithaca, N.Y.: Cornell University Press, 1995); David Lumsdaine, *Moral Vision in International Politics* (Princeton, N.J.: Princeton University Press, 1993); Nina Tannenwald, "Dogs that Don't Bark" (Ph.D. diss., Cornell University, Ithaca, N.Y., 1995).

[36] See, for example, Richard Best, *"Cooperation with Like-Minded Peoples"* (Westport, Conn.: Greenwood Press, 1986); Henry B. Ryan, *The Vision of Anglo-America* (Cambridge: Cambridge University Press, 1987); Randall B. Woods, *A Changing of the Guard* (Chapel Hill: University of North Carolina Press, 1990).

[37] For an attempt, see Robert Latham, "Liberalism's Order/Liberalism's Other: A Genealogy of Threat," *Alternatives* 20, no. 1 (Winter 1994).

in international relations. This study shares the interest of a growing number of scholars in ideational factors in world politics.[38] Most work in this area has established that ideas influence state policies and mediate between material factors and behavioral outcomes. This book goes one step further and argues that common values and norms affect not only policies, but also preferences and the definition of interests as resulting from these collective identities.

One should assume, however, that highly institutionalized security communities not only affect the interaction patterns among the participants but also the internal structures of the states themselves. The dense network of transnational relations in a highly integrated community of democratic systems should have repercussions for the domestic institutions of these democracies. Some work has been done in this context on how the integration in the Western community stabilized the domestic situation in newly democratizing countries.[39] But we know next to nothing about whether the transatlantic community—or the European Union, for that matter—has had any influence on the social and political coalitions of stable democracies such as the United States, Great Britain, or France. If, as I claim in this book, a strong sense of collective identity has emerged among these countries, this should have consequences for their domestic structures, in particular the political culture, the political institutions, and state-society relations.

The End of the Cold War and the Future of the Transatlantic Relationship

Since 1985 the European security environment has dramatically changed. The cold war is over, the U.S.-Soviet rivalry has given way to a new partnership among former opponents, Germany is united, the Warsaw Pact and even the Soviet Union have ceased to exist. Fundamental parameters in the international environment of the transatlantic relationship have been profoundly altered. The world of the 1990s is very different from the

[38] See, for example, Emanuel Adler, *The Power of Ideology* (Berkeley: University of California Press, 1987); Judith Goldstein and Robert Keohane, eds., *Ideas and Foreign Policy* (Ithaca, N.Y.: Cornell University Press, 1993); Ernst Haas, *When Knowledge Is Power* (Berkeley: University of California Press, 1990); Peter Haas, ed., *Knowledge, Power, and International Policy-Coordination*, special issue of *International Organization*, 46, no. 1 (Winter 1992); John Odell, *U.S. International Monetary Policy* (Princeton, N.J.: Princeton University Press, 1982); Kathryn Sikkink, *Ideas and Institutions* (Ithaca, N.Y.: Cornell University Press, 1991). See also the studies cited in note 35.

[39] See, for example, Michael Marks, "The Formation of European Policy in Post-Franco Spain" (Ph.D. diss., Cornell University, Ithaca, N.Y., 1993).

world of the 1950s. Can we extrapolate anything from the study of European-American relations during the height of the cold war for the future of the transatlantic ties? Will the Europeans continue to influence American foreign policy as they did during the cold war?

Answers to these questions depend, of course, on one's theoretical assumptions.[40] Waltzian realism, for example, probably expects the gradual disintegration of the North Atlantic Alliance. The answer of traditional realism following Hans Morgenthau depends on scope conditions, namely the future of American power and of threats to European security. Liberal theory expects the persistence of the transatlantic security community and its extension to the new democracies in Eastern Europe and even to Russia, depending on the future of that country's transformation. But liberalism is indeterminate regarding the institutional form of this community. If one adds institutionalist arguments, though, a strong case emerges for the preservation of NATO.

Realist balance of power theory maintains that alliances form and disintegrate in response to the emergence and the decline of external threats. Waltzian realists define "threats" solely on the basis of the distribution of power in the international system. Following this line of reasoning, Kenneth Waltz argued that the cold war structure was bipolar, since it consisted of only two great powers facing each other, as a result of which the smaller states were of little significance in the system.[41] The end of the cold war then resulted from the decline and ultimate disintegration of the Soviet Union as a great power.[42] Scholars following the structural realist analysis have argued, therefore, that the world is currently moving

[40] See, for example, Beverly Crawford, "Introduction: Causes of War and the Future of Peace in the New Europe," in *The Future of European Security*, ed. Crawford (Berkeley: University of California Center for German and European Studies, 1992), 1–41; Charles Glaser, "Why NATO Is Still Best," *International Security* 18, no. 1 (Summer 1993): 5–50; Gunther Hellmann and Reinhard Wolf, "Neorealism, Neoliberal Institutionalism, and the Future of NATO," *Security Studies* 3, no. 1 (Autumn 1993): 3–43.

[41] See Waltz, *Theory of International Politics*. For thorough critiques of the imprecise definitions of *bipolarity*, see R. Harrison Wagner, "What Was Bipolarity?" *International Organization* 47, no. 1 (Winter 1993): 77–106; Richard N. Lebow, "The Long Peace, the End of the Cold War, and the Failure of Realism," *International Organization* 48, no. 2 (Spring 1994): 249–78.

[42] The Waltzian analysis is rather vague, however, in defining what constitutes great power status. If, as the thrust of his argument implies, the defining feature is a state's economic basis for sustaining the global projection of force, the question arises as to whether the Soviet Union ever had this power and whether or when it disappeared. If one ascribes more weight to military capabilities, Russia is still in a league with the United States concerning nuclear power. As a result, the bipolar structure would persist, as Kenneth Waltz has recently argued. See his "The Emerging Structure of International Politics," *International Security* 18, no. 2 (Fall 1993): 44–79. On the contradictions in the realist analysis, see Lebow, "The Long Peace, the End of the Cold War, and the Failure of Realism."

from bipolarity to multipolarity with, maybe, a "unipolar moment" of American supremacy in between.[43] Most structural realists probably agree that American preponderance will not last very long, assuming that uneven rates of economic growth are likely to produce hegemonic challengers.[44] Waltzian realists should then not expect the transatlantic alliance to last much into the next century. Not only does the United States not need the European allies for its security in the post–cold war environment, the Europeans will also increasingly challenge American domination, since they no longer need the United States for their survival, either. While the United States might be able to mollify the growing transatlantic rivalry by accommodating the allies for some time, there is not much it can do about it in the long run. NATO is doomed and current efforts to adjust the alliance to the new international circumstances are likely to fail. As Kenneth Waltz put it in November 1990, "NATO is a disappearing thing. It is a question of how long it is going to remain as a significant institution even though its name may linger on."[45]

There are some indications for decreasing alliance cohesion such as the essentially uncoordinated troop cuts by the allies in response to a decreasing threat. But NATO as an institution remains alive and well so far. It does precisely what institutionalists rather than realists would expect, that is, it adjusts to a new international environment:

- Instead of heavily armored and mechanized divisions, member states are setting up intervention forces with increased mobility in accordance with the NATO decision to build an allied rapid reaction corps for "out-of-area" purposes.[46]
- In 1991 the North Atlantic Cooperation Council was instituted, linking the sixteen allies with Eastern Europe and the successor states of the Soviet Union.[47] Two years later, these countries were invited to join a

[43] Cf. John Mearsheimer, "Back to the Future: Instability in Europe after the Cold War," *International Security* 15, no. 1 (Summer 1990): 5–56; Charles Krauthammer, "The Unipolar Moment," *Foreign Affairs: America and the World* 70, no. 1 (1990/91): 23–33; Christopher Layne, "The Unipolar Illusion: Why New Great Powers Will Rise," *International Security* 17, no. 4 (Spring 1993): 5–51.

[44] See Robert Gilpin, *War and Change in World Politics* (Cambridge: Cambridge University Press, 1981).

[45] At a U.S. Senate hearing as quoted from Hellmann and Wolf, "Neorealism, Neoliberal Institutionalism, and the Future of NATO," 17. For the following see ibid., 22–26.

[46] If the alliance were disintegrating, one would expect the members to concentrate on the defense of their national territories rather than building light and mobile forces. On this point, see Hellmann and Wolf, "Neorealism, Neoliberal Institutionalism, and the Future of NATO," 22.

[47] See "North Atlantic Cooperation Council Statement," *NATO Press Service*, Dec. 20, 1991; Stephen Flanagan, "NATO and Central and Eastern Europe," *Washington Quarterly* 15, no. 2 (Spring 1992): 141–51.

"partnership for peace" creating institutionalized ties between NATO's integrated military command structure and the East European and Russian militaries.[48]

- The alliance increasingly plays a subsidiary role in UN-sponsored international peacekeeping and peace-enforcement missions. NATO ships patrol the Adriatic waters to enforce the economic sanctions against former Yugoslavia, while NATO aircraft monitor the no-fly zone over Bosnia-Herzegovina. In February 1994, NATO—authorized by the UN Security Council and the UN secretary general—issued an ultimatum to conduct air strikes in Bosnia if heavy weapons were not withdrawn from the area surrounding Sarajevo.[49]

A disintegrating alliance is unlikely to accept new commitments. Moreover, the structural realist notion of bipolarity and resulting alliance behavior fails to explain the dynamics of the transatlantic relationship during the cold war. Why should Waltzian realism be relied upon to predict the *future* of the Western alliance if the theory cannot explain its past?

Sophisticated traditional realism has at least been able to account for the outcome of European influence on U.S. foreign policy during the cold war. As to the future of the transatlantic relationship, the expectations of this approach depend on specific scope conditions.

Stephen Walt's "balance of threat" argument identified geographic proximity, offensive power, aggressive intentions together with aggregate capabilities as proximate causes that states align against external threats.[50] Two of these reasons for NATO no longer exist, while the Russian land mass and geopolitical location remain a potential threat to the country's neighbors. The Soviet withdrawal from Eastern Europe has ended the threat posed by Moscow's offensive conventional forces, while Soviet and Russian democratization have terminated the danger posed by aggressive intentions, at least for the time being. Sophisticated realism probably concurs with structural realism that, on the one hand, the purpose for NATO's existence has greatly decreased, resulting in a less cohesive transatlantic relationship. On the other hand, this version of realism

[48] For details see "'Partnerschaft für den Frieden' mit Osteuropa: Aber keine konkreten Zusagen für Mitgliedschaft," *Süddeutsche Zeitung*, January 11, 1994; "NATO Chiefs Hail New Era, but War Still Casts Clouds," *International Herald Tribune* (IHT), Jan. 12, 1994; "Clinton Hints NATO Would Defend East from Attack," *IHT*, Jan. 13, 1994.

[49] See, for example, "Report by Ad-hoc-Group of the North Atlantic Cooperation Council on Cooperation for Peacekeeping," *NATO Press Service*, June 11, 1993; Hellmann and Wolf, "Neorealism, Neoliberal Institutionalism, and the Future of NATO," 25; "The West Moves to Silence the Guns and Change a State of Mind," *New York Times*, Feb. 13, 1994; "Serbs Will Give Up Big Guns in Bosnia by Today, U.N. Says," *New York Times*, Feb. 19, 1994.

[50] See Walt, *Origins of Alliances*.

might argue that one should not dismantle NATO prematurely for several reasons:[51]

- While the threat from Russia is currently small, its reemergence as an aggressive power cannot be excluded. Its geographic proximity to Western Europe requires hedging against such a possibility.
- Preventing any great power from dominating the Eurasian rim continues to be in the supreme American interest and in that of its European allies.
- Wars in Eastern Europe and within as well as among the successor states of the Soviet Union are significantly more likely today than during the cold war and could spill over into Central and Western Europe.

In sum, prudent realists would probably agree with Charles Glaser that the case for NATO "is best viewed as an extended transition strategy—the preservation of NATO for a couple of decades into the post-Soviet era is prudent in the face of uncertainties surrounding both Russia and Western Europe."[52]

But the future of the transatlantic relationship also depends on the future of American *power*, if one follows hegemonic stability theory. Subscribers to a "declinist" point of view are likely to foresee a similar disintegration of the transatlantic relationship toward increasing conflicts as Waltzian realists.[53] Declining hegemonic powers are less likely to provide collective goods such as security, because doing so would enable potential challengers not only to "free-ride" on them, but also to gain power at their expense. At the same time, the hegemon's willingness to accept short-term costs for the benefit of maintaining its power status in the long run will change, too. Declining hegemons should be expected to cease ruling "by consent" and to retreat increasingly to isolationism or unilateral decisions. If American power relative to Europe and East Asia is declining, the European influence on American foreign policy is expected to decrease. Maintaining the transatlantic security institutions would become a burden rather than an asset for the United States, as a result of which these ties weaken.

Others disagree profoundly with the assessment of American decline and argue that U.S. primacy in a post–cold war environment can be maintained, if Washington adopts the right mix of domestic and international

[51] For the following see Glaser, "Why NATO Is Still Best;" Steven Van Evera, "Why Europe Matters; Why the Third World Doesn't: American Grand Strategy after the Cold War," *Journal of Strategic Studies* 13, no. 2 (June 1990): 1–51.

[52] Glaser, "Why NATO Is Still Best," 7.

[53] Cf., for example, Paul Kennedy, *The Rise and Fall of Great Powers* (New York: Random House, 1987); David Calleo, *Beyond American Hegemony* (New York: Basic Books, 1987).

policies.[54] The American "empire by consent" is expected to last and to continue providing European states with considerable influence on Washington's decisions.

In sum, as long as there are some security needs for maintaining the Western Alliance and as long as American power does not substantially decline, sophisticated realist arguments can be made that NATO will persist and the Europeans will continue influencing American foreign policy.

I have argued in this book, however, that conceptualizing NATO as just another military alliance misses the point. Rather, the Western Alliance represents a functional institutionalization of the transatlantic security community based on common values and a collective identity of liberal democracies.[55] From the perspective of liberal theory, neither Soviet power nor an objective Soviet threat as such led to the formation of NATO. Instead, the Soviet domestic structure and the values promoted by communism were regarded as alien to the community, resulting in a threat perception of the Soviet Union as the potential enemy. The democratization of the Soviet system initiated by Mikhail Gorbachev and continued by Boris Yeltsin started ending the cold war in Western eyes by altering the "otherness" of the Soviet system. The revolution in Soviet foreign policy and the liberalization of the Soviet system decreased the Western threat perception.

The end of the cold war not only does not terminate the Western community of values, but potentially extends it into Eastern Europe and maybe into the successor states of the Soviet Union, creating a "pacific federation" (Immanuel Kant) of liberal democracies from Vladivostok to Berlin, San Francisco, and Tokyo.[56] But liberal theory does not neces-

[54] See, for example, Nye, *Bound to Lead*; Samuel Huntington, "America's Changing Strategic Interests," *Survival* 33 (January/February 1991): 3–7; Huntington, "Why International Primacy Matters," *International Security* 17, no. 1 (Spring 1993): 68–83. For an early critique of the "declinist" perspective, see Bruce Russett, "The Mysterious Case of Vanishing Hegemony: Or Is Mark Twain Really Dead?" *International Organization* 39 (1985): 207–31.

[55] For a similar argument, see Steve Weber, "Does NATO Have a Future?" in *The Future of European Security*, ed. Crawford, 360–95. Emanuel Adler, "Europe's New Security Order," ibid., 287–326, shares the assessment, but comes to different conclusions regarding the desirability of NATO.

[56] On liberal and institutionalist visions of the future of European security, see Adler, "Europe's New Security Order"; Ernst-Otto Czempiel, *Weltpolitik im Umbruch* (München: Beck, 1991); James M. Goldgeier and Michael McFaul, "A Tale of Two Worlds: Core and Periphery in the Post–Cold War Era," *International Organization* 46, no. 3 (Spring 1992), 467–91; Charles Kupchan and Clifford Kupchan, "Concerts, Collective Security, and the Future of Europe," *International Security* 16, no. 1 (Summer 1991): 114–61; Dieter Senghaas, *Friedensprojekt Europa* (Frankfurt/M.: Suhrkamp, 1992); Steven Van Evera, "Primed for Peace: Europe after the Cold War," *International Security* 15, no. 3 (Winter 1990–1991): 7–57.

sarily expect NATO to last into the next century. It only assumes that the security partnership among liberal democracies will persist in one institutionalized form or another. Liberal theory is agnostic as to whether NATO, the Conference on Security and Cooperation in Europe (CSCE), or a common defense policy of the European Union provides the best framework for the security community.[57] Liberal theorists expect NATO to remain the dominant Western security institution and to regain its character as a defensive alliance, though, if the democratization process in Russia gives way to authoritarian nationalism. In this case, NATO should quickly extend its security guarantee to the new democracies in Central Eastern Europe.

While liberal theory is agnostic about the future of NATO except in the case of a new Russian threat, institutionalist arguments suggest that a transformed NATO should remain the overarching security community of the "pacific federation." First, it is easier to adjust an already existing organization encompassing an elaborate set of rules and decision-making procedures to the new conditions than to create new institutions of security cooperation among the liberal democracies in the Northern Hemisphere. The CSCE—not to mention the Western European Union—would have to be strengthened much further until they reach a comparable degree of institutionalization. The CSCE served a crucial purpose during the 1970s and 1980s by leaving the lines of East-West communication open during times of increased superpower tensions.[58] But it mainly relies on interstate bargains rather than transnational and transgovernmental coalition-building in a dense framework of norms, rules, and procedures. As a result, entangling the United States is easier in NATO than in the CSCE.

Second, the highly institutionalized structure of NATO and the integrated military command provide a unique opportunity of socializing the military and the defense policy apparatus of the former communist countries into a democratic alliance. This is perhaps the most important feature of the "partnership for peace" offered to the new democracies in Central Eastern Europe and the successor states of the Soviet Union, including Russia. The "partnership for peace" calls for joint training and military exercises and also invites officers to spend time at NATO's military command in Brussels. This could help to adjust military organizations used to authoritarian rule to democratic values and norms, thereby strengthening civilian control.

Third, the CSCE has the advantage over NATO that its purpose as

[57] I thank Andrew Moravcsik for clarifying this point to me.

[58] On the mostly overlooked role of the CSCE in helping to bring the cold war to an end, see Daniel Thomas, "When Norms and Movements Matter" (Ph.D. diss., Cornell University, Ithaca, N.Y., 1994).

prescribed in the 1975 Helsinki Final Act and the 1990 Paris Charter resembles a collective security institution and is thus already adapted to the post-cold war situation.[59] But a similar adjustment in the organizational goals is under way in NATO, too—from the 1990 "London Declaration on a Transformed North Atlantic Alliance," the 1991 "Rome Declaration on Peace and Cooperation,"[60] to institutional changes such as the North Atlantic Cooperation Council and the "partnership for peace." In addition and in contrast to the CSCE, only NATO has the integrated military structure to act as the regional security institution foreseen in Article 52 of the UN Charter and to carry out peacekeeping and peace-enforcement missions mandated by the UN Security Council.

Fourth, the preceding arguments imply that Article 4 of the North Atlantic Treaty prescribing timely consultation among the allies could be the future cornerstone of the organization rather than the mutual assistance clause of Article 5, which might recede to the background with the waning of external threats. Consultation norms have a long history in NATO and have served their purpose well as a prime instrument by which the allies influence each other. Close cooperation and policy coordination is nothing new for NATO and has been practiced among the members since the organization was founded in 1949.

Finally, NATO provides a unique institutional framework for the Europeans to affect American policies. As I argue in this book, liberal democracies successfully influence each other in the framework of international institutions by using norms and joint decision-making procedures as well as transnational politics. Playing by the rules of these institutions, they do not just constrain their own freedom of action, but they also gain access to the decision-making processes of their partners. Reducing the institutional ties might create the illusion of independence, but it certainly decreases one's impact. The French as compared to the British (or German) examples of the 1950s and 1960s are instructive.

At the end of the cold war, the Europeans face a choice similar to the one Britain and France had to make after the Suez crisis in 1956. They can reduce their ties to the United States in an effort to increase their independence. If so, they will decrease their impact in Washington, while potential American unilateralism will still affect them to a large degree. Alternatively, the Europeans can maintain their institutional ties across the Atlantic and continue to exert considerable influence on American foreign policy.

Which path the Europeans follow can easily become a self-fulfilling prophecy. If they reduce their institutional ties to the United States for fear of American dominance, they increase the power of those in Washington favoring unilateralism. Maintaining the institutions of the transatlantic security

[59] On this point see Adler, "Europe's New Security Order."

[60] See *NATO Press Service*, July 6, 1990, and Nov. 8, 1991.

community, however, is likely to sustain the transnational coalitions of internationalists who affected the foreign policies on both sides of the Atlantic quite successfully during the cold war. Preserving the transatlantic community goes a long way toward upholding the multilateral liberal order of the Western institutions and extending it toward new issue-areas and regions.

BIBLIOGRAPHY

PRIMARY SOURCES

Acheson, Dean. *The Korean War.* New York: W. W. Norton, 1969.

———. *Present at the Creation: My Years in the State Department.* New York: W. W. Norton, 1969.

Brandt, Willy. *Begegnungen und Einsichten.* München: Droemer, Knaur, 1978.

Chang, Laurence, and Peter Kornbluh, eds. *The Cuban Missile Crisis, 1962: A National Security Archive Document Reader.* New York: New Press, 1992.

Eisenhower, Dwight D. *White House Years: Mandate for Change, 1953–1956.* Garden City, N.Y.: Doubleday, 1963.

Eisenhower, Dwight D., Library (DDEL), Abilene, Kansas. Selected files on test ban negotiations (courtesy of Matthew Evangelista).

Kennedy, Robert. *Thirteen Days: A Memoir of the Cuban Missile Crisis.* New York: W. W. Norton, 1968.

Killian, James R. *Sputnik, Scientists, and Eisenhower: A Memoir of the First Special Assistant to the President for Science and Technology.* Cambridge, Mass.: MIT Press, 1977.

Kissinger, Henry. *White House Years.* New York: Weidenfeld & Nicolson, 1979.

Kistiakowsky, George. *A Scientist at the White House.* Cambridge, Mass.: Harvard University Press, 1976.

Library of Congress, Manuscript Division, Washington, D.C. W. Averell Harriman Papers (WAH).

Lloyd, Selwyn. *Suez 1956: A Personal Account.* London: Jonathan Cape, 1978.

Macmillan, Harold. *At the End of the Day, 1961–1963.* London: Macmillan, 1973.

———. *Pointing the Way, 1959–1961.* London: Macmillan, 1972.

———. *Riding the Storm, 1956–1959.* London: Macmillan, 1971.

National Archives (NA), Washington, D.C. Central Decimal Files and NSC Files.

National Security Archive, Washington, D.C. The Cuban Missile Crisis, 1962 (NSA:CMC). Microfiche collection. Washington, D.C.: Chadwyck-Healey, 1990.

———. Nuclear History Documents.

———. Nuclear Non-Proliferation Collection (NSA:NNP).

NATO: Fact and Figures. 2d. ed. Brussels: NATO Press Service, 1978.

"October 27, 1962: Transcripts of the Meetings of the ExComm." *International Security* 12, no. 3 (Winter 1987/88): 30–92.

Pineau, Christian. *1956 Suez.* Paris: Editions Robert Laffont, 1976.

Public Records Office, London. Cabinet Files (PRO:CAB).

Public Records Office, London. Diplomatic Correspondence Files (PRO:FO).

Public Records Office, London. Prime Minister Files (PRO:PREM).

Shuckburgh, Evelyn. *Descent to Suez: Diaries, 1951–1956.* London: Weidenfeld, 1986.

SPD Parteitag Hamburg, November 15–19, 1977. *Dokumente Frieden.*

Truman, Harry S. *Years of Trial and Hope*. Vol. 2 of *Memoirs*. Garden City, N.J.: Doubleday, 1956.

U.S. Department of State. *Foreign Relations of the United States, 1950 (FRUS 1950)*. Vol. 7. Washington, D.C.: GPO, 1976.

———. *Foreign Relations of the United States, 1951 (FRUS 1951)*. Vol. 7. Washington, D.C.: GPO, 1983.

———. *Foreign Relations of the United States, 1952–1954 (FRUS 1952–1954)*. Vols. 5, 6, 15. Washington, D.C.: GPO, 1979–1986.

———. *Foreign Relations of the United States, 1955–1957 (FRUS 1955-1957)*. Vols. 16, 20. Washington, D.C.: GPO, 1990.

"White House Tapes and Minutes of the Cuban Missile Crisis." *International Security* 10, no. 1 (Summer 1985): 164–203.

Zuckerman, Solly. *Monkeys, Men, and Missiles*. New York: W. W. Norton, 1988.

SECONDARY SOURCES

Abel, Elie. *The Cuban Missile Crisis*. New York: Lippincott, 1966.

Adler, Emanuel. "Europe's New Security Order: A Pluralistic Security Community." In *The Future of European Security*, edited by Beverly Crawford, 287–326. Berkeley: University of California Center for German and European Studies, 1992.

———. *The Power of Ideology: The Quest for Technological Autonomy in Argentina and Brazil*. Berkeley: University of California Press, 1987.

Adler, Emanuel, and Michael Barnett. "Security Communities." Paper prepared for delivery at the 1994 annual meeting of the American Polical Science Association, New York, September 1–4.

Allyn, Bruce, et al. "Essence of Revision: Moscow, Havana, and the Cuban Missile Crisis." *International Security* 14, no. 3 (Winter 1989/90): 136–72.

Ambrose, Stephen E. *Eisenhower: Soldier and President*. New York: Touchstone, 1990.

Axelrod, Robert. *The Evolution of Cooperation*. New York: Basic Books, 1984.

Baldwin, David A. "Power Analysis and World Politics: New Trends versus Old Tendencies." *World Politics* 31, no. 2 (January 1979): 161–94.

Baldwin, David A., ed. *Neorealism and Neoliberalism: The Contemporary Debate*. New York: Columbia University Press, 1993.

Barbier, Colette. "Les négociations franco-germano-italiennes en vue de l'établissement d'une coopération militaire nucléaire au cours des années 1956–1958." *Revue d'histoire diplomatique* 104, no. 12 (1990): 81–113.

Barnett, Michael. "Identity Politics and Security Communities in the Middle East." Prepared for *Norms and International Security*, edited by Peter Katzenstein. Forthcoming.

———. "Institutions, Roles, and Disorder: The Case of the Arab States System." *International Studies Quarterly* 37, no. 3 (September 1993): 271–96.

Baylis, John. *Anglo-American Defence Relations, 1939–1984*. 2d. ed. London: Macmillan, 1984.

Beschloss, Michael. *The Crisis Years: Kennedy and Khrushchev, 1960–1963*. New York: Edward Burlingame Books, 1991.

Best, Richard. *"Cooperation with Like-Minded Peoples": British Influence on American Security Policy, 1945–1949*. Westport, Conn.: Greenwood Press, 1986.

Betts, Richard. *Nuclear Blackmail and Nuclear Balance*. Washington, D.C.: Brookings, 1987.

Blight, James. *The Shattered Crystal Ball: Fear and Learning in the Cuban Missile Crisis*. Savage, Md.: Rowman & Littlefield, 1990.

Blight, James, and David A. Welch. *On the Brink: Americans and Soviets Reexamine the Cuban Missile Crisis*. New York: Hill & Wang, 1989.

Botti, Timothy. *The Long Wait: The Forging of the Anglo-American Nuclear Alliance, 1945–1958*. Greenwich, Conn.: Greenwood Press, 1987.

Boutwell, Jeffrey. *The German Nuclear Dilemma*. Ithaca, N.Y.: Cornell University Press, 1990.

Bowie, Robert. "Eisenhower, Dulles, and the Suez Crisis." In *Suez 1956: The Crisis and Its Consequences*, edited by William Roger Louis and Roger Owen, 189–214. Oxford: Clarendon Press, 1989.

Boyer, Mark A. *International Cooperation and Public Goods: Opportunities for the Western Alliance*. Baltimore: Johns Hopkins University Press, 1993.

Bremer, Stuart A. "Dangerous Dyads: Conditions Affecting the Likelihood of Interstate War, 1816–1965." *Journal of Conflict Resolution* 36, no. 2 (1992): 309–41.

Brugioni, Dino A. *Eyeball to Eyeball: The Inside Story of the Cuban Missile Crisis*. New York: Random House, 1991.

Bueno de Mesquita, Bruce. *The War Trap*. New Haven, Conn.: Yale University Press, 1981.

Bueno de Mesquita, Bruce, and David Lalman. *War and Reason*. New Haven, Conn.: Yale University Press, 1992.

Bull, Hedley. *The Anarchical Society*. New York: Columbia University Press, 1977.

———. *The Control of the Arms Race*. London: Weidenfeld & Nicolson, 1961.

Bundy, McGeorge. *Danger and Survival: Choices about the Bomb in the First Fifty Years*. New York: Random House, 1988.

Buteux, Paul. *The Politics of Nuclear Consultation in NATO*. Cambridge: Cambridge University Press, 1980.

Calleo, David. *Beyond American Hegemony*. New York: Basic Books, 1987.

Cameron, David. "Transnational Relations and the Development of the European Economic and Monetary Union." In *Bringing Transnational Relations Back In*, edited by Thomas Risse-Kappen. Cambridge: Cambridge University Press, 1995.

Carlton, David. *Britain and the Suez Crisis*. Oxford: Basil Blackwell, 1988.

Chernoff, Fred. *After Bipolarity: The Vanishing Threat, Theories of Cooperation, and the Future of the Atlantic Alliance*. Ann Arbor: University of Michigan Press, 1994.

Christensen, Thomas. "Domestic Mobilization and International Conflict: Sino-American Relations in the 1950s." Ph.D. diss., Columbia University, N.Y. 1993.

———. "Threats, Assurances, and the Last Chance for Peace." *International Security* 17, no. 1 (Summer 1992): 122–54.

Cioc, Marc. *Pax Atomica: The Nuclear Defense Debate in West Germany during the Adenauer Era*. New York: Columbia University Press, 1988.

Cline, Ray S. "Commentary: The Cuban Missile Crisis." *Foreign Affairs* 68, no. 4 (Fall 1989): 190–96.

Colard, Daniel, and Jean-Francois Guilhaudis, "L'option nucléaire, le problème des essais et la position de la France sur le désarmement." In *L'Aventure de la Bombe*, 281–308. L'Université de Franche-Comté et l'Institut Charles-de-Gaulle. Paris: Librarie Plon, 1985.

Conze, Eckart. "La coopération franco-germano-italienne dans le domaine nucléaire dans les années 1957–1958: Un point de vue allemand." *Revue d'histoire diplomatique* 104, no. 12 (1990): 115–32.

Cook, Don. *Forging the Alliance: NATO, 1945–1950*. New York: Arbor House/William Morrow, 1989.

Costigliola, Frank. *France and the United States: The Cold Alliance since World War II*. New York: Twayne, 1992.

———. "Kennedy, the European Allies, and the Failure to Consult." *Political Science Quarterly*, forthcoming.

Cotton, James, and Ian Neary, eds. *The Korean War in History*. Manchester: Manchester University Press, 1989.

Cox, Robert. "Social Forces, States, and World Order: Beyond International Relations Theory." In *Neorealism and Its Critics*, edited by Robert Keohane, 204–54. New York: Columbia University Press, 1986.

———. *Production, Power, and World Order*. New York: Columbia University Press, 1987.

Crawford, Beverly. "Introduction: Causes of War and the Future of Peace in the New Europe." In *The Future of European Security*, edited by Beverly Crawford, 1–41. Berkeley: University of California Center for German and European Studies, 1992.

Crawford, Beverly, ed. *The Future of European Security*. Berkeley: University of California Center for German and European Studies, 1992.

Cummings, Bruce, ed. *Child of Conflict: The Korean-American Relationship, 1943–1953*. Seattle: University of Washington Press, 1983.

Czempiel, Ernst-Otto. *Friedensstrategien*. Paderborn: Schöningh, 1986.

———. *Weltpolitik im Umbruch*. München: Beck, 1991.

Daalder, Ivo. *The Nature and Practice of Flexible Response*. New York: Columbia University Press, 1991.

Deutsch, Karl W., et al. *Political Community and the North Atlantic Area*. Princeton, N.J.: Princeton University Press, 1957.

Dingman, Roger. "Atomic Diplomacy during the Korean War." *International Security* 13, no. 2 (Winter 1988/89): 50–91.

Divine, Robert. *Blowing on the Wind: The Nuclear Test Ban Debate 1954–1960*. New York: Oxford University Press, 1978.

Dockrill, M. L. "The Foreign Office, Anglo-American Relations, and the Korean Truce Negotiations, July 1951-July 1953." In *The Korean War in History*, edited by James Cotton and Ian Neary, 100–119. Manchester: Manchester University Press, 1989.

———. "The Foreign Office, Anglo-American Relations, and the Korean War, June 1950–June 1951." *International Affairs* 62 (1986): 459–76.

Donfried, Karen. "The Political Economy of Alliances: Issue-Linkage and the German-American Relationship." Ph.D. diss., Fletcher School of Law and Diplomacy, Boston, May 1991.

Doyle, Michael. "Liberalism and World Politics." *American Political Science Review* 80, no. 4 (1986): 1151–69.

Driver, Christopher. *The Disarmers.* London: Hodder & Stoughton, 1964.

Duffield, John S. "Explaining the Long Peace in Europe: The Contributions of International Security Institutions." University of Virginia, November 1992. Manuscript.

Eichenberg, Richard. "Dual Track and Double Trouble: The Two-level Politics of INF." In *Double-Edged Diplomacy: An Interactive Approach to International Politics*, edited by Peter Evans et al., 45–76. Berkeley: University of California Press, 1993.

Evangelista, Matthew. "Cooperation Theory and Disarmament Negotiations in the 1950s." *World Politics* 42, no. 4 (July 1990): 502–28.

Evans, Peter, et al., eds. *Double-Edged Diplomacy: An Interactive Approach to International Politics.* Berkeley: University of California Press, 1993.

Farrar, Peter. "A Pause for Peace Negotiations: The British Buffer Zone Plan of November 1950." In *The Korean War in History*, edited by James Cotton and Ian Neary, 66–79. Manchester: Manchester University Press, 1989.

Farrar-Hockley, Anthony. *A Distant Obligation.* Vol. 1 of *The British Part in the Korean War.* London: HMSO, 1990.

Flanagan, Stephen. "NATO and Central and Eastern Europe: From Liaison to Security Partnership." *Washington Quarterly* 15, no. 2 (Spring 1992): 141–51.

Foot, Rosemary. "Anglo-American Relations in the Korean Crisis: The British Effort to Avert an Expanded War, December 1950-January 1951." *Diplomatic History* 10, no. 1 (1986).

———. "Nuclear Coercion and the Ending of the Korean Conflict." *International Security* 13, no. 2 (Winter 1988/89): 92–112.

———. *A Substitute for Victory: The Politics of Peacemaking at the Korean Armistice Talks.* Ithaca, N.Y.: Cornell University Press, 1990.

———. *The Wrong War: American Policy and the Dimensions of the Korean Conflict, 1950–1953.* Ithaca, N.Y.: Cornell University Press, 1985.

Fox, William R., and Annette B. Fox. *NATO and the Range of American Choice.* New York: Columbia University Press, 1967.

Freeman, J. P. G. *Britain's Nuclear Arms Control Policy in the Context of Anglo-American Relations, 1957–1968.* London: Macmillan, 1986.

Freiberger, Steven Z. *Dawn over Suez: The Rise of American Power in the Middle East, 1953–1957.* Chicago: Iven R. Dee, 1992.

Gaddis, John Lewis. *The Long Peace.* New York: Oxford University Press, 1987.

———. "The Unexpected John Foster Dulles: Nuclear Weapons, Communism, and the Russians." In *John Foster Dulles and the Diplomacy of the Cold War*, edited by Richard Immermann, 47–77. Princeton, N.J.: Princeton University Press, 1990.

Garthoff, Raymond. *Reflections on the Cuban Missile Crisis*. Rev. ed. Washington, D.C.: Brookings, 1989.

Gaubatz, Kurt Taylor. "Democratic States and the Duration of International Alliances." Paper presented at the annual meeting of the American Political Science Association, Washington, D.C., August 27–September 1, 1991.

Gilpin, Robert. *American Scientists and Nuclear Weapons Policy*. Princeton, N.J.: Princeton University Press, 1962.

———. *War and Change in World Politics*. Cambridge: Cambridge University Press, 1981.

Glaser, Charles. "Why NATO Is Still Best: Future Security Arrangements for Europe." *International Security* 18, no. 1 (Summer 1993): 5–50.

Goldgeier, James M., and Michael McFaul. "A Tale of Two Worlds: Core and Periphery in the Post–Cold War Era." *International Organization* 46, no. 3 (Spring 1992): 467–91.

Goldstein, Judith, and Robert Keohane, eds. *Ideas and Foreign Policy*. Ithaca, N.Y.: Cornell University Press, 1993.

Gowing, Margaret. *Policy-Making*. Vol. 1 of *Independence and Deterrence. Britain and Atomic Energy, 1945–1952*. London: Macmillan, 1974.

Grabbe, Hans Jörg. *Unionsparteien, Sozialdemokratie und Vereinigte Staaten von Amerika, 1945–1966*. Düsseldorf: Droste, 1983.

Graham, Thomas W. *American Public Opinion on NATO, Extended Deterrence, and the Use of Nuclear Weapons*. Cambridge, Mass.: Center for Science and International Affairs, Harvard University, 1989.

———. "The Politics of Failure: Strategic Nuclear Arms Control, Public Opinion, and Domestic Politics in the United States, 1945–1980." Ph.D. diss., Massachusetts Institute of Technology, Cambridge, Mass., June 1989.

Grayson, Benson Lee. *Saudi-American Relations*. Washington, D.C.: University Press of America, 1982.

Grieco, Joseph M. "Anarchy and the Limits of Cooperation: A Realist Critique of the Newest Liberal Institutionalism." *International Organization* 42, no. 3 (Summer 1988): 485–507.

———. *Cooperation among Nations*. Ithaca, N.Y.: Cornell University Press, 1990.

Groom, A. J. R. *British Thinking about Nuclear Weapons*. London: Pinter, 1974.

Grosser, Alfred. *The Western Alliance: European-American Relations since 1945*. New York: Continuum, 1980.

Haas, Ernst. *When Knowledge Is Power*. Berkeley: University of California Press, 1990.

Haas, Peter, ed. *Knowledge, Power, and International Policy-Coordination*. Special issue of *International Organization* 46, no. 1 (Winter 1992).

Habeeb, William M. *Power and Tactics in International Negotiations*. Baltimore: Johns Hopkins University Press, 1988.

Habermas, Jürgen. *Theorie des kommunikativen Handelns*. 2 vols. Frankfurt/M.: Suhrkamp, 1981.

Haftendorn, Helga. *Kernwaffen und die Glaubwürdigkeit der Allianz: Die NATO-Krise von 1966/67*. Baden-Baden: Nomos, 1994.

———. *Sicherheit und Entspannung: Zur Außenpolitik der Bundesrepublik Deutschland, 1955–1982*. Baden-Baden: Nomos, 1983.

Haggard, Stephan, and Beth A. Simmons. "Theories of International Regimes." *International Organization* 41, no. 3 (Summer 1987): 491–517.

Halliday, Jon, and Bruce Cummings. *Korea: The Unknown War*. New York: Pantheon, 1988.

Handel, Michael. *Weak States in the International System*. London: Frank Cass, 1981.

Hanrieder, Wolfram. *Germany, America, Europe: Forty Years of German Foreign Policy*. New Haven, Conn.: Yale University Press, 1989.

Hellmann, Gunther, and Reinhard Wolf. "Neorealism, Neoliberal Institutionalism, and the Future of NATO." *Security Studies* 3, no. 1 (Autumn 1993): 3–43.

Henderson, Sir Nicholas. *The Birth of NATO*. London: Weidenfeld & Nicolson, 1982.

Herz, John. *Political Realism and Political Idealism*. Chicago: Chicago University Press, 1951.

Hirschman, Albert. *Exit, Voice, and Loyalty: Responses to Decline in Firms, Organizations, and States*. Cambridge, Mass.: Harvard University Press, 1970.

Holloway, David, and Jane M. O. Sharp, eds. *The Warsaw Pact: Alliance in Transition?* Ithaca, N.Y.: Cornell University Press, 1984.

Holsti, Ole R., et al. *Unity and Disintegration in International Alliances*. New York: Wiley, 1973.

Hoppe, Christoph. *Zwischen Teilhabe und Mitsprache: Die Nuklearfrage in der Allianzpolitik Deutschlands, 1959–1966*. Baden-Baden: Nomos, 1993.

Horne, Alistair. *Macmillan, 1957–1986*. Vol. 2 of the official biography. London: Macmillan, 1989.

Hughes, Jeffrey L. "On Bargaining." In *Dominant Powers and Subordinate States*, edited by Jan F. Triska, 168–99. Durham, N.C.: Duke University Press, 1986.

Huntington, Samuel. "America's Changing Strategic Interests." *Survival* 33 (January/February 1991): 3–7.

———. "Transnational Organizations in World Politics." *World Politics* 25 (April 1973): 333–68.

———. "Why International Primacy Matters." *International Security* 17, no. 1 (Spring 1993): 68–83.

Ikenberry, G. John, and Charles F. Kupchan. "Socialization and Hegemonic Power." *International Organization* 44, no. 2 (Summer 1990): 283–315.

Immermann, Richard, ed. *John Foster Dulles and the Diplomacy of the Cold War*. Princeton, N.J.: Princeton University Press, 1990.

Ireland, Timothy P. *Creating the Entangling Alliance: The Origins of the North Atlantic Treaty Organization*. Westport, Conn.: Greenwood Press, 1981.

Jacobson, Harold K., and Eric Stein. *Diplomats, Scientists, and Politicians; The United States and the Nuclear Test Ban Negotiations*. Ann Arbor: University of Michigan Press, 1966.

Jervis, Robert. "Cooperation under the Security Dilemma." *World Politics* 30, no. 2 (1978): 167–214.

———. "Domino Beliefs and Strategic Behavior." In *Dominoes and Bandwagons*, edited by Robert Jervis and Jack Snyder, 20–50. New York: Oxford University Press, 1991.

———. "From Balance to Concert: A Study of International Security Cooperation." In *Cooperation under Anarchy*, edited by Kenneth Oye, 58–79. Princeton, N.J.: Princeton University Press, 1986.

———. "The Future of World Politics: Will It Resemble the Past?" *International Security* 16, no. 3 (Winter 1991/92): 39–73.

Jervis, Robert, and Jack Snyder, eds. *Dominoes and Bandwagons: Strategic Beliefs and Great Power Competition in the Eurasian Rimland*. New York: Oxford University Press, 1991.

Jong-yil, Ra. "Political Settlement in Korea: British Views and Policies, Autumn 1950." In *The Korean War in History*, edited by James Cotton and Ian Neary, 51–65. Manchester: Manchester University Press, 1989.

Jönssen, Christer. "Bargaining Power: Notes on an Elusive Concept." *Cooperation and Conflict* 16, no. 4 (1981): 249–57.

Kaiser, Karl. "Transnationale Politik." In *Die anachronistische Souveränität*, edited by Ernst-Otto Czempiel, 80–109. Köln-Opladen: Westdeutscher Verlag, 1969.

Kant, Immanuel. "Perpetual Peace: A Philosophical Sketch." In *Kant: Political Writings*, 2d. ed., edited by Hans Reiss, 93–130. Cambridge: Cambridge University Press, 1991.

———. "Zum ewigen Frieden: Ein philosophischer Entwurf" (1795). In *Immanuel Kant: Werke in sechs Bänden*, edited by Wilhelm Weischedel, 6:193–251. Frankfurt/M.: Insel-Verlag, 1964.

Kaplan, Lawrence S. *NATO and the United States*. Boston: Twague, 1988.

Katz, Milton S. *Ban the Bomb: A History of SANE, the Committee for a Sane Nuclear Policy, 1957–1985*. Greenwich, Conn.: Greenwood Press, 1986.

Katzenstein, Peter. *Disjoined Partners: Austria and Germany since 1815*. Berkeley: University of California Press, 1976.

Katzenstein, Peter, ed. *Norms and International Security*. Forthcoming.

Katzenstein, Peter, and Yutaka Tsujinaka. "'Bullying,' 'Buying,' and 'Binding': US-Japanese Transnational Relations and Domestic Structures." In *Bringing Transnational Relations Back In*, edited by Thomas Risse-Kappen. Cambridge: Cambridge University Press, 1995.

Kelleher, Catherine M. *Germany and the Politics of Nuclear Weapons*. New York: Columbia University Press, 1975.

Kennedy, Paul. *The Rise and Fall of Great Powers*. New York: Random House, 1987.

Kennedy, Thomas J. *NATO Politico-Military Consultation*. Washington, D.C.: National Defense University Press, 1984.

Keohane, Robert O. *After Hegemony: Cooperation and Discord in the World Political Economy*. Princeton, N.J.: Princeton University Press, 1984.

———. "The Analysis of International Regimes." In *Regime Theory and International Relations*, edited by Volker Rittberger, 23–45. Oxford: Clarendon Press, 1993.

———. "The Big Influence of Small Allies." *Foreign Policy* 2 (1971): 161–82.

———. "The International Energy Agency: State Power and Transgovernmental Politics." *International Organization* 32, no. 4 (Autumn 1978): 929–52.

———. *International Institutions and State Power*. Boulder, Colo.: Westview, 1989.

———. "International Liberalism Reconsidered." In *The Economic Limits to Modern Politics*, edited by John Dunn, 165–94. Cambridge: Cambridge University Press, 1990.

———. "Realism, Neorealism, and the Study of World Politics." In *Neorealism and Its Critics*, edited by Robert O. Keohane, 1–26. New York: Columbia University Press, 1986.

———. "Theory of World Politics: Structural Realism and Beyond." In *Neorealism and Its Critics*, edited by Robert O. Keohane, 158–203. New York: Columbia University Press. 1986.

Keohane, Robert O., ed. *Neorealism and Its Critics*. New York: Columbia University Press, 1986.

Keohane, Robert O., and Joseph S. Nye, Jr. *Power and Interdependence*. Boston: Little, Brown, 1977.

———. "Transgovernmental Relations and International Organizations." *World Politics* 27 (1974): 39–62.

Keohane, Robert O., and Joseph S. Nye, Jr., eds. *Transnational Relations and World Politics*. Cambridge, Mass.: Harvard University Press, 1972.

Kier, Elizabeth. *Images of War: Culture, Politics, and Military Doctrine*. Princeton, N.J.: Princeton University Press, 1995.

Kindleberger, Charles. "Dominance and Leadership in the International Economy." *International Studies Quarterly* 25, no. 3 (June 1981): 242–54.

———. *The World in Depression, 1929–1939*. Berkeley: University of California Press, 1973.

Klotz, Audie. *Protesting Prejudice: Apartheid and the Politics of Norms in International Relations*. Ithaca, N.Y.: Cornell University Press, 1995.

Knock, Thomas J. *To End All Wars: Woodrow Wilson and the Quest for a New World Order*. Oxford: Oxford University Press, 1992.

Knopf, Jeffrey W. "Beyond Two-level Games: Domestic-International Interactions in the Intermediate-range Nuclear Forces Negotiations." *International Organization* 47, no. 4 (Autumn 1993): 599–628.

———. "Domestic Politics, Citizen Activism, and U.S. Nuclear Arms Control Policy." Ph.D. diss., Stanford University, Stanford, Cal., June 1991.

Koen, Ross Y. *The China Lobby in American Politics*. New York: Harper & Row, 1974.

Kohl, Wilfried L. *French Nuclear Diplomacy*. Princeton, N.J.: Princeton University Press, 1971.

Krasner, Stephen, ed. *International Regimes*. Ithaca, N.Y.: Cornell University Press, 1983.

Kratochwil, Friedrich. *Rules, Norms, and Decisions*. Cambridge: Cambridge University Press, 1989.

Kratochwil, Friedrich, and John G. Ruggie. "International Organization: A State of the Art on an Art of the State." *International Organization* 40, no. 4 (Autumn 1986): 753–75.

Krauthammer, Charles. "The Unipolar Moment." *Foreign Affairs: America and the World* 70, no. 1 (1990/91): 23–33.

Krepon, Michael. *Arms Control in the Reagan Administration.* Washington, D.C.: University Press of America, 1989.

Kubbig, Bernd W. *Amerikanische Rüstungskontrollpolitik: Die innergesellschaftlichen Auseinandersetzungen in der ersten Amtszeit Ronald Reagans.* Frankfurt/M.: Campus, 1988.

Kunz, Diane B. *The Economic Diplomacy of the Suez Crisis.* Chapel Hill: University of North Carolina Press, 1991.

———. "The Importance of Having Money: The Economic Diplomacy of the Suez Crisis." In *Suez 1956*, edited by William Roger Louis and Roger Owen, 215–32. Oxford: Clarendon Press, 1989.

Kupchan, Charles A., and Clifford Kupchan. "Concerts, Collective Security, and the Future of Europe." *International Security* 16, no. 1 (Summer 1991): 114–61.

Kyle, Keith. "Britain and the Crisis, 1955–1956." In *Suez 1956*, edited by William Roger Louis and Roger Owen, 103–30. Oxford: Clarendon Press, 1989.

———. *Suez.* New York: St. Martin's Press, 1991.

Latham, Robert. "Liberalism's Order/Liberalism's Other: A Genealogy of Threat." *Alternatives* 20, no. 1 (Winter 1994).

Layne, Christopher. "The Unipolar Illusion: Why New Great Powers Will Rise." *International Security* 17, no. 4 (Spring 1993): 5–51.

Lebow, Richard N. *Between Peace and War: The Nature of International Crisis.* Baltimore: Johns Hopkins University Press, 1981.

———. "Domestic Politics and the Cuban Missile Crisis: The Traditional and Revisionist Interpretations Reconsidered." *Diplomatic History* 14, no. 4 (Fall 1990): 471–92.

———. "The Long Peace, the End of the Cold War, and the Failure of Realism." *International Organization* 48, no. 2 (Spring 1994): 249–77. Reprinted in *International Relations Theory and the End of the Cold War*, edited by Richard N. Lebow and Thomas Risse-Kappen. New York: Columbia University Press, 1995.

Lebow, Richard N., and Thomas Risse-Kappen, eds. *International Relations Theory and the End of the Cold War.* New York: Columbia University Press, 1995.

Lebow, Richard N., and Janice G. Stein. *We All Lost the Cold War.* Princeton, N.J.: Princeton University Press, 1994.

Legge, J. Michael. *Theater Nuclear Weapons and the NATO Strategy of Flexible Response.* Santa Monica, Calif.: RAND Corporation, 1983.

Leitenberg, Milton. "Chronology of the Cuban Missile Crisis." Oslo, 1989. Manuscript.

Liska, George. *Nations in Alliance: The Limits of Interdependence.* Baltimore: Johns Hopkins University Press, 1962.

Long, David E. *The United States and Saudi Arabia: Ambivalent Allies.* Boulder, Colo.: Westview, 1985.

Louis, William Roger. "Dulles, Suez, and the British." In *John Foster Dulles and the Diplomacy of the Cold War*, edited by Richard Immermann, 133–58. Princeton, N.J.: Princeton University Press, 1990.

Louis, William Roger, and Hedley Bull, eds. *The "Special Relationship": Anglo-American Relations since 1945.* Oxford: Clarendon Press, 1986.

Louis, William Roger, and Roger Owen, eds. *Suez 1956: The Crisis and Its Consequences*. Oxford: Clarendon Press, 1989.

Lowe, Peter. "The Settlement of the Korean War." In *The Foreign Policy of Churchill's Peacetime Administration, 1951–1955*, edited by John W. Young, 207–31. Leicester: Leicester University Press, 1988.

Lumsdaine, David H. *Moral Vision in International Politics: The Foreign Aid Regime, 1949–1989*. Princeton, N.J.: Princeton University Press, 1993.

Lundestad, Geir. *The American "Empire."* Oslo: Norwegian University Press, 1990.

L'Université de Franche-Comté et l'Institut Charles-de-Gaulle. *L'Aventure de la Bombe: De Gaulle et la Dissuasion Nucléaire*. Paris: Librairie Plon, 1985.

MacDonald, Callum A. *Britain and the Korean War*. Oxford: Basil Blackwell, 1990.

Macdonald, Douglas. "The Truman Administration and Global Responsibilities: The Birth of the Falling Domino Principle." In *Dominoes and Bandwagons*, edited by Robert Jervis and Jack Snyder, 112–44. New York: Oxford University Press, 1991.

Mai, Günther. *Westliche Sicherheitspolitik im kalten Krieg: Der Korea-Krieg und die deutsche Wiederbewaffnung*. Boppard: Boldt, 1977.

March, James G. "The Power of Power." In *Varieties of Political Theory*, edited by David Easton, 39–70. New York: Prentice Hall, 1966.

Marks, Michael. "The Formation of European Policy in Post-Franco Spain: Ideas, Interests, and the International Transmission of Knowledge." Ph.D. diss., Cornell University, Ithaca, N.Y., 1993.

Martin, Lisa L. "Interests, Power, and Multilateralism." *International Organization* 46, no. 4 (Autumn 1992): 765–92.

Mearsheimer, John. "Back to the Future: Instability in Europe after the Cold War." *International Security* 15, no. 1 (Summer 1990): 5–56.

Meier, Ernst-Christoph. *Deutsch-amerikanische Sicherheitsbeziehungen und der NATO-Doppelbeschluß*. Rheinfelden: Schäuble-Verlag, 1986.

Merritt, Richard. *Symbols of American Community, 1735–1775*. New Haven, Conn.: Yale University Press, 1966.

Meyer, David. *A Winter of Discontent: The Freeze and American Politics*. New York: Praeger, 1990.

Moravcsik, Andrew. *Liberalism and International Relations Theory*. 2d. ed. Working Paper Series. Cambridge, Mass.: Center for International Affairs, Harvard University, 1993.

Morgenthau, Hans J. *Politics among Nations: The Struggle for Power and Peace* (1948). Brief ed. New York: McGraw-Hill, 1993.

Mueller, John. *War, Presidency, and Public Opinion*. New York: Wiley, 1973.

Müller, Harald. *Die Chance der Kooperation: Regime in den internationalen Beziehungen*. Darmstadt: Wissenschaftliche Buchgesellschaft, 1993.

———. "Internationale Beziehungen als kommunikatives Handeln: Zur Kritik der utilitaristischen Handlungstheorie." *Zeitschrift für Internationale Beziehungen* 1, no. 1 (1994): 15–44.

Müller, Harald, ed. *A European Non-Proliferation Policy*. Oxford: Clarendon Press, 1987.

———. *How Western European Nuclear Policy Is Made: Deciding on the Atom*. London: Macmillan, 1991.

Munton, Don. "Getting Along and Going Alone: American Policies and Canadian Support in Korea and Cuba." Paper presented to the annual meeting of the International Studies Association, Atlanta, Ga., April 1992.

Navias, Martin S. *Nuclear Weapons and British Strategic Planning, 1955–1958*. Oxford: Clarendon Press, 1991.

Neustadt, Richard. *Alliance Politics*. New York: Columbia University Press, 1970.

Nunnerly, David. *President Kennedy and Britain*. London: Bodley Head, 1972.

Nye, Joseph S., Jr. *Bound to Lead*. New York: Basic Books, 1990.

Odell, John. *U.S. International Monetary Policy: Markets, Power, and Ideas as Sources of Change*. Princeton, N.J.: Princeton University Press, 1982.

Olson, Mancur, and Richard Zeckhauser. "An Economic Theory of Alliances." *Review of Economics and Statistics* 48 (1966): 266–79.

O'Neill, Robert. *Strategy and Diplomacy*. Vol. 1 of *Australia in the Korean War, 1950–1953*. Canberra: Australian Government Publication Service, 1981.

Ovendale, Ritchie. "Britain and the Cold War in Asia," In *The Foreign Policy of the British Labour Governments, 1945–1951*, edited by Ritchie Ovendale, 121–48. Leicester: Leicester University Press, 1984.

Oye, Kenneth, ed. *Cooperation under Anarchy*. Princeton, N.J.: Princeton University Press, 1986.

Peters, Susanne. *The Germans and INF Missiles: Getting Their Way in NATO's Strategy of Flexible Response*. Baden-Baden: Nomos, 1990.

Puchala, Donald J. "Integration Theory and the Study of International Relations." In *From National Development to Global Community*, edited by Richard L. Merritt and Bruce Russett, 145–64. London: Allen & Unwin, 1981.

Putnam, Robert. "Diplomacy and Domestic Politics: The Logic of Two-Level Games." *International Organization* 42, no. 3 (Summer 1988): 427–60.

Reston, James. *Deadline*. New York: Random House, 1991.

Reynolds, David. "A 'special relationship'? America, Britain and the International Order since the Second World War." *International Affairs* 62 (1986): 1–20.

Risse-Kappen, Thomas. *The Zero Option: INF, West Germany, and Arms Control*. Boulder, Colo.: Westview, 1988.

Risse-Kappen, Thomas, ed. *Bringing Transnational Relations Back In: Non-State Actors, Domestic Structures, and International Institutions*. Cambridge: Cambridge University Press, 1995.

Rittberger, Volker. "Research on International Regimes in Germany," In *Regime Theory and International Relations*, edited by Volker Rittberger, 3–22. Oxford: Clarendon Press, 1993.

Rittberger, Volker, ed. *Regime Theory and International Relations*. Oxford: Clarendon Press, 1993.

Rosenau, James N. *Turbulence in World Politics*. Princeton, N.J.: Princeton University Press, 1989.

Rotblat, Joseph. *Scientists in the Quest for Peace: A History of the Pugwash Conference*. Cambridge, Mass.: MIT Press, 1972.

Rothstein, Robert L. *Alliances and Small Powers*. New York: Columbia University Press, 1968.

Ruggie, John G. "Multilateralism: The Anatomy of an Institution." *International Organization* 46, no. 3 (Summer 1992): 561–98.

Russett, Bruce. "The Alleged Role of Nuclear Weapons in Controlling the Soviet-American 'Enduring Rivalry,' and in the Future." In *Nuclear Technology and International Politics*, edited by John Gelstad and Olav Norstad. London: Sage, 1994.

———. *Community and Contention: Britain and America in the Twentieth Century*. Cambridge, Mass.: The MIT Press, 1963.

———. *Controlling the Sword: The Democratic Governance of Nuclear Weapons*. Cambridge, Mass.: Harvard University Press, 1990.

———. *Grasping the Democratic Peace: Principles for a Post–Cold War World*. Princeton, N.J.: Princeton University Press, 1993.

———. "The Mysterious Case of Vanishing Hegemony: Or Is Mark Twain Really Dead?" *International Organization* 39 (1985): 207–31.

Ryan, Henry B. *The Vision of Anglo-America: The US-UK Alliance and the Emerging Cold War, 1943–1946*. Cambridge: Cambridge University Press, 1987.

Ryan, Mark A. *Chinese Attitudes toward Nuclear Weapons: China and the United States during the Korean War*. New York: M. E. Sharpe, 1989.

Sagan, Scott. "Nuclear Alerts and Crisis Management." *International Security* 9, no. 4 (Spring 1985): 99–139.

Schlesinger, Arthur. *Robert Kennedy and His Times*. Boston: Houghton Mifflin, 1978.

———. *A Thousand Days: John F. Kennedy in the White House*. Boston: Houghton Mifflin, 1965.

Schmidt, Helmut. *Verteidigung oder Vergeltung: Ein deutscher Beitrag zum strategischen Problem der NATO*. Stuttgart-Degerloch: Seewald, 1961. Translated to English as *Defense or Retaliation*. New York: Praeger, 1962.

Schwarz, Hans-Peter. "Adenauer und die Kernwaffen." *Vierteljahreshefte für Zeitgeschichte* 37, no. 4 (October 1989): 567–93.

Schwartz, David N. *NATO's Nuclear Dilemmas*. Washington, D.C.: Brookings, 1983.

Schwarz, Thomas. *America's Germany: John McCloy and the Federal Republic of Germany*. Cambridge, Mass.: Harvard University Press, 1991.

Seaborg, Glenn T. *Kennedy, Khrushchev, and the Test Ban*. Berkeley: University of California Press, 1981.

Senghaas, Dieter. *Friedensprojekt Europa*. Frankfurt/M.: Suhrkamp, 1992.

Sherwood, Elizabeth. *Allies in Crisis: Meeting Global Challenges to Western Security*. New Haven, Conn.: Yale University Press, 1990.

Sikkink, Kathryn. *Ideas and Institutions: Developmentalism in Brazil and Argentina*. Ithaca, N.Y.: Cornell University Press, 1991.

Simpson, John. *The Independent Nuclear State: The United States, Britain, and the Military Atom*. London: Macmillan, 1983.

Siverson, Randolph M., and Juliann Emmons. "Birds of a Feather: Democratic Political Systems and Alliance Choices in the Twentieth Century." *Journal of Conflict Resolution* 35, no. 2 (June 1991): 285–306.

Snidal, Duncan. "International Cooperation among Relative Gain Maximizers." *International Studies Quarterly* 35, no. 4 (December 1991): 387–402.

———. "The Limits of Hegemonic Stability Theory." *International Organization* 39, no. 4 (Autumn 1985): 579–614.

Snyder, Glenn H. "Alliance Theory: A Neorealist First Cut." *Journal of International Affairs* 44, no. 1 (Spring 1990): 103–23.

———. *Deterrence and Defense: Toward a Theory of National Security.* Princeton, N.J.: Princeton University Press, 1961.

———. "The Security Dilemma in Alliance Politics." *World Politics* 36, no. 4 (July 1984): 461–96.

Snyder, Jack. "Introduction" and "Conclusion." In *Dominoes and Bandwagons: Strategic Beliefs and Great Power Competition in the Eurasian Rimland*, edited by Robert Jervis and Jack Snyder, 3–19, 276–90. New York: Oxford University Press, 1991.

Stairs, Denis. *The Diplomacy of Constraint: Canada, the Korean War, and the United States.* Toronto: Toronto University Press, 1974.

Stein, Arthur. *Why Nations Cooperate.* Ithaca, N.Y.: Cornell University Press, 1990.

Stockholm International Peace Research Institute (SIPRI), ed. *World Armaments and Disarmament: SIPRI Yearbook 1972.* Stockholm: Almquist & Wiksell, 1972.

Stromseth, Jane E. *The Origins of Flexible Response.* New York: St. Martin's Press, 1988.

Stuart, Douglas, and William Tow. *The Limits of Alliance: NATO Out-of-Area Problems since 1949.* Baltimore: Johns Hopkins University Press, 1990.

Summer, Robert, and Alan Heston. "Improved International Comparisons of Real Product and Its Composition, 1950–1980." *The Review of Income and Wealth,* Series 30, no. 2 (June 1984): 207–62.

Talbott, Strobe. *Deadly Gambits.* New York: A. Knopf, 1984.

Tannenwald, Nina. "Dogs that Don't Bark: The United States, the Role of Norms, and the Non-Use of Nuclear Weapons in the Post–World War II Era." Ph.D. diss., Cornell University, Ithaca, N.Y., 1995.

Taylor, Richard. *Against the Bomb: The British Peace Movement, 1958–1965.* Oxford: Clarendon Press, 1988.

Thomas, Daniel. "When Norms and Movements Matter: Helsinki, Human Rights, and Political Change in Eastern Europe, 1970–1990." Ph.D. diss., Cornell University, Ithaca, N.Y., 1994.

Thomson, Janice. "Norms in International Relations: A Conceptual Analysis." *International Journal of Group Tensions* 23, no. 2 (1993): 67–83.

Thucydides. *The History of the Peloponnesian War.* Harmondsworth: Penguin, 1954.

Tiedtke, Stephan. *Die Warschauer Vertrags-Organisation: Zum Verhältnis von Militär- und Entspannungspolitik in Osteuropa.* München: Oldenbourg, 1978.

Trachtenberg, Marc. *History and Strategy.* Princeton, N.J.: Princeton University Press, 1991.

———. "A 'Wasting Asset': American Strategy and the Shifting Nuclear Balance, 1949–1954." *International Security* 13, no. 3 (Winter 1988/89): 5–49.

Triska, Jan F., ed. *Dominant Powers and Subordinate States.* Durham, N.C.: Duke University Press, 1986.

Vaisse, Maurice. "France and the Suez Crisis." In *Suez 1956*, edited by William Roger Louis and Roger Owen, 131–43. Oxford: Clarendon Press, 1989.

Vaisse, Maurice, ed. *L'Europe et la Crise de Cuba*. Paris: Armand Colin, 1993.

Van Evera, Steven. "Primed for Peace: Europe after the Cold War." *International Security* 15, no. 3 (Winter 1990–1991): 7–57.

———. "Why Europe Matters; Why the Third World Doesn't: American Grand Strategy after the Cold War." *Journal of Strategic Studies* 13, no. 2 (June 1990), 1–51.

Wagner, R. Harrison. "What Was Bipolarity?" *International Organization* 47, No. 1 (Winter 1993): 77–106.

Walt, Stephen M. *The Origins of Alliances*. Ithaca, N.Y.: Cornell University Press, 1987.

Waltz, Kenneth N. "The Emerging Structure of World Politics." *International Security* 18, no. 2 (Fall 1993): 44–79.

———. *Theory of International Politics*. Reading, Mass.: Addison-Wesley, 1979.

Wassermann, Sherri L. *The Neutron Bomb Controversy*. New York: Praeger, 1983.

Weber, Steve. "Does NATO Have a Future?" In *The Future of European Security*, edited by Beverly Crawford, 360–95. Berkeley: University of California Center for German and European Studies, 1992.

———. "Shaping the Postwar Balance of Power: Multilateralism in NATO." *International Organization* 46, no. 3 (Summer 1992): 633–80.

Wendt, Alexander. "The Agent-Structure Problem in International Relations Theory." *International Organization* 41, no. 3 (Summer 1987): 335–70.

———. "Anarchy Is What States Make of It: The Social Construction of Power Politics." *International Organization* 46, no. 2 (Spring 1992): 391–425.

———. "Collective Identity Formation and the International State." *American Political Science Review* 88, no. 2 (June 1994): 384–96.

Whelan, Richard. *Drawing the Line: The Korean War, 1950–1953*. Boston: Little, Brown, 1990.

Wolfers, Arnold. *Discord and Collaboration*. Baltimore: Johns Hopkins University Press, 1962.

Woods, Randall B. *A Changing of the Guard: Anglo-American Relations, 1941–1947*. Chapel Hill: University of North Carolina Press, 1990.

Wright, Michael. *Disarm and Verify*. London: Chatto & Windus, 1964.

Yost, David S. "France." In *The Allies and Arms Control*, edited by Fen O. Hampson et al., 162–88. Baltimore: Johns Hopkins University Press, 1992.

Young, John W. *France, the Cold War, and the Western Alliance, 1944–49*. New York: St. Martin's Press, 1990.

Young, Oran. *International Cooperation*. Ithaca, N.Y.: Cornell University Press, 1989.

INDEX